BEYOND LIBERTY AND PROPERTY

Professor Gunn presents a fresh, revealing picture of the public mind in Britain, from the Glorious Revolution to the First Reform Act, showing how British people of the eighteenth century came to a new understanding of politics. Departing from the usual approach based upon lengthy treatises by a few prominent commentators, he employs a wide range of documents: newspapers, magazines, parliamentary debates, sermons, pamphlets, judicial records, and private correspondence. He examines topics that have generally escaped even specialist notice and takes up questions long regarded as settled, casting a new and different light on them.

The themes explored include political liberty, "legal tyranny," defences of influence in government, recognition of the Opposition, and the development of organic categories of political analysis—the latter in a chapter that explodes the association often presumed between organicism and conservative modes of thought. A chapter on the "Fourth Estate" examines the gradual process of legitimation of "interests," culminating in the influence of the press. Central to the account of new political forces and their recognition is the idea of public opinion, which evolved during this period from the notion of public spirit.

Chapters on the classical legacy of the century and on the High-Tories examine two backward-looking aspects of the political culture. Tracing the persistent influence of High-Toryism, Gunn questions the conventional wisdom about eighteenth-century ideological consensus in general and Whig solidarity in particular. He demonstrates that theories of government from the seventeenth century survived to a degree not previously admitted by modern scholarship.

J. A. W. Gunn is head of the Department of Political Studies at Queen's University, author of *Politics and the Public Interest in the Seventeenth-Century*, and co-editor of *Benjamin Disraeli, Letters Volume I: 1815–1834* and *Volume II: 1835–1837.*

McGill-Queen's Studies in the History of Ideas

BEYOND LIBERTY
AND PROPERTY
The Process of Self-Recognition
in Eighteenth-Century Political Thought

J. A. W. Gunn

McGill-Queen's University Press
Kingston and Montreal

© McGill-Queen's University Press 1983
ISBN 0-7735-1006-0
Legal deposit 3rd quarter 1983
Bibliothèque nationale du Québec

Printed in Canada

This book has been published with the help of a grant from the
Social Science Federation of Canada, using funds provided by the
Social Sciences and Humanities Research Council of Canada.

Canadian Cataloguing in Publication Data

Gunn, J.A.W. (John Alexander Wilson), 1937-
Beyond liberty and property
(McGill-Queen's studies in the history of ideas, ISSN 0711-0995 : 6)
Includes index.
ISBN 0-7735-1006-0

1. Great Britain – Intellectual life – 18th century.
2. Great Britain – Politics and government – 18th
century.   I. Title.   II. Series.
JN327.G86   320.941   c83-094088-x

For James and Andrea

Contents

Acknowledgments

I AM GRATEFUL to what was once the Canada Council, and is now the Social Sciences and Humanities Research Council of Canada, for a leave fellowship in 1972–73. Several of the chapters presented here were planned or written in Oxford during that sabbatical leave. I wish also to pay tribute to the hospitality of the Warden and Fellows of Nuffield College, Oxford, in whose rewarding company I spent that year.

My thanks too to Eleanor Gunn, Dr. Nadia Khalaf, and Dr. Mary Jane Edwards, who read parts of the manuscript and contributed helpful advice. For reasons they will best understand, the book is dedicated to my children.

BEYOND LIBERTY AND PROPERTY

Introduction

THIS BOOK HAS GROWN out of a long-standing interest in mapping certain areas of the political thought of eighteenth-century Britain. The individual essays were written to explore themes that have not figured prominently in accounts by others, and so the book does not purport to be a complete and balanced history. Nor have I wished to revisit the subject of my own earlier work on ideas about party in the eighteenth century.

Each essay treats the development of an idea or a set of ideas over a period of time. In most of them, the entire century has served as the display-case, and indeed I have sometimes conceived the century to run from 1688 to 1832. Even in the one essay most obviously devoted to the thought of a single person (David Williams, in this case) my intent has been to show how political ideas emerged or changed. This too is true of the chapter concerned with the uses made of Mandeville's *Fable*. Generally I have wanted to learn what a succession of people had to say about some issue, and the large cast of characters—most of them, I confess, supporting players—is central to this ambition. If such an approach seems to slight the memory of the preconceived greats of the age—Hume or Burke—let it be said that such thinkers must continue to earn their way in relation to each successive question put by the student of ideas. We must take our evidence where we find it. Textual exegesis that extracts meaning by reading between familiar lines has its place. Here I have attempted something else.

Primarily, I have tried to write of innovations in thought, and especially those innovations that seem to have captured aspects of pol-

itics in such a way as to commend themselves to the modern student
of the subject. This approach, I know, has its risks, for it would de-
nature the thought of the past to portray its ideologists or publicists as
fledgling social scientists. Most were far from it, either in design or
in fact, and so I have reminded myself that previous thought is not
a prolonged struggle to give birth to our own parochial vision. Ana-
chronism, then, is a constant danger, but one may minimize the risk
by limiting the study to certain sorts of questions.

Ideas having to do with political institutions are more readily treated
than are abstract notions of justice, *virtù,* or other intimations of the
human condition, none of which is readily confined by an institutional
setting. Scholars rightly worry when political ideas are presented as
a lofty debate across the centuries, among participants who never met
and who shared neither a common language nor similar cultural
premises. By contrast, those eighteenth-century Englishmen who wrote
of, say, the office of prime minister or of "influence," of "legal tyranny," or of the press were contributing to a political culture in which
we still, in large measure, reside. Such ideas, it is argued, may prove
more manageable and invite less uncertainty than do more universal
concerns.

The reason is best seen by referring briefly to two of the major
sources of inhibition that weigh upon the intellectual historian of the
period. One of these is the normal outlook of the political historian,
well represented by Sir Lewis Namier and his school. The other is
the philosophically sophisticated position of Professor Quentin Skinner, as argued in a series of influential articles. It would not be fair
to attempt here to characterize these points of view fully, so I can
only record what I take to be their message for the present study.
Both, it seems, direct our interest to the intentions of those people
who expressed political opinions.

For Namier, the problem was that we were likely to be bamboozled
by the pretentious disguises assumed by selfish interests; this led him
to dismiss political ideas as epiphenomenal. Skinner's position is far
more difficult to put briefly, but he can be said to have argued for
the importance of our knowing, among other things, the intentions
of political writers while casting doubt on whether we could have any
confidence about what these intentions were, unless intellectual history were to obey standards much more stringent than had previously
obtained. Some of his critics have further burdened the ambitious
student of ideas with the judgement that not even the sort of contex-

tualist study favoured by Skinner can ensure knowledge of such intentions.

The answer to Namierism appropriate to present purposes is that political historians have been unmindful of the fact that some of the most important political ideas have been put forward for the purpose of redefining the boundaries of legitimate political conduct. Namier accepted self-interest in public life but deemed it destructive of the meaning of political ideas. However, some ideas lead us to reflect that "self-interest" is not the compromising skeleton in the closet that Namier would make it, for it is openly avowed. Some very significant examples of political concepts involved precisely the point that the game of politics was less a colloquium for eliciting truth than an arena for furthering interests. Pious protestations of virtue may well fall silent before this sceptical historian of places, pensions, and family connections, but his world-weary realism and his concerns about insincerity and self-delusion face a more demanding test with that political vocabulary that deals with the emerging means of articulating interests. Such a selection from political discourse serves to make sense of ideas about "interest" as a political concept, "party" as the vehicle for promoting shared designs, or "public opinion" as the outcome of the various concerns at large in a society. I have treated the first two elsewhere, so public opinion is the most prominent of the three in this collection and informs several of the chapters.

Since these essays are written from a contextualist point of view, my difficulties with Skinner's approach are really just matters of emphasis. I applaud his desire to depart from textual examination of the great books in isolation from their context in the traditions, conventions, and linguistic usages of their time. But some of his strictures on past efforts to write the history of ideas seem too inhibiting. When one examines eighteenth-century opinions about institutions and political processes, the "unit idea" is relatively well defined, and one's understanding receives constant nourishment from a multitude of sources, including anonymous pamphlets and the daily press. There is thus some assurance that people who used the same terms attached much the same meaning to them, and this is especially so when a term or a meaning was new and thus subject to comment. For this reason, the historian would be hard pressed to cite that text which announced to the world that there was a group of politicians, not just "in opposition" to government measures, but forming a body called the Opposition. But the language of the early 1730s reflected the presence of such an institution. Similarly, awareness of the phenomenon of public opinion did not come embodied in a single monumental text for which we must establish a linguistic context. Rather, the context itself may prove to be our only focus, and there may be no political equivalent to "the poem in itself" for which we must provide a context. In a sense, then, one may perhaps be even more contextualist than seems to have been contemplated by Skinner's corrective to historians of thought who were content to read only major works. But there are contexts and contexts; and if some forms of context are almost the whole of my concern, others are less relevant. I am certainly aware that Skinner too contemplates various sorts of context and that he does not limit himself to narrowly literary influences.

Professor Skinner's emphasis upon recovering the intentions of ideologists is of least help when some aspect of the political under- standing and vocabulary of a whole period is at issue. It need not matter for certain purposes whether writers wrote for love or for money, or indeed whether they were serious or playful, so long as they can be seen as contributing categories helpful for understanding politics. Nor need one necessarily be able to argue, as does Skinner, that an author's professed principles must have confined his actual behaviour. That no doubt helps, but it would suffice to show that by identifying important factors in politics a writer had affected the ex- pectations of others. The growth of a political culture may be less a process of being trapped into conforming to one's own rhetoric than a matter of educating one's fellow citizens. Their behaviour may then respond.

For example, the notion of a "fourth estate" in British government began as a pejorative epithet and matured to the level of a sober description of some of the novel features of the political order. The wry jokes of one decade are the solemn verities of the next, and the intention involved in marking such novelties may be a good deal less important than the fact that they were deemed worthy of notice at all. If one takes a sufficient number of samplings from a culture, the circumstances surrounding the writing of any one document are re- duced in importance. Of course, no scholar who has ever been led astray by the mock seriousness of some Augustan satirist will deny that it may be vital, at times, to ask what purposes an author had in mind and to what audience he appealed. But for some forms of inquiry, the mental state of the agent can usefully be subordinated to the activity of the society of which he was a part and to the measure in which that activity was understood by those people who wrote about public life.

The closest model in modern scholarship to the concerns treated in this book is provided by Professor Samuel Beer,[1] who uses the concept of "social self-knowledge," here understood as the process whereby a society obtained certain insights into its own workings. This was what was going on when politicians and journalists argued about the legitimacy of opposition to government, the genuineness of the liberty enjoyed under a parliament, or the efficacy of extra-parliamentary organization. The business of probing this self-knowledge as it existed in eighteenth-century Britain is assisted by those documents where contemporaries record that their time has witnessed something new. Care is needed here, of course, for such statements had uses other than historical understanding; and memories, then as always, were short. The story of High-Toryism and its survival amply demonstrates that one cannot always trust testimony about either the disappearance of old ideas or the novelty of supposedly new ones. Long ago, Dr. Johnson pointed out that the writers of epitaphs are not on oath, and the same applies to the promoters of new products. Nevertheless, there remains a valuable reflexive element in some forms of political thought, for there are occasions when people go beyond the task of assertion to dwell upon the measure in which their assertions were novel or commonplace. Such literature provides a guide to the emergence of ideas about luxury, "political liberty," or "public opinion." Indeed, it would be hard to imagine a process more reflexive than opinion about the place of opinion. However misleading statements of this sort may be, it is certain that such phenomena and consciousness of them do both have a beginning. A command of the literature can in principle identify that beginning, subject always to correction by further and better scholarship. It should also be emphasized that the enterprise of studying social self-understanding is not meant to be a means of doing social or political history without the drudgery imposed by archival research. The aim is not to document the development of such a phenomenon as, say, public opinion,

1. See Samuel H. Beer, "Political Science and History," in Melvin Richter, ed., *Essays in Theory and History: An Approach to the Social Sciences* (Cambridge, Mass.: Harvard University Press, 1970), pp. 68–71.

but rather to consider how the phenomenon came to be recognized and how it was understood.

There can be no meaningful grasp of innovation save against the background of some elements of continuity, and an awareness of the overlapping and interpenetration of intellectual traditions has always been necessary in the history of ideas. The same materials that allow a student of the period to become sensitized to departures from its orthodox positions will also serve to document survivals from an earlier time. Tracing the vestigial presence of a waning tradition has its own difficulties and is subject to that sort of prolepsis in which scholars wrongly anticipate the death of ideas that are, in fact, only in repose. All the prejudices of the social scientist enjoin him to seek his own habits of mind in earlier and perhaps inappropriate settings. It has seemed useful, then, to devote one very long essay to the reconstruction of a strand of seventeenth-century thought that stubbornly survived throughout the eighteenth century. Like many another student of the eighteenth century, I began my research with the previous century. Not only is this sequence of interests valuable for purposes of trying to say what was new after 1700; equally it affords a basis for discovering continuities. My only excuse for saying so much about Tory categories in the eighteenth century is that others have, to my mind, said too little. The essay on "legal tyranny" entails somewhat the same task of charting the course of survival, but in this case the theme of innovation is also present.

This foray into the current debate on how intellectual history should be written is no substitute for trying to write it. At best, it may serve to explain why I have chosen to write as I did; at worst, it deprives me of the comforting plea of complete innocence about questions of method.

I

Parliament and the Caesars:
Legal Tyranny in the Political Rhetoric
of Eighteenth-Century England

POLITICAL RHETORIC is always subject to a heavy discount on the part of the wary scholar; moreover, the language of the Opposition in eighteenth-century Britain strikes many historians as especially remote from reality. The "patriot" Opposition to Walpole and the Pelhams seems to have had few wants that a spell of office would not have satisfied, and their noisy vigil in the political wilderness was punctuated by strident claims about a revival of arbitrary rule. The theme admitted of many variations and included the "double cabinet" and the "secret influence" later alleged against the ministers of George III. It was often poor stuff, either as history or as literature, and it was numbingly repetitive.

Nevertheless, such discourse was a rich vein of opinion about the mechanics of free government and its attendant dangers. Nor were fears necessarily quite as empty as is sometimes supposed. One modern historian who wrote of these "pathless forests of ... Parliamentary verbiage" also pointed out that the administrations of the first two Georges forbade the printing of debates and division-lists, banished Convocation, curbed opposition through the City Act of 1725, prolonged the life of Parliament to protect themselves from the electorate, and systematically proscribed their political enemies.[1]

Because the bogey of tyranny never materialized, we must not as-

---

1. J. W. Jeudwine, *Religion, Commerce, Liberty: A Record of a Time of Storm and Change, 1683–1793* (New York: Longmans, Green and Co., 1925), pp. 96, 238. A sophisticated effort to rescue patriot rhetoric from irrelevance is Quentin Skinner's "The Principles and Practice of Opposition: The Case of Bolingbroke versus Walpole," in Neil McKendrick, ed., *Historical Perspectives: Studies in English Thought and Society in Honour of J. H. Plumb* (London: Europa, 1974), pp. 93–128.

sume that every eighteenth-century Cassandra was insincere. In a century of absolute governments, England with its Parliament was a marvel. But the very fact that the king's ministers could normally count upon a compliant parliamentary majority raised questions about the nature of the political system and particularly about the techniques of ruling through Parliament rather than against it. The centrality of this interest did much to redirect political speculation from the ethics of obedience and rebellion to the causal factors underlying British freedom. Through forty-five years of the Whig oligarchy and long after, the capacity of Parliament to resist the fate of the Continental legislatures, while maintaining a genuine freedom, was the subject of much effective writing and at least some concern that seems genuine.[2]

Those who sought historical parallels for their inquiries found an inexhaustible store of political precept in the fall of the Roman Republic. Application of the Roman story to British circumstances was the means whereby a host of writers was led to deny the reliability of constitutional forms as an indicator of liberty, thus prompting an appraisal of the nature of a free government. Roman experience was a natural starting-point for anyone concerned with political institutions. Providing a common fund of knowledge for all educated men, it afforded a stimulating record both of vigorous freedom and of the gloomy descent into tyranny. Englishmen knew well how the story ended, and because it suited their purposes, most emphasized, not the glorious dawn of Roman freedom, but the shadows of Julius Caesar and Tiberius.

Of course the prominence of the Roman example dated from before the eighteenth century; defenders of Stuart ambitions had even justified the admitted excesses of the emperors by extolling the order that some of them had brought.[3] But there were definite limits to the usefulness of Roman history to the events of the Civil War; Cromwell was difficult to associate with Roman usurpers, and the religious foun-

---

2. Professor James T. Boulton has treated this "powerful belief based on fear" largely as it appears in literary settings. There seems to be no way of knowing quite how powerful the belief was. See "Arbitrary Power: An Eighteenth-Century Obsession," *Studies in Burke and his Time* 9, no. 3 (Spring 1968): 905–26.

3. See Edmund Bolton, *Nero Caesar, or Monarchy Depraved* (London, 1623), p. 287.

dations of the parliamentary cause militated against the parallel.[4] Arbitrary government might indeed be linked to Rome, but more likely the church than the ancient polity, and pamphleteers who condemned Charles I as a tyrant sometimes went out of their way to distinguish between Roman tyranny and the meaning of the term relevant to events of the 1640s.[5]

There were indeed occasions in seventeenth-century England when people were moved to contemplate the difference between real and apparent liberties. John Pym did so in a speech of 1642. Later, when Parliament ostensibly had gained the day, it made sense to begin worrying about the dangers of that body's corruption, and men wrote of the irony of a threat posed to liberty by Parliament itself—the very foundation of English liberties. Marchamont Nedham, the sometime republican, explored certain possibilities of this argument.[6] Similar ideas appeared among Shaftesbury's followers in the years prior to the Exclusion Bills, as they portrayed Danby's Non-resisting Bill of 1675 as an effort at enslaving the nation under the forms of law.[7] The language was extreme, but the Whig opposition of the time was deadly serious, and the Place-bill of 1675, first of many intended to banish office-holders from the Commons, reflects their fears of corruption. As Algernon Sidney said of this period, the king had only recently gained the wherewithal to bribe parliaments, but since the

---

4. Certainly those eighteenth-century writers who were hostile to Cromwell—and that was most of them—resisted parallels between his treatment of Parliament and later tactics. But see *The Character of the Parliament Commonly Called the Rump* (London, 1721), where some effort was made to relate the two eras. A writer in the *Gentleman's Magazine* for 1750 (p. 467) gave an account of a plan, supposedly framed for Cromwell, to give "the appearance of parliaments without the reality of them." But this was probably just an eighteenth-century literary device.

5. See Anon., *A Brief Discourse upon Tyrants and Tyranny ... (London*, 1642), p. 7.

6. See *Two Speeches Deliver'd by the Earl of Holland, and Mr. John Pym ... Spoken in Guild Hall* (London, 1642); *The Answer of the Parliament of England to a Paper, Entitled, A Declaration of the King's Majesty ...* (London, 1650), pp. 28–29; and Nedham, *The True State of the Case of the Commonwealth* (London, 1654), pp. 9–10. Related comments by Nedham are quoted by James Burgh, *Political Disquisitions* (London, 1774), 1:359–60.

7. T.E., "A Letter from a Parliament-Man to his Friend ..." (1675), in *State Tracts* (London, 1693), pt. 1, p. 71; and "A Letter from a Person of Quality to his Friend in the Country" (1675), in *Parliamentary History*, 4, app., cols. xl, lxii. This second tract is sometimes attributed to Locke.

Restoration it had become feasible to turn Parliament into an instrument of slavery. Others chose 1672 or, less plausibly, 1688 as marking
the onset of large-scale corruption, but rarely did people offer any
period prior to the Restoration.

Until the Revolution, the theme of legal tyranny—as opposed to
the actual presence of corruption—was a minor one. Parliament might
indeed be corrupted, and was, but the threats of coercion or dismissal
were then too real to encourage the sort of speculation that flourished
in more settled times. Popery and French troops were not subtle
complaints; the era of refined analysis opened with the apparent enthronement of liberty in 1688.

The Moral Revolution of 1688

The so-called moral revolution produced more than societies for the
reformation of manners. It also unleashed a torrent of social and
political criticism that had, in some measure, been suppressed by the
previous régime. Drawing upon the experience with mercenary parliaments under the Stuarts, writers became ever more inclined to
speculate on the dangers of liberty's being undermined instead of
being swept away by force. After 1688, general laments by moralists
and by practical men with grievances abounded. One of these, Robert
Crosfield (or Crosfeild)—described by contemporaries as a "lace-
man"—bombarded the public and Parliament with accounts of pec-
ulation, influence-peddling, and general misuse of revenue in the
departments of government.[8] Parliament responded by committing
him to prison for writing a libel. Edward Stephens, writing on the
general state of government, and Sir William Hodges, on abuses in
naval administration, added to the chorus. Corruption was often perceived as essentially social, which led one commentator on the times
to record later that the "universal Corruption" of court, camp, and
city had infected Parliament itself.[9]

In 1692 a new place-bill was introduced but was not passed into
law. Corruption at various levels of government was the subject of a

8. See *House of Commons, Journals* (18 Jan. 1694–95), p. 211; and *House of Lords,
Journals* (21 Mar. 1694–95), p. 524. For a typical recital of abuses, supporting the
judgement that "the Nation is Sick," see [Crosfield], *A Dialogue Between a Modern Courtier,
and an Honest English Gentleman* (n.p., 1696), p. 16.

9. Roger Coke, *A Detection of the Court and State of England* ... (London, 1719), 3:7.

major parliamentary inquiry in 1694–95, and a tract of the day under-lined the parallel with the demise of popular government in antiq-uity.[10] Increasingly, bribery and influence were contrasted with more direct and violent methods, which, one writer warned, would alarm the people. But informal influence allowed arbitrary government to advance, with everything remaining "according to Form."[11] The Act of Settlement (1701) barred placemen from the Commons, but the clause was repealed before it was due to go into effect. Even had it remained, there is every reason to suppose that concern about liberty would have continued unabated. The paradox that would intrigue generations of publicists had been stated in a broadside of 1690. Liberty was now in greater danger than under the "suspected Stuarts," if only because the current government had been chosen by the nation, thus improving the means of blinding people to the tendency of events. Government being "more popular, and not *more limited, we are not more safe,* but our liberties more exposed."[12] Taken to its logical conclusion, the doctrine encouraged Britons to be most fearful when Whigs, not the Tory friends of prerogative, were in power. The point did not escape later oppositions.[13]

Much of the literature on corruption dealt with electors and the purchase of votes in counties and boroughs. Since this concomitant of representative government had no exact classical equivalent, there was less tendency to dwell here upon ancient history; anyway, such general indictments were far more innocuous than accusations against the Court, and so they could safely be made without benefit of veiled allusions. Of course, it was not uncommon for writers to trace the connections between corruption in high places and the debauching of the electorate. Members of Parliament who had to pay large sums to get elected would naturally, it was said, try to recoup by misusing their trust. Other critics chose to emphasize how corruption among the great would necessarily set a bad example for the masses. The watchword that promised a remedy for all abuses was "public spirit,"

10. Anon., *A Collection of the Debates and Proceedings ... Upon the Inquiry into the late Briberies and Corrupt Practices* (London, 1695), sig. A2.
11. N.N., *Some Reasons for Annual Parliaments in a Letter to a Friend* (London, [c. 1695]), p. 5.
12. Anon., *The English Man's Complaint* (n.p., [1690]).
13. See *Monitor* 37 (17 Apr. 1756). The theme was also standard fare in Tory pub-lications of the 1740s.

and churchmen plyed their trade by condemning its absence in all ranks of society. Spokesmen for successive administrations pointed to the impossibility of blaming government for the moral climate, since bribery flourished on the venality of private citizens. Spokesmen for the Opposition invariably reversed the argument, alleging that it was a corrupt government that must be held responsible for prevailing moral standards. The pattern was set for a century of inconclusive debate.

The fashion of identifying widespread corruption as the chief political ill was by no means a complete departure from the position of, say, Puritans of the 1640s with their cry against unregenerate opponents. But there was a difference in emphasis, as attention came more and more directed towards the state of society and less towards the acts of individual tyrants or the conscience of the ruler.[14] Vice and luxury, the bane of severe moralists in all ages, became political categories of unprecedented importance, and with the prominence accorded to structural defects in the political order, the importance of the ruler's conscience declined in proportion. The institution of limited monarchy assisted this transformation, for ministers of course replaced the sovereign as the focus of discontent. But there was more to it than an insistence that servants of the Crown not shelter behind their master. In 1758, the most popular censor of moral decay, the Reverend John Brown, actually suggested that Robert Walpole had been powerless to prevent the sea of corruption that had surrounded his administration.[15] That was certainly an extreme claim, and it found little favour with ardent partisans, but it attests to the enhanced importance of corrupt manners as a category of political analysis. Social corruption carried with it problems about causation that had no place in earlier talk of wicked rulers.

The passionate fixation on corruption that marked so much political writing pointed to changes in despotic technique and raised the possibility that the people might betray their own liberties. Examples of Roman tyranny and Roman virtue supplied the obvious historical model, and these were enthusiastically developed by the group of Old

14. For thoughts on this general tendency see James M. Buchanan and Gordon Tulloch, *The Calculus of Consent* (Ann Arbor: University of Michigan Press, 1965), pp. 310–11.

15. Brown, *An Estimate of the Manners and Principles of the Times* (London, 1758), 2:206–9.

Whigs, republicans, and Country Tories that included Walter Moyle, Andrew Fletcher, John Trenchard, and Charles Davenant. For all these men, the road to Rome was through Florence and Machiavelli. Understandably so, because the Florentine's prescription for a corrupt people—the restoration of a polity to its first principles—seemed to speak directly to the British situation. Of course, Machiavelli had known no institutional equivalent of the British Parliament, but in his concern for civic virtue and especially the reliance upon a militia, he did yeoman service within the commonwealth tradition.

Most of the elements of the theory of legal tyranny had already appeared in the writings of these men before the close of the seventeenth century. Moyle set the tone of much subsequent literature by writing an essay on the vicissitudes of the Roman constitution, and another work, in which he probably had a hand, treated the perils of a standing army sanctioned by Parliament. Whereas the army of James II had been but an "unlawful Assembly," a parliamentary army would see the land "enslaved ... by Authority."[16] His friend Andrew Fletcher, best known to posterity for a declared preference for writing ballads over legislating, painted an even gloomier prospect for a nation sunk in corruption: "Then it is that we must expect Injustice to be established by a Law, and all those Consequences, which would inevitably follow the Subversion of a Constitution, I mean, standing Armies, oppressive Taxes, Slavery, whilst the outward Form only of the ancient Government remains to give Authority."[17] In emphasizing the clandestine nature of arbitrary power, Fletcher went beyond the Whigs of 1675.

Other elements in the picture came from the pen of John Toland. Less interested than the others in using the fate of Rome to dramatize the condition of Britain, Toland made his most considerable contribution to the idiom of the time by popularizing the maxim that Britain could never be ruined but by a Parliament.[18] The author of this com-

---

16. *The Second part of an Argument shewing that a Standing Army is Inconsistent with a Free Government* (London, 1697), p. 23.

17. "Two Discourses Concerning the Affairs of Scotland; Written in the Year 1698," in *The Political Works of Andrew Fletcher, Esq.* (London, 1732), p. 76.

18. See *The Art of Governing by Partys* (London, 1701), p. 56; *The State-Anatomy of Great Britain*, 6th ed. (London, 1717), p. 39; and *Letters from the Right Honourable the late Earl of Shaftesbury to Robert Molesworth Esq.* (London, 1721), p. xx. The introduction to this last is by Toland.

ment—the probable parent of Montesquieu's ambiguous dictum about a loss of freedom when the legislature became more corrupt than the executive—was most often said to be Lord-Treasurer Burghley; but Bacon, and even Godolphin, was sometimes credited with it. The sentiment, Toland once said, was "in the Mouth of every Child"; certainly he had done his best to put it there. Toland also subscribed to the observation that far from ending the corruption begun under Charles II, the Glorious Revolution had extended it to such a degree as to have "chang'd the very Natures of Englishmen."[19] Toland developed no elaborate theory of tyranny and remained moderate in his views. A posthumously published work continued to rank packed and bribed parliaments a lesser danger than long ones.

In one of his pamphlets, Toland quoted Tacitus, that tersest of historians and the source of mottos for numerous publications of the eighteenth century: "Arcanum novi Status, Imago Antiqui, ... The Secret of setting up a new Government is to retain the Image of the Old."[20] The context had nothing to do with Toland's hostility to current mores; it was thus left to Charles Davenant to apply the motto to the issue of corruption.

A modern scholar has remarked that the Greek notion of preserving a constitution by trying to mould the citizenry to the appropriate character suffered "an almost total eclipse" until the advent of modern psychiatry.[21] This neglects the contribution of the Old Whigs of the 1690s and their numerous imitators. It is no doubt true that the bogey of corruption and legal tyranny was a better instrument for attacking governments than for actually altering the behaviour of Englishmen. Some men who pioneered this mode of discourse were genuine republicans who sought, if not popular participation, at least more effective checks to power. Their successors in eighteenth-century oppositions cherished ambitions for reform that were even more modest and institutionally imprecise. The era—spanning most of the eigh-

---

19. *The Danger of Mercenary Parliaments* (London, [c. 1695]), p. 3. Though this work has usually been credited to Toland, he seems only to have seen it through the press. The author was apparently the 3rd Earl of Shaftesbury. See Giancarlo Carabelli, *Tolandiana: Materiali bibliografici per lo studio dell' opera e della fortuna di John Toland (1670–1722)* (Florence: La nuova Italia, 1975), p. 42.

20. *Anglia Libera* ... (London, 1701), p. 19.

21. Martin Birnbach, *Neo-Freudian Social Philosophy* (Stanford: Stanford University Press, 1961), p. 222.

teenth-century—that separated the old religious struggles from the later ideological politics of class was relatively devoid of major domestic issues. It was thus tempting to see the prevailing calm and apparent freedom as pregnant with a future tyranny. Since the Opposition sought no major improvements in the lot of the poor and the powerless, it was also convenient to flesh out the programme of place-bills, a militia, shorter parliaments, and a reduced national debt by calling for a new civic spirit. Thus "patriot" politicians found transcendent purpose in what was otherwise a sordid pursuit of office.

"And Builds Imaginary Rome A-New"

The central element in Roman history that fascinated political writers was the process whereby the republic had been gradually transformed into the Empire. The facts were well known and had long been judged relevant to the experience of other states. Peter Heylin had written in 1632 of these events, paying particular attention to the manner in which the Roman people had been misled by "Appearances." In addition, Heylin expressed the conventional opinion that the reader of Roman histories "will judge them rather to contain the Acts of the whole World, than a particular Nation. ..."[22] But Heylin was a friend to Stuart government, and the times were not propitious for accounts of tyranny by stealth. In the reign of William III, Dr. Charles Davenant (1656–1714), economist and Country pamphleteer, returned to the theme with much more effect.

The year 1698 had seen a major new translation of Tacitus. It incorporated some of the vast scholarship already dedicated to the subject, but it owed its current form to the efforts of contemporary literary men—John Dryden, a Tory, and William Higden, a non-juror. All of Davenant's subsequent work bore the marks of Tacitus's description of Rome's loss of liberty. In a major indictment of corruption, appearing in 1699, Davenant pondered the fact that the Romans remained acquiescent under the growing imperial sway, and concluded that the cause lay in the attitude of the masses who "believed themselves still free, because, in show, the commonwealth had the

---

22. [Heylin], *Augustus:, or, An Essay of those Meanes and Counsels whereby the Commonwealth of Rome was Alter'd and Reduc'd unto a Monarchy* (London, 1630), p. 1. It was reprinted, without either the author's name or the date, around 1710.

same form as in elder times. ...." The weight of tyranny, Davenant explained, was borne largely by the upper ranks, while the common people, remote from an oppressive court, "could never be induced to oppose that power which still bore some resemblance to their ancient form of government."

Similarly, he claimed, English parliaments, once corrupted by a prince, would stagnate peacefully, the people blinded by "names and forms" and secure in the reassuring presence of the "outward show of the constitution." Sharpening a point already familiar in the writings of the champions of civic virtue, he denied that a corrupt commonwealth could hope for the same sort of deliverance that followed the death of bad kings. Indeed, he so refined the claim as to allege that mixed government, once corrupted, was "the greatest tyranny in the world, it is tyranny established by a law, it is authorized by consent, and such a people are bound by fetters of their own making."[23] The general sentiment that the corruption of the best things had the worst results was already familiar in the Christian adage *corruptio optimi pessima*, and often in the following century it was applied to the state of Parliament.

How could a people be brought to enslave itself? Part of the answer lay in the passive, self-deluding character of the public, careless in its attention to events and thus subject to being misled. Another factor was the measure in which many people might expect to profit from abuses. No doubt the sufferers from tyranny might indeed be drawn from the elite of the community, but the same stratum included many who would actively participate in shoring up the polity. Contrasting a crude despotism with the refined techniques of corruption, Davenant traced the process whereby influential people would come to terms with a tyrannical government, rendering it more secure:

A tyranny that governs by the sword, has few friends but men of the sword; but a legal tyranny (where the people are only called upon to confirm iniquity

---

23. "Of Private Men's Duty in the Administration of Public Affairs," sec. 5 of "An Essay upon the Possible Methods of Making a People Gainers in the Balance of Trade" (1699), in *The Political and Commercial Works of ... Charles D'Avenant*, ed. Sir Charles Whitworth, (London, 1771), 2:299–301. For an account of Davenant's thoughts about trade and society see J. G. A. Pocock, *The Machiavellian Moment* (Princeton: Princeton University Press, 1975), pp. 437–46. The entire work is of great value to the student of classical influences on the eighteenth century.

with their own voices) has of its side the rich, the fearful, the lazy, those that know the law and get by it, ambitious churchman, and all those whose livelihood depends upon the quiet posture of affairs. ...[24]

These words became a basic text in eighteenth-century political rhetoric. Davenant's portrait of how corrupt governors involved ever more people in their misdemeanors, thus linking the fate of these fugitives from justice with the prosperity of their protectors, was an essential part of the complaint about social corruption. The disease might originate with kings or ministers, but it had the effect of turning numerous private men into enemies of the public. Again, the message was not new. In the middle of the sixteenth century, the young Etienne de la Boétie had marvelled at how a corrupt people might be governed, and the parallel was not lost upon Englishmen of the eighteenth century. In fact the tyrannical pyramid of influence depicted in *Contr' Un* doubtless had much more relevance to England, undergoing what is now called the "financial revolution," than it had to the times in which it was written. The excellence of Boétie's book lay in its understanding of how a single ruler multiplied his dependents and his power; he had not written of legal tyranny and emphasized the use of military force in establishing arbitrary government.[25] By contrast, Davenant was able to show that the process of undermining freedom was already inherent in the sophisticated means of creating public credit and the concomitant growth of executive power.

One point, derived from Tacitus, was especially prominent in Davenant's writing and does much to explain its later popularity. After the clash of 1701, which saw a Tory Commons imprison petitioners from Kent, he defended Parliament against popular as well as ministerial power. For were the House ever to lose its independence and stature it would be much worse than useless, becoming a means of rendering absolute rule more onerous. That was the basic paradox that sustained the case for vigilance in a government already, to all intents and purposes, free:

It is not the name of a House of Commons that makes a nation free, but

24. Davenant, "Of Private Men's Duty," p. 301.
25. See la Boétie, *Discours de la servitude volontaire* [written c. 1549], ed. Maurice Rat, (Paris: A. Colin, 1963). For its use in British debate see *Fog's Journal* 360 (27 Sept. 1735).

their efficacy, power and authority, and the respect and reverence their consultations and proceedings meet with. But where all this is taken from them, the subjects are in worse condition, than if they were governed by the sword. For where there is nothing but the appearances of freedom left, the severest bondage is intended. 'Quantoque majore libertatis imagine tagabentur tanto eruptura ad insensius servitium'.[26]

Davenant's imaginative application of Tacitus was not the pattern of political argument that dominated the reign of Anne. The rekindled fires of party animosity and a succession of bitterly contested constitutional issues dictated other modes of debate. The case against corruption and legal tyranny was valuable in displaying a general pattern of conduct; specific issues were more readily discussed in direct fashion, without the assistance of history. John Toland continued to write during these years, but his most forceful pronouncements about corruption already had been made in the reign of William. With the status of the Church becoming a major issue, his attention was directed elsewhere. Davenant's writings from around the time of the second Partition Treaty (1700) were cited against the Tory government of 1710–14, and their legislation aimed at curbing the Dissenters was likened to the attempt of James II to introduce slavery by a law.[27] Addison's *Cato* was performed in 1713 as a tribute to the Duke of Marlborough, but the play had largely been written a decade before. Of course the public was attuned to discovering contemporary referents for historical figures, especially in the theatre. Nathaniel Lee's *Lucius Junius Brutus*, of 1680, had been accompanied by the same sort of furore that was caused by Addison's play. Still, some people denied that *Cato* had any political relevance, asking, "What does the Consti-

---

26. "Peace at Home and War Abroad" (1704), *Works*, 4:297. The quotation from Tacitus (*Annals*, bk. 1, par. 81) was commonly repeated in the eighteenth century. See, for instance, [Earl of Marchmont], *A Serious Exhortation to the Electors of Great Britain* (London, 1740), p. 10. This passage displays the genre known as "red Tacitism."·See Peter Burke, "Tacitism," in T. A. Dorey, ed., *Tacitus* (New York: Basic Books, 1969), p. 169. A recent treatment of Tacitus's influence suggests, surprisingly, his irrelevance to English politics after the Restoration. See Kenneth C. Schellhase, *Tacitus in Renaissance Political Thought* (Chicago and London: University of Chicago Press, 1976), p. 165.

27. See the anonymous pamphlets, *Dr. D—NANT's Prophesys* (London, 1713); and "Cato Brutus," *A Letter to the People of England, Occasion'd by the Letter to the Dissenters* (London, 1714), p. 124.

tution of Rome relate to us?"[28] Attempts to answer that question were forthcoming in abundance.

The high tide of Roman influence must surely have been the reign of George I. John Trenchard and Thomas Gordon, calling themselves "Cato," turned the *London Journal* into the most controversial newspaper of the day. Cato's theme was corruption—the prevailing morality displayed in the business of the South-Sea Bubble, presented against a background of the decline of classical commonwealths. It was not, in fact, as able a case as had been made by Davenant. Trenchard and Gordon seem to have been more reluctant than Davenant to portray the people as being misled by appearances, for many of the essays expressed a faith in the insight of the masses that had been absent in Davenant and, especially, in Tacitus. Desite occasional references to the people's being "trepanned" by their rulers, the point about legal tyranny was blunted in various ways, including the claim that the force wielded by a treacherous army might follow corruption and usher in tyranny.[29] Tacitus and Davenant, arguing that a continuing constitutional façade was possible, had been far more devastating.

Cato's best effort, written by Trenchard, did seem to grasp the nettle, though with a characteristic reluctance to admit that evil rulers could really disguise the nature of their government:

Names will not defend you, Gentlemen, when the Thing signified by them is gone. The Emperors of Rome were as absolute with the Shew of a Senate, and the Appearance of the People's choosing their Praetors, Tribunes and other Officers of the Commonwealth, as the eastern Monarchies are now without their seeming Checks, and this Shew of Liberty, and in some Respects they were more secure, as the Infamy of their Tyranny was shar'd by their Assemblies ... ; and the Condition of the People was rather the worse for these mock Magistrates and pretended Representatives, who, under the Colour and Title of the Protectors of the People, were, at the People's Expense, the real Helpers and Partakers of the Tyrant's Iniquity. The Kings of France have Parliaments, but Parliaments which dare not dispute their royal Pleasure,

---

28. [George Sewell], *Observations Upon Cato. A Tragedy by Mr. Addison*, 2nd ed. (London, 1713), p. 21.

29. See Cato letter 17, *London Journal* 72 (18 Feb. 1720–21); and letter 63, ibid. 131 (27 Jan. 1721–22). The most accessible source of these letters is the 3rd ed. of the full collection (reprinted, New York: Russell and Russell, 1969).

and the poor People would not fare one Jot the better, if these Parliaments were bribed not to dispute it.[30]

There are echoes here of Davenant, whose name does not appear in Cato's letters, and of Tacitus, whom they did occasionally quote. But in one respect Trenchard and Gordon went a little beyond their Old-Whig predecessors. Both Walter Moyle, mutual friend of Trenchard and Davenant, and Davenant himself had been intrigued with the way in which political power rested on opinion.[31] No student of Tacitus was unaware of the role played by names, titles, forms, and ceremonies in the famous account of political change at Rome. Accordingly, to say that power rested largely on opinion was but an extension of Tacitus.

Trenchard and Gordon took a particular interest in the social bearing of words, and several of their publications—the *Independent Whig* and the late numbers of Cato's letters in the *British Journal*—described how men were constantly being divided and governed by sounds and symbols. The bulk of these essays dealt with the way in which the clergy manipulated their flocks through purely verbal distinctions. Gordon translated Barbeyrac's assault upon priestcraft, and both he and Trenchard certainly found this sort of anticlericalism attractive. From Samuel Werenfels, a contemporary writer on logomachies, they could have obtained additional thoughts on the power of words.[32] One of the defining qualities of an independent Whig—the label with which Trenchard and Gordon were identified—was that he scorned the authority of mere names, and judged men by their actions.[33] Nevertheless, despite some effective comments by Trenchard on the manner of ruling by "Names" or "Sounds," Cato was rather disappointing on the subject. The bulk of the essays dealing with the role

30. Letter 70, *London Journal* 138 (17 Mar. 1721–22). A similar reluctance is apparent in "Britannicus" [i.e., Gordon], *The Conspirators on the Case of Catiline, Part II* (London, 1721), p. 21.

31. See Moyle, "An Essay upon the Constitution of the Roman Government" (1698), in *The Works of Walter Moyle Esq., None of which were ever before Published* (London, 1726), 1:30; and Davenant, "An Essay upon the Balance of Power" (1701), in *Works*, 3:318.

32. Werenfels even used the Roman example of cloaking slavery with the name of liberty. See *A Discourse of Logomachys, or Controversys about Words*, translated anonymously (London, 1711), p. 65.

33. [Gordon], "The Character of an Independent Whig" (1719), in Richard Barron and Thomas Gordon, eds., *A Cordial for Low-Spirits* (London, [1750]), p. 205.

of words in civil life were by Gordon, certainly the junior and weaker partner.[34] Thus the reader encounters some interesting speculations about the way in which rulers enhanced their authority through grand titles and how other merchants of illusion used words to create credit and generate economic activity, often relying, in the fashion of the time, on French terms to lend a meretricious glamour to their activity. The time was ripe for insights about the contribution of illusion to the maintaining of power; government, ostensibly free, seemed to grow more arbitrary every day, while the terrible power of opinion created and destroyed fortunes. In May 1721, John Darby, printer and bookseller, advertised a publication entitled *A Discourse Shewing that most of the Disputes in the World are Nothing but Contentions about Words*. This may have been the synthesis that the subject required, but, assuming that publication did take place, no copy seems to have survived.

As in so many other facets of current political argument, the source of the insight lay in the works of Tacitus, in this case, his explanation of the specious continuity lent to a political order by the retention of old names—*eadem magistratuum vocabula*. In a century when theory failed singularly to keep pace with changes in political institutions, it was an observation that remained popular, three words that with unparalleled brevity summarized the Opposition view of power.[35]

Despite an apparent regard for Tacitus—he provided the motto of the *Independent Whig*—Trenchard did him a major disservice in attributing one of his major themes to Machiavelli: "Machiavel advises any one, who would change the Constitution of a State, to keep as much as possible to the old Forms; for then the People, seeing the same Officers, the same Formalities, Courts of Justice, and other outward Appearances, are insensible of the Alteration. ..."[36] The account is garbled in several respects, for Machiavelli gave exactly the opposite advice, cautioning a new prince to make everything new. His advice

---

34. See Gordon's essays: "Of the Abuse of Words," *Humourist* (London, 1720), 1:195–201; *Independent Whig* 1 (20 Jan. 1719–20); 28 (27 July 1720), and 36 (21 Sept. 1720); and *An Essay on the Practice of Stock-Jobbing* (London, 1724), p. 5.

35. *Annals* 1, 3. For instances of its use see Michael Kearney, *Lectures Concerning History Read During the Year 1775, in Trinity College, Dublin* (London, 1776), p. 58; and Jeremiah Gill, *Thoughts on a Reform in the British Representation* (Gainsborough, 1785), p. 35.

36. *Independent Whig* 12 (6 Apr. 1720).

to those who tried to introduce liberty into a state previously without it was indeed to retain some familiar forms, but Trenchard employed the idea in the context of demonstrating how tyranny and superstition were maintained.[37] On the other hand, the lesson could certainly be gained from a reading of Tacitus, but hardly in the form of advice, since Tacitus invariably perceived the difference between form and substance as the essence of refined tyranny. Still, it was a fruitful error, and many others later cited Machiavelli to the same purpose.[38]

Predictably, Cato's forays into Roman history provoked numerous answers from Walpole's administration; indeed, a number of newspapers were probably funded by the government for the express purpose of counteracting Cato's influence. Cato's mode of argument was identified as a specific genre that originated early in the reign of William III. The technique of alluding to parallels between Britain and Rome seemed unfair—"a wrong Way of arguing"—just because distant times were so very different. As one Whig journalist put it, he admired Livy and Tacitus, but he could have wished the two placed on some *Index Expurgatorius* for the previous two or three years.[39] A stout refusal to meddle with the writings of subtle foreigners was probably the best strategy for Cato's opponents.

But some chose to meet Trenchard and Gordon on their own ground. Cato's use of the Roman experience was intended to demonstrate that a gradual descent into tyranny had happened before. However, Tacitus's now famous comments about retaining the façade of the old order when establishing a new one was amenable to other interpretations. The *imago antiqui* of Tacitus became the traditional form of British institutions, where despite all appearances, power had settled irrevocably and safely in the hands of the Commons. Even John Toland in his *Anglia Libera* had already put Tacitus to that use, though it was entirely foreign to the original meaning. In similar fashion,

37. Cf. Machiavelli, *Discourses*, bk. 1, chaps. 25–26.
38. See *Weekly Journal or, Saturday's Post* (better known as *Mist's Journal*) 131 (12 Aug. 1727); *Fog's Journal* 265 (1 Dec. 1733); and *Craftsman* 865 (22 Jan. 1742–43). A comparable confusion was Jeremiah Dyson's attribution to Machiavelli of Davenant's translation and quotation of a passage in Tacitus. See [Dyson], "A Fair Trial ... or, the Rights of Electors Asserted" (1769), in *A Collection of Some Scarce and Interesting Tracts* (London, 1788), 3:370.
39. See *St. James's Journal* 29 (15 Nov. 1722); Anon., *The Censor Censur'd: or, Cato Turned Catiline* (London, 1722); and *Whitehall Journal* 25 (6 Nov. 1722).

Davenant's quotable passages about corruption appeared in the government press in contexts calculated to reverse their normal impact.[40] Perhaps men in office wished to give the impression that they had nothing to fear from polite learning about ancient tyranny. This would help to account for Walpole's encouragement of Gordon's later publication of a successful translation of Tacitus, replete with commentary on such matters as "Why under such Tyrants the Senate Continued to Subsist."[41] For, by this time Gordon was said to be a tame pensioner—"Silenus," the ministerial toady later to be brilliantly mocked by Pope for having finally become, with help from the Treasury,[42] an "independent Whig." It was difficult to recruit Tacitus to Walpole's cause, and Gordon did not really try, but there was an undoubted reluctance to concede such a popular author to the Opposition.

The same ambivalence that afflicted the ministry is apparent in the ranks of Country Tories. They too proclaimed their unwillingness to swap classical allusions, as when Archibald Hutcheson's *Freeholder's Journal* announced that it would not rely upon Machiavelli and Tacitus to retell British history. Instead, it offered Addison's proclaimed ambition to look directly at the laws and history of the English people. In truth, the writers of the *Freeholder's Journal* were no more consistent than Addison himself.[43] There was certainly a rational case for avoiding Tacitus and his modern friends, for Cato appeared to have effectively appropriated antiquity on behalf of independent Whiggery. In the reign of Anne, the Tories had already disliked appeals to

40. *Englishman's Journal* 3 (20 June 1722); and *Supplement to the St. James's Journal* 33 (12 Dec. 1722).

41. Gordon, *The Works of Tacitus, I: Containing the Annals to which are prefixed Political Discourses upon that Author* (London, 1728), p. 89. John Nichols claimed that Gordon's commentaries were derivative from the work of "Malvezzi Scipio Ammirato" and "Don Balthazar Alamos Banientos" [*sic*]. See *Literary Anecdotes* (London, 1812), 1:710. This account muddles the names of three commentators on Tacitus. The one whose work most closely resembles that of Gordon was Virgilio Malvezzi. This author did argue that it was significant that magistrates continue in office and with their titles, though without authority, but his emphasis was entirely different. See *Discourses upon Cornelius Tacitus*, trans. Sir Richard Baker (London, 1642), pp. 155–58.

42. For a credible attempt to explain Gordon's supposed apostasy see David L. Jacobson, ed., *The English Libertarian Heritage* (Indianapolis: Bobbs Merrill, 1965), pp. xxviii–ix.

43. *Freeholder's Journal* 5 (28 Feb. 1721–22). Cf. ibid. 48 (21 Nov. 1722).

Roman history because of the associations with republicanism.[44] Matthias Earbery, a Jacobite, was even more decisive in his rejection of Rome as a vehicle for hounding Walpole. Earbery spoke the language of legal tyranny, as current reality and not as an image from the past, but he applauded Hobbes's judgement that the ancient historians had poisoned the minds of the English gentry.[45] High-Churchmen and Jacobites felt that they had a genuine history upon which they could draw, and in this respect they differed from the Old Whigs, whose republican doctrines had no English roots that could safely be examined. Hostility to a period that offered no possible support for their cause continued to be characteristic of the friends of royal prerogative; English history afforded much friendlier soil.

But even Tories and alleged Jacobites, such as Nicholas Mist, learned to speak the fashionable language of the day. The voice of the eighteenth-century commonwealthman was not entirely stilled, even after Gordon's apostasy, but it was becoming indistinguishable from that of the rest of the opposition to Walpole. Here Davenant's writings found an honoured place within a considerable range of opinion, which included the Jacobite Duke of Wharton.[46] But Davenant was not a popular figure with High-Churchmen, since he had deserted that cause to serve Harley. Davenant's works were quoted too in *Mist's Weekly Journal* and in *Fog*, its whimsical successor, but he was generally identified only as the writer of a work against the Partition Treaty or the author of "a Treatise upon Government, written soon after the Revolution."[47]

The writers of the *Craftsman* in the 1730s preferred to use *Cato's Letters* or Gordon's *Tacitus* in order to dramatize the fate of a corrupt people. In one respect, however, Bolingbroke and his associates did not hesitate to pursue a point further than their predecessors; and so whereas Cato had questioned the value of corrupt parliaments, the

44. See *Examiner* 18 (23–30 Nov. 1710); and *Tory Tatler* 16 (3 Jan. 1710–11). The *Examiner* was then written by Swift.

45. [Earbery], *The Occasional Historian* (London, 1730), 2:4; and *The Universal Spy or, The Royal Oak Post Reviv'd by "John Perspective"* [i.e., Earbery] 1 (29 Apr. 1732), and 2 (6 May 1732).

46. *True Briton* 11 (8 July 1723).

47. *Mist's Journal* 145 (27 Jan. 1727–28); number of 18 Jan. 1728–29, in *Select Letters taken from Fog's Weekly Journal* (London, 1732) 1:27–31; and *Fog* 271 (12 Jan. 1733–34).

Opposition of the 1730s said flatly that it was better to dispense with parliaments entirely. Since the Opposition had been unsuccessful in swaying the electorate, it was becoming difficult for Walpole's enemies to deny that the people might indeed be led to mistake the forms of a free government for the substance. During the 1730s, the terms "legal slavery" and "parliamentary tyranny" became firmly established in political vocabulary. An essay by a Jacobite, James Erskine of Grange, was one of the influential documents in pressing to its conclusion the point about the virulence of disguised tyranny: "If we must choose, it would be better for us to have an absolute Monarchy, founded upon the Principles of passive Obedience and Non-resistance, and supported by superstitious Priests ... than an absolute Monarchy, founded upon Corruption and supported by mercenary Parliaments."[48] The Old Whigs of a previous generation would have seen the object of such an argument but would not, one suspects, have cast themselves with such abandon into the arms of superstitious priests. To speak of the value of jettisoning parliaments was to contemplate very strong medicine, especially at a time when there still were people who genuinely doubted the efficacy of the institution and who took divine right and absolute monarchy as valid claims.

John "Orator" Henley, one of the more colourful ministerial journalists, was particularly merciless in his attacks on the Roman politics of the time. Ignoring the real difference in emphasis between Trenchard's views and those of the *Craftsman*, Henley dismissed Bolingbroke and company with the quip that "Caleb is Cato Common-plac'd."[49] His irreverent wit did not spare the dead, as he poked fun at "Brigadier Trenchard," who had died, he claimed, in the wars between Cato and Caesar. Henley's distrust of Gordon—not an uncommon reaction—knew no bounds, but Tacitus, the "Grub Journalist of Old Rome," also shared in the abuse. Without Tacitus, he said, a number of the journals of opposition would never have seen the light. Tacitus alone was the parent "of *Mist* and *Fog*, those *Bales* and *Waggon-Loads* of *Common Senses*, that have broke down so many Stage-coaches ... in the Country Interest."[50]

Undoubtedly the Opposition press was pedestrian and derivative,

48. [Erskine], *The Fatal Consequences of Ministerial Influence* (London, 1736), p. 22.

49. *Hyp-Doctor* 44 (5–12 Oct. 1731). Caleb D'Anvers was the pseudonym of the writers of the *Craftsman*.

50. Ibid. 458 (21 Aug. 1739).

but Bolingbroke did, in fact, rework the materials of English history in order to frame his condemnation of corruption. He once called Tacitus a favourite author, but Bolingbroke refrained from presenting the undigested chunks of other writers in the manner of his colleagues in opposition. Even when arguing the most conventional theme—the revival of Roman experience with tyranny under the forms of liberty—he found an imaginative way of making an old point:

Q. What is *become* of the Scipio's and Cato's of Rome?
A. They sing now on the *English* stage.[51]

The jibe has particular force when one considers that a government journalist of the period said that all he wanted to hear of Rome was the Italian opera.[52]

Prior to the election of 1741, the concern about corruption was intense. Parliamentary debates were full of descriptions of the techniques of legal tyranny, and references to Rome were certainly not rare.[53] A protest by the minority in the House of Lords, following the loss of the Place-bill of 1740–41, put the Country position with a directness usually lacking in current journalism. Without a place-bill, the Opposition Lords asserted, the remaining forms of the constitution would "by creating a fatal Delusion" become the nation's greatest grievance.[54] The press was often inhibited about addressing itself to issues without a measure of historical allusion, no matter how transparent. Members of Parliament were not under quite the same restraints, but they too resorted to recitals of past events, if only because their prophecies of slavery and general ruin had not materialized. Journalists were often forced to employ the lame excuse that it was necessary to prepare institutions to resist bad rulers while time still remained under an indulgent government. The conventions of Par-

51. Bolingbroke, "The Freeholder's Political Catechism" (1733), in *A Collection of Political Tracts* (London, 1748), p. 270.

52. [Aaron Hill], *Prompter* 12 (20 Dec. 1734).

53. See, for example, *Parliamentary History* 11, cols. 564–65, for the speech attributed to the Earl of Chesterfield, 19 March 1739–40. Accounts of the speeches by other members of the Opposition record comparisons between the British government and that of France and Spain, but not Rome. Opposition speeches on the occasion were issued in 1772 as an appendix to a pamphlet. See [F. Webb], *Thoughts on the Constitutional Power, and Right of the Crown, in the Bestowal of Places and Pensions* (London, 1772).

54. For the full text see *Parliamentary History* 12:2–6.

liament allowed greater candour, though without any hard evidence of a conspiracy against liberty there was little to be added to the veiled insinuations of the press. There is also the difficulty that in the absence of official records of debates, the same journalists who wrote the newspapers may well have attributed their own language to Members of Parliament.

These years belonged most of all to Davenant. For writers of the Opposition he was, in truth, what Henley had dubbed him in jest— "that Father of Politicks."[55] The *Craftsman* and the *Daily Gazetteer* vied with each other to claim his authority.[56] Davenant had written against factions and against interference with Parliament by the public, so ministerial writers had reason to use his works. His economic writings belonged to everyone, of course, and his estimates on population, dating from the turn of the century, were still being used a full century later. Whether it was the penchant of evil ministers to hide behind the king or the powers of Parliament over treaty-making, Davenant's thoughts continued to sustain the newspapers. But most important were the passages about legal tyranny. To a careless journalist of the decayed *Craftsman* of 1744, he was "Sir William D'Avenant," but the message about dangers at the heart of free institutions survived unchanged.[57] Especially memorable was his portrait of new forms of tyranny, taken from his *Private Men's Duty*. There were telling phrases too in his *Balance of Power*: "The beginnings of arbitrary power are always light and easy. ..." "Opinion is the principal support of power ... for all things subsist more by fame than any real strength."[58] With the obvious familiarity of the public with the basic assumptions of legal tyranny, some writers suggested only the main elements, leaving to the reader the business of spelling out details. This was obviously so when journalists said after 1745 that had the pretender been successful, the nation would have no Parliament or worse than none.

55. *Hyp-Doctor* 195 (13 Aug. 1734).
56. See *Craftsman* 665 (7 Apr. 1739); and *Daily Gazetteer* 1189 (13 Apr. 1739).
57. *Craftsman* 936 (2 June 1744). The same error occurred in Anon., *An Essay on Civil Government* (London, 1743), p. 25. For a sampling of other explicit references to Davenant's political arguments see *Westminster Journal* 347 (23 July 1748); and 354 (17 Sept. 1748); *London Evening Post* 4522 (30 Oct.–2 Nov. 1756); and *Craftsman, or Say's Weekly Journal* 838 (27 Aug. 1774).
58. These passages were quoted in *Extraordinary North Briton* 9 (9 July 1768), and 24 (15 Oct. 1768).

To Oliver Goldsmith, writing in 1759, Davenant and Trenchard were ranked as the "standards" in a particular way of writing—the enlistment of antiquity to combat current abuses.[59] When a collected edition of Davenant appeared in 1771, it was quite clear that it was less a revival than a measure of his continuing influence. Of course, the press of the early 1770s was given to presenting shabby copy; only the intrusion of unprecedented events seems to have spared readers a wholesale recapitulation of essays penned seventy years before. In fact several of the scurrilous Opposition papers edited by William Moore lived largely from the works of the Old-Whig tradition and cannibalized each other by borrowing the borrowings. However, it was not only the hacks who found their columns pre-digested in Davenant. John Thelwall, the democrat of the 1790s, had kind words for the political economist's good sense and clear insight on the issue of corruption.[60] Only Harrington, Locke, and the non-juror Charles Leslie were equally successful in bridging the entire century. In fact, Sir Francis Burdett, speaking in the Commons in 1809, quoted the same passage from Tacitus that Davenant had used in 1704—and for roughly the same purpose.[61]

The Limits of Aristocratic Politics

Long before men ceased to quote Davenant, the tradition of which he was a part had worn thin. Part of the reason was undoubtedly a loss of the appeal that had long belonged to Roman history. Admittedly, some writers and politicians always had been hostile, and, on the other hand, major reconstructions of Roman history—those of Gibbon and Ferguson—were still to come. The fact remains that Roman heroes were no longer in fashion. Whether one attributed this to something as portentous as the onset of the movement called romanticism or simply to the natural reaction to a surfeit of Catos and Catilines is a difficult question. Whatever the reason, complaints, not just of the unwarranted use of the ancients, but of the substance

59. *Bee* (London, 1759), p. 242.
60. *Tribune* 3 (London, 1796), p. 9.
61. *Parliamentary History* n.s. 14 (1809): 1045–46.

of the originals, multiplied.[62] After 1750 concern about the deficiencies of a classical education was increasingly heard,[63] and it undermined the common foundation of the prevailing form of rhetoric. In
the 1730s even pro-administration writers had been given to dipping
into the bottomless fund of familiar allusion; Henley himself had
found it expedient to reflect upon the liberty of the press and its limits
in ancient Rome—conveniently overlooking the fact that the Romans
had lacked a press, free or otherwise!

A decade or two later found essayists who questioned the relevance
of the Roman model not just in literature and the arts—the focus of
the quarrel between ancients and moderns—but also in relation to
public life. The myth of Roman freedom came under attack, as when
Samuel Johnson greeted Thomas Blackwell's *Memoirs of the Court of
Augustus* with devastating indifference: "He is come too late into the
world with his fury for freedom, with his *Brutus* and *Cassius*. We have
all on this side of the Tweed long since settled our opinions. ..."[64]
Though Johnson's brand of Toryism might seem naturally unfriendly
to political lessons from republicans and thus not a compelling example, his sentiments were echoed by people with different opinions.
An enthusiast for the Old-Whig scheme of a militia sought to distance
himself from the normal associations of the idea, pleading that it
"carries its own conviction, without resorting to Greece or Rome. ..."[65]

62. For adverse comment on Tacitus see Thomas Hunter, *Observations on Tacitus*
(London, 1752); on Cicero, *Marcus Tullius Cicero, His Offices*, trans. William Guthrie
(London, 1755).

63. See, for instance, Samuel Butler, *An Essay upon Education* (London, [1750)]; and
[John Gordon], *Occasional Thoughts on the Study and Character of Classical Authors* (London,
1762), p. 145. In the 1760s, Adam Smith and Joseph Priestley both expressed their
doubts about the relevance of classical rhetoric for British public life. See Wilbur Samuel
Howell, *Eighteenth-Century British Logic and Rhetoric* (Princeton: Princeton University
Press, 1971), pp. 570–71, 644–45. Howard D. Weinbrot, *Augustus Caesar in "Augustan"
England* (Princeton: Princeton University Press, 1978), examines, from a literary perspective, one aspect of the decline of classical influence.

64. *Literary Magazine: or, Universal Review* 5 (15 Aug.–15 Sept. 1756), p. 239. For
Johnson's authorship see Donald J. Greene, *The Politics of Samuel Johnson* (New Haven:
Yale University Press, 1960), p. 173. Less virulent expressions of the same feeling are
[William Melmoth, the Younger], *Letters on Several Subjects by the late Thomas Fitzosborne,
Bart* (London, 1748) 1:7, 2:11; and [Richard Flecknoe], *An Essay on Wit: to which is
annexed, a Dissertation on Ancient and Modern History* (London, 1748), p. 28.

65. "Eboracensis," *A Letter to the Right Hon. Charles Townsend ... being Thoughts on the
Militia Laws* (London, 1762), p. 30.

If true on the question of defence, it applied as well to the general political state of the nation. Charles Lucas, the Dublin patriot of the Pelhamite era, must have been one of the last of the malcontents whose arguments (in the *Censor*) consisted mainly of parallels with Roman tyranny.

The emergence of John Wilkes as a national political figure of the 1760s brought with it new issues, including a concern for remedying those abuses that required no hypothetical spectres of future tyranny. Oddly enough, it is from the eve of the emergence of genuinely radical reform movements that one can date a new sort of appeal to Rome. Tacitus had written of popular tumults as well as bad emperors, and it was in this vein that Oliver Goldsmith's *Citizen of the World* hinted at the possibility of Parliament's seeking tyranny through the ostensible defence of popular privileges. The argument, part and parcel of the campaign to strengthen the hand of a young king, was supported by a lame analogy with supposed misbehaviour by the Roman Senate. More extreme was the warning of a newspaper in the Court interest. Paraphrasing a statement by Davenant, it intoned: "What Rome has felt, Britain may feel. ... We have had our Sylla; a Catiline, a Clodius are making their appearance; may we never see a Caesar."[66] So much for Pitt! It is also true that by 1766 there were signs of a temporary resurgence of interest in Rome on the part of the Opposition, for Roman colonial policy came to be contrasted with current treatment of America. In any event, the American crisis was more immediate and genuine than the causes that had exercised the patriot Opposition, and the propaganda less frequently leaves one with the impression, so apparent in earlier writings, of a set of clever maxims in search of suitable application.

The cry of public spirit as a barrier to tyranny had been ideal for those gentlemen in opposition who sought nothing more than passive support from the people. Since the existing government had not usually been portrayed as tyrannous, the accent had been on forestalling future disasters. But the amounting demands for a reform in the representation transcended anything that had previously been sought. As late as 1771, Obadiah Hulme expressed the traditional wish for short parliaments as a means of obtaining honest government. Supporting his argument with Roman parallels, he concluded that if Par-

66. [Goldsmith], *Citizen of the World* ... (London, 1762), 1:218. See too *Plain Dealer* 5 (10 June 1763), and 7 (25 June 1763).

liament were but independent, it would not matter who elected it.[67] By contrast, John Dunning's motion of 1780 protesting the influence of the Crown was in no way dependent on the traditional arguments; asked to defend his stand, he merely cited the wants of thousands of citizens as expressed in petitions tabled in the Commons. The old patriot Opposition had never received comparable extra-parliamentary support and so found it necessary to appeal to Rome. Probably it did later reformers a disservice, since opponents of Dunning's motion noted the long history of complaints about influence and the fact that both the influence and its supposedly malign effects remained unproven.[68] Crying wolf, either in Latin or in English, had the usual unfortunate consequences. Lord George Germain, one of the major opponents of Dunning's resolution, had previously expressed his aversion to political argument drawn from Livy and Tacitus. By 1780 that sort of objection had ceased to tell against a modern case for reform. One does find references to the situation of Rome in publications of the county associations or the later Society of the Friends of the People, but they are far outweighed by recitals of specific structural inequalities. When the desire to broaden the franchise was joined by a very un-Whiggish interest in the fate of the poor, the hold of the old political idiom was further weakened. Hewling Luson, civil servant and profound social thinker, argued in 1787 that disputes about governments were misplaced, the only difference between free and arbitrary ones being their original constitution. Even discussing past rights was "trifling" since the only pressing questions were concerned with what government ought to do for the poor. His tract, appropriately entitled *Inferior Politics*, deserves to be better known.

Major John Cartwright was one of the later reformers who eventually embraced the paradoxes of legal tyranny with some enthusiasm. But Cartwright used modern European writers—Gravina and Filangieri—in order to argue his case.[69] Cartwright had come late to the cause of parliamentary reform and was relatively ill-read in earlier

67. [Hulme], *An Historical Essay on the English Constitution* (London, 1771), p. 194.
68. See the remarks of Lord Nugent, *Parliamentary History* 21 (1780–81):349–52.
69. See *A Letter from John Cartwright Esq., to a Friend at Boston* (London, 1793), pp. 22n., 26n. Filangieri's work, first published in 1784, had been translated into English in 1792. See *The Science of Legislation*, translated from the Italian of the Chevalier Filangieri by Wm. Kendall (London and Exeter, 1792). Cartwright's familiarity with Gravina's little-known work on the Roman Republic was probably also derived from Filangieri.

British political literature. Hence he was probably unaware of the extent of previous efforts to employ the Roman analogy. Since he cited neither Tacitus nor his British interpreters, it seems unlikely that Cartwright gained much material on the mechanisms of tyranny from other than the European sources.

Foreigners had much more to contribute to the investigation of modern government than texts recounting the misfortunes of ancient Rome. In France, Spain, Denmark, and Sweden, the medieval estates had been defeated in various ways by the executive power. Englishmen were aware of these developments. Popery and wooden shoes had been a typical seventeenth-century image for French government. At a more refined intellectual level, Viscount Molesworth's *Account of Denmark* (1694) had been a relatively subtle attempt to warn of possible dangers to the English Parliament. There was a problem in arguing from Continental experience with absolutism, for though the Gothic constitution was undoubtedly either destroyed or in retreat throughout Europe, its mode of passing did not lend itself to convenient comparative analysis. Most of Europe had long lacked the freedom to require corruption; nor could it plausibly be argued that a corruption of manners, of the sort relevant to British commercial society, had been the source of the misfortunes of the Danes and the Swedes.

The problem of putting European experiences to good use had been evident as early as 1681 when Thomas Rymer, future historiographer-royal, published a book called *A General Draught and Prospect of Government in Europe: Shewing the Antiquity, Power, Decay, of Parliaments*. Here Rymer presented a strongly Whiggish account of the decline of European legislatures and praised England's parliamentary tradition as the most perfect surviving example of Gothic liberty. Rymer wrote an able description of the growth of absolutism in France, but in a parenthetical comment on the gap between constitutional forms and reality he flew, predictably, to antiquity: "The Caesars were never so absolute, as when the Senate had the Show, and Name of all. But afterwards when their Power declined, then did their Shadows lengthen, and their Titles swell beyond all Sobriety and Proportion."[70]

70. [Rymer], *Of the Antiquity, Power and Decay of Parliaments, Being a General View of Government, and Civil Polity in Europe* (London, 1714), p. 6. This was the 2nd ed. For the complete printing history of the work see Curt A. Zimansky, *The Critical Works of Thomas Rymer* (New Haven: Yale University Press, 1956), pp. 279–80.

Rymer's book was not very influential in its own time, perhaps because the people most given to discussing the fate of legislatures—Moyle, Davenant, and their set—were hostile to Rymer's literary criticism.[71] James Ralph, one of the more skilful Opposition writers on corruption and tyranny, gave the book its widest audience when he reprinted it as part 1 of his *Of the Use and Abuse of Parliaments*. Ralph attributed the book to Algernon Sidney, but William Bollan, writing a generation later, named Lord Somers as the author.[72] Even though he did not correctly identify the author, Ralph had used Rymer's study of European conditions to support his basic contention that the obvious form of despotism was to govern without parliaments, whereas the tactic best suited to Britain was to govern "by Parliaments."[73] Ralph surpassed most of his fellow hacks by his capacity to invest the usual business of discrediting the government with an awareness of the general fate of legislatures in the period. To that attractive sense of epoch Rymer made a large contribution, both here and in a variety of periodicals.

There can be little doubt, however, that the partisan intent of writings about modern legislatures limited their value as history. It was not unusual in the late eighteenth century for historians to note that the treatment of the origins of legislatures had been grossly distorted by tendentious accounts; the same was true of materials connected with the decline of parliaments in the modern era. But with the weakening of the classical hegemony over studies of political change, there was increased scope for effective comparative studies. Indeed, it may be that the development of an ambition to refine the "science of government" contributed to the waning of interest in finding lessons in the fate of republican Rome. The British response to the Swedish Revolution of 1772 was in terms of this ambition of scientific analysis rather than rhetoric. Charles Francis Sheridan, a member of the staff of the British embassy in Stockholm, shared the passion for liberty that Rymer had shown a century before. Indeed, with that much more knowledge of the progress of despotism, he was probably even more

71. See Caroline Robbins, ed., *Two English Republican Tracts* (Cambridge: Cambridge University Press, 1969), p. 24.
72. [Bollan], *The Free Briton's Supplemental Memorial ... wherein the Origin of Parliaments in Europe and other Interesting Matters are Considered* (London, 1770), pp. 26–34.
73. Ralph, *Of the Use and Abuse of Parliaments; in Two Historical Discourses* (London, 1744), 2:715.

alarmed. But as Sheridan's excellent book demonstrates,[74] the merit of comparative analysis was a sensitivity to real differences between nations. The most salient weakness of the rhetoric of legal tyranny was precisely its failure to document genuine parallels—a natural consequence of the striving for emotional effect.

Because of its apparent commitment to Roman virtue and the trappings of classical republicanism, the rhetoric treated here has been described as "reactionary" in a sense that was not true of the political language that predominated in the seventeenth century.[75] Certainly Britain was already, in the eighteenth century, adopting the mores of an industrial society, and these were resisted by the friends of civic virtue. Similarly, influence and organized opposition might usefully confront each other in the House of Commons. Certainly, that system was still too heavily weighted on the side of the ministry, and so there was some reason to complain of the influence of the Crown. It is no less true, however, that a *modus vivendi* did emerge in the relations between Crown and Parliament, and it did not take the form of the independent Parliament sought by Old Whigs. Again, the rhetoric of civic virtue seemed to stand in the path of history.

A more sympathetic viewpoint would emphasize, however, that in seeking a model for political life in the ancient world, the tradition actually emphasized those elements of politics that had emerged at the end of the seventeenth century. Again and again, the writers on legal tyranny insisted that they were not offering government based on force as the substitute for rule through influence. The Old Whigs and their ideological descendants liked neither, and so it became all the more plausible to seek their ideal in the distant, not the recent, past. Although it is undoubtedly true that understanding of some aspects of the eighteenth century—parties, for instance—was impeded by their being viewed through Roman eyes, it is worth mentioning that appeals to King Alfred and the mythical Commons in early English parliaments constituted no improvement. But this was an alternative tradition in eighteenth-century argument, one sometimes employed by the same people who so greatly admired Livy and Tacitus. Indeed, the defences of an ancient constitution usually did rather

74. Sheridan, *A History of the Late Revolution in Sweden*, 2nd ed. (London, 1783), esp. pp. 1–31.
75. J. G. A. Pocock, "Machiavelli, Harrington and English Political Ideologies," in *Politics, Language and Time* (New York: Atheneum, 1971), p. 133.

more violence to historical fact than did appeals to Tacitus. Thus the claim of the seventeenth-century common lawyers, echoed by some in the eighteenth century, that the ancient constitution had to be restored or observed involved a gross distortion of history. In seeking bedrock in Roman practice, civic virtue was disentangled from specific misconceptions about English history and its proponents left free to argue the relevance of timeless political wisdom and general human values—such as the requirement that things be in reality as they were in external appearance. That was not an insignificant cause.

Form and Substance

Since the sombre prospect of legal tyranny was never realized, we must look elsewhere for the contribution to political understanding inherent in the theme. Although the possibility of discrepancies between profession and performance was never absent from political thought, the politics of eighteenth-century Britain were such as to lend special significance to the admonition that the externals of a form of government might not correspond to its essential nature. It was natural enough, when parliaments were in retreat, to contrast polities having active legislatures with those where a king and his advisers ruled unopposed. It cannot have escaped anyone that parliaments and juries might do their work well or ill; but the situation of seventeenth-century Englishmen made them most concerned that free institutions be recognized and given a chance to work at all. If one consults Rymer's survey of 1681, it becomes obvious that he was most interested in the composition and powers of the various estates that existed in European governments. The reason was obvious: the legal definition of the estates was then a major issue in English politics, since it had to do with the legal competence of the monarch and the bench of bishops. The common lawyers' desire to have a government of laws and the maverick Harrington's faith in "good orders" both show the same desire to settle the government upon firm legal foundations—old or new.

The whole point of the talk of legal tyranny was that forms could not be trusted as indication that all was well. This message was not confined to malcontents in opposition, but figured prominently in the appeals of men in office. Richard West, a prominent Whig jurist, wrote an essay that minimized the importance of the outward forms of government, stressing instead the need to curb excessive visions of liberty lest they be inconsistent with what he called "any regular Administration of Government." Using familiar ideas of plenitude in creation, he noted that forms of government were indeed very different; still "insensibly they may slide One into the Other, and by what imperceptible Degrees these Alterations may come about; it will be found very difficult to determine the precise Point, where one Form ends and Another begins. ..."[76] The general point was not inconsistent with what enemies of the Whig government were saying, but the emphasis on avoiding the extremes of a commonwealth form changed the nature of the argument entirely. Government writers were not calling for public spirit to infuse the dead shell of form; they were adamant in their distaste for panegyrics on public spirit, even to the extent of complaining testily that it should not matter if there were some dishonesty in government if the rights and privileges of private citizens were protected.

When Pope gave memorable voice to these sentiments in his famous couplet of 1733–34, he was cultivating common ground between ministry and Opposition. If only fools chose to contest for forms of government, then some sectors of opposition—classical republicans and indefeasible-right Jacobites—were indeed foolish. But since Pope himself stood out against corruption, he was equally in a position to endorse his friend Bolingbroke's obsession about decay beneath the façade of constitutional government. The ambiguity of Pope's most famous observation about politics ensured that it would continue to be put to diverse purposes. Pope probably had a bent towards the authoritarian position on forms, suggesting that one obey the established rulers irrespective of the precise nature of the régime, though with the assumption that the government would be, in some sense, a mixed one.[77] Since he wrote of good administration and not of spirit, Pope really steered between partisan positions.

This did not prevent his couplet's being woven into the tangled skein of allusions that formed the case against legal tyranny. A typical

76. *Free Thinker* 194 (29 Jan. 1719–20), reprinted in *Gentleman's Journal and Tradesman's Companion* 6 (6 May 1721). West is identified as the writer of this piece by Nicholas Joost, "Authorship of the *Free-Thinker*," in Richmond E. Bond, *Studies in the Early English Periodical* (Chapel Hill: University of North Carolina Press, 1957), p. 133.

77. See William Warburton, *A Critical and Philosophical Commentary on Mr. Pope's Essay on Man* (London, 1742), p. 134; and Pope, *An Essay on Man*, in *Works*, ed. Maynard Mack (London: Methuen and Co., 1950), 3:123n.–124n.

essay of this sort introduced obligatory references to emperors of Rome and the "shadow" of freedom by claiming that liberty consisted not so much in "constitution or form, as in the execution or administration of government."[78] Pope's oracular pronouncement continued to give comfort both to reformers and to anti-reformers at the time of the American Revolution, though sometimes the reformers quarrelled mildly with his formulation, pointing out that while forms guaranteed nothing as to good government, each form did have its peculiar evil.[79] An odd indication of Pope's influence on the age occurs in William Ellis's translation of Aristotle's *Politics* where the translator rendered Aristotle's views on the best form of government as "that by which a State may be best administered."[80]

The message about forms and their questionable significance was prominent in several of the more perceptive theoretical works on government that appeared in the middle of the eighteenth century. The label "theoretical" is none too precise but serves to distinguish writings that contained high analytical content and seem not to have been written solely with immediate partisan intent, as was the bulk of political literature.

William Horsley, known to posterity chiefly as an essayist in the *Daily Gazetteer*, seems to qualify as a relatively theoretical writer. Horsley's main argument was that sages on government had directed the bulk of their attention to the forms of political rule and especially to the nature of the sovereign authority. In reality, he argued, climate, national character, the revenue, the administration of justice, and the nature and duties of lesser magistrates were all significant factors. Machiavelli, so often now hailed as a great realist, failed to impress Horsley, who was armed with a new standard for judging insight. The Florentine erred in treating the sovereign as though he were a

---

78. See "Of Publick Liberty," by "The Whimsical Philosopher," *London Magazine* 18 (May 1749), p. 206.

79. For Opposition use of Pope see *Crisis* 62 (23 March 1776); and a late and elaborate example of the genre about legal tyranny, *An Inquiry into the Origin and Consequences of the Influence of the Crown over Parliament* (London, 1780), p. 2. Although this pamphlet has been attributed to Lord Nugent, his strenuous opposition to Dunning's motion makes the claim most unlikely. Pope figured too in the arguments of people who were well affected to the administration. See *Weekly Magazine, or Edinburgh Amusement* 29 (14 Sept. 1775); and [John Lind], *Three Letters to Dr. Price ... by a Member of Lincoln's Inn* (London, 1776), p. xv.

80. Aristotle, *A Treatise on Government*, trans. William Ellis (London, 1776), p. 380.

"common Hangman." The objection was not, in fact, that princes were lent too little dignity but that they were perceived by Machiavelli as instrumental in situations over which they had little control. For this reason, Machiavelli dwelt "in the Clouds," joined by the rest of mankind in pursuing the "Form or Shadow of Government" while neglecting the substance.[81]

The same concern for replacing accounts of the acts of rulers with attention to structural factors is evident in some of Horsley's later essays. Here, he had become increasingly partisan, and his methodological quarrel with Machiavelli had become fused with the rhetoric of legal tyranny. As part of the argument, Horsley denied the effective differences between arbitrary and free governments and introduced a hint of an economic radicalism that was rather unusual for the times. In so-called arbitrary government, the people were slaves in law; in free government, they were so in fact. "A People notionally free, that enjoy not the full Benefit of their Art and Industry, are like the Parliaments of France, who please themselves with an empty Name. ..." Artistry and "the seeming Voice of the People" had replaced the sword as *instrumenta regni*. Britons were no doubt governed by law in "Civil Affairs," but in the "Political State" of the nation the public debt in fact governed, with the directors of great trading companies serving as "Janizaries" under a prime minister.[82]

A cooler tone is evident in the remarks by a Tory lawyer and political writer, John Campbell, when he discussed problems in establishing the true state of a nation:

I say the true state; for the exterior and nominal Constitution is to be found in every Compendium of Geography or History. But if an arbitrary Monarch confides in a *Junto*, his Government is, in effect, an Aristocracy. If a limited Prince either governs, or is governed by the *Heads* of a *Party*, the Constitution becomes from that Moment an *Oligarchy*. ...[83]

Obviously Campbell was saying that Britain qualified as an oligarchy;

---

81. [Horsley], *Lord Theodore's Political Principles* (London, 1744), pp. 6, 10.

82. *The Polite Politician* (London, 1759), pp. 57–59. The essay cited here is one of many in this compilation drawn from the series called "The Fool," of which Horsley was apparently the author.

83. [Campbell], *The Present State of Europe; Explaining the Interest, Connections, Political and Commercial Views of its Several Powers*, 5th ed. (London, 1757), p. 9.

in addition, he left no doubt that the traditional categories for identifying governments were bankrupt. Although it would be easy to exaggerate the hold ever exercised by these categories, their future place would be greatly reduced.

Probably the followers of Harrington were as faithful to form as any thinkers of the eighteenth century. Moyle had been extremely insistent on the preservation of legal safeguards for liberty and resisted the claim of governors that the manners of the people served as a constraint on the prevailing level of virtue. Classical republicanism remained consistent in claiming that it was the government that formed the manners of the people in the first instance. This was precisely the basis on which Dr. David Fordyce, a professor at Aberdeen, insisted that it was indeed the constitution, not the administration of government, that rendered it good or bad. Governments formed people and not the reverse.[84] Fordyce was perhaps one of the first to employ the expression "political culture," but unlike Herder, another eighteenth-century user of the term, Fordyce was not engaged in any quasi-sociological endeavour. Rather, he remained firmly in the republican tradition of conscious establishment of good orders and citizen training to ensure their respect. The same vehement opposition to any casualness about forms appeared in the work of George Ensor, no ordinary Harringtonian, but clearly a republican. In his disdain for Pope's couplet, he indicated that he had probably read the Ellis translation of Aristotle. "If I could imagine, that Pope sought his opinions in Greek literature, I should refer the following empty verses to an Aristotelian source. ..."[85] The answer was probably much simpler: the translator of Aristotle had read Pope.

At the other end of the political spectrum Pope appears to have been no more popular. Forms were important to High-Churchmen, for, as previously noted, they had a stake in a long tradition. As Owen Ruffhead, compiler of the statutes at large, said of the British constitution, "Form ... is in fact substance."[86] Other defenders of prerogative, many of whom were a good deal more extreme than Ruffhead, shared the same antiquarian impulse and loved to dwell upon the niceties of ancient constitutional practice. But the more extreme ver-

---

84. [Fordyce], *Dialogues Concerning Education* (London, 1748), 2:21.
85. Ensor, *On National Government* (London, 1810), 1:84.
86. [Ruffhead], *An Appeal to the People in which the Prerogative ... with the Rights of Parliament ... are Considered*, 2nd ed. (London, 1760), p. 22.

sions of High-Church politics flourished more at the beginning and the end of the century and were comparatively inconspicuous in the middle decades.

From the early days of the first assaults on Walpole it had been clear, as Thomas Gordon noted, that there was literally no one ruler in an absolute monarchy. Of necessity, the titular head would have a host of accomplices.[87] Nor was that other abstract possibility—the rule of all—much contemplated. Most politicians found it convenient at some point in their careers to thank their stars that, by convention, the voice of the people was to be collected only within the walls of Parliament. Certainly in the heyday of the theory of legal tyranny the people who quoted Tacitus on the fate of Rome were sensitive to any attempt to undermine liberty by demagogic appeals to poor and dependent voters. So there was little occasion to remark upon the oligarchical character of government; in large measure, it was simply taken for granted. This explains why one finds no Augustan equivalent to twentieth-century theories about the prevalence of elites. In order for such a position to be worth stating, it had to be contrary to expectations. In addition, since most Englishmen allowed that, for better or for worse, the British government was not one of the three pure forms, but mixed, there was again no need to dwell upon the traditional classification.

Pope's formula had served a variety of masters in eighteenth-century debate, but its value for a later age would be largely confined to the realm of literature. Forms might indeed be unimportant, but injunctions to seek honest administration were of limited value too. One of the abler radical newspapers of 1816–17 contains an essay entitled "Error in the Division of Governments." Here the writer agreed that all known governments were in fact mixed and that there were no such things as fixed and immutable forms. The cardinal error of the ancient classification had been that it looked to the nature and number of the governors; far better to consult the character of the governed. This criterion produced two major types of government: those in enlightened nations and those in unenlightened ones. All other talk of forms was a matter of "theatrical representations."[88] In

---

87. Cato letter 72, *London Journal* 141 (7 Apr. 1722).

88. *Spirit of the Press* 6 (28 Dec. 1816). The Bodleian holdings of this paper seem to be the only run extant. The tone is rather similar to John Wade's *The Gorgon*, which appeared in 1818, but this radical paper seems more sophisticated in argument.

its concentration upon the social characteristics of a nation and on the measure in which the people were capable of exercising political roles, the essay conveys perfectly the concern of a new era. At the same time, in his quest for the reality that lay behind illusion—and even in some comments on tyrants who used the "name of freedom" to mislead—the essayist continued to draw upon the literature about legal tyranny.[89] With all its faults, it was a resilient tradition.

In a sense, of course, the bogey of legal tyranny was curiously premature. The message that the forms of consent made government safer and more economical appears more appropriate to the age of plebiscites. Constant, with his description of a régime that did not so much deny liberty as parody it, was recording not a vision but an image—that of Bonapartism.[90] But it was unnecessary to have the experience of plebiscitary rule before one in order to perceive the potential. The makings of such a government were already thought to be present in the politics of eighteenth-century England. Since the demise of republican Rome lacked the vital elements of representation and of modern public finance, it could at best hint at a condition the details of which were peculiar to the eighteenth century. That hint was necessary, however, to allow the Opposition to refer openly to dangers not yet fully illustrated by English experience.

To see in this the much-sought seeds of totalitarianism is excessive, and it would serve no purpose to add to the chorus tracing this form of government to elements in the English Civil War, the Reformation, and earlier. The eighteenth-century experience does, however, establish that a lesson presumably not learned until later already was known in the freest society in Europe. Modernity is an elusive quality, but surely it was a watershed in political development when all political designs came to terms with the forms of constitutional and representative government. Lord Lyttelton, a close student of both classical and modern politics, was conventional in placing the crucial period of transition at around the Glorious Revolution: "whereas before, *to govern by parliaments* was the policy only of good and wise princes, after this period, it may be considered in a different light, because all expedients of *governing otherwise* are plainly impracticable, and it may

89. *Spirit of the Press* 1 (23 Nov. 1816).
90. "De l'esprit de conquête" (1813), in *Oeuvres de Benjamin Constant*, ed. Alfred Roulin (Paris: Gallimard, 1957), pp. 1014–39.

not always imply a conforming the government to the sense of the people."[91] It is not clear that we have yet gone much beyond that formulation of the problem.

91. Persian letter 63, in *Works* (London, 1776), 1:336–37.

II

The Fourth Estate:
The Language of Political Innovation

THE EIGHTEENTH-CENTURY CONSTITUTION embodied a complex series of compromises that had to be expressed in a form suitable for popular consumption. The formula that expressed the Revolution Settlement had but three terms—King, Lords, and Commons—and these three served for most of the century as a succinct description of the form of government. True, the High-Churchmen and Tories recognized the bishops as an estate. But rather than complicating the picture, this position encouraged a perception of a political order with but two prime units: at the head was the sovereign; all the rest—the lords spiritual, the lords temporal, and the commons—were subjects. With the Whig triumph of 1714 such Tory notions became much less conspicuous.

The major consequences of such a parsimony with categories was that the perceived constitutional framework excluded a number of significant political units, both governmental and social. Since the major aspects of political life had to be accounted for within the secular trinity, the crucial problems in political discourse lay in the business of relating situations and structures to the formal organs of government. Here lay the frontiers of eighteenth-century political understanding. Officially, King, Lords, and Commons were the whole realm—everybody. But a rigorous commitment to formal theory meant that the constitution had nothing to say about some of those bodies to which people actually gave their loyalty. One measure of the growth of sophistication about politics is available in the process whereby the constitution was gradually extended to capture organizations or political factors other than the branches of the legislature.

The State and Its Competitors

The conventional view of the constitution had been hard won; at the accession of George I it had apparently been finally settled after seventy-five years of passionate debate. It was not a position that Englishmen were likely to relinquish without grave misgivings. In order to protect the scheme of King, Lords, and Commons, various arguments were employed to discredit the claims of other political units,[1] and these arguments were in fact current even while the sovereign was still considered to have a status superior to that of the various estates of the realm.

Suspicion of bodies that might compete with the sovereignty of Parliament was no new thing, for many of the fundamental divisions of the seventeenth century had turned on exactly that consideration. No Act of Indemnity could erase the impression that the troubles leading to the execution of Charles I had sprung from the various forms of Low-Church organization. Even John Locke had to admit that assemblies of Dissenters had once been "hotbeds of sedition and nurseries of faction."[2] This was no necessary barrier to tolerating their existence, for, as a contemporary of Locke's put it, conventicles were least likely to "nuzzle up a Faction" when they were allowed to meet in public places where their views could most readily be ascertained. Every church was necessarily a "Society or Body Politick," but if treated sensibly, no dangerous consequences need follow from that.[3]

Given the experiences of the Civil War, it was understandable that High-Churchmen should cherish their cry of "the Church in danger." Indeed, the civil constitution also appeared to be threatened, and the Dissenters' case for Occasional Conformity—the practice whereby they qualified themselves for public offices—provoked elaborate visions of their ultimately using political office to undermine the political order. Since dissenting congregations were held to pose danger, it followed that any efforts to promote their principles were equally threatening. Thus the conventional Anglican judgement on the dissenting academies was that they were "Nurseries of Rebellion," a phrase much

---

1. The point has been noted before. See Wilfred Harrison, *Conflict and Compromise: History of British Political Thought, 1593–1900* (New York: Free Press, 1965), p. 92.

2. Locke, *Epistola de Toleranta: A Letter on Toleration*, ed. R. Klibansky and J. W. Gough (Oxford: Oxford University Press, 1968), p. 135.

3. William Denton, *Jus Caesaris et Ecclesiae vere dictae* (London, 1681), p. 53.

in vogue around the time of the Sacheverell trial.[4] The prevailing attitude towards Dissenters softened somewhat as the eighteenth century progressed, assisted perhaps by Hume's conclusion that Dissenters had preserved British liberties. But the opinion that Roman Catholics belonged to a state within a state continued to flourish; the familiar arguments about whether full legal recognition of Catholic subjects would strengthen faction or disband it were all rehearsed during the debates on Catholic emancipation in the 1790s.

But for much of the century, the Dissenters, not the Roman Catholics, posed the major problem. For their organizations, real or supposed, were a thorn in the flesh of all those whose loyalty to the established church and the Tory party made recognition of competing organizations very difficult. Nor was it necessary for organizations to be overtly either Low-Church or Whiggish for them to fall under that ban. The Societies for the Reformation of Manners had gained official support in the form of royal proclamations. This did not prevent their being condemned, by Sacheverell and others, for promoting "Faction and Rebellion."[5] Even the newly fashionable places of common resort, such as coffee-houses, were often identified as emanations of those interests inimical to the High-Flyers and their political allies. A satirical piece of 1673 poked fun at the varied clientele of such haunts, but the author unmistakably conveyed his position in describing the institution as "a *Lay-Conventicle*, Good-fellowship turned *Puritan*."[6] The mood persisted in Sackville Tufton's condemnation of coffee-houses as "Shops of Sedition and Anvils of Rebellion." Sir Humfrey Mackworth's likening of taverns, frequented by Whigs and Dissenters, to

---

4. [Edmund Curll], *The Case of Dr. Sacheverell Represented in a Letter to a Noble Lord* (London, 1710), pp. 30–31; and *The Moderator* 7 (9–12 June 1710). The moderation of this last is not very pronounced.

Henry Sacheverell (d. 1724) was a flamboyant preacher and baiter of Dissent. He is remembered chiefly because the Whigs of 1710 impeached him for seditious libel. He was convicted on a party vote, subjected to a very light penalty, and became a popular hero. See below, chap. 4.

5. See W. R. Bahlman, *The Moral Revolution of 1688* (New Haven: Yale University Press, 1957), pp. 92–95.

6. "The Character of a Coffee-House ..." (1673), reprinted in Gwendolen Murphy, ed., *A Cabinet of Characters* (London and Oxford: Oxford University Press, 1925), p. 315.

standing armies against the nation's liberties was but an adaptation of the charge to suit the situation of the Tory Opposition of 1717.[7]

More obviously political in their nature were the various clubs that brought together like-minded gentlemen. Though Augustan England was not without Tory bodies of this sort, the bulk of them catered to men recognizable as Whigs. Thus when William Shippen, destined to become the pet Jacobite of Walpole's parliaments, wrote in his poem *Faction Display'd* that the Kit-Kat Club "gave Direction to the State," he was alluding to a constitutional irregularity that many saw as typically Whig. If the Kit-Kats seemed to some a revival of Shaftesbury's Green-Ribbon Club of the seventeenth century, the supposed Calves-Head Club preserved the republican tradition of Harrington's Rota. There have been scholars who doubted the existence of this gathering of militant republicans, but if one allows for a rather loose meaning of the word "club"—and that was the primary meaning in the early eighteenth century[8]—there is evidence of gatherings in taverns and houses to celebrate the execution of Charles I. In fact, the republican Sylas Neville records the survival of the practice early in the reign of George III.[9] Vulgar Tory journalists, such as Ned Ward, no doubt exaggerated when they wrote of the Calves-Head, but their alarms had apparently at least a slim foundation in fact.

Although the commitment of many pre-1714 Tories to the Revolution Settlement seems to have been at best tenuous, it was these same Tories who felt most threatened by elements of society that fell outside the bastions of church and state. Tory horror at the growth of a commercial society is now a familiar theme, conceivably an exaggerated theme, considering the number of Tories who were prominent in trade and the fact that even Defoe gave primacy to the landed interest. Undoubtedly, however, new forms of commerce posed a danger to the rural society of the squires and the clergy. Translated into public discourse, this feeling of unease took the form of arguing that the Bank of England was becoming a danger to the constitution,

7. [Tufton], *The History of Faction, Alias Hypocrisy, Alias Moderation* (London, 1705), p. 162; *Plain Dealer* 3 (26 Apr. 1712), for similar remarks; and Sir H. M. [i.e., Mackworth], *Down with the Mug: or Reasons for Suppressing the Mug-Houses* (London, 1717).

8. Robert J. Allen, *The Clubs of Augustan London* (1933; reprinted, Hamden, Conn.: Archon Books, 1967), p. 5.

9. *Diary of Sylas Neville, 1767–1788*, ed. Basil Cozens-Hardy (London: Oxford University Press, 1950), pp. 3, 90–91.

towering over the formal organs of government. Control over credit might raise the Bank so high that it would dwarf Parliament—a form of hegemony made plausible by the affinity claimed between a society such as the Bank and the Whig faction in Parliament. Invoking the suggestion of an *imperium in imperio,* John Broughton thus argued that the Bank was an unacceptable "Solecism in Politicks," for it was an extra-constitutional body on which the constitution was made to depend.[10]

Suspicion of corporations of various sorts was of course already a familiar part of British culture. Thus when Charles II had challenged the charters of various bodies—local governments, livery companies, colleges and schools—his position could be defended by reference to a familiar concern. Sir Robert Sawyer, the attorney-general, stated the essence of the legal case when he insisted that unless the corporations could be required to forfeit their charters, they would be "so many Commonwealths by themselves, independent on the Crown and in defiance of it."[11] A judge of the time designated such bodies as "little republics" and similarly repudiated their claims. The "concession" theory of corporations thus enjoyed support where it counted—in the courts. Clearly, the Tory fear of competing jurisdictions had roots that stemmed from the major events of Stuart times.

Again, the Whigs stood for a proliferation of associations, though not, in this case, new ones. It is also true that one can easily overstate Whiggish loyalty to the principle of associations. Writers such as Thomas Hunt certainly did their best to defend the City of London's independence, but hardly, as is sometimes claimed, by depicting borough corporations as "repositories of democracy and the bulwarks of the Constitution." Hunt argued, rather, from the other direction, noting that only arbitrary governments so restricted local autonomy.[12] Fear of a papist plot against liberty far outweighed any positive and overt

---

10. [Broughton], *Remarks upon the Bank of England* ... (London, 1707), sig. A3, pp. 36, 39; and [Broughton], *The Vindication and Advancement of our National Constitution and Credit* (London, 1710), pp. 6, 45–46, 77. See too P. G. M. Dickson, *The Financial Revolution in England: A Study in the Development of Public Credit, 1688–1756* (London: Macmillan, 1967), p. 26.

11. Quoted in Jennifer Levin, *The Charter Controversy in the City of London, 1660–1688, and its Consequences* (London: Athlone Press, 1969), pp. 48–49.

12. Ibid., p. 77. Cf. Thomas Hunt, *A Defence of the Charter, and Municipal Rights of the City of London* (London, 1682), sig. A2, pp. 2, 4.

commitment to what we could now call "pluralism." The dispute about
the status of corporations came closest to being one about the general
nature of government when the two sides used their respective positions to support arguments about the place of the Commons in early
parliaments. Robert Brady's statement of the concession theory was
thus part of the general case that humble people had enjoyed no
recognized place in Parliament. James Tyrrell's championing of local
autonomy was even more closely tied to his unhistorical claims for the
rights of the Commons.[13]

Much of the political history of the Whigs was compressed into the
single word "association." The paper that led to the downfall of
Shaftesbury called upon subscribers to defend the Protestant religion
and the existing government against papists. In the manner of the
time, the document itself, and not just the body of men whose existence it contemplated, was called an "association." Though Whigs attempted to establish kinship between this paper and one drawn up
for the same purpose in the reign of Elizabeth, Tories perceived it as
a revival of the Solemn League and Covenant of 1643.[14] Nor did the
widespread popularity of the association of 1696—intended to protect
William III and the Protestant religion—dispel the sinister connotations of the term. When Henry Sacheverell wrote, in 1702, of a "new
Association" of the enemies of monarchy and of the Church, he was
appealing to sentiment nurtured in High-Churchmen over the previous two generations. The term no doubt retained some of its unfavourable connotations, even through the eighteenth century, for in
1780 Charles James Fox had to assure a meeting at Westminster that
there was nothing unconstitutional in the word. The last decade of
the eighteenth century gave rise to the need for similar assurances
on the part of the great lawyer Thomas Erskine. By this time, however,
the term requiring naturalization was "convention," the innocence of
which could be established by referring to its emergence in the lan-

13. Brady, *An Historical Treatise of Cities, and Burghs, or Boroughs*, 2nd ed. (London, 1704), sig. A2; and Tyrrell, *The General History of England, both Ecclesiastical and Civil* (London, 1704), 3, pt. 2:188, 204.
14. Anon., "Remarks upon the New Project of Association, in a Letter to a Friend" (1681), in *Somers' Tracts*, 2nd ed. (London, 1812), 8:309.

guage of the county associations of the 1780s or, much better, by reference to the Convention Parliament of 1688–89.[15]

Returning now to the early eighteenth century, it is clear that the Tories of the time were among the least disposed to tolerate new forms of social organization. Only in defence of the established church were Tories prone to speak favourably of social organization independent of the state; even on that issue, the most effective case took the form of according to the Church of England formal status as a central part of "the Constitution in Church and State." For the most militant High-Churchmen sought not independence from the formal organs of secular government but superiority over them in relation to ecclesiastical matters. This of course entailed their arguing the constitutional rights of Convocation against those kings or bishops who might presume to ignore it. It was not an easy case to make, especially for men who, before the Revolution, had argued the divine right both of kings and of episcopacy.

Unavoidably, High-Churchmen sometimes overstated their claims. Thus the Jacobite William Oldisworth argued that some enemies of the Church would make it no more than an "Out-house" and considerably less in stature than a tavern, coffee-house, or club. So far, so good, but his skilful blending of Tory prejudices went dangerously far when he appealed to the acknowledged presence of many "little Supremacies" that rightly insisted on their legal autonomy. "Have not the *Lord Mayor*, the *Lords* and *Commons*, nay every Society and Club, their particular Powers, which they claim as Rights, unalterable, and Independent of all others?"[16] Such a plea might indeed save the Church, but it would simultaneously justify the survival of many social units whose presence was most unwelcome. Of course Oldisworth conceived of the privileges of the Church of England as far more ample than those of other jurisdictions, and this no doubt accounts for his apparent lack of concern at the implications of the argument.

Apart from such defences of ecclesiastical power, there were few

---

15. For a report of Fox's speech see *London Courant, and Westminster Chronicle* (3 Feb. 1780). Erskine's discussion of the terminology of radicalism was made during the trial of Thomas Hardy. See *The Speeches of the Hon. Thomas Erskine ... on Subjects Connected with the Liberty of the Press* (London, 1810), 3:398–99.

16. [Oldisworth], *A Dialogue Between Timothy and Philatheus* 2nd ed. (London, 1709), pp. 181, 186.

other occasions to call forth Tory or Jacobite arguments in behalf of organized interests. The Tories appear to have identified themselves with the central organs of church and state and thus to have seen no need to argue in favour of any lesser units. Not even the October Club seems to have required defence as an organization, for the Whigs had been first in the field with this sort of association, and, though they mocked the tenets of this High-Tory gathering, they seem not to have questioned its right to exist. Tories followed Whigs into clubland, just as they competed in the new world of commercial corporations. But all the while the Tories—when they expressed opinions at all—tended to repudiate such innovations.

The political right has often been pictured as being more sympathetic to organized complexity than the doctrinaire left, and such may well be so if one contrasts attitudes in post-revolutionary France. However, there is much evidence to suggest that in eighteenth-century England it was the Tory and Jacobite traditionalists who stood out against novel forms of social organizations. The upsetting experience of cherishing lost causes no doubt weakened High-Churchmen's regard for the paramountcy of "Church and King." After all, there was but faint satisfaction in asserting the claims of a king belonging to the wrong dynasty, a parliament full of Whigs, and a church that resolutely allowed the strongest adherents of the Stuarts to create a schism. However, the long-term tendency was for High-Tories to become reconciled to the nature and occupants of the central organs of the nation, not for them to establish their own counter-institutions.

But their long spell in the political wilderness did little to reconcile Tories to the diversity of British society. Opposition simply meant that traditional prejudices about Dissenters and urban life were reinforced by the normal animus of "Country" politicians against ministries, standing armies, and financial institutions. Indeed, it is fair to say that there were no champions of pluralism in eighteenth-century England, for the Whigs who had come to power with the death of Anne proved to be extremely jealous of all centres of opposition to the Hanoverian establishment. Chief of these were those sectors of the clergy who preached up the rights of Convocation and that stronghold of non-juring and Jacobite sentiment—Oxford University. Abstract propositions about independence of the Church of England were condemned in the Whig press as treasonable, as were the more concrete signs of disaffection by an Oxford mob.[17] Whig bishops were

17. See such Whig papers as *Flying-Post: or, Post Master* 3342 (21–23 Jan. 1713–14);

firmly in agreement with the Whig politicians about the relative positions of mitre and crown, but it was the politicians whose Erastian premises were most often expressed in the early years of the reign of George I as they echoed Matthew Tindal's charge in his famous *Rights of the Christian Church* that the High-Churchmen threatened an *imperium in imperio*. This implied considerably more than the long-standing ambition of High-Tories to have the bishops universally recognized as representing an estate of the realm. Exactly what was implied in terms of the rights of Convocation is not easy to say. Since a literal instance of *imperium in imperio* was generally accepted as a political impossibility, such a description of the aims of the High-Church was limited to its enemies.

Whiggish views on the proper relations between church and state dictated no change in actual practice, which recognized the place of the king as head of the Church, thus giving effective control of ecclesiastical affairs to Parliament. The only question was the tone in which secular supremacy ought to be stated. Warburton's *Alliance Between Church and State* (1736) set the dominant pattern, for his rendering of the different ends of church and state avoided the Hobbesian truculence of Tindal and Sir Michael Foster while making no concessions to High-Flyers. The notorious disloyalty of large elements within Oxford University was a more practical matter. Jacobite rioters in Oxford led to demands "for purging the Church and the Universities," though the ministers did not in fact proceed with the Universities Bill of 1716.[18] It must have been a painful time for men such as Sacheverell, who used to complain bitterly that High-Churchmen were seen as simply as one party in the state. At the outset of the Whig supremacy, men of his leanings were commonly dismissed as "the Faction."

Nor was all the energy of the Whigs expended merely in restraining the extremists within the Church of England. The havoc caused by

---

Medley 23 (1–4 Oct. 1715); and Philip Horneck's *High-German Doctor* (4–7 Jan. 1714–15) and (11–14 Jan. 1714–15).

18. *Flying-Post* 3654 (4–7 June 1715); George Waldron, *A Persuasive Oration to the People of Great Britain* (London, 1715), p. 61; and E. Bennet, *Considerations on the English Constitution in Church and State ...* (London, 1721), pp. 22–23, 30. See too W. R. Ward, *Georgian Oxford: University Politics in the Eighteenth Century* (Oxford: Clarendon Press, 1958), pp. 77–80, 87.

the South-Sea Bubble was interpreted by the government as a result of the presence of numerous commercial bodies that had come into existence without the sanction of the Crown. The Bubble Act of 1720 made such contractual and unincorporated bodies illegal; had it been strictly enforced, it would have had somewhat the effect of the Le Chapelier law of revolutionary France.[19] John Trenchard, writing as "Cato," condemned the political role of "Corporations or political Combinations of Men, that ... have Bodies, but no Souls, nor consequently Consciences."[20] A legal dictum of the previous century had held that such bodies, because of their lacking souls, could not be held to commit treason. Trenchard, however, was more in keeping with the times in emphasizing how various bodies might serve the cause of unrest or disloyalty.

Another observation that was also typical of a prevailing point of view came from a ministerial newspaper of 1722. Noting Trenchard's concern about corporations and admitting that he seemed mainly to be referring to literal corporations that sued and were sued by virtue of their seals, the writer insisted still on a caveat. The expression "political Combinations of Men" could, he complained, easily be adapted to the purposes of enemies of the Lords and Commons; Trenchard should then have taken pains to exempt these bodies from his assault.[21] Arguments about the legitimacy of social organization always seemed to come back to the bedrock of King, Lords, and Commons. Anglicans and Dissenters might haggle about whether the Church of England might ever be deemed a "mere voluntary Society," the rectitude and political significance of clubs and taverns might remain a subject for debate, but no one doubted that King, Lords, and Commons, in some relation or other, were the essence of the constitution. The status of all other bodies had to be decided by reference to their likely impact on these all-important units.

The jealous centrality of the bodies forming Parliament was bol-

19. For accounts of the act's operation see Alexander Mundell, *The Influence of Interest and Prejudice upon Proceedings in Parliament Stated* ... (London, 1825), essay 7; and A. B. DuBois, *The English Business Company after the Bubble Act* (New York: Commonwealth Fund, 1938), chap. 1. The ethos of such legislation is succinctly presented in C. T. Carr, *The General Principles of the Law of Corporations* (Cambridge: Cambridge University Press, 1905), pp. 171–72.

20. *London Journal* 162 (1 Sept. 1722).

21. *A Supplement to the St. James's Journal* 33 (12 Dec. 1722).

stered by the individualism that pervaded eighteenth-century social thought. Men in opposition apparently chose to assume that concentrated economic power necessarily posed a danger to liberty. Accordingly, one such argument documented the specifically economic objections to exclusive companies but took as axiomatic that such "wealthy Combinations" were politically threatening.[22] A debate in the House of Lords on the Mortmain Bill of 1736 further illustrates the point. Here, an unidentified speaker apparently claimed that great care was needed to prevent a large share of the landed interest from falling into the hands of any one "society," sacred or profane. Not only were such bodies obviously less stalwart in defending the realm there were the trusty freeholders, but they were also lent a "sort of unity"[23] by the laws and might therefore come to dominate the government. This was precisely the blend of power without personal moral responsibility that had bothered Trenchard. The very fact of an interest's being identified as such, especially if it were in any way set apart by the law, seemed sinister to at least some people in public life. Impervious to the argument that it was only through impartial treatment that militant religious interests could be dissolved, the self-appointed guardians of church and state fought every concession to minorities. In 1753, High-Church sentiment and the animus against economic interests were fused in the hysteria against the so-called Jew Bill. Naturalization of the British Jews, it was alleged, would allow them eventually to engross the land and thus to control the government. Similar considerations were voiced, especially in Ireland, on the issue of Catholic emancipation.

No issue better exemplifies the range of eighteenth-century opinions about interests in the state than the prolonged debate over the status of the standing army. Representing concentrated power potentially destructive to the people, and perhaps even to the Ministry, the standing army was easily depicted as a sinister monolith in stark contrast to the benign and diffuse force of the individuals who would compose a citizen militia. Since there was little danger after the Revolution that a standing army would ever again exist in defiance of Parliament, eighteenth-century argument dwelt upon the army's possible place in the legitimate political order. John Trenchard, writing

22. *Craftsman* 341 (13 Jan. 1732–33).
23. *Parliamentary History* 9 (1736):1121, 1138–39.

in 1698, had raised a relevant point in suggesting that an army with the consent of Parliament would present the peculiar danger of becoming a part of the constitution. Though this might appear a somewhat cerebral and bloodless complaint—compared, for instance, to papism and Stuart tyranny—it was entirely consistent with the dominant desire to identify the legitimate political organs and to eliminate those that seemed to challenge their supremacy.

The standing army consequently emerged in the vocabulary of the Opposition as one of the major outposts and harbingers of that tyranny whose coming was vociferously proclaimed by all men out of place. One Country pamphleteer likened a standing army to the papists, for both seemed to be examples of that morbid political condition known as *imperium in imperio*. Reflecting on the long-standing danger of competing foci of power, this writer expressed an understandable embarrassment that the wolf, whose arrival had so long been cried up, had yet to appear.[24] What did appear were the Militia Acts of 1757–58, which served, for a time at least, to reduce loose talk about tyranny under a standing army. Since the revised militia scheme was difficult to make effective, worries about the army never really disappeared.

It was not entirely clear what arrangement, if any, would have suited eighteenth-century malcontents, save the entire disbanding of a professional army in time of peace. As Trenchard's argument shows, an army fully integrated into constitutional practice might appear to be more objectional than one sheltered only by the royal prerogative. It was this particular cleft stick that the Opposition presented to the Whig Ministry of the mid-1730s when the minority in Parliament proposed that the commissions of army officers be secured against ministerial interference. This raised the question whether the real complaint was an army independent of government—and hence free to turn upon its civilian employers—or one that was too subservient to the Ministry of the day. More than once, ministerial spokesmen expressed their frustration at seemingly impossible demands made by the proponents of a pristine and uncluttered constitution. In 1737, for instance, Henry Pelham argued that the danger associated with a standing army would also exist with a militia, for it too would constitute

24. Anon., *Seasonable and Affecting Observations on the Mutiny Bill ... in a Letter from a Member of Parliament to a Noble Lord* (London, 1750), pp. 64–65.

a separate interest in the kingdom. Government necessarily had to legislate for the unique needs and demands of particular interests. "Every corporation, every society, almost every sort of tradesmen ... have the same reason to think themselves a body of men different from the rest of the people. ..."[25]

On the issue of the alleged need to make the army more independent of the Crown, the Ministry of the 1730s was adamant. Any interference with the right of the executive to remove officers would have the most serious consequences for the system of government, creating a "fourth power," when previously there were but three. This riposte, initially made by Lord Hervey, came to be vulgarized in the ministerial press as the charge that the Opposition sought to turn the army into one of the estates of Parliament.[26] Although the two sides of the House obviously differed on specific issues, both reflected the powerful belief that there could be no tampering with the supremacy of the three branches of the legislature.

When men spoke of the possibility that the army might come to act in the manner of a fourth estate, they were indulging in a form of discourse that was highly characteristic of the eighteenth century. The term carried more than a hint of condemnation, since it implied that some section of the community was presuming to assert its right or capacity to affect public policy. A common understanding of the hallmark of an estate of Parliament was that it have a veto on legislation, and, by extension, this status might be seen as being sought by any overmighty body of subjects. Not surprisingly, many political forces that were sometimes described as additional estates were also deemed to threaten the condition of *imperium in imperio*. The latter suggested competing supremacies or areas of immunity where the legislative sovereignty of Parliament would not be recognized. The image of a fourth estate served best to indicate a new presence in the field that might be expected to complicate the business of governing. An empire within an empire could exist only if there were no contact between the two—a seeming impossibility. A fourth estate, presumably attempting to act as though co-ordinate with the other three, suggested interaction rather than independence. Since general opinion ordained that the supreme power should rest with three branches, it was dif-

---

25. *Parliamentary History* 9 (1737):1341.
26. Ibid., (1734):331; and *Daily Gazetteer* 2055 (25 Dec. 1741).

ficult to see how business could proceed unless these bodies co-operated. This exact point informed much official journalism in the Walpole years; his writers continually insisted that three totally independent powers would bring all government to a standstill. In fact, even the Country demand for an independent House of Commons visualized some connections between legislature and executive. If three separate and interacting bodies proved compatible with sovereignty and effective government—and only the most resolute enemies of mixed government consistently said otherwise—then there was no logical barrier to visualizing a fourth contributor to the process. A fourth estate might be legally unprecedented (in England) and objectionable, but unlike the presence of two supreme powers in a single state, it was not a logical and practical impossibility.

Undoubtedly though, it was contrary to all current accounts of the constitution that there could be a legitimate fourth estate. The orthodox Whiggish position was that each of the three estates represented one of the prime forms of government and that there was no room for the recognition of any "Fourth Estate."[27] Englishmen who identified the estates differently were no more inclined to recognize more than three. Thus, when Whigs and Tories clashed on constitutional issues during the reign of Anne, each accused the other of encouraging the opinion that there could be a fourth estate.[28] Whigs insisted that the king was an estate, which would make four if the claims on behalf of the bishops were recognized. Against this background, it was certainly not a good thing to be called a fourth estate. However, when we read, in the *Flying-Post* of early 1714, that the Convocation sought to be "one of the Estates of Parliament, or something greater," it is clear that there existed a hierarchy of evils.

Convocation did not, of course, create a separate sovereignty, but rather disappeared as an active body and carried on no effective activity between 1717 and 1847. But ecclesiastical policy was not thereby settled, and in the middle of the eighteenth century there were still wordy battles such as that between the Dissenter Micaiah Towgood and John White, of Cambridge. Towgood was bent on contesting

27. Matthew Zampini de Recanti, *Treatise of the Three Estates, and their Power* (London, 1680). This was a sixteenth-century book, reissued with an "Advertisement" addressed to issues of the day in England.

28. See, for the Tories, J. S., *Peace and Union* (London, 1704), p. 18; and for the Whigs, *The Observator* 4, no. 2 (4–7 Apr. 1705).

High-Church presumption about the co-ordinate status of church and state. The church was not, said Towgood, half the civil constitution; rather, it was no more essential a part than "the treasury, the army, or either of the courts of Westminster-hall." Though less than White wanted, this was no inconsiderable role in the constitution.[29] Such accommodation can be explained only by the fact that champions of the church might aspire to something greater than a position comparable to an estate of Parliament. In the event, of course, Anglicans settled for a good deal less.

Since a fourth estate could be contemplated—though with varying degrees of horror—and since there had already existed more than three possible candidates for inclusion among the three estates, the notion of a fourth estate persisted. Indeed, when much the greater part of informed opinion came to accept the estates as King, Lords, and Commons, the history of the fourth estate was only beginning. Not only did allusions to such a body grow in number as the century advanced, but their tone became more moderate with growing appreciation that the formal theory of the constitution was incapable of doing justice to the richness and variety of day-to-day politics. Through all the dreary bickering of the first two Hanoverian reigns there was at least some recognition that the nation was experiencing innovations in the machinery and processes of government. These years, in particular, saw much discussion of whether certain obvious aspects of politics rightly belonged in the system. The years of Anne and of George III no doubt had rather more dramatic issues, but in fact the processes of innovation had already begun under Anne and were far from complete in 1760. The bodies labelled during the century as a fourth estate comprise a catalogue of the political organizations and organs of government that rose to prominence in that period. Some, of course, were much more important than others.

The Opposition and the Ministry

Eighteenth-century political history may not have been party history as we now understand "party"; undoubtedly, though, it was dominated by the struggle between the Government of the day and those

---

29. [Towgood], *A Dissent from the Church of England Fully Justified* ... (1746), 12th ed. (London, 1811), p. 143.

who, in some organized way, opposed the ministers. Not only was party in general obnoxious to orthodox political assumptions, but the bodies called Ministry and Opposition,[30] each in its own way, posed challenges to constitutional propriety. Throughout the greater part of the century questions about the status of these two bodies remained, as it were, on the agenda. Eventually, in a very unsystematic way, they got answered.

Ministry and Opposition were rather different from the other interests that Englishmen found disturbing. A solution to the possible hegemony of the Bank would have been not to renew its life; the Church of England could be clearly subordinated to Parliament; and the army, though not practicable to disband, could be supplemented and balanced by the counterweight of a militia. No such solutions presented themselves with respect to the major antagonists within the state. Ministries might be replaced, but the king had to have ministers. The members of an unsuccessful faction might be banished from even minor offices or, in the case of Jacobites, even executed, but the supply of Grumbletonians was inexhaustible. Perhaps surprisingly, of the two foci of political loyalty it was the Opposition that most readily found an accepted place in the political system.

Opposition

Opposition was not initially even recognized as an important interest in the state. Rather, it was an activity in which politicians occasionally indulged; if they over-indulged, it became treason or sedition. Early in Anne's reign, Dr. Charles Davenant and Mary Astell, feminist and Tory, described party—especially involving men against the Court— as exemplifying the solecism of *imperium in imperio*. This was natural enough at a time when elements within the parties did tend to disagree about which dynasty ought to rule the nation. With stakes so high, the charge of treason was never far away. The Whigs of 1715 voiced that fear about a Tory party, sections of which were rightly suspected of leaning towards the king across the water. Such a party was per-

---

30. At the risk of inconsistency, I have capitalized the words "Ministry" and "Government," when dealing with those institutions throughout this chapter. In other chapters, the words are rendered in lower case. "Opposition," in referring to the body as distinct from the practice, has been capitalized throughout.

ceived as contending with the Crown for supremacy or as one that "at least would set up *Imperium in Imperio.*"[31]

Once the threat of an anti-Hanoverian revolution had diminished, the activity of opposition flourished under a régime that was, on the whole, exceptionally tolerant about such matters. "The Opposition" as a body was recognized by the early 1730s. Bolingbroke, its effective leader, laboured well to justify the same mobilization of talent on the part of the minority as necessarily took place on the Government side. He did not, of course, contemplate a permanent Opposition, for its very purpose in organizing to turn out bad ministers suggested that when good men were in control no such check would be necessary.[32]

When one considers what extraordinary intolerance greeted certain new interests on the political scene, some explanation is needed to account for the relative mildness with which ministerial writers treated the overt threat of organized opposition. For the practice of opposition, even the body carrying on the practice, was not roundly condemned, though their motives and the nature of their complaints did provoke systematic abuse and strenuous denial respectively. There is no denying the fact that Bolingbroke's Opposition chose the terms of debate and placed Government writers in a defensive posture that left little room for thoroughgoing condemnation of the place of an Opposition. For the last decade of Walpole's Ministry, the constitutional issue was the independence of the House of Commons, not the legality or responsibility of an Opposition. Forced to justify the control exercised over the House by the ministers, Treasury journalists found it entirely satisfactory to be able to point to so-called patriots within the House who could be relied upon to oppose the ministerial phalanxes.

Indeed, there emerged the very striking paradox that it was men in power, or their minions, who were most articulate in explaining the function of a parliamentary Opposition. This remained true in the era of Lord North. Of course, there were other considerations,

---

31. Anon., *An Important Letter Relating to the Affairs of Great Britain* (London, 1715), p. 18. Tracts like this provoked some early defences of party competition, one of which is attributed to Defoe. See *The Secret History of State Intrigues in the Management of the Scepter, in the late Reign* (London, 1715), p. 13.

32. Here, and elsewhere below, I have drawn upon documents contained in my collection *Factions No More: Attitudes to Party in Government and Opposition in Eighteenth-Century England* (London: Frank Cass, 1972).

including the fact that no one really suggested that all votes in Parliament must be *nemine contradicente*. Thus the acceptability of an Opposition, as distinguished from open rebellion, had always been a matter of degree. But the existence of the "choir" in Elizabeth's parliaments had not brought forth any defence of organized Opposition. Things had changed. An Opposition that presented itself as a response to specific ills was less threatening than one frankly aiming at power; an Opposition allegedly spontaneous was more acceptable than one obviously "formed." Opposition that endangered the unity needed for war and diplomacy was often condemned; in fact, the qualifications were endless. But what is conspicuously missing is any large or coherent body of argument to the effect that an Opposition had no place in the system.

By 1739 Bolingbroke was commonly referred to in the ministerial press as the "Anti-Minister," though he was in fact, no longer on the scene. The literature that accompanied Walpole's downfall in 1742 only served to strengthen the credentials of an Opposition, especially an apparently "principled" one such as moved many of the Tories. Five years after Walpole's resignation, Henry Fielding wrote facetiously of a "new Science or Profession ... well known by the Name of THE OPPOSITION."[33] But further triumphs lay ahead. Even the admitted distaste expressed by Court politicians for a formed Opposition may be exaggerated. A strongly ministerial pamphlet from early 1756, purporting to be an explanation of the constitution for the edification of a foreigner, shows a supporter of Newcastle defending the Opposition. The aim of the work seems to have been to defend simultaneously the personnel of the current administration and the existence of the Ministry—a term "vague and ill-understood in our Language"— as an institution. Duplicating the feat of Walpole's writers, the pamphlet granted credentials to the Opposition as part of the process of rendering the Ministry legitimate:

An Opposition is no bad Thing in the main: is now, from long Use and Experience systematized into our Constitution, and affords a most excellent school for future Statemen. It is a short Obstruction only to the good Purposes of a Ministry, and a proper Guard against their entering on bad ones. It can, in short, do very little Hurt, but by being misunderstood by your Counsellors.

33. *Jacobite's Journal* 9 (30 Jan. 1747–48).

This document of 1756 was written in one of the troughs of English politics, scarred by petty factional intrigues on the part of the followings of Pitt and Henry Fox, and indeed the tone of the pamphlet may perhaps be explained by the emergence of an Opposition within the Ministry. But it contained an unambiguous assertion that Opposition need not be a dangerous state within a state, need not even be dismissed as a profession, but was becoming a recognized part of government. Arguments that served the cause of an administration might also render Opposition legitimate, as this tract demonstrates. The author, striving to explain the body called the "Ministry," said that if the individuals in office were good men, their "confluence" was also good, for he would not allow such a logical fallacy as "bene divisis ad male composita."[34] The same argument was implicit in the growing recognition of Opposition, though neither application would have satisifed students of the law of conspiracy, who would have had no difficulty in showing how acts involving collusion became offensive. It is also true that the institutions of both Ministry and Opposition benefited from the notion that a clash of evils might produce good; but that is another story.

When the Opposition laid its long seige to the government of Lord North, the same pattern apparent in the time of Walpole reappeared. Rarely did the malcontents assign to their kind a lasting place in the system. By contrast, administration writers continued to follow the technique of deflecting attacks by justifying opposition in general while attempting to defuse the specific complaints. This was to say, in effect, that the men in opposition were engaged in a respectable function so long as they stayed at it and remained out of office. This cannot have given much solace to the minority, but it signalled a major advance in the official recognition of real political forces. A recognition of opposition in the country and in Parliament was not too great a price to pay for an opportunity to defend the sort of "influence" needed to secure for king and Treasury their parliamentary majority.

Proclaimed in 1756 as part of the constitution, the Opposition reached new stature in a pamphlet by George Chalmers, Scottish antiquary and hired pen of North's Government. Arguing against the views of

---

34. Anon., *A Letter to the King of * by an Englishman, not a Member of the House of Commons* (London, 1756), pp. 12, 24, 20.

both Burke and the Earl of Abingdon that the Opposition should emulate that of 1739 and secede, Chalmers urged them to stay in Parliament. Theirs was an indispensable function:

> Is it too strong to say that our Constitution, so long as it continue free, must, literally speaking, consist of four parts, King, Lords, Commons, and—Opposition? But it certainly is not too strong to say that every nation consists, more or less, of three parts—the body governing, the body governed, and the body opposing the government. We speak here of free countries.[35]

Once again, it had been made clear that it was not alienation from the political order but commitment to it that bred a firm appreciation of the permanent function of opposition. Even a temporary success by the Opposition could be turned to good account by those in power. This was evidenced when men cited the passage of Dunning's motion of 1780 against influence as proof that no effective royal influence existed. The Opposition had begun the century as an *imperium in imperio*; by 1777 it had been honoured with the dignity and responsibilities of a fourth branch of government and, as Chalmers went on to say, was "one of the two things" whose collision produced the "sacred fire of freedom." The other thing was of course the governors—the Ministry.

The Ministry

The Ministry too needed to prove itself within the eighteenth-century constitution. For one must not forget that whereas politics late in the century was increasingly perceived as the clash of Government and Opposition, neither of these units rested easily within the framework of King, Lords, and Commons. One clause of the Act of Settlement of 1701 forbade those with offices under the Crown from sitting in the Commons, and another clause of the same statute required the sovereign to use his Privy Council, and no smaller body, for matters properly in its competence. The measure, originating in a Tory-dominated House of Commons, occasioned relatively little comment

---

35. [Chalmers], *Second Thoughts: or, Observations upon Lord Abingdon's Thoughts on the Letter of Edmund Burke to the Sheriffs of Bristol*, 2nd ed. (London, 1777), p. 34. Another example of the genre is [James Macpherson], *A Short History of the Opposition during the last Session of Parliament*, 3rd ed. (London, 1779).

in the press, perhaps because the provisions of the act were not due to go into effect until the Hanoverian succession, or perhaps because the place clause seemed excessive even to some Country members. The repeal of the offending clauses by the Regency Act, in the winter of 1705–6, was greeted with even less reaction in the press, though it was opposed by a "Country" minority composed of both Whigs and Tories and attracted a very full house.[36]

In a decade of raging partisan loyalties, the exclusion from the Commons of future servants of the Crown and their subsequent reinstatement offended less than the issues raised by the Kentish Petition, Occasional Conformity, and the Aylesbury election case of 1702–4. Nevertheless, the years 1701–6 decided the fate of the ministers of the Crown. Henceforth they might sit in the House of Commons, supported by a following of placemen. Bishop Burnet's objection that nobody would care to be a privy counsellor on the original terms of the act obviously did not reflect the views of all public men of the time. It is significant, however, that when the Tories later in the century regaled the public with Whig crimes, they listed the Riot Act of 1715, the Waltham-Black Act of 1723, the repeal of the Triennial Act in 1716, and the various manoeuvres used to kill place-bills. But rarely did they contemplate the sort of general place-bill that would bar ministers from the Commons, nor had they much to say about the gutting of the Act of Settlement, apart from some references as a prelude to the unsuccessful place-bill of 1739–40.[37] The king's ministers would long be abused as a bizarre constitutional phenomenon, but both the use of a Cabinet Council and the presence of some of its members in the lower House were increasingly recognized in the silence of the law.

---

36. G. S. Holmes, "The Attack on 'The Influence of the Crown', 1702–16," *Bulletin of the Institute of Historical Research* 39 (1966):47–68. See too Holmes, *British Politics in the Age of Anne* (London: Macmillan; New York: St. Martin's, 1967), p. 131; and Jennifer Carter, "The Revolution and the Constitution," in Geoffrey Holmes, ed., *Britain after the Glorious Revolution, 1689–1714* (London: Macmillan, 1969), pp. 46–47. A revealing contemporary report, stressing the absurdity of excluding all placemen, is found in Dr. Charles Davenant's letters to his son, Harry. See letters of 22 Jan., 8 Feb., and 22 Feb., 1705–06, in B.L. Add. Ms. 4291, fols. 43r 48v and 54v. The same case had been made in a broadside of 1701 that commented on the strange absence of opposition to the original clause. See *Officers Good Members; or the late Act of Settlement Consider'd* (London, 1701).

37. *Craftsman* 671 (19 May 1739); and 702 (22 Dec. 1739).

Permitting the Cabinet to exist with members in the House of Commons was not the same thing as giving it legal definition, and on many occasions in the eighteenth century the politicians recorded their uncertainty about the body.[38] In January of 1711–12 there was a very full, if inconclusive, debate in the House of Lords about the wording of a motion blaming the "Cabinet Council" for the military failure in Spain. The Duke of Devonshire objected to the changing of the original phrase to the word "Ministers." Others preferred "Ministers" or "Ministry" as being better known. Some liked neither; some objected to neither. Lord Ferrer described the Ministry as "more copious" than the Cabinet Council. The Duke of Argyle thought that all ministers were of the Cabinet Council but that not all members of that body were ministers, while the Earl of Peterborough, with characteristic eccentricity, contributed the thought that "Privy-Counsellors were such as were thought to know everything, and knew nothing; and those of the Cabinet Council thought nobody knew anything but themselves."[39]

There were then uncertainties about the advisers of the king, and modern students of the subject are not assisted by the fact that one does not always know when exactly certain stages in the institution appeared. One could easily exaggerate the degree to which eighteenth-century people were concerned with such complex matters. There is not only the surprising equanimity with which Country Tories and Old Whigs accepted the amendments to the Act of Settlement—with less extra-parliamentary fuss than was manifested over a partisan manoeuvre such as the "Tack" of 1704. One discovers too that politicians in the House of Commons evinced no desire to pass self-denying ordinances that might later mar their own careers. There were, of course, continuing jibes about the notorious fact that the king's speech was not his own.[40] In point of fact, no other arrangement would readily have allowed the Opposition to attack the measures proposed in the speech, maintaining all the while their loyalty to the throne. Indeed,

38. See Edward Raymond Turner, *The Cabinet Council of England in the Seventeenth and Eighteenth Centuries, 1622–1784* (Baltimore: Johns Hopkins Press, 1932), 2:41–47.

39. *A Collection of the Parliamentary Debates in England, from the Year M,DC,LXVIII to the Present Time* (London, 1741), 5:371–78. This is often called Torbuck's Debates, after the name of the publisher.

40. See, for example, Anon., *A Dialogue Between a New Courtier and a Country Gentleman* (n.p., 1712), p. 13; and a speech by the Duke of Argyle in *Parliamentary History* 11 (1739–41):276.

Walpole himself was sometimes credited with introducing the practice of assuming that the words of the speech were the ministers', not the king's—this in 1718, after the Whig split. However, a measure of propriety had to be observed in referring to the speech from the throne; Wilkes in 1763 was deemed to have gone too far. A source of resentment more genuine than that provoked about the authorship of the king's speech involved the address of thanks. Opposition writers dwelt on the indignity whereby the House was to "echo back" the substance of the speech. Thus both the king's puppet-like performance and the response to it were orchestrated by the ministers.[41]

With whatever reservations, parliamentary minorities had little choice but to accept the Cabinet on its own terms. It was all very well to complain that the constitution knew no such body, but the very people who complained also insisted that ministers be held responsible and that no wrong be attributed to the king. It was only the corporate identity of the ministers, then, and their situation in Parliament that could be sources of grievance. Impeachment would no doubt have served as a means of punishing individual ministers, but that procedure fell into disuse. Nor would its revival have served Opposition purposes, since its leaders normally hoped to turn out the current administration, not simply to punish erring individuals. To insist that the king employ his Privy Council no longer carried any weight after the repeal of 1706, so the burden of Opposition rhetoric fell upon the allegation that the sovereign was the slave of his ministers. Opposition writers pretended that it was dangerous to spell out the word "Cabinet" in full, but this was usually a coy affectation.

From the perspective of the ministers, there must always have been a temptation to claim that opposition to their measures was an attempt, in the well-known phrase, "to wound the sovereign through the sides of his servants." Under Walpole, however, the Whigs seem to have deserted this standard defence, in some measure at least. It was not uncommon among Whig publicists to assert that there was an "essential Difference between the King and his Ministers" and that it would be unworthy of a good administration to "join the Ministers with the

---

41. Reports about the organization of the ministerial majority under Walpole include [William Pulteney, Earl of Bath], *An Humble Address to the Knights, Citizens, and Burgesses ... by a Freeholder* (London, 1734), esp. p. 13; and *Historical Manuscripts Commission*, 18th report, *Diary of the First Earl of Egmont, II* (1730–33), (London: H.M. Stationery Office, 1920), pp. 365–66.

King."[42] Naturally, Whig political argument was not homogeneous, and the strategy of skulking behind the throne continued to have its practitioners and would later be revived in 1762 by admirers of Lord Bute.

In searching for images of constitutional impropriety, the Opposition hit upon the same language that served on other issues to rally support for traditional political forms. The Ministry had improperly become a fourth estate. Sir Lewis Namier once said that this charge was "generally current" in the press between 1735 and 1761,[43] but he cited no examples. The earliest such use to come to light is a Jacobite's objection, both to the word "Ministry" and to the reality of its power. "Ministers of State" were known and respectable, but a ministry prefigured the demise of the constitution:

> The Word to me, seems injurious to the Honour of a crowned Head; it makes a fourth Estate in the Kingdom, and the most weighty of all; if the Prince should ever fall under the Disadvantages mentioned before. We know but three Estates, the Lords Spiritual and Temporal, and the Commons, are the native Counsellors of the Kingdom.[44]

Matthias Earbery, the probable writer, was no doubt assisted in his intransigence against the Ministry by his impartial contempt towards both Whigs and Hanoverian Tories, plus the knowledge that whichever side held the advantage, his cause was excluded from the Court. The expression may also owe something to Earbery's characteristically Jacobite denial that the king could ever be an estate. Had he perceived the king to be one of the estates, it might have been more difficult to allege that his servants were also one, especially since there was not the same reason then, as there was later, to claim that the sovereign felt imposed upon by his ministers.

In the reign of George II the same or comparable expressions were quite often employed to discredit the ministers. Sometimes it was said

---

42. *Free Briton* 54 (10 Dec. 1730); and Anon., *A Letter to a Friend in the Country, upon Occasion of the Many Scurrilous Libels, which have been lately Publish'd* (London, 1743), p. 18.

43. Namier, *England in the Age of the American Revolution* 2nd ed. (London: Macmillan, 1963), p. 59n.

44. *Loyal Observator Revived; or Gaylard's Journal* 13 (2 Mar. 1722–23).

that the Cabinet Council was an independent sovereign power, "a Society within a Society," and a conspiracy against the freedom of a nation whose constitution knew only the Privy Council.[45] The high point of virulent anti-ministerial writing came at mid-century, a period graced by only a weak Opposition but one inspired by the fact that it had witnessed a most graphic instance of the king's being ruled by his servants. In 1746, George II had tried to rid himself of some of them and, following Henry Pelham's very brief resignation, had been ignominiously forced to take them back. The languid Opposition of Leicester House and the Tories could take heart in the possibility that a breach between king and ministers might afford an alternative to the cultivation of the heir apparent as a road to power. The relative political innocence of an Opposition increasingly composed of men who had grown up alienated from the Court also encouraged an attack upon the Cabinet. Imprecations on the wickedness of ministers sounded best when the accusers could not themselves be taxed with the same offences. Bolingbroke's attacks could always be answered by reference to his memorable misdemeanors in Harley's Government of 1710–14. It probably gave them scant solace, but there were few glass houses in the wilderness inhabited by the forlorn Opposition of the late 1740s.

At a time when parliamentary debates could be reported only as thinly veiled accounts of an imaginary state, the case against the ministers also spoke the awkward language of political allegory. Sometimes the requirement of supposedly distant lands and barbarous-sounding offices produced very bizarre results. Thus the description of the mythical Coralban constitution noted the distress that ensued when the "highest Degree of a Tri-une Legislature, became oppressed by a Fourth arising from the two lower."[46] Earbery had put it better.

Similar charges, more openly stated, were directed at Pitt in the period 1757–61. In these instances, however, there was unprecedented emphasis upon the impropriety of the office of prime minister. The actual "fourth estate" was generally identified as a cabal of min-

---

45. See *Common Sense* 146 (19 Nov. 1739); and Anon., *A Constitutional Riddle* ... (London, 1750), p. 4.
46. *Old England: or, the National Gazette* 10 (8 June 1751).

isters,[47] but in tribute to Pitt's personal hegemony, he was perceived as bestriding the whole system. Indeed, sometimes Pitt himself was depicted as having engrossed "all the different Powers of Government" and thus, in effect, functioning as a fourth estate that loomed over the other three.[48]

The animus against a chief minister already had quite a long history. An ancient misunderstanding has it that Henry Pelham was the first man to be called prime minister in other than a derogatory sense; but this will not do. For one thing, opponents were really none too happy about Pelham's position—shared in this case with his brother, the Duke of Newcastle—and this led to persistent Opposition sniping at a sinister "Coalition of Brothers." More to the point, a number of ministerial pamphleteers had shown no hesitation in describing Robert Walpole as "Prime Minister."[49] If, on the other hand, the necessary degree of notice is taken to be acclamation by the Opposition, recognition had to await a later day than Pelham's. At the time of the elder Pitt's resignation, his enemies canvassed the full range of arguments against an all-directing minister, including the thought that such a person was more offensive in terms of traditional constitutional practice than even an arbitrary king. Meanwhile, the retired minister's admirers replied that, however unsanctioned by the constitution, such an office was necessary.

When Bute became First Lord of the Treasury, in 1762, the situation was greatly changed. No longer could critics of the administration purport to seek the emancipation of a captive sovereign, for the

---

47. See, for example, [Henry McCulloh], *The Fatal Consequences of the Want of System in the Conduct of Public Affairs* (London, 1757), p. 54. The author was a place-seeker who eventually gained employment in America. Emphasis on the French system of public boards, a favourite idea of his, identifies the pamphlet as McCulloh's. James Ralph identified him as a writer on this subject in reporting to Newcastle on McCulloh's activities. B.L. Add. Ms. 32,737, fols. 272–75.

48. [Philip Francis, the elder], *A Letter to a Right Honourable Person and the Answer to it, Translated into Verse* (London, 1761), p. 26.

49. See *Flying-Post* 5792 (8 Dec. 1730); and [Thomas Curteis], *An Appeal to the Reason and Consciences of all Englishmen ...* (London, 1735), pp. 45, 48. Curteis was a Kentish clergyman who cleared his tract with the Duke of Newcastle. The great man required certain changes prior to publication. See B.L. Add. Ms. 33,344, fols. 69–90. A recent study demonstrates that the office of prime minister was not really accepted until after 1780. See Robert A. Smith, *Eighteenth-Century Politics: Patrons and Place-hunters* (New York: Holt, Rinehart and Winston, 1972), pp. 169–74.

complaint against Bute was simply that the king wanted him too much and the people too little. Ministerial writers did not, however, emulate earlier administrations in defending the office of prime minister. Rather, one finds in the pamphlets of Owen Ruffhead and Sir James Marriott an attempt to fuse king and minister. In Ruffhead's *Ministerial Usurpation*, published in 1760 while Pitt was still in office, this involved likening the ministers to the king's personal household. Mariott's writings revived the threat that obstacles thrown in the way of ministers would necessarily be seen as opposition to the king.[50] Both the arguments that figured in attacks on the Great Commoner and those supporting his successor denied that there was any room in the constitution for a chief minister who would threaten any of the three branches of the legislature. Bute's Ministry minimized its own parliamentary moorings, disavowed reliance on the people, and preferred to rest its case upon the favour of the sovereign. Indeed, Bute's admirers were far more hostile to the presence of a prime minister than they were to ordinary opposition, and some Court literature simultaneously affirmed that nothing was so constitutional in England as an Opposition, but that some limits would have to be placed on its presumption.[51] Specialists still argue whether a new political creed emerged at the outset of George III's reign, but certainly men in power expressed certain attitudes that did not fit the language of Walpole's administration. The time was ripe for talk of the "King's Friends."

One myth about the advisers of the Crown has it that the menace of the "King's Friends" arose only because of a special relationship between George III and Bute and survived only through careful tending by the Rockingham faction.[52] Now, there is evidence suggesting something new in the ministerial language of this time, but it is equally certain that the phrase, at least, was an old one. Namier discovered the expression in use in 1755, but it was already known in the reign

50. [Marriott], *Political Considerations; being a few Thoughts of a Candid Man at the Present Crisis* (London, 1762), p. 34. See too John Brewer, *Party Ideology and Popular Politics at the Accession of George III* (Cambridge: Cambridge University Press, 1976), pp. 115–18.

51. *Plain Dealer* 9 (9 July 1763), a different paper from that cited in note 7 above.

52. On the difficulty of giving substance to Burke's complaint about such a sinister cabal see I. R. Christie, *Myth and Reality in Late-Eighteenth-Century British Politics and Other Papers* (London: Macmillan, 1970), pp. 211–12.

of William III when Country spokesmen denied that the king needed any special friends in Parliament. As a moderate Tory put it, those in office sought an untenable distinction between "the King's and the Nation's Friends." No merely accidental conjunction of words, the expression also appeared in the ministerial press of the 1730s. It served too, with rather different connotations, as a genteel way in which Jacobites within Britain referred to their loyalty.[53] No doubt the unusually rapid turnover in ministries gave the phenomenon of the "King's Friends" greater visibility in the 1760s.[54] But in all fairness to the Whigs, the assumption that the king would, in some measure, be his own minister placed unprecedented weight on his unofficial sources of inspiration. Nor should it be forgotten that such notions persisted beyond the early years of the reign. North's rather modest conception of his responsibilities confirmed the practice, known as "Department Government,"[55] whereby individual ministers could communicate directly with the king. In the 1770s the status of the Opposition, though not their fortunes, seemed better defined and more secure than that of the king's first minister.

When political rhetoric again brought the ministerial estate to the fore, the circumstances recalled those of 1746, 1757, or 1761. The king was again imposed upon by unwelcome advisers—this time the Fox-North Coalition of 1783—and so once again the interests of the ministers and the throne became distinguishable. Enemies of the coalition predictably called it a fourth estate, a group of borough-mongers in opposition to King, Lords, and people. A perceptive writer in the *English Review* recalled that "the same objection was particularly urged against the administration of the Pelhams in the late reign."[56] Indeed,

53. See [James Drake], *A Justification of the Proceedings of the Honourable the House of Commons in the last Session of Parliament* (London, 1701), p. 26; [Drake], *The History of the Last Parliament* ... (London, 1702), sig. A2v; *Daily Gazetteer* 95 (17 Oct. 1735); and *The Lockhart Papers: Containing Memoirs and Commentaries upon the Affairs of Scotland from 1702 to 1715, by George Lockhart* (London, 1817), 1:408, 439.

54. As pointed out by John B. Owen, "George II Reconsidered," in Anne Whiteman et al., eds., *Statesmen, Scholars and Merchants: Essays in Eighteenth-Century History presented to Dame Lucy Sutherland* (Oxford: Clarendon Press, 1973), p. 120.

55. For use of the term see *Westminster Gazette; or, Constitutional Evening-Post* 37 (3–7 Dec. 1776); and the sources quoted in Betty Kemp, *King and Commons, 1660–1832* (London: Macmillan; New York: St. Martin's, 1968), p. 126.

56. Francis Dobbs, *A Letter Addressed to Lord North and Mr. Fox* (London, 1784), p. 6; and *English Review* 3 (Feb. 1784), p. 140.

modern friends of the king—Tories to others—had continued to describe the Whig oligarchy of the reign of George II in precisely those terms. Thus, Leonard Smelt, speaking at the great Yorkshire meeting of December 1779: "In the days of Whiggism, the minister, distinct from the crown, formed a fourth branch of legislature, which had absorbed within itself the power and office of the crown. ..."[57]

As an alternative to pilloring the coalition itself as a fourth estate, one might so describe the body contemplated by Fox's India Bill. Foxites, smarting from the defeat of 1784, replied in kind, sometimes alleging that Pitt's own Board of Control for India was equally offensive, sometimes finding the unwanted estate among "secret advisers" or placemen. Richard Brinsley Sheridan, the playwright and close associate of Fox, noted that the jargon of "fourth estate" and *imperium in imperio* had been applied to the governance of India long before Fox's bill.[58] The regency crisis of 1788–89 afforded another opportunity for constitutional lessons administered by the Opposition, and it was not lost. Thus they damned the ministerial plan for a regency for so dividing the powers of the Crown as to create a new estate of Parliament.[59] The reign of George III was rich in putative fourth estates issuing from the executive branch. The complicated constitutional situation of Ireland before the reforms of 1782 led to claims that the Privy Council in England, or in Ireland, or perhaps both of them, formed an unwarranted "fourth estate."[60]

Eventually, concern for the status of the Ministry subsided, without there being any dramatic reversal of opinions. Throughout the century there continued to be reformers, such as James Burgh and Granville Sharp, who called the Treasury Bench an abomination and sought a stringent place-bill. But banishing ministers from the House of Commons was simply not feasible, and not even the sponsors of the last

57. Smelt's words were recorded by his political opponents, but all accounts agree in this respect. See Anon., *The Yorkshire Question, or Petition, or Address* (London, [1780]), p. 15; and *London Courant & Westminster Chronicle* (10 Jan. 1780).

58. See the exchange between Burke and Thomas Powys, *Parliamentary History* 24 (1784):347, 350. Other examples include a speech by Spencer Stanhope in Christopher Wyvill, *Political Papers* ... (York, n.d.), 2:340; *English Review* 21 (May 1793), p. 397; and Sheridan, *A Comparative Statement of the two Bills for the better Government of the British Possessions in India* (Dublin, 1788), pp. 15, 34–41.

59. See *Parliamentary History* 27 (19 Jan. 1789):1033–34. Various pamphleteers took up the theme.

60. *Public Register: or, Freeman's Journal* (Dublin) 7, no. 79 (15–17 Mar. 1770).

major effort of 1740–41 had sought such a drastic solution. The position of the king's ministers could never be resolved in the same manner as was that of the Opposition. The latter body gained acceptance by proving both its loyalty and its usefulness over a long period of time. Neither of these qualities was really in dispute with respect to the Government. The problem was simply that over the course of more than a century the political system was changing from one in which the king was, or could be, the mainspring of government to one in which he was not. During the transition, the king's ministers were neither his alone nor solely responsible to Parliament, since parliamentary practice has yet to impose practical limits to the king's formal power of appointment. The popularity of the king's actions in dismissing the coalition and the unceremonious dumping of the Talents in 1807 showed that ministers supported by an unreformed House of Commons were not secure against royal displeasure.

Paradoxical as it may seem, the place of the Opposition was more readily defined. With the development of parties, the Opposition simply inherited the role, previously seen as belonging to the whole legislature, of checking the executive power. This change took time to effect, but its nature was apparent to some people from quite early in the eighteenth century. Of course, the very ambiguity that surrounded the nature of the Cabinet assisted in entrenching the institution of Opposition, for it was usually ministerial defenders who felt compelled to justify the ministerial interest and the Treasury Bench by welcoming organization on both sides of the House. This process had been going on since the early 1730s, but the constitutional crisis of 1783–84 did much to consolidate both Ministry and Opposition as permanent institutions, leading to an understanding of parliamentary business as an adversary process between the two. No one document seems to have captured the whole picture. However, the *Political Herald and Review*, a very sophisticated publication edited by Dr. Gilbert Stuart and Dr. William Thomson, indicates the lines along which informed opinion was invited to move. Two unsigned articles that followed the events of 1784 were entitled "The Grounds of a Constitutional Opposition Stated" and "Idea of a Constitutional Prime Minister of England."[61]

The latter article, written by no friend of Pitt the Younger, is es-

---

61. *Political Herald* 2 (Aug. 1785):111–20, and 9 (Mar. 1786):197–200.

pecially interesting in its allowance that, whatever the demerits of the incumbent, a prime minister was "a necessary agent" in the government. The same decade established the term "Leader of the Opposition"[62] as a sober description of another sort of office, and so the battlelines of constitutional government were drawn. Corresponding to the description of the office of "Prime Minister" was a later admission by another of Pitt's critics that the "Ministers of State" or Cabinet were also essential to the system, since they "form that constitutional bond of union between the two grand branches of government." This was what Walpole's writers had been saying seventy years before—the very words "Bond of Union" could have been culled from a Treasury print[63]—but the Opposition had rarely been receptive to such explanations. Bagehot's famous reference to a hyphen or a buckle is but a more studied metaphor.

So the two anomalous bodies—one commonly accused of hatching treason, the other of plotting tyranny—began, at last, to fit the scheme of government. Had the energy of Walpole's writers been sustained by their successors, or had malcontents claimed more readily for themselves the function accorded them by others, this measure of insight might have been achieved much sooner. But understanding is only one of the aims of political argument, and not the major one at that, so we cannot say that a century of dispute was unnecessary.

The People

That entity known as the "People" had long been a familiar part of English political rhetoric, but it was unknown to formal statements about the parts of the constitution. Even in the seventeenth century there had been vigorous debates about the identity and powers of the people,[64] for Whig philosophy founded nothing less than the origin of government upon the consent of that body. Not surprisingly, those

62. See *Public Advertiser* 14,131 (24 Jan. 1780); and Lord Montmorres, *The Letters of Themistocles* (London, 1795), letter of 22 Dec. 1788.

63. William Belsham, *Essays Philosophical and Moral, Historical and Literary* (London, 1799), p. 384. Cf. *Daily Courant* 5776 (8 Oct. 1734).

64. One of the few treatments of eighteenth-century literature on the subject deals only with material after 1760. See Jacob Viner, "Man's Economic Status," in James L. Clifford, ed., *Man Versus Society in Eighteenth-Century Britain: Six Points of View* (Cambridge: Cambridge University Press, 1968), pp. 28–29.

who appealed to the current power of the people were judiciously imprecise about the nature of the entity. Critics were more precise, and Sir Roger L'Estrange filled his *Observator*, the Tory publication of the 1680s, with verbal darts against such undefined generalities as the "People" and *vox populi*. Since not even republicans such as Algernon Sidney were favourable to political activity by the masses, most articulate Englishmen must have had a fairly small proportion of the nation in mind in their appeals to the people. Certainly the purposes of the law were served by a conservative understanding of the term. Arguing the place of Roman Catholics in England, the Whig William Atwood said that "they are not in Law, in this respect, any Part of the People; for People is always taken for them that have legal Interests. Thus when the Statute provides, that the People of Counties shall chuse their Sheriffs, it relates not to all the People in general but onely to Freeholders."[65]

The "People" was on the political scene early in the eighteenth century in the persons of the Kentish Petitioners of 1701. The ferocious response of a Tory House of Commons to their address committed the Whigs to support the people "without doors"—and a generous support it was. Lord Somers was credited with writing the major Whig justification of the petition and, although he neither attributed any special wisdom to the people nor allowed them any right to command the House of Commons, he did wholeheartedly endorse their right to express their views. What is more, Somers claimed that the House of Commons represented only those who had chosen its members, leaving the bulk of the people still unheard. "But what are they to the whole Body of the People, who are represented in the Political State, and are entituled to all the Benefits and Advantages of it?"[66] The Lords too could represent the people, and, Somers claimed, it was they who currently spoke the sense of the people. For all his supposed concern for the non-voting masses, the suggestion that the upper chamber as much represented the nation as did the lower is now open to an ironical interpretation that would have been lost on Lord Somers.

Daniel Defoe also defended the Kentish Petitioners and explored

65. Atwood, *The Lord Chief Justice Herbert's Account Examined* ... (London, 1689), p. 46.

66. [Somers], *Jura Populi Anglicani: or, the Subjects' Right of Petitioning* (London, 1701), p. vi.

different aspects of the subject. Unlike Somers, Defoe supported the right of the people to instruct their representatives, with the sole proviso that Members of Parliament could not be elected on the condition that they obey those instructions. Still the members of the Commons—"the Abridgment ... *the Freeholders* of England in *Miniature*"—had a moral obligation to respond. In another respect, Defoe was considerably less generous in his concessions to the people, since he was unusually explicit about the composition of that body whom he identified as the fountain of all legitimate authority and whose interests and welfare provided the end of all political activity. The "People" were not to be confounded with the "Inhabitants"; the two were quite distinguishable. "When therefore I am speaking of the Right of the People, I would be understood of the Freeholders, for all the other Inhabitants live upon Sufferance. ..." Other inhabitants were either servants of these freeholders or paid for their privileges by renting property. The freeholders were, quite literally, "the proper Owners of the Country."[67]

The most cogent case against an appeal to the people was put by Dr. Charles Davenant in an essay that apparently puzzled contemporaries. Davenant's discovery of "The Danger of Appealing to the People from their Representatives in Parliament" embodied the argument of the Tories of 1701 but formed part of a work not published until 1704. When it appeared, it had become notorious that Davenant had emulated his literary creation "Tom Double" and had deserted the cause of the High-Church party to accept office under Godolphin in a coalition of Whigs and moderate Tories. The timing of a publication, part of which had apparently been written in response to events in the reign of King William, can only have been an embarrassment to Davenant's new masters.

The most memorable phrase in Davenant's condemnation of an appeal to the people was his objection that any such action detracted from the power and dignity of the Commons and served, in fact, "to set up a fourth Estate." The charge was answered by Defoe, still the champion of the people outside Parliament. Denying that the collective body of the people constituted any improper fourth estate, Defoe insisted that they were rather the basis of "the other three Estates."

67. [Defoe], *The Original Power of the Collective Body of the People of England, Examined and Asserted* (London, 1702), pp. 22, 18.

In keeping with his earlier candour, Defoe also had more to say about who the people were:

Its proper to enquire who are these People, of whom this original Power is thus asserted. Negatively, not all the Inhabitants, but positively all the Free-holders, the Possessors of the Land have certainly a Right in the Government of it, and if these are called the People, to these there is a Case wherein an Appeal to them is absolutely necessary.[68]

Defoe was aware of the reputation of the people among the better sort; they were the "Rabble," the "Mob." He proclaimed his loyalty to them, whatever epithets they might attract, but was also careful to specify that political power really belonged only to the landowners.

Later Whig documents display a somewhat reduced commitment even to the freeholders. Defoe remained interested in the business of petitioning, especially as it arose over the union with Scotland, but became increasingly cautious about extending any general mandate to direct the decisions of the Commons. Whigs continued to grant to the people the safe prerogative of having been the origin of power, but here the term "Community" served as a synonym for the people. "Vox Populi" thus came to be contracted into the decisions of Parliament, "the whole People of England in Epitome."[69] Following the Sacheverell trial of 1710, with its moral victory for the High-Tory position, Whigs became fearful of the verdict of the people, for quite apart from the obvious displeasure of Queen Anne, shown in a change of ministers, the enormous sale of Sacheverell's sermon and his triumphal procession following the trial showed that he had massive support in the country. Benjamin Hoadly did his best to discourage a new election, part of a resolute Whig attempt to discredit the loyal addresses that poured into London in the spring of 1710. The same arguments that Whigs had used against the Tory addresses in 1680 at the time of the dissolution of Parliament were revived in more

68. Davenant, "The Danger of Appealing to the People from their Representatives in Parliament" (1704), in *Works*, 4:292; and [Defoe], *Some Remarks on the First Chapter of Dr. Davenant's Essays* (London, 1704), p. 23.

69. *Review* 3, nos. 167, 168 (25, 28 Jan. 1706–7); and Anon., *Judgment of Whole Kingdoms and Nations* (London, 1710), p. 46. For the printing history and a long list of possible authors, including Defoe, see W. T. Morgan, *Bibliography of British History (1700–1715)* (Bloomington, Ind., Indiana University Press, 1937), 2:69.

violent form, and Tories were suddenly discovered to be seekers for democracy based on "Mob-Principles."[70]

A tract attributed to Defoe remarked on the development of new ways to bias the people's judgement, while at the same time "the People themselves have taken up so many New Ways to express themselves, that we are obliged to take *New Ways also*, to understand them by."[71] Defoe distrusted the "Thing call'd the *Sense of the Nation*" and tried to demonstrate that it was unreal, since belied by the obvious intent of men's actions. Tory professions of loyalty to the succession were meaningless, inconsistent, exaggerated in language, and thus devoid of sense. The Whigs of 1680 had likened the addresses of the time to the empty claims of loyalty given to Richard Cromwell before his fall; in 1710 the obvious parallel was the apparent support expressed for James II just prior to the Revolution. The effort was an unusually transparent piece of party writing; understandably it did not enter into the official canon of Whig philosophy, but it did cast some light on what Defoe called such "Phaenomena in our Politick Philosophy."

An even more searching appraisal soon followed. Equally hostile to the addresses—"*Vox Populi*, one of the most wicked *Vox*'s [*sic*] in the World"—John Oldmixon took pains to spell out how addresses were actually drafted, all with the intent of dispelling the almost irresistible impression that the supporters of Sacheverell really did express a popular cause. For one thing, Oldmixon urged, mere addresses, intended to convey a sentiment rather than asking for specific actions, carried less weight than did petitions.[72] More seriously, he alleged that the addresses, such as that from Gloucestershire, did not express the true sense of that county. It all came back again to the freeholders who chose knights of the shire. The knights were the ones who would most likely speak the sentiments of the men who had chosen them, not a grand jury chosen by the sheriff. In the case of Gloucestershire, he produced an earlier address of 1708, signed by the lord lieutenant, the lord bishop, justices of the peace and other dignitaries and pre-

---

70. [Hoadly], *The Fears and Sentiments of all True Britains with Respect to National Credit* ... (London, 1710), p. 13; and his *The Voice of the Addressers* (London, 1710).

71. *The Character of a Modern Addresser* (London, 1710), p. 6.

72. [Oldmixon], *A Complete History of Addresses, from their First Original under Oliver Cromwell, to this Present Year 1710*, 2nd ed. (London, 1710), p. 13. According to Defoe, the distinction was not often observed, the terms being used interchangeably. *Review* 3, no. 166 (23 Jan. 1706–7).

sented to the House of Commons by knights of the shire. A poor Tory document, signed only by the sheriff and the grand jury, and delivered only by the burgess of a borough, was distinctly inferior evidence. It was especially suspect when the local Members of Parliament did not associate themselves with it, since a knight not delivering an address could be assumed to disown it. Even the timing of some of the addresses served to limit confidence in them, since "if a County has addrest as often as there are Market-Towns in it, yet if it is not done at the Assize, it does not seem to have a regular Execution. ..."[73] Further irregularities had been involved in assembling panels and in obtaining signatures to the addresses, and the complaints of local Whigs documented these facts. "We do not pretend that the Sense of A City is infallibly lodg'd in its Deputy Lieutenants; but when they have Reason and Law of their Side, 'tis very probably they speak the mind of all loyal and reasonable Persons."[74]

It was not a good time for the claims of the "People." The Whigs had been pressed to disown most of their extravagant claims for the public without doors; and the Tories, enjoying the benefits both of royal favour and, after October, of electoral success, saw no need to add theoretical embellishment by proclaiming the majesty of the people. Atterbury, the Jacobite, surely expressed something closer to Tory sentiments when he denied that the voice of the people could ever be the voice of God. Nor did the people improve their low degree when the Whigs returned to power in 1714. An administration that did not hesitate to repeal the Triennial Act because of the danger that a deluded people would vote against them held no brief for popular involvement in government. The comment of a Jacobite agent of 1717 that Tories and Whigs now spoke the same political language[75] might also have mentioned that the Whigs of the day were confident that all their revolutions lay behind them. An unusually authoritarian

---

73. [Oldmixon], *The History of Addresses: Part II* (1711), p. 249. Scholarly literature on the crisis of 1710 appears to have neglected Oldmixon's contributions. See Lee Horsley, "*Vox Populi* in the Political Literature of 1710," *Huntington Library Quarterly* 38 (1975):335–53, where the *History* is not mentioned.

74. [Oldmixon], *History of Addresses*, p. 44. Defoe and the Earl of Sunderland were among the supposed authors of this two-volume work. Oldmixon eventually claimed authorship. See his *Memoirs of the Press, Historical and Political, for Thirty Years Past, from 1710 to 1740* (London, 1742), p. 7.

75. Quoted in Dame Lucy Sutherland, *The East India Company in Eighteenth-Century Politics* (Oxford: Clarendon Press, 1952), p. 20.

Whig paper even insisted that the current danger of Tory mobs meant that *"Vox Populi* can no longer be called *Vox Dei.*"[76]

In 1734 the constitutional status of the people was again an issue when the Opposition won a rare victory in the withdrawal of the Excise Bill. The patriot cause of instructing members was thus a topic of animated debate prior to the election of that year. The Whig press chose to view the right to instruct members of the Commons both as derogating from the law-making power of Parliament and as impracticable. "Should these Gentlemen constitute a fourth Estate, consisting of all the Freeholders and Freemen of Corporations in England, where shall they meet?"[77] In the early summer of 1734 it had become clear that the people had not come to the aid of the Opposition; the *Craftsman*, rising to the occasion, insisted that the sense of the people could not be accurately collected from a corrupt electoral process. Members elected from the boroughs were especially likely to have triumphed through the use of unfair methods.

Walpole's writers struck back decisively. They denied that the counties were the people or expressed the sense of the people. Information on that subject was to be had only within Parliament. Indeed, had the people been so misled as to support the Opposition, that outcome would merit no regard. The *Craftsman* was accused, rather unfairly, of finding "four Powers" in the constitution prior to the election, but only three afterwards.[78] This was intended to suggest that the Opposition had deserted the people—a most tendentious reply to the perfectly just charge of electoral corruption. The new Whig history, not unlike the Tory history of the previous century, punctured the claim that the people had ever enjoyed a significant constitutional status. "Populus" in ancient documents had meant, not the commons, but the great laity as opposed to the senior clergy. It meant not the whole people, but "only the People of Property at that Time." Judging themselves safe for another seven years, the Whigs went so far as to say that the folly of the masses was a certain argument against that claim of merit that supposedly followed from popularity.[79]

Rarely can the supporters of any victorious party have been so

76. *Commentator* 8 (25 Jan. 1719–20).

77. *Daily Courant* 5651 (15 May 1734).

78. *London Journal* 787 (27 July 1734); *Daily Courant* 5702 (13 July 1734); and *Hyp-Doctor* 196 [really 199] (10 Sept. 1734).

79. *Daily Gazetteer* 90 (11 Oct. 1735); and 24 (26 July 1735).

ungrateful or come so close to proving too much for their own comfort. In effect the Whigs had argued against any test of popular feeling beyond the brute votes expressed within the conventions of the age, a form of election that terminated when the majority in the House of Commons ruled on controverted elections in a predictably partisan way. The sense of the people was shown in choosing Whigs; apparently no other outcome could express that sense:

If the Nation itself, the great collective Body of the People, were brought to poll, without Exception to Age or Condition, even this would not determine the Sense of the People, though the Majority were *three to one* on the Numbers. The People must be distinguished from themselves; the Wise from the Weak and Simple; the Honest from the Unsound and Corrupt.[80]

Defoe's divine right of freeholders begins to appear a neutral system, by contrast. The question of the identity of the people and their prerogatives declined in importance between elections. But when it did arise, Whigs remained ready with Davenant's argument of 1704 about the impossibility of a "fourth Estate."[81]

With the coming of the Pelhams, oppositions continued to present themselves as spokesmen for the people, and governments continued to deny that any such unit needed to be considered beyond the confines of the House of Commons. In 1749, Henry Pelham, then prime minister, described the people as "a sort of ghost or hobgoblin" used to frighten. Pelham was rebuked in the Commons for his disrespect for the people of England, but his sentiment was by no means unique. Lord Barrington said the same thing, somewhat more tactfully, when he argued that opposition to the Bill for Registering Numbers of People was misrepresented as being that of the people themselves. For when anyone attributed opinions to the people, he meant—could only mean—his own opinions and those of his own small circle of acquaintance.[82]

Contemporary journalism reflected the same attitude. Henry Fielding, for instance, partook of that contempt for vulgar opinion that seems to have been *de rigueur* among men of letters. Fielding poured scorn on the political pretensions of what he was pleased to call "the

---

80. *Free Briton* 242 (20 June 1734). See too 255 (19 Sept. 1734).
81. *Daily Gazetteer* 938 [really 946] (6 July 1738).
82. *Parliamentary History* 14 (1749):585, and (same vol.) (1753):1341.

mob"—a body he dubbed, with facetious solemnity, "the fourth Estate."[83] Here Fielding fancied himself highly original, apparently unaware of the long history of so describing the people outside Parliament. Nor, of course, was the term "mob" an uncommon epithet; Defoe had remarked on its comparative novelty some fifty years before. In one respect only had Fielding any claim to novelty. Normally writers had the respectable electorate in mind when they wrote critically of an unwarranted fourth estate. As he himself pointed out, the mob had yet to claim that "negative Voice" belonging to all branches of the legislature. Nor, in fact, was it likely to do so, since mob activity remained still too rare and, by its very nature, too random in its intervention to deserve even the mock title of fourth estate. Fielding's sally was, however, prophetic, as the years after 1752 saw increased political activity by the populace.

Fielding's inspiration had probably been the riots that accompanied calendar reform, but more important manifestations of popular feelings came thereafter in quick succession—the Jew Bill, the case of Admiral Byng, and Pitt's emergence as first minister. The people "without doors" were showing more political animation than usual, which prompted a writer of the next decade to wonder whether the meaning of the word "public" had changed since the reign of Anne. In the 1760s, he complained, the term was equated with the mob and consequently was not respected.[84] A further comment on the new political volatility was expressed by a partisan of Lord Bute, commenting upon his unpopularity as prime minister. Bute's critics, he averred, spoke for "a certain body corporate, who want to be considered not only as one branch of the legislature, but that to which the other three, *viz* king, lords and commons, ought to be subservient." It was improper, however, for the people to deem themselves "a principal branch of the legislature."[85]

83. *Covent-Garden Journal* 41 (5 Oct. 1752), and 47 (16 Nov. 1752).

84. Letter from *St. James's Evening Post*, reprinted in [Francis Blackburne? ed.], *A Collection of Letters and Essays in Favour of Public Liberty, First Published in the News-papers in the Years 1764, 65, 66, 67, 68, 69, and 1770* (London, 1774), 1:82.

85. *A Select Collection of the Most Interesting Letters on the Government, Liberty, and Constitution of England, which have appeared in the Different Newspapers from the Elevation of Lord Bute, to the Death of the Earl of Egmont*, 2nd ed. (London, 1768), 1:99–100. This was one of several such collections published by, and probably also compiled by, John Almon.

The "People" as spoken of here formed a body corporate only in the figurative sense, but there was a literal corporation that often presumed to speak in their name. This was the City of London. The City was perhaps not usually described, in so many words, as a fourth estate, but Professor Butterfield seems correct in his observation that it had the right credentials. This is made plain from the fact that a document of 1741 intended to counter excessive political involvement on the part of Londoners made very great concessions. The crucial statement was that, save for periods of emergency, Londoners were "in the common Case of Subjects, without a Negative upon, or any Jurisdiction over, the *Legislative* or the *Executive* Power."[86] Recalling that accepted doctrine defined an estate as a body that possessed such a negative, the upshot seemed to be that sometimes the City might act as though it had quite unusual legal privileges. The statement too was made well before the alliance between John Wilkes and the City, at which time the political resources of London were most conspicuous. An emergency, showing the City's power, came when it allied itself with the printers in 1771–72. It was then clear that Parliament would be ill-advised to insist upon its legal prerogatives—in this case, its right to bar reports of its proceedings. Already in 1764 one finds a ministerial writer accusing the City of threatening "to erect *imperium in imperio*."[87] Administrations that denied being Tory were coming to sound suspiciously Tory-like.

The repeated efforts by Wilkes to take his seat in the Commons as representative for Middlesex was one further issue that stressed the tension developing between Parliament and the constituencies, but debate did not move perceptibly beyond familiar questions. When Joseph Priestley, however, argued that political power was originally and properly the gift of the people, his position eventually raised questions that went beyond that sort of traditional and rather inoffensive Whiggism that claimed a theoretical popular sovereignty. John Wesley's mocking question to Priestley, "Who are the people?" had been part of Court rhetoric from at least the late seventeenth century.

86. Sir Herbert Butterfield, *George III, Lord North and the People, 1779–80* (London: Bell, 1949), p. 181; and Anon., *An Historical Essay, wherein the Example, Influence and Authority of Londoners in Publick Affairs ... are Occasionally Considered* (London, 1741), p. 9.

87. [Owen Ruffhead], *Letter to the Common Council of the City of London* (London, 1764), p. 3.

Wesley adroitly contrasted the "People" of political rhetoric with the reality of a population of approximately eight million, of whom he reckoned five hundred thousand to be adult male freeholders.[88] The estimate was surely generous. Though the exchange was ordinary in its substance, a new intensity of feeling presaged further developments.

On 30 December 1779, some freeholders met in Yorkshire, and a movement of county associations was born. Many different interests were fused in the movement—economical reform, a redistribution of parliamentary seats, and simple desire, on the part of some politicians, for office. But in addition, the cause brought to the fore the place of the "People" in the political order. Spokesmen for the associations insisted, like their predecessors the petitioners of 1769–70, that they had with them the wealth of the counties. However, for some of the reformers the "People" now meant all adult males. From some quarters, at least, Wesley had his answer. One of the advocates of a greatly extended franchise was John Jebb, who raised another spectre that was far more real and worrisome to the Government.

He proposed that the associations see themselves not as importunate petitioners but as potential rivals to the House of Commons. If Parliament refused to co-operate, the associations should act on their own, forming a national convention or congress with full powers to execute reforms. In some quarters there was talk of an "out-of-door Parliament," but the leaders of the movement kept such possibilities well in the background. Throughout the century, men in office had repeatedly invoked the threat of a new centre of power that would overawe the formal organs of government. At last it threatened to materialize. In the light of such sinister talk, one can hardly doubt the sincerity of the alarm sounded in the ministerial press about sedition, unconstitutional acts, and the possibility that Parliament might be reduced to registering the edicts of self-appointed cabals. Inevitably, the ministers responded with the familiar charge that they were threatened with a "new unauthorized fourth estate." Lord Hillsborough, newly appointed secretary of state, adhered to this position, perhaps even without being familiar with the most ominous strain in

88. [Wesley], *Thoughts Concerning the Origin of Power* (Bristol, 1772), pp. 7–9.

the associators' vocabulary—the contemplated national convention.[89] In later public statements, Hillsborough made it clear that he objected to the associations, not to the act of petitioning.

Both the enthusiasm and the fear generated by the associations were much reduced by the summer of 1780. Even before the Gordon Riots, the county associations were linked to that other manifestation of popular clamour, Gordon's Protestant Association; after the riots, the dangers of popular organization were much more apparent.[90] But the presence of the county associations seems not to have depressed the prestige of the "People" as a political force. In 1733–34, the people had been described as an impossible fourth estate; in 1780, comparable, perhaps rather greater, concern was caused by the attempt to organize a national association, independent of Parliament and, in some measure, hostile to the majority in it. By comparison, the fact of petitioning at all attracted rather little criticism, and even the presumption about querying public expenditure, while deemed dubious practice, seems not to have scandalized North's supporters either in Parliament or in the press. The prospect of an extra-parliamentary convention could never been seen by orthodox Englishman as other than unconstitutional, indeed revolutionary. Nor did most reformers at this time view adult male suffrage either as a safe issue or a desirable goal. In raising the stakes to an unacceptable level, some writers for the county associations may actually have rendered more modest appeals relatively respectable.

Events in England came to be repeated in Ireland, as the Ulster Volunteers, initially formed to fend off a threatened French invasion, took on civil functions and called for a variety of reforms. Attorney-General Scott played Lord Hillsborough in the Dublin drama, for it was he who led the horrified response to the Volunteers' entry into politics. When the Volunteers sent Henry Flood, armed with a draft

89. *Parliamentary History* 20 (1780):1352; and Anon., *A Letter to the New Parliament ...* (London, 1780), p. 3. For a survey of this idea see T. M. Parssinen, "Association, convention and anti-parliament in British radical politics, 1771–1848," *English Historical Review* 88 (July 1973):504–33.

90. Ian Christie has noted the role of the Gordon Riots in provoking hostility to the reforming associations. See *Wilkes, Wyvill and Reform: The Parliamentary Reform Movement in British Politics, 1760–1785* (London: Macmillan; New York: St. Martin's, 1962), p.115. Long before Gordon's movement turned violent, the two kinds of association were linked together as dangerous causes. See *Morning Chronicle* 3336 (27 Jan. 1780).

bill, from the floor of their convention to that of the Irish House of Commons, courtiers were aghast. An English parallel would be the claim, in 1713, that Richard Steele had a parliamentary speech dictated by the Kit-Kat Club. The Volunteers were widely accused of attempting to overawe the legislature or, at least, to act as though they constituted another house.[91] Influential men drifted away from the Volunteers, and the cause of reform in Ireland subsided.

Henry Flood's defence of the Volunteers' presumption forms an interesting challenge to eighteenth-century suspicions about organized bodies. Countering the charge of unconstitutionality, Flood argued that the legislature sought or received the advice of gentlemen of the law or merchants to supplement its own knowledge.[92] In some sense, then, these groups were made legislators without any claims of impropriety. This was considerably more moderate than talk in Dublin that the Volunteers were the real legislature, and so Flood made their stand appear more attractive and less peremptory than it really was. His words do serve, however, to indicate the difficulties, especially at that time, in distinguishing between a legitimate interest and a rival to Parliament. As a military body, the Volunteers were obviously more subject to suspicion than most, for they seemed to evoke all the fears normally expressed about an army, an opposition, and a popular extra-parliamentary organization. Judging from past British experience, any one of these might have sufficed to raise anxiety.

Though the counties movement failed to sustain its momentum, the presence of the "People" as a significant political unit did survive the early 1780s. The Fox-North Coalition of 1783 was genuinely unpopular in the country, and the very people who had most ardently embraced reform felt most betrayed by the opportunism of the alliance. The upshot was an election in which both reformers and friends to the royal prerogative could find common cause. It may well be true that royal influence and Treasury funds were the immediate instruments of Pitt's victory of 1784; public opinion, like Providence, does not work without means. Pitt was not the choice of a spontaneous, uninfluenced public opinion, though it seems reasonable to assume

91. *The Parliamentary Register: or, History of the Proceedings & Debates of the House of Commons of Ireland*, 2nd ed. (Dublin, 1784), 2:226–43; and Francis Hardy, *Memoirs of the Public and Private Life of James Caulfield, Earl of Charlemont*, 2nd ed. (London, 1812), 2:133 [really 115], 145–46 [really 127–28].

92. *Parliamentary Register* 3:20.

that the public voice called him to office far more clearly than it had his father in 1757. In 1784 there had at least been an election. When Pittites in the new House of Commons said that it was the most "popular" house ever chosen, Fox's Martyrs had no answer; Lord North had at least the satisfaction of showing consistency in arguing, both before and after the coalition, that opinion in the country should not dictate policy to the House of Commons.

The most audacious conclusions drawn from 1784 came from the *English Review*. Damning the coalition from the start, it had joined the chorus of Pittite addresses for a dissolution, beginning as soon as Pitt came to power. The defeat of the India Bill showed the presence in the state of "a party ... different from King, Lords, and House of Commons"—the party of justice and wisdom. Anticipating Pitt's electoral triumph, this new force gained the status of "a fourth estate," composed of the people "and all that can influence the people, justice, self-interest, and the love of the public. ..."[93] The writers of this most politically aware of magazines were not so naïve as to assume that the people drew from a pure spring of public good; it sufficed that they produced an acceptable conclusion to what would otherwise be a constitutional stalemate.

There was more to this invocation of the public voice than the normal human feeling that one's own cause will appeal to all reasonable people. Typically an administration and its supporters resisted any appeal from the people outside the normal septennial election and approached even such elections with some trepidation. Though the Crown never lost an eighteenth-century election, ministers often feared for their majorities. Even in 1710, when Queen Anne replaced her Whig ministers and called a new election, there was no room for tension between the choice of the Crown and that of the Commons. For the departing Whig ministers had never possessed a firm hold of the Commons and had leaned heavily on a Whig majority in the Lords. But in 1784 there was a clear and obvious conflict between the wishes of the sovereign and the loyalties of the House of Commons. The "People" thus were to serve as the final arbiter in disputes "among the different members of the government."[94] Interpreting the defeat

93. *English Review* 2 (Dec. 1783):476, and 3 (Mar. 1784):238. The writer may well have been Dr. William Thomson. See *Annual Biography and Obituary* 2 (1818):101. Further information on the authors of this publication is to be found in chap. 7, below.

94. *English Review* 3 (Mar. 1784):238.

of the coalition as displaying the power of the "general voice of the nation" to check encroachments by the Commons, the *Review* claimed that there could then be no resisting this popular power. The House of Commons was stronger than either Crown or Lords, or indeed both together, so any likely combination of the branches of the legislature was effectively within the control of the people. Wisely, the writer chose not to contemplate the situation claimed by the more outspoken reformers of the day, that all branches of the legislature be found conspiring against the people, thus requiring a separate organization to oppose Parliament.

Nor did the *Review*'s enthusiasm flag after the election. The people remained the ultimate balance of the constitution—"a fourth estate of the kingdom, different from King, Lords, and their own representatives in Parliament."[95] This estate was fortified by various elements of social progress, chief among which were those factors, such as the growth of the press, that assisted the quick communication of ideas.

Such enthusiasm did not banish all reservations about political intervention by the people. For one thing, the events of 1783–84 placed in office a Government that saw good reason to rejoice in the voice of the people, but at the inevitable cost of creating an Opposition that condemned as demagogic the appeal beyond Parliament. Pitt was often accused of playing prince and people off against one another, to the detriment of both. A view characteristic of Fox's party was put by an able pamphleteer who commented on the decline of the House of Commons. Such novelties as the associations borrowed from America and Ireland had established as many Houses of Commons as there were opportunities for public discussion. The new possibility of separating the House and its constituents was perceived as leaving the multitude unprotected "and extends the Royal prerogative in the *inverse ratio* of a Country-meeting to the British senate."[96] Acclamation of the new popular fourth estate by Pittites still left ample scope for traditional views, as displayed by Sir Brooke Boothby. A Whig with

95. Ibid. 5 (Jan. 1785):80.
96. Anon., *Letters on the Politics of France ... by an English Gentleman at Paris* (London, 1788), pp. 45–46. The writer may have been W. A. Miles, who was in France at this time and who certainly was the author of another work bearing considerable resemblance to this one. See [Miles], *Cursory Reflections on Public Men and Public Manners on the Continent* (London, 1790).

radical tendencies, best remembered for his rejoinder to Burke's *Reflections*, Boothby wrote of the popular estate in the old pejorative way.[98] Tories too remembered how to condemn the popular voice—when it suited their purposes. Resistance to the Reform Bill in 1831–32 would sometimes raise the spectre of a new fourth estate that would dominate the three traditional branches of the legislature.[98]

Those who joined the *English Review* in applauding the role of the electorate as constitutional arbiter made quite modest claims of the newly recognized unit. Far from picturing the people as looming over all other bodies, they contemplated nothing more than the use of the electorate as a last resort. The expectation of septennial elections had suffered a blow with the very premature dissolution of 1784. However the notion of a popular tribunal was new, and thus some care had to be taken in specifying what was involved. The French Revolution imposed a need for further caution. Thus people who described the electorate as the major partner in "a sort of FOURTH ESTATE" were at pains to demonstrate that this was a counsel of moderation in defence of the established constitution.[99]

Special Cases: The Press and the Poor

To twentieth-century readers the fourth estate *par excellence* is the press; indeed, only in that expression does the notion of an estate of the realm survive in modern parlance. The press emerged as a putative estate much later than had most of the other supposed estates, and so the "fourth estate" as we know it is actually a nineteenth-century contribution to a habit of mind that had flourished most in the previous century.

Admittedly, the freedom of the press had been recognized for most of the eighteenth century as an advantage peculiar to British liberty, a point commonly made quite early in the reign of George I. By 1740 the notion that an unfettered press was the "palladium" of liberty—

---

97. Boothby, *A Letter to the Right Honourable Edmund Burke ...* (London, 1791), p. 9.

98. Anon., *The Three Estates, their Relative Rights and Duties* (London, 1831), pp. 9, 15.

99. [William Bruce and Henry Joy, eds.], *Belfast Politics: or, a Collection of the Debates, Resolutions, and other Proceedings of that Town* (Belfast, 1794), p. 178. For similar use of the expression by a moderate Whig see *The Works, Literary, Moral and Medical of Thomas Percival, M.D. ...* (London, 1807), 1:clxxv, from a letter of 1793.

an expression later popularized by Junius and others—was already being heard.[100] But an appreciation of the overall role of the press in political life was slower in emerging. Typically, writers on behalf of Opposition praised the principle of a free press in the interests of even greater freedom of expression. Those on the side of the Ministry claimed to support the same principle but emphasized the need to prevent a debasing of liberty into licence. However, for all the discussion of the need for a free press, little was said until late in the century about the newspapers as a political force. The issue of personal libels and the presence of some very amusing misprints attracted more comment.

The probable reason for this course of development is that, save for comparatively short periods when the columns of major papers such as the *Public Advertiser* or the *Public Ledger* were open to all shades of opinion, the London press was easily identifiable as either ministerial or anti-ministerial. This situation was often presented as an aid to the process of airing all possible views, but it also militated against the growth of a corporate identity for the newspapers, especially in terms of their political impact. As a publication edited by the radical Benjamin Flower once put it, "The press is divided against itself," each paper flying to a party for patronage.[101] Defenders of a free press often argued that it would be unreasonable for only one side in the party struggle to have an audience for its opinions. Nevertheless, when such people were moved to contemplate the press as a central organ of society, they most readily conceived of a major journal of opinion that was equally accessible to all parties.[102] The factors that eventually led people to perceive the press as a unified political force were no doubt part and parcel of the favourable attitudes towards the phenomenon of public opinion, a trend particularly noticeable after 1784.

If public opinion was deemed benign—or even just important—

100. See, for instance, *Common Sense* 49 (7 Jan. 1737–38). Here and elsewhere, I am indebted to G. Stuart Adam's unpublished Ph.D. thesis, "The Press and its Liberty: Myth and Ideology in Eighteenth-Century Politics" (Queen's University, 1978).

101. *Political Review and Monthly Mirror of the Times*, n.s. 1 (Aug. 1812):306. For a more positive view of the same situation see Anon., *The Periodical Press of Great Britain and Ireland* (London, 1824), p. 101.

• 102. Examples of both opinions are to be found in *English Review* 11 (Feb. 1788):157–58, and 9 (Apr. 1787):316–17.

then the organs that shaped it gained new stature and might be identified as a single force contributing to public enlightenment. It is also
worth observing that what was apparently the first noteworthy instance of the press's being called the "fourth estate" took place in the
House of Commons. As Charles Ross, long a *Times* gallery corre-
spondent, remembered it, Brougham used the phrase in referring to
the reporters covering the debates. This incident, which seems to have
taken place around 1823–24, coincides with a recognition that, despite
the partisan quarrels among the various papers, there had emerged
a large body of political reporters with sufficient *esprit de corps* to create
a new and politically influential profession.[103] Edmund Burke is sometimes credited with a much earlier use of the expression, also in relation to the parliamentary reporters; but considering his relations
with the press, that story is probably apocryphal.

Whatever Burke may or may not have said, modern historians continue to date the rise of the press as the fourth estate from the effective
acknowledgment after 1772 of the press's right to publish parliamentary debates.[104] If such an event requires a text, it comes, not from
Burke, but from Jean Louis de Lolme's discovery that the censorial
power in England lay in the people, supported by a free press.[105] In
a century in which more than one moral reformer had proposed the
revival of the Roman censorial power, de Lolme's conclusion of 1771
was significant and influential. Sometimes, however, it was reproduced
in garbled form, as when a newspaper credited "Mr. De Solmes" with
arguing that "the press may be considered as part of the executive
power. ..."[106] A sloppy censor, this. For while the quotation captured
the spirit of de Lolme's effort to bestow an official function upon the
press, it failed miserably to retain the central idea that it was precisely

---

103. This is particularly noted in a comprehensive review of the press in *Westminster Review* 2 (July 1824):194–212. The author was probably Gibbons Merle.

104. See A. Aspinall, "The reporting and Publishing of the House of Commons' Debates, 1771–1834," in Richard Pares and A. J. P. Taylor, eds., *Essays Presented to Sir Lewis Namier* (London: Macmillan; New York: St. Martin's, 1956), pp. 227–57; and Kennedy Jones, *Fleet Street and Downing Street* (London: Hutchinson, 1920), p. 36. A recent treatment of the concept of the press as the fourth estate underestimates the prestige of the press before 1840. See George Boyce, "The Fourth Estate: the Re-appraisal of a Concept," in Boyce et al., *Newspaper History From the Seventeenth Century to the Present Day* (London: Constable, 1978), p. 20.

105. de Lolme, *The Constitution of England* (London, 1775), p. 277.

106. *Craftsman: or Say's Weekly Journal* 806 (15 Jan. 1774).

the independence of the press that gave it such importance. Just because it could never be safely identified with the formal organs of government, the press invited comparison with those other extra-constitutional bodies that had earned the title of a fourth estate. A pamphlet of 1780 described the newspapers as "centinels" placed on the outposts of the constitution, and that made the point effectively.

Setting aside Burke's undocumented allusion and de Lolme's notion of a censorial power, the *English Review*'s discovery of a fourth estate in the "people" was the most apparent form of recognition devoted to the press prior to the French Revolution. It was the press that was perceived as focusing issues and animating the public for its task in arbitrating among the branches of Parliament. That press, reified into a potent monolith, was credited not only with influencing political life, but with dominating it, though this judgement was no doubt premature. "The press has almost swallowed up the political conse-quence of the pulpit, and awes and controls even members of parlia-ment and ministers of state."[107]

Already in 1780 the press was facetiously called an *imperium in imperio*. But this was merely a tribute to its governance in matters of literary taste and came as part of the trite thought of an essayist that Pope's literary dominance had yet to settle upon the shoulders of any unchallenged successor.[108] Unfavourable notice of the political role of the Opposition press was a favourite theme in ministerial papers in the period of reaction, Perry's *Morning Chronicle* and the *Edinburgh Review* being obvious targets. One such assault consisted in flaying the *Review* for its association with Whig debating societies, thus forming a "fourth branch" of government in defiance of the other three.[109] Hazlitt's quip of 1821 to the effect that William Cobbett was, in him-self, a "fourth estate" was much friendlier in tone, though not un-critical.

The power of the press came, on the whole, too late to qualify it as a fourth estate comparable to the others treated here. The mag-isterial *Times*, with its power and independence, received the appel-lation, but only well into the nineteenth century. In the eighteenth century most newspapers were too obviously the transmission-belts of

107. *English Review* 9 (Apr. 1787):315.
108. Robert Nares, *Periodical Essays* 2 (9 Dec. 1780).
109. Anon., *The Scotiad, or Wise Men from the North: A Serio-Comic Poem* (London, 1809), pp. 8–9.

some party to gain recognition as autonomous powers. By the late 1830s,[110] when the press became widely known as the fourth estate, the point of the comment was close to being lost. Government, Opposition, and the electorate had gained commanding positions in the recognized scheme of things, and historians were beginning to reinstate the bishops—purely to put the record straight—as one of the original three estates. The glorious centrality of King, Lords, and Commons had suffered major inroads; thus the significance of adding another estate to their company was much reduced. It is ironical that the surviving use of the expression "fourth estate" began life as an outdated metaphor.

One striking omission from the list of candidates for a fourth estate serves to distinguish British from European political thought. The poor and generally unprivileged do not appear to have figured in this company, though the problems presented by that sector of society was a topic of discussion throughout the period under consideration. There has been, indeed, an attempt to credit Sir Robert Sawyer with discovering a "fourth estate" in the mass of peasants and workers not represented directly in Parliament.[111] But Sir Robert's comments in the Convention Parliament of 1688–89 will not bear this interpretation. He had referred to the fact that freeholders and burghers, those who had presumably chosen a body he wished to discredit, were not "the fourth part of the Kingdom." This meant only that they numbered less than one quarter of the whole population, probably considering only adult males. The allusion to the unrepresented segment was solely for purposes of casting doubt on the right of Parliament to change the succession, and no label was provided for the nonvoting masses.

Henry Fielding had certainly identified the mob as an estate, but the point of his jocular quip was that it had, to his mind, begun to play a significant role in government; he had been unconcerned with the socio-economic status of its members. The same can be said of

---

110. For early uses of the term to refer to the press see [William Carpenter], *The Rights of Nations: A Treatise on Representative Government, Despotism and Reform* (London, 1832), p. 358; *Court Journal: Gazette of the Fashionable World* 193 (5 Jan. 1833):10, and 271 (5 July 1834):472. All three references were specifically to the presence of reporters in Parliament.

111. See Stuart Prall, *The Bloodless Revolution: England, 1688* (Garden City, N.Y.: Anchor Books, 1972), p. 260.

references—favourable or otherwise—about the people as an estate. Only by serving, either officially or informally, as an organ of government could any body be identified—even in jest—as an estate. Continental estates had some claim to be social orders, but the estates in England had long ceased to embody discrete status-groups in any precise sense.[112]

There was no British equivalent to the estate of peasants in Swedish government, nor did British political vocabulary follow German and Austrian practice in recognizing vocational estates of intellectuals or bureaucrats. A tendency late in the seventeenth century to distinguish estates of the realm and those of Parliament could be seen as a reversion to earlier English usage when "estate" had a less precise constitutional meaning. The usage was part of a tactful effort to smooth over the question of the bench of bishops and its claim to be an estate. It failed, and little further was heard of vocational estates.

At the outset of the French Revolution, claims for consideration of the poor, peasants, mothers, and other neglected groups sometimes took the form of stating that they were in fact a *quatrième ordre*. An anonymous pamphlet, probably by Restif de la Bretonne, raised the possibility of even a fifth estate.[113] An increased awareness of the plight of the indigent is apparent in British literature of the same period, but generally they were identified only as the poor. Nor does it appear that the nineteenth-century German expression *vierte Stand* had any standard equivalent in British references to the proletariat.

Benjamin Disraeli was presumably copying Continental practice when, in a speech of 1843 at Shrewsbury, he referred to the "estate of the poor."[114] He went on to declare it an error to suppose that the constitution consisted only of Queen, Lords, and Commons but confused the picture by identifying the estate of the poor with that of the Church of England. Since Disraeli was prominent in the effort to label as a Whiggish heresy the opinion that the monarch was an estate, his

112. See A. F. Pollard, *The Evolution of Parliament*, 2nd ed. (London: Longmans, Green and Co., 1926), pp. 61–80; and David Ogg, *Europe of the Ancient Régime, 1715–1783* (London: Collins, 1965), pp. 62–63.

113. P. Dufourny de Villiers, *Cahiers du quatrième ordre ... de l'ordre sacré des infortunés* (Paris, 1789); and [N. E. Restif de la Bretonne], *Le plus fort des pamphlets, l'ordre des paysans aux Etats-Generaux* (Paris, 1789), p. 67.

114. *The Wisdom of Disraeli*, arranged by T. Comyn-Platt (London: National Review, 1920), p. 29.

position was typically Janus-faced. Striving to resurrect the ancient formula of the monarch and the estates, he simultaneously sought to adapt the theory to nineteenth-century society. But the language of estates was not the idiom for understanding social classes, and Victorians did not follow Disraeli's example.

Estates and Interests

The title of an estate said something about the political status of an organized interest, and it could not apply to just any interest. It is worth noting, however, that the language knew the word "interest," referring to an organized group, long before most of the new "estates" were talked about in the terms typical of the eighteenth century. Interests, in the modern sense, were widely discussed in the period of the English Civil War, when these were the City, the Army, and various religious sects. The landed and trading interests were soon added and later the monied interest, to describe investors in the funds. Only by acting in a particular way or by posing a special sort of threat, could these be spoken of as claiming the privileges of a new estate. The language of interests certainly replaced that of estates—in the long run—but there was a very long period when the two coexisted.

Men referred to a fourth estate for a variety of purposes. Initially, the expression was usually ironical, an attempt to deflate the pretensions of political opponents with a recourse to sarcasm. Nothing more conclusively reveals the vacuity of Shaftesbury's famous criterion of ridicule as the test of truth. For the ridicule directed at the various fourth estates was usually but one stage in the recognition of new political forces and bodies. King, Lords, and Commons all spawned additional units that had somehow to be assimilated into the tripartite scheme. The position of the lords spiritual had been, in a sense, settled in the uneasy compromise that granted them the name of an estate in some of the traditional language of government but none of the real power that belonged to an estate of the realm. The Ministry, sprung from the Crown but seated in the houses of Parliament, could never come to be perceived favourably as a fourth estate but, with the taming of the prerogative, assumed most of the political functions of the Crown. The third estate, as was proper, was the most productive of new or competing identities. The Opposition within doors and the people without displayed the protean nature of the one branch of the legislature that was meant to embody the rich diversity of the population.

A literal fourth estate was hardly more probable than was that greatest of all constitutional aberrations, a state within a state. The major difference between the two was that a new challenger as one of the estates of Parliament could be greeted in a positive and sympathetic way that could never be applied to the *imperium in imperio*. The range of responses to unfamiliar phenomena varied from utter rejection—because they threatened to form a separate sovereignty— to ridicule as a fourth estate, and ultimately to acceptance as necessary and legitimate. When the Cabinet had won acceptance, despite its failure to conform to the scheme of three estates, and both the loyal Opposition and the people found respectability as estates by courtesy, the fetters imposed by eighteenth-century language were broken. The outcome might have been a reinterpretation of what the estates meant in the political system. In fact, recognition of the various units served notice that the scheme of three estates no longer explained the most important processes of government.

If this recognition seems a long time in coming, one can only offer the thought that the process of attaining it required the convergence of several independent developments. There was no one theorist of the "fourth estate." Thus each separate instance gained notice in apparent isolation from the others, and the political vocabulary for describing each such anomaly had to be rediscovered anew. The fact that the century witnessed a series of fourth estates testifies to the nature of the prevailing political assumptions. It is not surprising that tradition specified no mode of responding to new features of politics; rather, the logic of the political culture simply led to common responses to different phenomena. On that happy regularity hangs the tale of political innovation and its acceptance in the eighteenth century.

III

Mandeville: Poverty, Luxury, and the Whig Theory of Government

BERNARD MANDEVILLE (1670–1733) is a difficult figure in the history of social thought. The historians of economic doctrine, having decided that he does not belong exclusively to the realm of *belles-lettres*, are still not sure quite what to do with him. Thus we have continuing debate about whether or not he was *dirigiste* or *laissez-faire* in his general outlook.[1] This particular controversy has survived the growth of the opinion that mercantilism, at least in its English setting, had large elements of what would later be called economic liberalism.

Such debates about the appropriate way of identifying Mandeville's views are not very fruitful. If indeed we can speak at all of a definable creed called "mercantilism," then Mandeville was certainly a mercantilist in his understanding of the proper attitude of government vis-à-vis the poor. If, however, we consult his notorious defence of the indulgences of the rich, it is comparatively easy to make a case for his *laissez-faire* leanings. Only by committing ourselves to the unlikely assumption that Mandeville wanted all classes treated alike is it plau-

This chapter was presented as a paper at a meeting of the Conference for the Study of Political Thought in 1974, and it is cited in some of the recent literature. See M. M. Goldsmith, "Mandeville and the Spirit of Capitalism," *Journal of British Studies* 17 (Fall 1977):71; and Thomas A. Horne, *The Social Thought of Bernard Mandeville: Virtue and Commerce in Early Eighteenth-Century England* (London: Macmillan, 1978), p. 87. I have made some revisions, chiefly for purposes of noticing publications since 1974.

1. Mandeville's *laissez-faire* position was argued by F. B. Kaye, the modern editor of the *Fable*; Jacob Viner disagreed in several publications. More recent scholarship has again swung towards Kaye's original argument, though with qualifications. See Nathan Rosenberg, "Mandeville and Laissez-Faire," *Journal of the History of Ideas* 24 (Apr.–June1963):183–96; and Friedrich A. Hayek, "Dr. Bernard Mandeville," *Proceedings of the British Academy* 52 (1966):125–41.

sible to make global judgements about his economic philosophy. Another perspective on our subject will yield the same sort of conclusion. It is sometimes claimed that Mandeville was an economic individualist because he undoubtedly favoured considerable latitude for the pursuit of personal and selfish interests. On the other hand, we have incontrovertible evidence that he perceived the national good in terms of the traditional "mercantilist" values of national power and grandeur, glory abroad, and a full treasury at home. Again reality is richer than our limited categories.

Both of the foregoing arguments suggest that an adequate grasp of Mandeville dictates looking for something more than fragments of economic theory. The controversies among historians of economic thought about Mandeville's intentions turn, in part, on a failure of scholars to concern themselves very much with the political context of the *Fable*. Of course, it has long been taken for granted that the economic ideas of the eighteenth century had a political dimension; even without the studies by Furniss and Buck,[2] it was obvious that some assignment of costs and benefits was the point of the whole business. J. G. A. Pocock has called the administrations of the early eighteenth century "mercantilist government,"[3] and if we do not press the adjective too hard, the expression usefully reminds us that the government was then adapting to major economic changes. Sometimes dismissed as an era without political thought, the times actually saw a new political economy that provided the state with its rationale. In several respects Mandeville contributed to the formation of the attitudes that accompanied this form of government, and this is seen especially if we consult the use made of his ideas in political debate.

Nor is it gratuitous to view Mandeville's theme of luxury as directly related to the political order. Mandeville first defined luxury as anything "not absolutely necessary to keep a Man alive." Elaborating on this understanding, he presented a traditional account of luxury as an issue that entailed both a complete code of personal conduct and a theory of history. In the wisdom of the ages, the phenomenon of luxury was by no means confined to that narrowly economic significance the term had acquired by the middle of the eighteenth century.

---

2. See E. S. Furniss, *The Position of the Labourer in a System of Nationalism* (New York and Boston: Houghton and Mifflin, 1920); and P. W. Buck, *The Politics of Mercantilism* (New York: H. Holt and Co., 1942).

3. J. G. A. Pocock, *Politics, Language and Time* (New York: Atheneum, 1971), p. 140.

Sometimes, indeed, luxury had meant not the consumption of goods but "lechery," and normally in past usage it had borne the meaning of a revolt against the necessary bonds imposed by moral self-restraint and the requirements of hierarchy and social order. Since the complaint had been so general in character, authors were not very careful about distinguishing luxury from what we might now call its effects. Mandeville, who of course was hostile to the traditional indictment, was more meticulous than some others when he cited the association of luxury with avarice and rapine, and those vices, in turn, with a condition where "Offices of the greatest Trust are bought and sold; the Ministers . . . corrupted, and the Countries [*sic*] every Moment in danger of being betrayed to the highest Bidders. . . ."[4] But still Mandeville took no pains to articulate causal links, for it had been a truism that luxury and political corruption were almost one. The same tendency to slough over the consequences was present in efforts by Mandeville and others to identify luxury with happier circumstances. In this way the defence of luxury could readily serve the cause of justifying the techniques of rulers, such as the use of "influence," that were the hallmarks of the Walpole era.

Civic Humanism: In Praise of Poverty

There is not much conventional political theory—as understood by the greats of the previous century—in Mandeville. We can make the most of what there is by putting his remarks in context. The setting is peopled less by the Jacobites and Tories who had lost in 1714 than by the purveyors of virtue as practised in the ancient republics of the Mediterranean. In Mandeville's time and for most of the eighteenth century the rhetoric of Opposition teemed with allusions to public spirit in the ancient world and the terrible effects of a corruption of manners. The classical tastes of the Augustan age were nowhere more apparent than in paper volleys levelled weekly against Caesar, Catiline, and Sejanus—a rhetorical device made all the more sensible by dangers involved in openly defaming the ministers of the Crown. The classical-republican inspiration of the eighteenth-century Country party

---

4. *The Fable of the Bees*, ed. F. B. Kaye (Oxford: Oxford University Press, 1924), 1:115. My discussion of luxury is drawn largely from John Sekora's valuable study, *Luxury: the Concept in Western Thought, Eden to Smollett* (Baltimore: Johns Hopkins Press, 1977), pp. 73, 81, 100.

produced an odd faith. Its devotees despised tyrants, loathed corruption, and hailed a militia as a guardian of the virtue of a blameless people. However, this professed commitment to the welfare of the "People" was frequently joined by a distinct coolness towards the lower orders.[5] The people were most admirable at a distance; civic humanism was, on the whole, rather an aristocratic creed. It embodied the heroic postures of Cincinnatus and Cato, without seeking much by way either of political involvement or of material benefit for the mass of the population. Andrew Fletcher's suggestion that the poor of Scotland be enslaved for their own good illustrates, albeit in exaggerated form, the social teaching of classical republicanism. Although other commonwealthmen did not follow Fletcher in his desire to alter the legal status of the poor, neither did they share his evident concern for their physical welfare.

Strangest of all was the connection—cited in text after text—between political liberty and poverty. This relationship was present already in Machiavelli, whose relative lack of interest in the economic setting of politics extended to disparaging riches even in their vaunted role as the sinews of war. With apparent reluctance, Machiavelli had allowed that some material resources were indeed indispensable for warfare, but still he insisted that the character of a people was of greater weight. This prejudice led him to subscribe to the primitive mercantile assumption that in a free city the treasury should be rich but the individual citizens poor.[6] It seems like a difficult faith to sustain, but no doubt the conditions of the time—in which freedom and virtue had more to do with the goal of national independence than with sustained general participation—gave an air of reality to the claim. Rich, luxurious nations fell prey to their hardy, impoverished neighbours, who were scarcely likely to attract predators anyway, having little to lose. Adding to this consideration the familiar Roman story of a decline caused by wealth and effete manners, the exponents of civic virtue found in Spartan austerity the economic foundations of freedom. The martial Swiss, secure in their forbidding mountains,

5. For examples, see Ian R. Christie, *Wilkes, Wyvill and Reform* (London: Macmillan; New York: St. Martin's, 1962), p. 8. Caroline Robbins, who is more sympathetic to the school, takes a comparable position in *The Eighteenth-Century Commonwealthman* (Cambridge, Mass.: Harvard University Press, 1959), pp. 15–16, 184.

6. Machiavelli, *Discourses*, bk. 1, chap. 37; bk. 2, chap. 19.

added a modern parallel to the ample fund of classical allusion. A tradition had been forged.

That equality of condition that was supposedly preserved by the Spartan model was redefined less stringently in Harrington's balance of property. In requiring a balance in the people, Harrington set a condition that could easily be satisfied without banishing riches. By the same token, his system did not require affluence among the people, since the crucial factor lay in the relative shares of property and power in the various orders, not in the absolute amount of wealth. Later Harringtonians shared the master's assumption of an agrarian economy and were sometimes more explicit in their respect for poverty. Thus Henry Nevile regretted the corruption of the people in ancient Rome, for "if they had kept their poverty, they had kept their government and their virtue too."[7]

In the republican martyr Algernon Sidney we find much stronger stuff. Here, unabated, was the Machiavellian taste for the stern virtues of Sparta and early Rome, joined by a disdain for riches gained otherwise than through plunder. Amid his praise for honest poverty, Sidney did indeed find room to note that the riches of Rome had perished with its freedom. But he left no doubt that these riches were in themselves dangerous, for the presence of concentrations of wealth and luxury bred corruption by making intolerable that poverty that was the fountain of virtue. The safest social climate remained one in which riches "were either totally banished, or little regarded."[8] Sidney specifically attacked vices that were profitable to private men, deeming them inimical to the general good.

Sidney's teaching was enshrined in Old-Whig orthodoxy by Trenchard and Gordon and formed a central assumption in their denunciation of public morality in the era of the South-Sea Bubble. In a long succession of papers, the pens behind "Cato" insisted that prosperity could not flourish without liberty and that, indeed, all the embellishments of life, the arts included, flowed from political freedom. Trenchard and Gordon sometimes courted incoherence just because

---

7. "Plato Redivivus" (c. 1681), in *Two English Republican Tracts*, ed. Caroline Robbins (Cambridge: Cambridge University Press, 1969), p. 97. Nevile's fellow-republican, Walter Moyle, was less certain. Cf. "An Essay upon the Lacedaemonian Government" (1698), in *The Whole Works of Walter Moyle, Esq., that were Published by Himself* (London, 1727), p. 51.

8. Sidney, *Discourses Concerning Government* (London, 1698), pp. 201–2.

they insisted on giving reasons for valuing freedom and public virtue, for the very factors that they saw as insecure or impossible without freedom seemed actually to threaten its very existence. Only by assuming at least a frugal sufficiency could they continue to argue that all the good things in life were contingent upon maintaining freedom from corruption. Not only the ideal level of wealth but also its distribution was left uncertain when they argued, with Harrington, that "a free people are kept so, by no other Means than an equal Distribution of Property; every Man who has a Share of Property, having a proportionable Share of Power."⁹ This was scarcely equality as others understood it. The difficulties in the argument were the result of refusing to choose between two sticks with which to beat the government. Thus sometimes they availed themselves of the seventeenth-century threat of popery and wooden shoes—the symbols and substance of tyranny and poverty. But these Old Whigs were equally attached to another scenario—one featuring the evils of inequality, envy, and the resulting decay of barriers against arbitrary government. In this respect they faithfully followed Sidney and differed in no essential respect from the opinion expressed by Vertot, the reigning historian of Rome. Attributing the freedom of the republic to an acceptance of individual poverty as a virtue, Vertot praised "une pauvreté presque égale entre les citoyens."¹⁰

The Political Message of the "Fable" and Its Immediate Reception

Mandeville published the 1723 edition of the *Fable* in the wake of the furor over the Bubble. Cato, having reached the height of his popularity in the previous year, had moved from the *London Journal* to the *British Journal* but continued to fulminate against the government. This was precisely the time identified by later writers as the one in

9. *Cato's Letters*, 3rd ed. (1733; reprinted, New York: Russell and Russell, 1969), 1:26 (22 Apr. 1721).
10. Vertot, *Histoire des révolutions arrivées dans le gouvernement de la république romaine* (The Hague, 1727), 3:176. There had been an English translation as early as 1720. All students of "civic humanism" must acknowledge the magisterial presence of J. G. A. Pocock's *The Machiavellian Moment*. Of specific interest here are his comments on the treatment of luxury by Fletcher (pp. 430–31), Davenant (pp. 443–45), and Montesquieu (pp. 491–92).

which the manners of a commercial society became established. The revolution in public finance had even created a new social order—the "money'd interest," taking its place beside the established interests of land and trade.[11] It was a time too when the champions of the Whig establishment felt compelled to warn the public that security against popery and tyranny and the relative calm in public life still required what Mandeville called a supreme "arbitrary Authority" and "unlimited Obedience"; for even limited Whig governments had still to govern. A Tory paper of the day drew attention to abuses of power, reminding its readers that a popular government was not the golden age of "Sweetness and Liberty." More surprisingly, the government press in these years inveighed against the "rabble," promoted a Whiggish version of reason of state, and adopted as its message to the people a favourite scriptural text of Queen Anne—"study to be quiet."[12]

Mandeville's *Fable* explored another dimension of government—the function of the politician. At a time when Jacobites purported to believe in government from the hand of God, and Old Whigs praised the virtues of a bloodless abstraction called "the People," Mandeville celebrated the contribution of very human governors, though credit had to be shared with institutions built up over time. Man's very socialization was the work of "skilful Politicians," and "dextrous Management" by that same breed kept private foibles from becoming public abuses, thus rendering men useful to each other.[13] The hand

11. See a letter in the *General Evening Post* (11 Jan. 1750). On the interests of the time see *Freeholder's Journal* 43 (19 Dec. 1722). Three decades later it was a matter for discussion that the distinction between the trading and moneyed interests was still not consistently observed. See [Patrick, Lord Elibank], *An Inquiry into the Original and Consequences of the Public Debt* (London, 1754), p. 3. For modern comment on the monied and other interests see Michael Kammen, *Empire and Interest* (Philadelphia: Lippincott, 1970), pp. 60–62; and, for the standard account of the changes in government finance and public credit, P. G. M. Dickson, *The Financial Revolution* (London: Macmillan, 1967).

12. Mandeville, *Free Thoughts on Religion, the Church and National Happiness* (London, 1720), pp. 297–300. Tory comment is taken from the *Weekly Journal, or Saturday's Post* 135 (1 July 1721). Typical Whig statements, similar in tone to Mandeville's, may be found in the *Weekly Journal, or British Gazetteer* (15 Apr. 1721); *Pasquin* 56 (13 Aug. 1723); and various issues of the *St. James's Journal* for March and April 1723.

13. *Fable*, 1:47, 116, 145, 208. Professor M. M. Goldsmith has helpfully reminded me that Mandeville's use of "politician" sometimes included moralists as well as statesmen. I agree, but often the modern and narrow meaning seems to be intended. His further suggestion that Mandeville's politician must be taken as a symbol of society in

of the politician was particularly evident, for good or evil, in managing the poor, and Mandeville noted how those social ills, often attributed to luxury, proceeded in fact from maladministration. Mandeville cheerfully allowed that the selling of offices was a fault in the polity and corrupt ministers a danger.[14] But more importantly, he gave significant credentials to the elected politicians of a free government, at a time when the role of the politician was in low repute, at least among literary folk.

Of course, Mandeville was not inclined to salvage the personal reputations of politicians. In the first edition of the *Fable* in 1714 he already had said that it was an unhappy nation that left its welfare to the "Virtues and Consciences of Ministers and Politicians." This was standard Whiggish doctrine, the whole point of the balance of the constitution being that ambitions were set against one another for the benefit of the whole. Mandeville spelled out his meaning in the major publication that appeared between the first two editions of the *Fable*, in 1714 and 1723. Again he remarked on the failings of politicians— their insincerity and petty ambitions. But Mandeville sought also to reconcile his readers to the necessary inconveniences of a limited monarchy. Kings who were blessings to their people had to be indulged in their need for retainers: "So many Services require abundance of People of various Employments, who are well vers'd in all manner of Elegancy and Politeness, the several Branches of the public Administration demand Officers of different Ranks and Capacities . . . of whom several have huge Salaries and other Emoluments, and not a few great Opportunities of enriching themselves."[15]

Irrespective of the personal frugality of the monarch, then, courts had to be "Places of Pomp and Luxury." To his credit, Mandeville scotched the argument that rulers needed a great panoply to strike

---

general is enlightening but does not, I believe, rule out a more literal (and Whiggish) interpretation. See M. M. Goldsmith, "Public Virtue and Private Vices: Bernard Mandeville and English Political Ideologies in the Early Eighteenth Century," *Eighteenth-Century Studies* 9 (Summer 1976):510. After all, Mandeville's argument did strike at Opposition rhetoric, and he was perceived as a Court Whig. See Isaac Kramnick, *Bolingbroke and his Circle* (Cambridge, Mass.: Harvard University Press, 1968), pp. 201–4; and W.A. Speck, "Bernard Mandeville and the Middlesex Grand Jury," *Eighteenth-Century Studies* 11 (1977–78):368.

14. *Fable*, 1:114–15, 287.
15. *Free Thoughts*, pp. 336–37.

awe into their subjects.[16] Such considerations carried no weight with the author of the quip that the humility of bishops must be a very ponderous virtue, since it had to be drawn by a coach and six. Pomp was necessary to courts simply because those in power enjoyed it. Although it might well be true that all ministries strove to engross the available places of trust and profit among themselves and their friends, Mandeville argued that the very ubiquity of such abuses should moderate criticism. Where, he asked, were the people who could judge without prejudice? A further factor that should curb criticism of politicians was the complexity of politics and the distance separating affairs of state from the normal concerns of private men. In fact the sudden "Contingencies" and novelties to which political life was subject made even experienced politicians the victims of unforeseen consequences.[17] Here Mandeville's characteristic way of viewing the business of merchants, rakes, and whores was turned to the impact of unintended consequences on public policy. Mandeville's final offering in defence of the Hanoverian line and its ministers blended themes from his Whiggish politics and his economic observations. Malcontents, out of place, had complained of the Court's wealth going, in some cases, to German courtiers. But really, sighed Mandeville, the charges of disgruntled politicians were exaggerated. "When Courtiers, that are Foreigners enrich themselves with our Money, their Heirs spend it among us, and the Sons often with the same Application, that the Fathers scrap'd it together."[18] Such observations need to be borne in mind, given the more muted testimony of the *Fable*.

Mandeville seems not to have been as interested in the commonplaces of politics as were many of the literary men of the age; this has left his modern readers unsure about the measure in which the *Fable* addresses issues of the day as distinct from the general development of institutions, and the tension pervades current interpretations. We do know that Mandeville's patron, Lord Macclesfield, the Lord Chancellor from 1718 to 1724, quarrelled with Walpole.[19] This left Mande-

---

16. *Fable*, 1:163–65.

17. *Free Thoughts*, pp. 345–46.

18. Ibid., p. 351.

19. Kaye explains some points in the second part of the *Fable*, published in 1728, in terms of the relationship between Mandeville and his patron. *Fable*, 2:326–27n. The edition of 1723 may have been similarly affected, since Macclesfield was then already feuding with Walpole. See John M. Beattie, *The English Court in the Reign of George I* (Cambridge: Cambridge University Press, 1967), p. 150.

ville in the uncomfortable situation of a pro-administration Whig who may have felt no admiration for the most powerful Whig. Moreover, Mandeville had conventional reservations about the emerging office of prime minister, the basis of Sir Robert's power. Yet even as he denied the legal existence of a prime minister and belittled the capacities of those who presumed to fill the office—tendentiously, he deemed it much less challenging that that of Lord Chancellor— Mandeville recognized the contribution of the adroit politician. As for the calling of statesmen, according to Cleomenes, who spoke for Mandeville at this point in the text, it required nothing less than "the highest Qualification human nature is capable of possessing. . . ." Mandeville went on to say that such ability was unnecessary in mere politicians, for common sense, resolution, energy, and honesty would largely suffice. Faint praise perhaps, but it can be seen as presenting the ministers as competent for the performance of their tasks, thus deflecting Opposition attacks.[20]

Admittedly, Mandeville dreamed of a government that would work well even if the governors were evil. All Whigs did, and Mandeville with his penchant for finding social value in evil persons, as much as any. But it is difficult to believe that he hoped for much if evil politicians were also fools.[21] The contingencies of politics made great demands upon wisdom, foresight, and a general familiarity with society: "nothing in human Affairs requires greater knowledge than the Art of Governing."[22] It was not an original lawgiver who received this supreme accolade, for as a good Whig, Mandeville saw the constitution as already determined. Yet regulations for the proper administration of trade were still wanting, and Mandeville probably thought that judicious administration would always be needed. With all his fail-

20. *Fable*, 2:330–31. A balanced interpretation of this passage, noting both its modest expectations for politicians and its legitimizing of the Whig government, is provided by H. T. Dickinson, "The Politics of Bernard Mandeville," in Irwin Primer, ed., *Mandeville Studies* (The Hague: Martinus Nijhoff, 1975), pp. 91–93.

21. Professor Rosenberg has, it seems, exaggerated the *laissez-faire* element in Mandeville by citing comments on the modest abilities required for the posts of prime minister and Lord Treasurer. See Rosenberg, "Mandeville," p. 192; and *Fable*, 1:325. We must not forget Mandeville's animus against Walpole and the fact that it was Walpole who, from 1721, held both of the offices that had been disparaged.

22. *Fable*, 2:318. It is Cleomenes, not the more naïve Horatio, who is speaking at this point.

ings,[23] the politician in power was a figure on whom the happiness of society depended, for Mandeville appreciated that ministers there had to be.

Quite apart from his hymn to political management, Mandeville's explicitly partisan comments were a significant statement of Whig constitutional theory—certainly the best since the Whig victory at the elections of 1715. For the theorizing over the Peerage Bill of 1719, although abundant, was often confusing, owing to the complexity of the issue. But Mandeville's greatest contributions lay in the future.

To understand the real significance of Mandeville's writings we must turn again to their political context. No reading between the lines, no tracing of arch allusions or interpretations of pregnant silences need claim our attention. The defence of the Court and its luxury are among the most straightforward, least paradoxical of Mandeville's pronouncements. The argument said exactly the right things: that the people themselves or human nature was the source of corruption, not the government; that the national strength was not jeopardized by the pleasures of the rich, prominent among whom were Whig place-holders, but that careful administration was needed to keep vice innocuous; that the nation was great and rich and free. Cato's philippics against the government had urged equality, virtue, and at least a measure of poverty on the nation. Mandeville's alternative transformed the politician from corrupter-general to the agent of civilization, whose adroit management left the people with their vices and bestowed, as well, an unprecedented liberty. The politician's price consisted in the perquisites of office, and so a bond was formed between private indulgence and the new pattern of politics based on the systematic use of influence.

The *Fable* could not, of course, have been written against Cato, but even before the edition of April 1723 it was used against that self-righteous composite-critic. Kaye's careful researches into Mandeville's influence found virtually no response to the 1714 edition.[24] In fact,

23. Contemporary pamphlets bore titles such as *The Anti-Politician* (1734) and *The Advantages of Politicks to this nation* (1729), the latter being intended to suggest that such advantages were minimal.

24. Neither Kaye nor Paul Sakmann's *Bernard de Mandeville and die Bienenfable-Controverse* (Freiberg, 1897) mentions an early and important response to Mandeville, such as Tindal's, cited here. Some of Defoe's essays for Mist's *Weekly Journal* indicate that he too was familiar with the first edition of the *Fable* as early as 1719, and Defoe already used the formula "private vices, public benefits" to account for struggles between state-factions.

it did make an impact, for Mandeville's arguments took their place in the defensive armoury of the Whig ministers. Cato's assault on the prevailing political mores had changed the style and content of political debate, and from arguing about the original contract, the succession, and indefeasible hereditary right, men found themselves involved in a much closer examination of the nature of contemporary institutions. The Whig stalwart Matthew Tindal was responsible for several of the more forceful answers to Cato. Tindal repudiated Cato's charges about the effects of luxury and corruption, adding, for good measure, a blow at the malcontent fixation on the ancient world:

Private Vices, in this Case, are far from being publick Inconveniences, as is admirably made out by a late ingenious Author: And our Law, for this very Reason, abhors *Perpetuities*. And I may add, That vast Numbers of Trades People and Artificers wou'd soon starve, were we oblig'd to live as the Romans did, in those Times most celebrated for their Frugality; when they had no Manufactures, no Trade, no Ships ... and their Riches chiefly consisted in their Cattle. ...[25]

Tindal's frank praise for the *Fable* affords us only a glimpse of its importance for the political struggles of the time. Then the curtain rang down as conventional religious sensibilities condemned Mandeville's naturalistic and cynical treatment of morality and his unsettling account of the workings of Providence. The Whigs had recruited some of the ablest political writers from the ranks of churchmen—Benjamin Hoadly, Francis Hare, Francis Squire, Thomas Sherlock—and theirs was a more dependable form of support than Mandeville's elusive and disturbing wit. The government press did contain some favourable references to Mandeville's ingenious ideas about vice and its consequences,[26] and the *London Journal*, then a government paper,

25. [Tindal], *A Defence of our Present Happy Establishment; and the Administration Vindicated* (London, 1722), p. 19. In a pamphlet of 1729 Tindal continued to affirm his attachment to Mandeville's position. See *An Address to the Inhabitants of London and Westminster*, cited in Horne, *Social Thought*, p. 108.

26. See *Pasquin* 34 (13 May 1723). For much later instances of praise for Mandeville's social insight see *Prompter* 146 (30 May 1736); and *Adventurer* 29 (13 Feb. 1753). It is not difficult to find other favourable references, but most of these have a bantering tone that makes their intent suspect.

was open to Mandeville when he wished to answer his critics. But more typical of the reaction was the comment of another ministerial Whig that Mandeville was a man of sense, whose conclusions were "pretty right" but nonetheless dangerous material with which to fill the heads of the common people. Indeed, most of Mandeville's conclusions were already familiar to men of affairs, but they knew better than to strip society of its "Pretensions." Even while distancing the administration from the *Fable*, this writer tried to improve upon the occasion by attacking "Cato," here described as Mandeville's "humble Imitator and Follower"[27]—a claim contrary both to fact and to logic. Thomas Gordon did certainly use Mandeville on later occasions,[28] but *Cato's Letters* upheld resolutely antithetical opinions.

John Dennis the critic had that horror of corruption typical of civic humanism, but he also defended Walpole against all comers. Dennis took fright at Mandeville's attribution of the evils of luxury to "Male-Administration" and "bad Politicks." In his condemnation of the *Fable* Dennis was especially insistent on the fact that the government was not at fault, that indeed, political ills followed from luxury, and that luxury itself must be banished.[29] No doubt Dennis, for all his independent Whiggery, was the more partisan of the two, and no doubt he earned the small pension finally bestowed by Walpole. However, he misrepresented Mandeville in treating him as a severe critic of the administration.

Following the condemnation of the *Fable* by the Middlesex grand jury (in the summer of 1723), Mandeville's logic became much more prominent than favourable use of his name. Numerous government supporters were prepared to argue that liberty and trade were naturally the cause and effect of each other and that, if poor, a people would not deem their few resources worth defending against op-

27. *Tea-Table* 25 (15 May 1724).

28. [Gordon], *Humourist* 20 (London, 1725) 2:114–15.

29. Dennis, *Vice and Luxury Publick Mischiefs* (London, 1724), pp. 56–58, 70–72. The assigning of fault for corruption was a major issue in political argument. The very title of another of Dennis's works puts one side of the case. See *Julius Caesar Acquitted and his murderers Condemn'd. In a Letter to a Friend. Shewing that it was not Caesar who destroy'd the Roman liberties. . . . To which is added a second letter, shewing that if ever the liberties of Great Britain are lost, they will be lost no other way than by the corruption of the people of Great Britain themselves.* (London, 1722).

pressors. The eclectic William Arnall sometimes employed Harringtonian arguments in defence of Walpole, but he also found opportunities
to argue in the manner of Mandeville. Resisting the Opposition formula that political liberty was protected by uncompromising standards
of virtue, Arnall instead argued that the lesson to be learned from
the attempt to introduce an agrarian law at Rome was that "publick
Frugality" was potentially fatal to a state, whereas it might flourish
with a "moderate Largess."[30]

Only Mandeville's abstract moral propositions about the sources of
virtue and justice can account for hostility on the part of contemporaries who saw much to admire in his specific observations about society. The socializing mechanism of human relations and the role of
the politician in orchestrating human frailty seemed not at all objectionable to clergymen who could not swallow the general satire on
moral rigorism.[31] Objections arose because of Mandeville's perverse
insistence that certain activities were both vices and necessary to society. Some critics rendered the message of the *Fable* relatively un-
subtle by assuming that it was a simple rationale for the profit of a
few politicians masquerading as the public.[32] It is true, of course, that
Mandeville was justifying the administration—a point largely neglected in modern studies. But there seems no good reason to argue
that he was not sincere in his mercantilist understanding of national
strength, independent of the welfare of specific individuals. Others
saw Mandeville as an ordinary apologist for the beau and the belle
and felt it necessary to insist that when luxury diffused riches, benefit
accrued "not to the luxurious Man, or to a sensual luxurious People,

---

30. [Arnall], *Clodius and Cicero* ... (London, 1727), p. 26. Sekora tends to overlook
arguments of this sort, claiming that Walpole's writers usually attacked the integrity of
the Opposition, rather than defending luxury. Sekora, *Luxury.*, p. 111. Possibly Arnall
intended to apply Mandeville's arguments but shrank from naming his source of inspiration. See Thomas Horne, "Politics in a Corrupt Society: William Arnall's Defense
of Robert Walpole," *Journal of the History of Ideas* 41 (1980):613.

31. See Robert Burrow, *Civil Society and Government Vindicated from the Charge of being
Found'd on, and Preserv'd by, Dishonest Arts* (London, 1723), p. 12n.; and his *A Dissertation
on the Happy Influences of Society Merely Civil* (London, 1726), p. 19. Both are texts of
sermons.

32. See Anon., *The True Meaning of the Fable of the Bees* (London, 1726); *Mist's Weekly
Journal*, n.s. 59 (11 June 1726); and *Weekly Miscellany* 379 (29 Mar. 1740).

but to those who take Advantage of supplying others with the Materials of Luxury."[33]

Mandeville would have agreed in the main, even to the extent of
discouraging the importing of certain foreign luxuries. The very essence of his theory stressed how the gain both of some individuals
and of the public was built upon the ruin of others. The old fears
about tyranny and wooden shoes could now be fitted for commercial
life by another pedal image—clogs to clogs. This was appreciated by
some people who still held to the ideal of virtuous equality. One of
these pointed out the inconsistency of Opposition complaints that
Britain suffered from "universal Poverty" and that the cause was the
prevailing luxury. Far better to argue in specifics and thus admit that
"the Children of those ruined by Luxury in this Age, must toil for
the Children of the Industrious in the next."[34] This verdict was wholly
in accord with Mandeville's sympathies. For he had even softened his
harsh opinions about the labourer to allow that any exceptional person
who by pinching his belly managed to save on subsistence wages de-
served to rise in the world.[35]

Luxury in Later Political Argument

Mandeville has been called the high-priest of luxury in the eighteenth
century,[36] and undoubtedly his one characteristic position is what kept
his ideas before the public for most of the century. The judgement
that a society could not turn its back on refinement and remain great
was at the heart of the interminable debate about the causes, extent,

33. William Shorey, *Fourteen Discourses Preach'd on Several Occasions* (London, 1725),
p. 111.

34. Anon., *Important Considerations on the True Nature of Government* (London, 1741),
pp. 36–37. Cf. *Fable*, 1:319, 354–55; and Mandeville, *A Letter to Dion* (1732), introduction by Jacob Viner, The Augustan Reprint Society, 41 (Los Angeles: University
of California, William Andrews Clark Memorial Library, 1953), p. 39. In these passages
Mandeville noted how the public good was necessarily founded on the ruin of some
individuals and families.

35. *Fable*, 1:193.

36. Malvin R. Zirker, *Fielding's Social Pamphlets* (Berkeley and Los Angeles: University
of California Press, 1966), p. 78. The same consideration probably accounts for Professor Hayek's opinion that Mandeville was one figure whose ideas could be assumed
to be known by all well-informed people of the time.

and meaning of corruption—a debate that produced very nearly the whole substance of British political argument in the forty years after 1723. The argument reflects all the confusion and inconsistency normally encountered when people continue to write in an idiom that is imperfectly adapted to changed circumstances. Caught between a romantic primitivism that seemed ever less meaningful for a commercial nation and Mandeville's full-fledged acceptance of commercial modernity, many polemicists tried to use both without endorsing either.

The commonwealth rhetoric that hailed the virtuous poverty of Sparta and republican Rome was an early casualty. For although some of the tenets of civic humanism lingered into the nineteenth century, admiration for virtuous poverty was one of the less resilient strains in the tradition. A first step in modifying opinion was made when Opposition writers came to soft-pedal the merits of poverty, concentrating instead on a supposed plot to enslave the people by developing their taste for luxury. Thus it was commonly observed in the 1730s that luxury and poverty went hand in hand, since people who lived above their means would ultimately be ruined. In letter 19 of his *Dissertation upon Parties*, Bolingbroke argued this position to explain how luxury led envious men into the arms of corruption, "for there is imaginary as well as real poverty." In the corresponding passages in their works, Machiavelli, Sidney, and (sometimes) Cato advocated real poverty as the antidote. Nor did Mandeville deny that luxury and poverty might successively visit the same persons, but he was more precise than Bolingbroke, and of course he resisted the connection with tyranny founded upon corruption. Frequently luxury and poverty were linked in other contexts as well, as people wrote, with Mandeville, of the "luxury of the poor," meaning any consumption or activity of this class not connected with their work. The expression conveys Mandeville's tendentious understanding of luxury as anything beyond the bare requirements of survival.

Other Opposition writers went farther than Bolingbroke in shaking off the connection between virtue and poverty—even to the extent of invoking the classical ideal in mock praise of Walpole. The minister, they said, kept the people poor solely out of regard for their moral welfare. Furthermore, they intoned with ironic solemnity, Rome was ruined by its wealth. Opposition writers published what purported to be ministerial essays in which they quoted Vertot, the apostle of pristine virtue, on the value of general poverty in securing liberty. Such sallies remained in fashion after the fall of Walpole.[37] It is difficult to assess the meaning of these essays. Normally one might think that a writer would not resort to irony unless the object of his attack were clearly ridiculous. However, one of the problems of understanding this great age of satire is that mores changed very rapidly. Consequently the texts of satirists do not appear exaggerated when placed beside the same propositions in the works of people who wished to be taken seriously. It seems safe to say, however, that there was less serious talk about virtuous poverty in the 1730s than in the previous decade.

Nor should this be surprising, for it is easy to overestimate the strength of the hostility generated by commercialism and the financial revolution. Swift and Bolingbroke did indeed resent the emergence of new claims to power and status. But we must also recall that some of the most cogent analyses of trade had come from the pens of Tories in the reign of William III. Nicholas Barbon and Dudley North had even defended luxury for its value in giving employment,[38] and North had been more consistent than Mandeville himself, for the former also supported high wages so that the worker might share in the general prosperity. Charles Davenant, the best-known writer on trade for most of the eighteenth century, had seen nothing wrong with the accumulation of private wealth, accepting it as a contribution to the national stock and one of the signs of a "prosperous people."[39] Davenant was famous for his pedantic display of classical allusion, but his admiration for republican Rome stopped short of recommending the sharing of poverty. At the time of writing, he too was a Tory of sorts. It is not Davenant's demand that the people share in the balance of trade that needs explaining, nor the revival of such sentiments in the 1730s. The Old-Whig interlude seems rather to be the anomaly. Had Mandeville published at a time other than that of Cato's great popularity, his case for self-interest might have seemed less important. The relative obscurity of *The Grumbling Hive* in 1705 and the 1714 edition of the *Fable* attest to this.

37. See *Fog's Journal* 308 (28 Sept. 1734); *Craftsman* 493 (13 Dec. 1735), and 888–91 (2–23 July 1743).

38. See, for example, Nicholas Barbon, *A Discourse of Trade* (1690), ed. Jacob H. Hollander (Baltimore: Johns Hopkins University Press, 1905), pp. 31–33.

39. See "Discourses on the Public Revenue, and on the Trade of England, Part II" (1698), in *Works*, 1:357–58.

In the 1730s the Spartan cause was on the wane, but Mandeville had not won. At times, the Opposition press did indeed argue that luxury was not the social evil that it was sometimes thought to be. For though it "may ruin *Individuals*, ... whatever One loses Another gains, and the *National Stock* cannot be thus exhausted."[40] Walpole's writers were jubilant, boasting that finally the Grumbletonians had been "hunted out of that fallacious Trick" of condemning luxury. In point of fact, the ministry had itself only recently grown bolder in its position on luxury, assisted no doubt by the appearance in 1738 of an English translation of Jean-François Melon's book on commerce.[41] The Frenchman, who had published in 1734, was probably the first European to popularize Mandeville's economic doctrine, replete with a disdain for the irrelevance of Lacedaemonian simplicity. Released from the apparent dilemma of wishing to use Mandeville's argument, while fearing association with his name, the *Daily Gazetteer*, the chief ministerial paper, acclaimed David Bindon's translation of Melon.[42] The government's arguments about economic conditions became noticeably more forceful as its writers gave the ministry full credit for the combination of freedom and prosperity that had luxury as a necessary by-product. Ministers were no more culpable than was a father who made adequate provision for his children, knowing that they might use their patrimony unwisely. All good ministries, it was now claimed, sought peace, freedom, and plenty, and such luxury as existed was but the "scab of Riches." A measure of voluntary restraint might well be useful in curbing excessive consumption, but no free government should use its power to force frugality on its citizens. Such action would unjustly deprive of their livelihoods those who catered for luxury. Walpole himself set the tone when the government went on the offensive:

40. *Craftsman* 675 (16 June 1739). This issue was identified in the government press, but I have not as yet been able to consult the original.

41. We still do not know that Melon had read Mandeville, but it is generally assumed that he had. See André Morize, *L'Apologie du luxe au xviii*ᵉ *siècle et "Le Mondain" de Voltaire* (1909; reprinted, Geneva: Slatkine Reprints, 1970), p. 120.

42. *Daily Gazetteer* 1275 (23 July 1739). Earlier numbers indicate a much more conventional distaste for luxury. See ibid. 120 (15 Nov. 1735), and 801 (27 Jan. 1738). In his preface to the translation, Bindon qualified in some respects Melon's praise of luxury. *A Political Essay on Commerce* (Dublin, 1738), pp. xxv–vi.

A minister is answerable, Sir, in some measure; for the wealth of a nation; but he is not answerable for the abuse of that wealth. And when gentlemen exclaim against the luxurious living of a nation, they are mistaken if they think that thereby they hurt the reputation of a minister in the eyes of considerate men. No, Sir, they bestow a tacit encomimum upon the minister. ...[43]

By the end of the Walpole era there had emerged a fairly coherent theory of government and society, justifying a number of the components of Walpole's political system—royal influence through use of places and pensions, as a means of keeping a rich House of Commons dependent, and parties that served as foci of both the administration and its opponents. Luxury was an important part of the pattern. Men in opposition still linked it to corruption and faction. Spokesmen for government expressed the point differently by pointing to the numerous lucrative offices available in a commerical society and the consequent growth of parties to contest those offices.[44] Influence too, in the form of places and pensions, was increasingly linked to the prosperity of the nation as writers followed Mandeville in calculating the unavoidable costs of greatness. No one author seems to have adequately synthesized all these factors, though Hume, with his essays of 1741–42 on luxury and on the independency of Parliament, grasped the main elements. Henceforth, the jeremiads of patriots in opposition would be subject to the objection that their code was unsuited to the ways of refined nations. The ties now perceived between private luxury and institutional change grew stronger.

Not all of this of course, can be laid at Mandeville's door, either in praise or in blame. He had never been very explicit about parliamentary institutions, nor could he have been aware of the mid-century vogue of discovering stages in the development of human societies. By 1750 the opinion that luxury stimulated trade was said, by one severe moralist, to be in mouth of "every petty politician."[45] But

43. *Parliamentary History* 10 (1738):441. For sources of other comments see *Daily Gazetteer*, 1289 (8 Aug. 1739), 1507 (18 Apr. 1740), 2015 (2 Dec. 1741), and 2285 (29 Oct. 1742).

44. For causal connections among such factors as prosperity, luxury, and opposition to government see [John Perceval], *Faction Detected by the Evidence of Facts* (London, 1743), pp. 5–7.

45. "Of Avarice and Luxury," *British Magazine* (Sept. 1750), p. 344.

Mandeville continued to be recognized as the major spokesman for the political economy of a commerical society. In 1757 Soame Jenyns, who shared Mandeville's taste both for paradoxes and for brutal realism in social theory, wrote his *Enquiry into the Nature and Origin of Evil*, which included a section on the inevitability of sundry forms of political corruption. In the same year, Dr. John Brown, in his *Estimate of the Manners and Principles of the Times*, continued his efforts, begun in the 1740s, to rouse the nation against luxury, corruption, and parties. Still, a contemporary journalist chose to describe the revival of debate as pitting Mandeville against Montesquieu![46] Since those two did not differ dramatically in their attitudes to luxury—Montesquieu denied that riches necessarily corrupted and saw no striking virtue in poverty[47]—apparently the writer identified Mandeville with the general cause of corruption. This is perhaps understandable, since Mandeville's general mode of argument—the systematic defence of apparent abuses through ingenious efforts at causation—lent itself to a variety of applications. Almost any departure from the traditional patterns of government could be treated in this way.

It was Mandeville's fate to be blamed for the opinions of others and to be ignored, even disavowed, by those who borrowed his ideas. One is not surprised, then, when the author of a Pittite journal wrote essays in praise of luxury and against the model of Spartan virtue and then remarked that "the writings of Mandeville are but little read or read with contempt and disgust."[48] But his influence was undeniably great. Sophisticated expositions of the flawed constitution of the 1790s still benefited from his arguments. Thus one confessed admirer rebuffed efforts at parliamentary reform by alleging that the numerous placemen did little harm and, since they were large consumers of the

---

46. *Herald* 2 (24 Sept. 1757).

47. Later commentators on Montesquieu basically agreed with his tolerance of luxury, but stated the irrelevance of doctrines on the subject more forcefully than had he. See [David Williams], *Lectures on Political Principles* (London, 1789), lecture 7; and [Destutt de Tracy], *A Commentary and Review of Montesquieu's Spirit of Laws*, trans. William Duane (Philadelphia, 1811), p. 189.

48. *Looker-On ... by the Rev. Simon Olive-Branch* [i.e., William Roberts] 35–36 (5–12 Jan. 1793), and 69 (7 September 1793). See too the dismissal of arguments about avoiding riches and about the relation of prosperity to vice as "so destitute of solid reflection, that it has not probability enough for a *Fable*." [E. Wynne], *Eunomus: or, Dialogues Concerning the Law and Constitution of England*, 3rd ed. (London, 1774), 3:336. The conclusion owed more to Mandeville than the author admitted.

superfluities of life, served as a valuable fillip to trade.[49] Henry James Pye, the Poet Laureate of the day, was another anti-reformer who admitted his admiration for Mandeville's cogency.[50] In fact, the name of Mandeville was probably more prominent in this brilliant salvo of cynical realism than in the comparable period at the close of Walpole's government fifty years before.

The aspect of Mandeville's thought that provoked least comment among his contemporaries was his acceptance of a life of unremitting poverty for the labourer. Only after 1750 did informed opinion begin to take seriously the possibility that high wages might actually be a part of national prosperity.[51] From the viewpoint of Adam Smith, a believer in high wages, Mandeville's worry about the scarcity of poor to do the world's work would seem rather odd. However, the increased concern about the ills of poverty probably did nothing to make Mandeville's case for luxury less attractive; if one assumed growing refinement and increased consumption among all ranks of society, luxury became more defensible. As Gibbon put it, luxury served to redistribute property into the hands of the "diligent mechanic."[52] With writings on this progress of society becoming commonplace, luxury increasingly came to be endorsed without any comments on its social and political effects and without reference to Mandeville.[53]

The Discovery of Society?

Comparing Mandeville with his natural opponents—the classical republicans or Old Whigs—one can only say that Mandeville was re-

---

49. Anon., *Dialogues between a Reformer and an Anti-Reformist* (London, 1794), pp. 51–54, 61–62.

50. Pye, *Sketches on Various Subjects; Moral, Literary, and Political*, 2nd ed. (London, 1797), essay 35.

51. On this trend, see A. W. Coats, "Changing Attitudes to Labour in the Mid-Eighteenth Century," *Economic History Review*, 2nd series 11 (1958–59):35–51.

52. Gibbon, *History of the Decline and Fall of the Roman Empire* (London, 1815), vol. 1, chap. 2, p. 87. The first edition appeared in 1776. On the decline of the Spartan ideal in this period see Elizabeth Rawson, *The Spartan Tradition in European Thought* (Oxford: Oxford University Press, 1969), pp. 347–51.

53. See, for instance, Anon., *An Essay on Luxury, Written originally in French by Mr. Pinto* (London, 1766); [Dr. John Trusler], *Luxury no Political Evil* (London, [1780]); William Russell, *The History of Modern Europe, Part I* (London, 1779); 2: 592; and James Dunbar, *Essays on the History of Mankind in Rude and Cultivated Ages*, 2nd ed. (London, 1781), p. 368.

sponsible for a much more compelling analysis of society. He can usefully be seen as unpacking their holistic statements about the "People" versus their rulers or about nations that were poor and virtuous or luxurious and corrupt. For although Mandeville was undoubtedly interested in demonstrating how society was knitted together, he also excelled most contemporary political writers in the measure in which he tried to be specific about who precisely was poor, corrupt, or self-indulgent, who won in social transactions, who lost, and why. Too often the admirers of Sparta were satisfied with woolly historical allusions set in a context of moral indignation. It was all too simple to refer earnestly to equal commonwealths, especially since adherence to Harrington allowed people to vacillate uneasily between a literal equality and the undemanding condition that the commons hold the balance of property. Citing the virtues of Sparta and republican Rome was of little relevance, unless there were some coherent scheme for duplicating those conditions. An agrarian law seemed out of the question, and unlike recurrent attempts by the Opposition to obtain stronger place-bills or to repeal the Septennial Act, there seems to have been no genuine effort in this direction. There was perhaps more serious talk of reviving the sumptuary laws, but again, nothing happened.[54] Concern about excessive inequalities was channelled most usefully into support for higher wages and efforts to hold down the price of "provisions"—a prime interest of practical men at the time of the scarcity and consequent hunger riots of 1766–67. A less relevant echo of the quest for a virtuous simplicity was the agrarianism of Dr. William Thomson and others in the 1790s.[55] The one part of Mandeville that reformers sometimes accepted—with evident embarrassment—was his strictures on overeducating the poor.[56]

No doubt Mandeville was in many respects brutally insensitive to the needs of the powerless. Nevertheless, the avowed enemies of tyranny and corruption seem rarely to have paid the poor any attention at all, especially in the period before 1750. The prerequisite for a better society was surely taking seriously the social and economic setting of the existing one—including its abuses. Appeals to the past, as

---

54. All such interference with consumption had lapsed in the seventeenth century. See Frances E. Baldwin, *Sumptuary Legislation and Personal Regulation in England* (Baltimore: Johns Hopkins Press, 1926).

55. See [Thomson], *Letters from Scandinavia* (London, 1796), 1:352–53, 361.

56. A good example, both of the influence and the accompanying distress, is David Williams, *Claims of Literature* (1801; reprinted, London, 1816), pp. 64–65n.

in the commonwealth tradition, provided no insights into the relations of polity and economy. But Mandeville's analysis, and especially his habits of mind, contributed significantly to an understanding of such factors as luxury, the scope of government regulations, the business of the politician, and the sort of corruption that others called "influence." In addition, he addressed himself to the relations among these factors and thus provided significant insight into something that could not readily be called an abuse—the nature of society itself. Scouring the period between the writings of Locke and those of Lorenz von Stein in 1850, modern scholars have presented numerous candidates for the title of the social theorist who effectively focused social inquiry upon "society." Adam Ferguson, we are sometimes told, was the first to write of "civil society"[57]—an absurd claim that arises in a search for the background of Marx's bürgerliche Gesellschaft. Rousseau,[58] Fichte, and Novalis[59] all have their proponents, as has Joseph Townsend, writing of goats and islands in 1786.[60]

The merits of these candidates vary, but a strong case can be found for seeing in Mandeville an unusually effective probing of the nature of the social bond. His writings demonstrated a specific connection between two widely noted forms of social corruption: luxurious consumption and political influence. Meanwhile his general formula about vices and benefits invited further efforts at justifying political innovations. Despite his apparent lack of concern for the poor, Mandeville's satire even served to emphasize the suffering and hypocrisy on which prosperity was founded. For those of us who believe that social science exists to tell us truths that are paradoxical and unobvious, Mandeville carries impressive credentials.

It was the tragedy of eighteenth-century thought that the bulk of sophisticated efforts at social causation were directed to the cause of sanctifying abuses, though Mandeville's efforts of this sort show a healthy irreverence too often lacking in his imitators. However, it is

57. Dick Howard, *The Development of the Marxian Dialectic* (Carbondale, Ill.: Southern Illinois University Press, 1972), p. 179, n. 22.

58. See Marshall Berman's corrective to Ernst Cassirer's judgement in Berman, *The Politics of Authenticity* (New York: Atheneum, 1970), p. 156n.

59. See P. E. Kraemer, *The Societal State* (Meppel, Netherlands: J. A. Boom, 1966), p. 4.

60. As argued by Karl Polanyi, *The Great Transformation* (Boston: Beacon Press, 1957), p. 11.

this conjunction of social analysis and partisan commitment that explains current uncertainties about Mandeville's point of view. Those who portray him as embodying the logic of modern functionalism are quite correct.[61] Mandeville's eye for patterns in human conduct and the undesigned growth of institutions was remarkable. But his ideas were also useful to the Court Whigs of the 1720s and after, and he is unlikely to have been entirely insensitive to that possibility. The final irony is that scholars continue to debate the intentions of this first student of the unintended consequence.

61. See *International Encyclopedia of the Social Sciences*, s.v. "Mandeville"; and Louis Schneider, ed., *The Scottish Moralists on Human Nature and Society* (Chicago: University of Chicago Press, 1967), p. xlix.

IV

The Spectre at the Feast:
The Persistence of High-Tory Ideas

WRITERS ON THE HISTORY OF IDEAS must always be on their guard against the error of distorting the past in such a way that it is made to resemble our own times. A dangerous thrust towards the present, and what is familiar, has led often enough to assigning a modernity to texts that can not sustain the burden. A related problem is the tendency, not unknown among historians, to write the epitaph to some era in human affairs, thus lending coherence and structure to stories that seem otherwise too complex to be told. There is a certain satisfaction in being able to clear the slate as a preliminary to grasping new ideas. But just as it is hazardous to see everywhere anticipations of modernity, still it is unwise to forget that old ideas die slowly, are capable of extraordinary resiliency, and thus often escape the coffins fashioned for them by the impatient prophets of a new era.

If historians of the eighteenth century in England have been agreed on anything, it has been the proposition that the Revolution marked the end of those theories that had supported the Stuarts' absolutist experiment. We all "know" that the eighteenth century belonged to Whiggish ideas, eventually giving birth to democratic ones. But this view, for all its virtues, neglects two factors: the opinions associated with absolutism did not quit the stage, while triumphant Whiggism continued to speak in many voices. Generations of scholars have bade farewell to disturbing notions of divine right, passive obedience, and the other trappings of absolute government, all supposedly overthrown by the Revolution.[1] The way for such a conclusion has sometimes been prepared by the discovery that mixed monarchy was an

---

1. For a bold and unqualified version of this claim see J. L. Duncan, "Juristic Theories of the British Revolution of 1688," *Juridicial Review* 44 (1932):30–38.

ideal shared in some considerable measure by the Tories of the Restoration.[2] A reassuring moderation has been accorded even to the opinions of the Jacobites of the Convention Parliament, using as exemplars the Earl of Nottingham and Francis Turner (the non-juring bishop of Ely until his refusal to swear allegiance led to his being deprived of office). Neither of these assists in making the case effective.[3] Specialists in the politics of the reigns of William and Anne have appreciated that there was more continuity in political attitudes than was consistent with the general change of heart mysteriously credited to the Revolution, but rarely has the span of time during which old ideas persisted been stretched farther than the period under immediate examination. An excellent biography of Atterbury makes the point that most Englishmen of the generation that made the Revolution probably deemed Locke's ideas as irreligious and anarchical, thus explaining the currency of competing ideas. Still, the death of Atterbury in 1732 provides the occasion for reflecting that issues such as passive obedience belonged to the past. Another able survey of political ideology places the final demise of Tory loyalties at much the same time, pronouncing last rites for traditional Toryism early in the reign of George II.[4]

Because such things have often been said, and because the picture with which we are left seems distressingly incomplete, it is worth while to suggest some qualifications. For if most Englishmen were intellectually unprepared for violent Whiggism at the Revolution, it may be

---

2. B. Behrens, "The Whig Theory of the Constitution in the Reign of Charles II," *Cambridge Historical Journal* 7 (1941):42–71.

3. George L. Cherry, "The Legal and Political Position of the Jacobites, 1688–89," *Journal of Modern History* 22 (Dec. 1950):309–21. Nottingham's moderation can only be illustrated by his acceptance of the Revolution; his opinions remained High-Tory. Turner, on the other hand, was well known to contemporaries for combining, in eccentric fashion, adherence to the original contract and traditional divine right. See Anon., *Tories and Tory Principles Ruinous to both Prince and People* (London, 1714), pp. 75, 77.

4. G. V. Bennett, *The Tory Crisis in Church and State, 1688–1730* (Oxford: Oxford University Press, 1975), pp. 104, 307; H. T. Dickinson, *Liberty and Property: Political Ideology in Eighteenth-Century Britain* (London: Weidenfeld and Nicolson, 1977), p. 164. Elsewhere, Professor Dickinson suggests that the demise can be dated from the failure of the 1715 rebellion. See "The Rights of Man from John Locke to Tom Paine," in Owen D. Edwards and George Shepperson, eds., *Scotland, Europe and the American Revolution* (Edinburgh: Edinburgh University Student Publications, 1976), p. 39.

that a significant number of them took a very long time to adapt.[5] We cannot, it is true, know conclusively what most people thought, for only the articulate stratum has left a record. But that point precludes all speculation about the intellectual furniture of the masses. It seems sensible, then, to assume that more people held to every conceivable opinion than one would gather from the writings and speeches that have survived; but it is these survivals with which one must work. Sometimes actions, rather than words, can document the case, but at a time when the Crown virtually determined the outcome of elections, the political success of one party or another gives only a slender basis for inferring the state of the public mind. Furthermore, since some elements of the seventeenth-century Tory creed were matters of symbolic significance, rather than a programme of action, no hasty conclusions can be drawn from the silence or inactivity of most citizens.

1. CONSTITUTIONAL THOUGHT
AFTER THE REVOLUTION: 1688–1714

A useful starting point for the inquiry is the founding document of the order established by the Revolution—the Bill of Rights. The preamble described the Convention as "representing all of the Estates of the People of this Realm," a phrase obviously intended to refer to "estates" in the sense of "orders of the population" and not "property." The studied ambiguity of the document has been noted even by a modern scholar who has assumed that the era of the Bill of Rights signalled the triumph of the Whiggish notion that estates were King,

---

5. Some recent and influential efforts at revising the history of the Tory party make a case for its being essentially Jacobite during its decades of proscription. See Eveline Cruickshanks, *Political Untouchables: The Tories and the '45* (New York: Holmes and Meier, 1979), *passim*; and, with emphasis more on the perception of Jacobitism than on the reality, J. C. D. Clark, "The Decline of Party, 1740–1760," *English Historical Review* 93 (July 1978):499–527. Though this form of revisionism has had to face a formidable challenge from Linda Colley, Dr. Colley has herself stressed the endurance of seventeenth-century political ideas among eighteenth-century Tories. See Colley, *In Defiance of Oligarchy: The Tory Party, 1714–60* (Cambridge: Cambridge University Press, 1982), esp. pp. 115–17.

Lords, and Commons.[6] This, we are told, stilled contrary ambitions
to make kings superior to all the estates, which had also entailed
recognizing claims of the bishops to be a clerical estate. Charles I had
once associated himself with the Whiggish position—in his *Answer to
the Nineteen Propositions* (1642), written by Sir John Colepepper—and
two generations of Tory apologetics had not undone the damage. A
close parallel to the language of the preamble occurs in the remarks
attributed in the debates of the Convention to Sir Robert Sawyer, one-
time attorney-general and prominent in the Jacobite membership of
that body. Speaking against the parliamentary status of the Convention, Sawyer said of its members, "We are Representatives of the
People in the three Estates of the Nation, and the King."[7] This was
Tory language, and Oxford University, in 1683, had condemned as
republicanism the claim that the king was a mere estate. At the time
of the Revolution, the university tacitly disavowed its decree by removing the printed copies, but it made no retraction.[8] Now it seems
that this High-Tory formula survived even in the birth certificate of
the new order. An intention to placate the least Whiggish members
of the Convention would be consistent with the course of this most
conservative of revolutions and especially with the suppression of
radical sentiments from early versions of the Declaration of Rights,
of which the bill was the statutory embodiment.[9]

The bill and its preamble were much quoted in future years, but
only those people who wished to argue for the persistence of the
seventeenth-century constitution were prepared to say what the
preamble actually meant, and they were confident that the estates did
not include the king. Often enough, impeccable Whigs had occasion
to allude to the powers of resistance or of political regeneration resident in the people, and on these occasions they not infrequently noted

6. Corinne C. Weston, *British Constitutional Theory and the House of Lords, 1556–1832*
(London: Routledge and Kegan Paul, 1965), p. 115n. A later work makes co-ordinate
power of King, Lords, and Commons the touchstone of the new orthodoxy and assigns
its permanent ascendency to the years after 1715. See C. C. Weston and Janelle Renfrew
Greenberg, *Subjects and Sovereigns: The Grand Controversy over Legal Sovereignty in Stuart
England* (Cambridge: Cambridge University Press, 1981), pp. 373–79.

7. *Debates of the House of Commons, from the Year 1667 to the Year 1694. Collected by the
Honourable Anchitell Grey Esq.* (London, 1769), 9:22.

8. [White Kennett], *A Complete History of England*, 2nd ed. (London, 1719) 3:413.

9. See Robert J. Frankle, "The Formulation of the Declaration of Rights," *Historical
Journal* 17 (1974):265–79.

how the "Estates" might assemble to reconstitute the government. Or in a more radical vein, it might indeed be argued that in the event of a king's misbehaviour power would revert not to the "Estates" but to the body of the people.[10] The simple fact is that existing political vocabulary made it rather difficult to avoid contrasting "Kings" and "Estates," thus leading to the inference that the king was no estate of the realm but was superior to all of them. Historical precedents, drawn from England's past, favoured the practice, as of course did political arrangements in other Gothic constitutions, where the monarch was not generally deemed to be an estate. The same was true of the Scottish Parliament until its disappearance at the Union, for there the estates consisted of the lay nobility, the barons, and the commons. It was, to be sure, possible to write of estates in the population without thereby denying that the king was one of the three estates of Parliament. This had been the position of Denzil, Lord Holles, in his contribution of the early 1680s to the dispute about the status of the bishops. However, the idea that there were estates of Parliament as opposed to estates of the realm found little support after the Revolution. A variant of the idea did figure in Henry Care's very influential book *English Liberties*—a standard source on the constitution throughout the eighteenth century. Care had refused to quarrel with those who designated bishops as an estate, so long as they meant by the term only a degree or condition of men. By this reckoning, however, there would be considerably more than three estates, for the knights, citizens, and burgesses in the House of Commons would each then be an estate. In a more precise sense, however, the term referred to a definite function in English government, and that capacity belonged only to King, Lords, and Commons. In words still being quoted in the nineteenth century, "'tis such a Poize in the Ballance, or such an *Order* or *State*, as hath a *Negative Voice* in the *Legislative Power*."[11]

10. Examples abound. See William Atwood, *Reflections Upon a Treasonable Opinion, Industriously Promoted, Against Signing a National Association* (London, 1696), p. 45; [Daniel Defoe?], *A Speech Without Doors* (London, 1710), pp. 12–13; [William Newton], *Revolution Principles Fairly Represented and Defended*, 2nd ed. (London, 1717), pp. 16, 20; and "English," *Considerations on the Present State of England by a Country Layman* (London, 1717), pp. 10, 12, 17.

11. [Care], *English Liberties or, the Freeborn Subject's Inheritance* (London, [1680]), p. 80. For later use of the dictum see Anon., *The Manner and Method of Proceeding against Bishops for High-Treason* (London, 1722), p. 12; Walter Honywood Yate, *Political and Historical Arguments Proving the Necessity of a Parliamentary Reform* (London, 1812), 1:159–60; Anon., *The British Constitution Analised ... by a Doctor of Laws*, 2 vols. (London, 1811), vol. 1, where the whole volume was frankly based upon Care.

Care had therefore been subject to no doubts about the proper designation of estates, but then of course his position was among those responsible for the Oxford decree and its condemnation of any views that suggested no more than co-ordinate status for the King. Whigs after the Revolution had less to lose than had embattled figures of the 1680s, such as Care. But they were, in fact, a good deal more circumspect in committing themselves on an issue of such practical and symbolic significance, perhaps because William III was not receptive to hearing that his prerogatives or his status as king had been much confined by the Revolution. One need not rely here upon evidence of fleeting and ambiguous comments about English government; rather some of the most significant and detailed constitutional treatises by Whigs reveal a distinct tendency to minimize the changes that the Revolution had wrought. Perhaps it was because the Whig champions had been accustomed to working in ancient records in their vain search for the Commons in early parliaments, but for whatever reason, their constitutional positions could not have given much offence to those High-Tories who purported to fear a republican revival. George Petyt, who is credited with a sort of constitutional handbook for the use of the Convention Parliament, was perfectly uncritical in his references to the estates, using Finch to say that estates were King, Lords, and Commons, Coke to identify the three estates of the realm in traditional terms, and Sir Robert Atkyns to refer to three estates of Parliament, which again included the king.[12] If he intended his readers to understand some distinction between estates of the realm and those of Parliament, he kept this assumption to himself. William Atwood, an early admirer of Locke's political writings, cited precedents against any suggestion that the king of England was a mere estate like the others and allowed his Englishness to overcome his Whiggishness to the extent of elevating the royal prerogative over both Ireland and Scotland.[13] Finally, James Tyrrell, a most as-

---

12. G. P., *Lex Parliamentaria* (London, 1690), pp. 4–10. In linking Petyt's book to the Convention, Gerald M. Straka refers to an edition of 1689 that I have been unable to locate. See Straka, *Anglican Reaction to the Revolution of 1688* (Madison, Wisc.: University of Wisconsin Press, 1962), p. 9.

13. W. A., *The Fundamental Constitution of the English Government* (London, 1690), pp. 3, 63, 101; *The History and Reasons of the Dependency of Ireland upon the Imperial Crown* ... (London, 1698), p. 6; and *The Superiority and Direct Dominion of the Imperial Crown of England over the Crown and Kingdom of Scotland* (London, 1704), pp. 318–19.

siduous student of the ancient constitution, showed some hesitation
on the issue but usually adhered to the position that the ancient statutes showed the king to be other than one of the three estates.[14]
Pressing this notion to its practical conclusion, Tyrrell credited the
king with the major share of the power of legislation, with Lords and
Commons having a "co-operative" but not a co-ordinate power with
the king.[15]

It is certainly not the years immediately after the Revolution to
which one may look for the emergence of a clear-cut Whig consensus
on the constitution. The quality shared by the Whig historians was a
marked disinclination to endorse those doctrines that had been a
major source of division prior to the Revolution. One might be tempted
to explain this by arguing that it was the irrelevance of such technical
questions that led to their seemingly careless or inconclusive treatment, but the extraordinary significance accorded to the issues in the
polemics of the 1680s makes the hypothesis an unlikely one, especially
with respect to writings that dealt with the constitution other than
incidentally. The identity of the three estates remained crucial because
it provided the most readily recognizable indication of political leanings. Did one endorse the constitutional position of Bishop Laurence
Womock, who deemed the houses of Parliament to share in law-
making as a beggar shared in alms? Or did Henry Care's vision of a
limited monarchy carry the day? Was the king superior to the other
branches of the legislature or was he not? The issue of the estates
served as a shibboleth here and was a more precise and definitive one
than talk of passive obedience, power from the "People," an original
contract, or divine right, all of which served less well to capture a set
of political preferences in a succinct formula. If some writers failed
to bite the bullet, it was probably because they wished not to offend.

The reign of William III, ending in 1702, was distinguished more
by Court-Country divisions than by those of Whig and Tory, and this

14. Writings by Tyrrell that suggest a Whiggish view of the estates include *The General
History of England* 3, pt. 1 (London, 1704):4. But see, by contrast, *Bibliotheca Politica*
(London, 1694), pp. 891, 917. The edition of 1718 continued to adhere to this position;
see pp. 437–38.

15. *Bibliotheca* (1694), p. 317; 1718 ed., pp. 218, 221. Tyrrell's position on "co-
operative power" was sometimes taken to be authoritative by Whig writers. See Anon.,
An Introduction to a Treatise Concerning the Legislative Power (London, 1708), p. 14.

meant that the more extreme ideological positions had been temporarily muted. A Whig pamphlet in support of the Kentish petitioners of 1701 suggested that there was an ecclesiastical estate, which would have left no room in their number for the king. At the same time, an answer from a defender of the Tory majority in the House of Commons appeared to argue the reverse of this position, thus subscribing to the doctrine condemned by Oxford University.[16] Clearly, the constitutional alternatives of pre-revolutionary England were not uppermost in the minds of *these* writers, nor in fact is it easy to find militantly Whiggish sentiments intended to restrain the power of kings. An outspokenly High-Tory pamphlet of 1702 was reduced to confuting objectionable Whiggish opinions in the writings of Thomas Hunt, who had been active in the reign of Charles II, and Samuel Johnson, an alleged republican whose relevant works dated from immediately after the Revolution.[17] John Toland, commonwealthman and deist, was the only contemporary Whig to attract much of this writer's attention. Indications of the prevailing moderation can be drawn from various points on the political spectrum. Following the attempted impeachment of the Whig Junto—one of a series of clashes between Lords and Commons towards the end of William's reign—Sir Humphrey Mackworth wrote a notable defence of the Tories in the Commons. Here he presented King, Lords, and Commons as together forming the supreme power while simultaneously checking each other.[18] This argument has rightly been seen as a strong endorsement of mixed government to which was added an unusually early instance of commitment to a functional separation of powers.[19]

16. Anon., *Jura Populi Anglicani: or the Subject's Right of Petitioning* (London, 1701), p. vii. Lord Somers has often been credited with authorship. For the reply see *Jura Populi Anglicani ... Answer'd Paragraph by Paragraph* (London, 1701), pp. 21–22.

17. Anon., *Saul and Samuel or, the Common Interest of our King and Country* (London, 1702). Sometimes attributed to Charles Davenant; but he cannot have been the author, since the text contains unfavourable references to him.

18. Mackworth, *A Vindication of the Rights of the Commons of England* (London, 1701), pp. 3, 5, 9. For comment on Mackworth's career see Mary Ransome, "The Parliamentary Career of Sir Humphrey Mackworth, 1701–1713," *University of Birmingham Historical Journal* 1 (1948):232–54.

19. See Isaac Kramnick, *Bolingbroke and his Circle*, pp. 142–43. But Mackworth did not, in fact, "begin" the identification of the branches of government with different functions. For a clear example dating from the Revolution see [Edward Stephens], *Authority Abused by the Vindication of the Last Years Transactions* (London, 1690), sig. a3v.

In that same year a position rather similar to Mackworth's was expressed by John Humfrey, an octogenarian Nonconformist clergyman. Humfrey was most concerned that the supreme power of the state be recognized as lying in Parliament. Like Mackworth, he recognized special powers and peculiar rights of King, Lords, and Commons and indeed pointed out that it would be an error to suppose that the received distinction between executive and legislative power should prevent acceptance of the supremacy of Parliament, for all other powers were exercised according to acts passed by that body. Branches of the legislature, he insisted, did not each enjoy a portion of sovereignty; rather it rested "jointly" in all three. Corresponding to Mackworth's earlier argument about "Checks" was Humfrey's observation that the various rights enjoyed by the branches of the legislature were "distinguished, divided, scrambled." Failure, then, to recognize the unity of the supreme power in Parliament would create not just checks, but "Check-mate," and for this reason Humfrey refused to speak of "co-ordinate" powers, since each was subordinate to the authority of the three combined.[20]

Within a very short time, the Tory assault on Dissenters through a series of unsuccessful Occasional Conformity bills (1702–4) had sharpened the positions of both men and signalled a growing polarization in political opinion. Humfrey had suggested in 1701 that it was a pity that the Act of Settlement contained no unequivocal statement about the identity of the supreme authority. In 1702, he returned to the point with greater urgency. Humfrey had been stung by the High-Church assault on Occasional Conformity, and this led him to express particular suspicion of the established Church and its bishops. Dissenters were naturally chary of bishops, though most of these were good Whig bishops who resisted the dangerous elements among the lower clergy. However, for Humfrey, a man of the seventeenth century who had already been an adult at the time of the Civil War, the identity of the three estates was a question "of some Heat." With the Act of Settlement already passed, he sought a "Supplemental Bill," clarifying the issue that King, Lords, and Commons were the three estates.[21] The issue continued to disconcert him, and as late as his

20. J. H., *Letters to Parliament-Men, in Reference to some Proceedings in the House of Commons* (London, 1701), pp. 18, 22–23.

21. Humfrey, *The Free State of the People of England Maintained* (London, 1702), pp. 19–22.

ninety-fourth year he was arguing that it had been the representatives of the fifty counties who had convened in the Convention Parliament to choose a king;[22] this, presumably, to avoid the common manner of referring to that gathering as one of the "Estates." If Humfrey reflected a growing concern on the part of Dissenters about their place in political life, Mackworth revealed the effects of mounting High-Church militancy. He wrote a defence of the Tories' Occasional Conformity Bill, which said not a word about divided power or shared supremacy. Addressing Queen Anne, he assured her that she was neither one of the three estates nor a fourth estate, but the "Sovereign Head" of the body politic.[23]

Mackworth's political views were subject to considerable comment, for he had expressed himself on all the major issues of the day. The change in tone between 1701 and 1704 needed some explanation, and one admirer—it may even have been Mackworth himself—tried to exonerate him from the charge of gross inconsistency. Arguing that Mackworth had been misinterpreted, his defender wrote: "but it is plain, he did not intend thereby to destroy the Sovereignty of the Crown, and make the King to have a Co-ordinate Power with the *Lords* and *Commons*, but he distinguished between the *Legislative* and *Executive Authority*."[24] Mackworth's words of 1701 suggested an intention to uphold that version of mixed government, with a clear separation of powers, that might well have developed had the original provisions of the Act of Settlement not been repealed. The language of 1704 was irreconcilable with that of 1701, for the second pamphlet looked back towards the anti-parliamentary Toryism of the 1680s. Times had changed again, and High-Tory thoughts were once more in fashion. Obviously there had been a point in Humfrey's desire to entrench his sophisticated Whiggism in some prominent statute.

Mackworth had rehabilitated his reputation with the guardians of Tory orthodoxy, and there were others who needed to accommodate themselves to the new ideological climate. Francis Atterbury, future

22. [Humfrey], *Free Thoughts Continu'd upon Several Points ...* (London, 1712), p. 60; and J. H., *Of Subjection to King George. Being a Brief Essay for Reconciling Whigs and Tories* (London, 1714), p. 10.

23. Mackworth, *Peace at Home*, 2nd ed. (London, 1703), sig. Br.

24. J. S. [Mackworth?], *Peace and Union: or, a Defence of Sir Humphrey Mackworth's Treatise on the Occasional Bill* (London, 1704), p. 18. Defending himself in 1707 over. some commercial speculations, Mackworth wrote under cover of being someone else.

Jacobite and then dean of Carlisle, fell afoul of his bishop, William Nicolson, and the bishop charged his subordinate cleric with having attacked royal supremacy over the Church. Neither participant in the quarrel was noteworthy for constitutional consistency, for Atterbury's desire to challenge ecclesiastical control had become much less intense with the enthronement of Queen Anne and her High-Church convictions. Nicolson, for his part, was moving away from an initial Tory loyalty towards a Whiggism more consistent with his episcopal status. Part of the bishop's case against Atterbury entailed reference to others who had vacillated in their views of the constitution, in which connection he cited Mackworth's change of heart. But no similar contrition could be found in another writer who had described a "civil Ballance" among the three estates as the basis of freedom.[25] This miscreant, though not named, was none other than Dr. James Drake, medical man and pamphleteer. Drake is sometimes presented as a Tory ultra, an opinion based on his joint authorship (with Henry Poley, M.P.) of *The Memorial of the Church of England* and his editing the Tory paper *Mercurius Politicus*, one issue of which led to his prosecution for attacking the Dissenters. But whatever feelings he harboured against Dissenters, Drake's notions about the structure of English government were far too moderate for High-Church circles. This moderation is reflected in other publications in which he wrote of the "co-ordination and Essence of a House of Commons as an Estate,"[26] and though he never again invited censure by treating the Crown on a par with the other branches of the legislature, even the

---

25. [William Nicolson], *A True State of the Controversy Betwixt the Present Bishop and Dean of Carlisle, Touching the Regal Supremacy* (London, 1704), p. 19. For the background to the dispute see Francis Godwin James, *North Country Bishop: A Biography of William Nicolson* (New Haven: Yale University Press, 1956), pp. 154–61; also see below, pp. 137–38. An authoritative account of the whole Convocation controversy is Norman Sykes, *Edmund Gibson, Bishop of London, 1669–1748* (London: Oxford University Press, 1926), chap. 2.

The passage quoted from Drake was from his *History of the Last Parliament, Begun at Westminster, the Tenth Day of February, 1700* (London, 1702), p. 86. See too his *Some Necessary Considerations Relating to all Future Elections of Members to Serve in Parliament* (London, 1702), p. 22.

26. *Mercurius Politicus* 13 (21–24 July 1705), p. 51. Drake's dismissal by J. A. Downie as a "lowly scribbler" is probably not unjust. See *Robert Harley and the Press* (Cambridge: Cambridge University Press, 1979), p. 87. However, hired pens such as his might still convey important currents of political opinion.

famous *Memorial* described English government as a mixed monarchy. Drake's relative coolness towards the farther reaches of Toryism seems to have earned him the reputation of being a hireling who wrote against the Whigs only because he had failed to gain preferment under them, an innuendo that loses some of its force when one realizes that it was Drake's early criticism of the Parliament that cost him his employment. A better answer is that he was essentially a Country pamphleteer who had not refurbished his vocabulary to fit with the High-Toryism re-emerging in Anne's reign.[27]

Another figure caught in the surge from Country ideology to High-Toryism was Charles Davenant. One of the best of the Country pamphleteers against the Partition treaties, he was even once in the 1690s refused office because of the suspicion that he was a Jacobite. The accession of Queen Anne found him flirting with right-wing Tories, such as Nottingham, about a possible seat in Parliament; but by 1703 he was securely tied to Harley and Godolphin,[28] at the price of twelve hundred pounds a year, his enemies alleged. In 1704 Davenant published his famous *Essays Upon Peace at Home, and War Abroad*, one chapter of which defended the practice of Occasional Conformity. Retribution came rapidly in the form of constitutional lessons from a number of members of the High-Church party. Davenant's studied "moderation" not only protected the enemies of the Church but temporized on precisely those constitutional issues that were again coming to the fore. "He tells you the Lords Spiritual and Temporal and the Commons, *are what some have stil'd the Three Estates of Parliament*; by the Word *Some*, insinuating that it was far from being a receiv'd Opinion and that he was indifferent as to the Belief of it Himself. ..."[29] Moderation was not the fashion, for the reign of Anne belonged to

---

27. See Narcissus Luttrell, *A Brief Historical Relation of State Affairs from September 1678 to April 1714* (Oxford, 1857), 5:315, 327. This may be the reason for the "ill usage" Drake apparently suffered at the hands of his own party. The cause of it has never been explained. See James O. Richards, *Party Propaganda Under Queen Anne: The General Elections of 1702–1713* (Athens, Ga.: University of Georgia Press, 1972), p. 31n.

28. BL, Add. Ms. 29,588, letter of 24 June 1702 from Davenant to Nottingham. Later we find him seeking Godolphin's approval of the *Essays* and worrying about *"Disobliging my old Friends"*. Add. Ms. 28,055, fol. 14r.

29. Anon., *Tom Double Against Dr. D-v-n-t* (London, 1704), p. 12. Davenant's most persistent critic was Mary Astell, one of the rare female writers of political polemics. She too was exercised at Davenant's failure to raise the Queen above the estates. See "Tom Single" [Astell], *Moderation Truly Stated* (London, 1704), p. xxxv.

the merchants of abuse and, too often, to silly specialists in veiled political allusions, such as John Dunton of the Whigs and the Tory Mrs. Manley.

Had the views expressed by Mackworth (in 1701), Drake, and Davenant continued to be acceptable, that constitutional consensus so often credited to the Revolution might well have been in existence by the beginning of the eighteenth century. As it was, however, the most firmly held constitutional views of Anne's reign were those voiced by the more extreme Tories. The most eloquent spokesman for these ideas was Charles Leslie (d. 1722), Jacobite and non-juror, whose writings were destined to carry the banner of High-Toryism through to the accession of George III and beyond. Leslie had been a prolific writer of pamphlets from the time of his public exposure of the Glencoe massacre in a work of 1695. Beginning in 1704, he wrote a weekly paper called the *Rehearsal*, aimed at refuting the Whiggisms of John Tutchin's *Observator*; some other Tory papers are also attributed to him.[30] Leslie owned no very unusual opinions on the English form of government, being content to belabour all the real or supposed Whig-tenets with an array of precedents and skilfully argued logical objections. Power from the people, the state of nature, the status of an English monarch, and the consequences of co-ordinate power were the grist for his mill. No statute embodying Leslie's sense of the constitution escaped his notice; thus he dredged up the act, still then in force, for the attainder of the regicides (12 Car. II c. 30) with its statement that neither people nor Parliament possessed any coercive power over the person of the king. All eighteenth-century enemies of co-ordinate power would follow in his wake. Nor did the contribution of the Bill of Rights and the prayer-book (service for 5 November) go unnoticed.[31]

Leslie has been called the first Englishman to attack John Locke's

---

30. See Anon., *Revolution Principles: Being a Full Defence of the Bishop of St. Asaph's Preface to his Four Sermons* (London, 1713), p. 25, where the *Moderator* and the *Plain Dealer* are both credited to Leslie. Neither appears to be his work, nor are they mentioned in the only biography, which cites many of his writings. See Rev. Robert J. Leslie, *Life and Writings of Charles Leslie, M.A., Nonjuring Divine* (London, 1885). To be a non-juror did not in itself imply Jacobite loyalty, for a number of principled clergymen refused to swear allegiance to William III, although they made no effort to restore the Stuarts. However, Leslie was both non-juror and Jacobite.

31. Examples of this form of argument appear in [Leslie], *The Right of Monarchy Asserted* (London, 1713), p. 3; and *Rehearsal* 1, no. 110 (5 June 1706).

understanding of the relations among the organs of English government.[32] The claim neglects the contribution of Samuel Parker, High-
Churchman and editor of the review *Works of the Learned*. Parker had
discovered adherence to co-ordinate power in scattered comments in
the *Second Treatise* on the respective powers of the people, the executive power, and the legislative. Locke then stood accused of claiming
supremacy for each of these in turn: "Legislative, hold up thy Head;
'tis thy turn in the next Line to come uppermost." Such, claimed
Parker, was Locke's "Cerberus Common-wealth."[33] Leslie seems to
have preferred to poke fun at Locke's state of nature, and for instances
of the attachment to co-ordinate power he relied upon the *Observator*
and Benjamin Hoadly, later famous as the bishop of Bangor. Hoadly
was quite conspicuous as a Whig who clearly and frankly avowed that
the king and the two houses of Parliament were "co-ordinate." Since
equally Whiggish but more thoughtful people such as Tyrrell and
Humfrey denied this proposition, Tory ultras were sometimes at a
loss to identify living exponents of the doctrines they condemned.
But Hoadly spared them any need to fly to that generalized bogey
"the men of forty one," meaning the republicans who had overthrown
Charles I. Even before a famous sermon of 26 July 1708, which put
co-ordination in the clearest terms, Hoadly had obviously espoused
the position, and Leslie had duly upbraided him for it.[34] A few anonymous pamphleteers joined Hoadly in this exposed position, but it
cannot be said to have figured unambiguously as a Whig tenet. When
Leslie wished to epitomize Whig theory, however, he naturally used
Hoadly. One of Leslie's most effective pieces was conducted in the
form of an imaginary dialogue among Hoadly, William Higden, a
lapsed non-juror who had come to argue for acceptance of the Revolution, and a Hottentot, whose role was to comment authoritatively
on the state of nature.[35]

32. John Dunn, "The Politics of Locke in England and America," in J. W. Yolton,
ed., *John Locke: Problems and Perspectives* (Cambridge: Cambridge University Press, 1969),
p. 61.

33. [Parker], *Essays on Divers Weighty and Curious Subjects, Particularly Mr. Lock's and
Sir William Temple's Notions* ... (London, 1702), pp. 50–55. Parker had put his name to
the 1701 edition, entitled *Sylva*.

34. Hoadly, *The Measures of Submission to the Civil Magistrate Consider'd*, 4th ed. (London, 1710), p. 223; *Rehearsal* 3, no. 17 (29 May 1708).

35. [Leslie], *The Finishing Stroke. Being a Vindication of the Patriarchal Scheme of Government* (London, 1711).

Time after time Leslie returned to the theme of the relations between the major organs of government, spelling out with varying
emphasis, the dangers of what he alleged to be the Whig position.
Co-ordinate power created three sovereigns, not one, and so was an
impossible scheme of government. It was inherently unstable, absolute
equality of power being impossible; thus one of the contending bodies
was sure to come uppermost. Furthermore, two of the elements in
the scheme consisted of subjects, who could not intelligibly be called
either superior to or equal to the monarch. A standard objection to
popular sovereignty, still current in the twentieth century, echoes
Leslie's complaint. The answer, well put by Hoadly, and by surprisingly few others—that "it doth not make a Servant his Master's Master,
to allow him the Liberty of defending himself"[36]—did not entirely
succeed in dispelling all doubts about co-ordinate power. Leslie excelled in demonstrating both the logical and the practical difficulties
in this formulation of mixed government and was at his best when
attempting to puncture assertions about a balance of power.

Of course, the image of a balance was then old in the language of
limited monarchy, but the early eighteenth century had seen an up-
dating of the formula—already present in Charles I's *Answer to the
Nineteen Propositions*—about the balance among the three estates hang-
ing evenly. Jonathan Swift, a good churchman, and later to become
a good Tory, wrote *The Contests and Dissensions Between the Nobles and
Commons in Athens and Rome* and assumed throughout that a balance
obtained among the various parts of the state. Indeed, so prominent
was the idea of balance in this work that a Victorian edition bore the
title *The Balance of Power in the State*. Leslie used Swift's book as the
occasion of presenting all the problems associated with an imprecise
notion of political balance. How, he asked, could the Commons (or
by implication any power participating in the balance) know what
their proper share was, and if ignorant of that, what would guide
their action?

Is it not Possible, in so Nice a Case as this, That the several Parties who held
this Ballance, may Differ in Opinion ... as to one another's Share? And is

36. Hoadly, *The Original and Institution of Civil Government Discuss'd* (London, 1710),
p. 32.

there no Umpire? ... When CHILDREN Agree in SCRAMBLING for APPLES; and Jealous LOVERS about their MISTRESS; then expect to find RIVALS for POWER, Agree in each Other's SHARE of the BALLANCE![37]

Leslie repeated the same arguments in answer to a Whig who had defended both Swift's book and the case for Occasional Conformity. Here Leslie demonstrated more vividly than had most High-Tories what exactly was so objectionable in such ideas. Talk of balance meant claims for co-ordinate power, which was dependent upon showing that the king was only one of the three estates of Parliament. Such a reduction of the king's authority would be but a preliminary to enthroning the people; for the balance was inherently unstable and would end with the destruction of all but one of the three contending bodies.[38]

Leslie himself stood for principles—partriarchal power, the absolute character of English government, passive obedience, and indefeasible hereditary right—the truth of which were far from obvious. He was therefore at his best when excoriating the Whigs for the supposed defects of their political philosophy. On issues such as the balance of the constitution and co-ordinate power some Whigs were certainly a good deal more cogent than others; certain versions, in their incoherence, gave hostages to fortune. No Whig thinkers appeared in the reign of Anne to bestow the same care in promoting the idea of balance among the estates as Leslie and others took in dismantling it. Indeed, few of the criticisms levelled at the idea of balance during the remainder of the century escaped its critics of the first decade. Already it had been appreciated that a mechanical balance needed some power to hold it, and that power awaited identification. Some Tories could think, then, in terms of a balance held by the king, who thus retained his supremacy over other parts of the legislature.[39] Already the alternatives of constant disorder or total immobilism were prophesied

37. [Leslie], *The New Association ... Part II* (London, 1703), p. 11.

38. [Leslie], *Cassandra (but I hope not) Telling what will come of it* (London, 1704) 1:10–24.

39. See Dr. Thomas Gooch, chaplain to the Lord Bishop of London, *A Sermon preach'd before the Honourable House of Commons* (London, 1712), pp. 6–8.

for any system founded on these mechanical principles.[40] Not until the 1770s would the darling notion of balance again be subjected to comparable analysis, by which time sixty additional years of experience would have documented that the theory was belied by the facts of eighteenth-century politics. By no means did the Tory creed consist only of ideas that had outlived their time. Even the most ancient of their absolutist claims—that of the divine right of kings—was to prove extremely resilient. As for Tory scepticism about the value of a constitutional balance, its time was yet to come.

Leslie began his *Rehearsal* because he had felt that apart from newsletters there were no organs of Tory opinion. When the last issue appeared in the spring of 1708, Tory opinions were in the ascendant and continued to flourish in more coherent form and were expressed with a greater confidence than were Whig alternatives. The Whigs seem to have had more newspapers at their disposal, though the quality of their political argument was not high. In 1702 Tories had sought legislation to confirm the government by King, Lords, and Commons against the threat of republicanism. After the Whigs' Pyrrhic victory in the trial of Henry Sacheverell and the ensuing Tory success in the elections of 1710, expectations ran much higher. One unnamed member of the lower house of Convocation wrote in February 1710–11 of his distress that neither the Tory parliamentary majority nor Convocation had made any move to "consecrate" the doctrines of passive obedience and hereditary right, and an opportunity had thus been lost.[41] Nevertheless, Whig political ideas appear to have been in retreat, not for lack of outlets for these opinions—even after the stamp tax of 1712—but owing to uncertainty over what opinions should be expressed and timidity about offending the queen. Even the speech by Nicholas Lechmere at Sacheverell's trial—described as setting forth an extreme Whig view of the constitution[42] —involved nothing more

40. A point stressed in another Tory critique of Swift's enthusiasm for balance, this one attributed to James Drake. *The Source of our Present Fears Discovered: or, Plain Proof of some late Designs Against our Present Constitution and Government*, 2nd ed. (London, 1706), pp. 54–55. The sentiments are not those expressed elsewhere by Drake; perhaps he changed his tune.

41. Letter quoted in [White Kennett], *The Wisdom of Looking Backward, to Judge the better of one Side and T'Other ... for the Four Years Last Past* (London, 1715), pp. 113–15.

42. Geoffrey Holmes, *The Trial of Doctor Sacheverell* (London: Eyre and Methuen, 1973), p. 131.

than the argument that sovereignty rested with the legislative power composed of King, Lords, and Commons. The Whig managers no doubt gave way to their feelings in disparaging Sacheverell's abilities, but their constitutional position was moderate.

Indicative of the different measures of confidence belonging to the two parties was the issue of Convocation and its status. Atterbury and others had begun in 1697 to promote the rights of Convocation as a body of the Church corresponding to Parliament in the state. For the next twenty years there was a struggle between the lower house of Convocation, with its strong Tory bias, and the Whig bishops. The issue cut across the grain of normal constitutional debate, for it saw High-Tory spokesmen arguing for the powers of a representative assembly while opposed by bishops who were quite content if they heard as little as possible from the zealots among their junior brethren. Atterbury's case was dependent upon discrediting the notion that the bishops were in Parliament to represent the clergy. Rather, he said, their presence only reflected the fact of their baronies, and in the absence of Convocation, the clergy as an estate of the realm wanted representation.[43]

Atterbury had been answered by a formidable array of talent including future bishops Kennett and Gibson and future archbishop Wake. Whereas Atterbury, the High-Churchman, had used an old Whiggish argument for reducing the constitutional status of the bishops, the Whigs replied by emphasizing the supremacy of the monarch over the Church and also the place of the bishops as one of the estates of Parliament, though they seemed uncertain whether the bishops represented the clergy.[44] Both of the main assertions were contrary to the spirit of the party's constitutional ideas as they appeared in relation to other issues. Tories too had contradicted positions taken elsewhere, but despite charges to the contrary,[45] no writer on behalf of the in-

---

43. [Atterbury], *A Letter to a Convocation-Man Concerning the Rights, Powers and Privileges of that Body* (London, 1697), p. 15.

44. See William Wake, *The Authority of Christian Princes over their Ecclesiastical Synods Asserted* (London, 1697), pp. 222–23; [Edmund Gibson], *The Pretended Independence of the Lower-House upon the Upper a Groundless Notion* (London, 1703), *passim*; and White Kennett, *Ecclesiastical Synods and Parliamentary Convocations in the Church of England* (London, 1701), pp. 9, 218. Kennett's book epitomizes the awkwardness of the situation.

45. See [Gibson], *The Marks of a Defenceless Cause in the Proceedings and Writings of the Lower House of Convocation* (London, 1703), p. 11, an attack on George Hooper's tract, *The Narrative of the Lower House of Convocation . . .* (London, 1702).

ferior clergy seems to have made the king (or queen) one of the three estates. As we have seen in the case of Atterbury's quarrel with Bishop Nicolson, High-Church anxiety about the powers of the monarch were tempered under Queen Anne, and so the issue became less conspicuous. The trying business of attempting to have one's own way in ecclesiastical affairs, without confusing understanding about the civil constitution, continued in the writings of Matthew Tindal. As a loyal Whig, Tindal argued for the superiority of the king in Parliament over the Church. But his Erastian opinions had entailed saying also that the supreme power had to be indivisible, a lapse he vainly tried to explain away and for which he was cruelly mocked by William Oldisworth.[46] The High-Church party was fated to lose its effort to revitalize Convocation as an organ for making policy, but in losing, their writers presented a more consistent doctrinal front than did the Whigs. There were, admittedly, telling Whig jibes about the sort of co-ordinate power being sought by High-Tories; however, these Tories showed no equivalent to the confusion displayed by White Kennett or Matthew Tindal.

The uncertainty that had prevailed before the Whig debacle of 1710 was compounded after the electoral defeat. The party was demoralized and bereft of some of its abler writers. Tutchin, whose *Observator* had featured an unsophisticated but effective brand of Whiggism, was dead, victim of a Tory mob in 1707; Hoadly stopped writing political pamphlets for several years after 1710; Defoe now wrote for the Tory ministry. George Ridpath's *Flying-Post* was loyal to that form of extreme Whiggism once represented by Henry Care, and Care's work was frequently quoted in its pages. But Ridpath was also oddly cautious in his constitutional pronouncements, and in an otherwise quite outspoken pamphlet written from the safety of exile, he equivocated on the identity of the three estates, using the silly excuse that he lacked time to resolve the issue.[47] Another Whig publication, written at the time of the election of 1713, breathed a similar tentativeness. "The Constitution is mix'd, and consists of Three Estates, (some say Four) Queen, Lords, and Commons, tho' the Queen is Independent of the

46. [Tindal], *Rights of the Christian Church Asserted* (London, 1707), p. 56; [Tindal], *A Second Defence of the Rights of the Christian Church* (London, 1708), p. 70; and Oldisworth, *A Dialogue between Timothy and Philatheus*, 2nd ed., (London, 1711), 3:87–88.
47. [Ridpath], *Parliamentary Right Maintain'd, or, the Hanoverian Succession Justify'd* (n.p., 1714), p. 35.

rest. ..."[48] Having offended Anne by trying Sacheverell, the Whigs were very nervous about seeming to rein in the prerogative. The unity demonstrated by the party on the question of the succession was not accompanied by much confidence or clarity in its other political opinions.[49] Richard Steele continued to maintain a truculent Whiggism, but he was no political theorist and did not try to answer the sophisticated arguments of Leslie, Oldisworth, and their imitators. John Shute, later Viscount Barrington, did support Whiggism in relevant terms, paying attention both to logic and to legal precedents; and (judging from internal evidence) his popular pamphlet, with its strong affirmation of co-ordinate power and subordination of the executive to the legislature, was certainly written before Anne's death.[50] But Barrington was exceptional.

Tory doctrine, by contrast, was relatively firm, though admitting differences of emphasis. The Country Toryism once displayed by Mackworth, Davenant, and Drake had lost its prominence with the sharpening of issues. True, extreme views sometimes assumed an uncourageous, shuffling quality, apparent in some of the statements made by Sacheverell and illustrated by his vagueness as to whether the supreme power to which obedience was owed was the king or the legislature.[51] Such a fault of character was duly noted by Hoadly, along

48. Anon., *Instructions to Freeholders: Drawn from her Majesty's Most Gracious Speech from the Throne* (London, 1713), p. 17. Other Whigs obviously remained of the opinion that the monarch was not an estate. See [John Willes], *The Present Constitution, and the Protestant Succession Vindicated* (London, 1714), pp. 41, 71. The pamphlet has been attributed both to John Willes, the future judge, and to Dr. John Willes of All Souls. Both, as it happens, were Whigs.

49. On the unity of the Whigs see Geoffrey Holmes, *British Politics in the Age of Anne*, pp. 245–46. Their ideological disarray is noted in J. P. Kenyon, *Revolution Principles: The Politics of Party, 1689–1720* (Cambridge: Cambridge University Press, 1977), pp. 155–57.

50. [Barrington], *The Revolution and Anti-Revolution Principles Stated and Compared* (London, 1714), pp. 30, 48–51, 57.

51. For an example prior to his trial see [Henry Sacheverell and John Perks], *The Rights of the Church of England Asserted and Prov'd* (n.p., 1705), pp. 47–49. The relevant section seems to have been by Sacheverell. See Thomas Herne, *Remarks and Collections* (1705–7), ed. C. E. Doble (Oxford, 1885), 1:11. After the Revolution, Tories and Anglicans managed to maintain innocuous versions of non-resistance and passive obedience by accepting Parliament as that supreme power to which the subject owed obedience. See Straka, *Anglican Reaction*, pp. 83–88; and H. T. Dickinson, *Liberty and Property*, pp. 47–50. Dickinson's whole first chapter is an excellent guide to the nuances of language after 1688.

with the High-Tory tendency to employ terms such as "hereditary right" in disingenuous ways. The genre of political dictionaries, ostensibly summarizing Whig principles, also betrayed the fact that some versions of the Tory case depended upon the vulgar labelling of their opponents as republicans. Joseph Trapp was responsible for some such efforts. Nor did the debate about the power of Convocation—a dreary wasteland of strained argument over legal precedents—help to preserve the consistency of Tory political doctrine. Nevertheless, in the writings of the cleverer men of the Tory side—Leslie and Oldisworth, for instance—there was a coherence that gained its strength both from the weight of precedent and from the skill with which these writers exploited Whig uncertainties. Holding that the government had not changed at the Revolution, the High-Tories enjoyed the advantages of one who argues from a traditional position. Little wonder that they sometimes fared rather well against Whigs who had to explain a system of government for which there was no traditional or well-prepared rationale. For the Tory ultras, the government remained an absolute monarchy, though at the same time it might be described as "limited," by virtue of the sovereign's condescending to employ parliaments. The government they claimed to recognize in existing institutions was not then arbitrary, but neither was it "mixed" in the manner favoured by Whigs. Co-ordinate power was an impossibility, and the sovereign was supreme. The state of nature was a dangerous fiction and the original contract an invitation to unrealizable visions of power emanating from the people and recoverable by them. Leslie and Oldisworth were particularly valuable for the Tory cause because they were so uninhibited in their assaults on Whiggish ideas, and thus they served as the shock troops of an alternative political order. Not their least merit must have been that, as unregenerate Jacobites, they might be repudiated if necessary.

It would be a mistake, however, to assume that these sophisticated extremists were isolated in their accounts of English government, for the same teaching appeared in the writings of Abel Roper, the most senior of Tory journalists; of Thomas Dawson, vicar of New Windsor; and of Conyers Place, until 1736 the master of Dorchester grammar school[52]—to name only a few. Judging from the volume of polemical

---

52. For Roper's views, see *Supplement* 673 (28–30 Jan. 1711–12); Dawson, *A Treatise of Loyalty and Obedience; Wherein The Regal Supremacy is Asserted* (London, 1710), pp. 13–27; Place, *The Arbitration: or, The Tory and Whig Reconcil'd* (London, [1710?]), pp. 40–42.

literature and from the readiness with which men associated their names with these opinions, the assault on Whiggish notions of government was a popular cause. It was also a set of ideas that managed to survive, virtually unchanged, for a remarkably long time.

The Jacobite attachment eventually withered for lack of a suitable object, but traditional doctrines in defence of the Church (High-Church) and the state (High-Tory) remained attractive to many, especially when they could be compared advantageously to some free-thinking or democratic alternative. As an unspoken loyalty, Jacobitism was often devoid of doctrine and served at times as a desperate response to disappointed expectations. Jacobites might flirt with fomenting the latent unrest of the poor and dispossessed or speak even the language of Country-party republicanism.[53] For that reason, the people called here "High-Tories" are of greater intellectual interest if only because they usually had doctrines, not just a secret love.

2. SURVIVAL

What happened to the doctrines of Toryism after Anne's death in 1714? Undoubtedly these ideas retreated before the victorious Whigs and indeed became far less visible than the Tory party itself. For though Tories remained in Parliament, and apparently predominated in the country for some time to come—else why the Septennial Act?— the political ideas associated with the party in the reign of Anne are generally held to have suffered a proscription more complete than any applied to persons. Individuals might continue to believe what they wished in private, but discretion silenced most of the sort of language associated with Sacheverell and Leslie. The penalties were especially heavy for avowedly Jacobite publications, and in one instance early in the reign of George I the common hangman received not only a seditious publication—the famous *Vox Populi, Vox Dei* of 1719—but also the printer who was implicated.

It would still be wrong, however, to assume that any overt utterance of sentiments hostile to the new king and his party disappeared without trace. For one thing, there was no formal code of orthodoxy to

---

53. See Linda Colley, "English Radicalism Before Wilkes," *Transactions of the Royal Historical Society*, 5th series, 31(1981): 1–19; and Colley, *In Defiance of Oligarchy*, pp. 101–2.

which those who ventured political expression had to conform; this meant that the government was less than consistent in prosecuting offenders. It is equally true that opinions hostile to the royal family or to the Revolution Settlement were deemed much more offensive than were political statements of a more abstract character. When one adds to this the very ambiguous nature of some of the most controversial partisan positions, and the consequent confusion into which even sound Whigs were liable to fall, the scope for continued use of traditional idiom, whether High-Tory or Jacobite, was considerable.

A case in point is the response to the new regime of Luke Milbourne, famous for his ranting sermons in memory of Charles I. Milbourne's annual effusions after 1714 remained true to their High-Church tone, with the most obvious adaptation to circumstances being a new emphasis upon the duties owed to lawful princes. This was accompanied by a reduced concern for preaching non-resistance—the theme of his sermons during the reign of Anne. The most sensitive topic was the title of the Hanoverians, and there were no unambiguously disloyal statements about this matter. But hostility to Whig ideas of popular sovereignty continued unabated, chiefly in the form of digs at their state of nature. Milbourne's parishioners at St. Ethelburga also continued to hear that the king was not an estate, though the point came to be made so as to avoid any offensive attack upon co-ordinate power, and in this respect the sermons of the Georgian era were pale things compared to their predecessors. In one later publication, Milbourne even made a concession to the possibility that "Assemblies of Estates" might be vested with sovereign power, though the effect must have been much lessened by the defence of patriarchalism that marked the same work. In 1725, Milbourne published the texts of many of his sermons, including all of those from prior to 1714 that had been published at the time of their delivery; so he obviously cannot have felt very cramped in expressing his opinions.[54]

Milbourne was not alone in presenting unrepentant High-Flying ideas. The *Examiner* under William Oldisworth became more outspoken with the accession of George I, since it was now relieved

---

54. Milbourne, *A Vindication of the Church of England from the Objections of Papists and Dissenters* (London, 1726), 1:380–81, 398. Milbourne was such an outspoken cleric that his response to the new era is of some interest. Professor Kenyon's judgement that the transition was an easy one may be true enough, but one must use a test other than the titles of sermons. See Kenyon, *The Politics of Party*, p. 224.

of that moderate Toryism previously imposed on the paper by Harley. Sneers at the original contract, interspersed with similar dispraise of co-ordinate powers, served as the stock-in-trade for most of its remaining life. A straw in the wind, however, was the reference to a cavalier pamphlet of 1644 that had followed Charles I in identifying the three estates as the king, a house of peers, and one of commons.[55] Though the denial of such a constitutional arrangement was to prove the hardiest of Tory principles, it also afforded almost as graceful an exit as was available in framing an acceptable form of non-resistance. At least Charles's own document of 1642 had allowed for a withdrawal on the issue of the estates. By contrast, equivocation about whether non-resistance was owed to kings alone or to the government as a whole was no older than 1688.

The years immediately following the Whigs' triumph saw some rather short-lived publications that promoted opinions decidedly out of step with Whiggish orthodoxy. Of these, the *Freeholder Extraordinary* was close to being simply Hanoverian Tory in its sympathies, especially since it excelled in its contempt for Whiggish rhetoric. However, solemn pronouncements about the constitutional supremacy of the king[56] and a tendency to revert to the events of 1641 both suggested that Toryism had yet wholly to sever its Jacobite associations. Still less ambiguous in its message was the revival of *Heraclitus Ridens*, a title that had first appeared on Thomas Flatman's Tory paper of 1681–82. William Pittis had also employed the name for a Jacobite paper of 1702–3, to which Charles Leslie probably contributed. The version of 1717–18, published by one William Boreham, showed its colours by affirming that legislative power resided exclusively in the king, parliaments, being but his "Productions and Creatures."[57] The superiority of the monarch to the estates of the realm followed naturally from the basic principle. Arguments of a similar nature sustained

---

55. *Examiner* 3, no. 46 (15–18 Feb. 1715–16). Oldisworth fired a final salvo, replete with some characteristic arguments about the logical difficulties inherent in Whig government, in his *Miscellanies in Prose and Verse* . . . (London, 1720), vol. 1. There appears to have been no second volume.

56. *Freeholder Extraordinary* 2 (29 Jan. 1717–18); not to be confused with Archibald Hutcheson's *Freeholder's Journal*, which used the sort of Country rhetoric about corruption later employed by Bolingbroke.

57. *Heraclitus Ridens* 7 (13 Mar. 1717–18). The title had also been before the public in 1713, but only in the form of the eighty-two members of Flatman's original effort.

George Flint's weekly papers of 1716: *Robin's Last Shift* and the *Shift Shifted*. These were not the engines to dislodge the tightening grip of the Whig oligarchy, but when one considers that the Whigs lacked journals of opinion of a comparable sort until the early years of the next decade, the prominence of these opposition sheets may better be appreciated.

Although this sort of political dissent waned with the passage of the years, undeniably it was slow in disappearing. The rallying-point of the early 1720s was known as the *Loyal Observator Revived*, published, it seems, by a Doctor Gaylard. Less historical and nostalgic than some of its predecessors, it assailed the pretensions of the Whig ministry while defending the prerogatives of the office of kingship.[58] An impartial distaste for both Whigs and Tories showed the way towards that Country distrust of men in office that allowed some Jacobites to sound increasingly like commonwealthmen of the "Old-Whig" sort.

A similar point of view informed the numerous writings of Matthias Earbery, one of the very few of the Jacobite remnant who possessed some talent for political argument. Earbery made no secret of his preference for republicans over Whigs if only because they too were against a foreign king.[59] He had set out his principles in bold and unambiguous fashion in 1716 in a pamphlet where, in the manner of Charles Leslie, he attempted to demonstrate the impossibility of placing supreme power in any hands but those of a single ruler.[60] In 1732 he was still at it, writing under the name "John Perspective." His paper, the *Universal Spy: or, The Royal-Oak Journal Reviv'd*, appears to have had no more than three issues, and the irrepressible Earbery later recorded Newcastle's order of September 1732 for his arrest.

---

58. *Loyal Observator Revived; or Gaylard's Journal* 13 (2 March 1722–23), and 14 (9 March 1722–23). Gaylard was later jailed for his connection with the *Weekly Journal or, Saturday's Post*, published by Nicholas Mist. See Abel Boyer's *Political State of Great Britain* 26 (July 1723), p. 119.

Work needs to be done on the question of what publications were deemed seditious and why. Most sources on the press cite the same few cases. But see the information on government repression in 1717–18, based on the *Historical Register* and PRO materials, in Paul S. Fritz, *The English Ministers and Jacobitism between the Rebellions of 1715 and 1745* (Toronto: University of Toronto Press, 1975), p. 62.

59. Earbery, *An Historical Account of the Advantages that have Accrued to England by the Succession in the Illustrious House of Hanover, Part I* (London, 1722), pp. 12–13.

60. M. E., *Elements of Policy Civil and Ecclesiastical, in a Mathematical Method* (London, 1716), pp. 4, 22, 26, 33.

The government, in turn, seized and burned that further publication in which he recorded his earlier brushes with authority.[61] Though Earbery's extra-parliamentary pinpricks were not granted the same immunity as those of William Shippen inside Parliament, it still speaks volumes for the relative liberality of Walpole's administration that such a doughty opponent enjoyed a long career.

Nor was Earbery alone in his resolution to keep alive the political faith of High-Toryism. Oxford University, the scene of rioting early in the new reign, provided a home for Matthew Hole of Exeter College and John Lindsay of St. Mary Hall, two clerics who continued to assail the Whig articles of faith. Hole, with his Dissenter-baiting and his furious defence of the rituals of 30 January[62]—known to others as the "madding day of the Black-coats"—was actually the more circumspect of the two. Lindsay declared his commitment to divine right, non-resistance, and passive obedience while simultaneously denying the validity of talk about a state of nature, an original contract, or any other notion that challenged the "Absolute" character of kings and their clear superiority to the estates of the realm.[63] As always in such assertions, the sound was at odds with the sense, for the message about the irresistible power of kings was a most eloquent avowal of loyalties incompatible with the Hanoverian succession. Normally, however, the government appears to have ignored these theoretical sallies unless they were allied with a clear challenge to those clauses of the Act of Settlement that defended the succession. Denial of the constitutional role of Parliament was equally incompatible with the Bill of Rights, for instance, but this question did not carry the same practical consequences as did the foundations of Hanoverian rule. It was also notoriously difficult to determine what was being said about the constitution in general, for the language of absolute power might allow for equivocation about whether the legislative or executive power was intended. Moreover, it was a simple matter to engage Whigs and

---

61. *English Reports* 94:544; and Earbery, *The Whole System of English Liberty* (London, 1738), p. 28. The Bodleian copy contains Rawlinson's note recording the fate of most of the other copies.

62. Matthew Hole, *The Second Part of the Antidote Against the Poison of some late Pamphlets* (Oxford, 1717), pp. 14, 61.

63. J. L., *The Short History of the Regal Succession . . .* (London, 1720), sig. c3, pp. 41, 57.

Dissenters about contracts and states of nature without thereby touching the more delicate matter of title to the throne.

For those who chose to avoid a frontal assault on Revolution principles, there was the subtler art of writing history. Bevil Higgons employed this medium and fought Bishop Burnet, issue by issue, through the events of the previous century. Higgons wrote from an unsophisticated cavalier perspective in which kings towered above all others as the central actors. He thus avoided theoretical propositions of any sort.[64] A similar spirit moved Zachary Gray, whose *bête noire* was John Oldmixon's Whig history. Gray had much to say about Charles I "the royal Martyr" but again addressed himself to none of the more difficult issues of principle. It was left to a moderate Churchman such as Laurence Echard, one-time archdeacon of Stow, to spell out the place in history of doctrines such as passive obedience. Echard was sufficiently acceptable in his political opinions to benefit from the patronage of George I. Obviously, then, he accepted the Revolution Settlement. He did, however, appear to come down on the Tory side of doctrines about resistance and obedience, which Echard defended in the name of reason of state. At the same time, he allowed how difficult it was to support any general formula without qualification, for the doctrine of passive obedience was necessarily subject to fluctuation, sometimes contracted and at other times extended mightily.[65] Or, as Tories of the previous reign had been fond of saying—whether as an excuse for accepting the Revolution or as a threat of future conduct was not always clear—that nature might sometimes rebel against principle. Echard had to counter critics who thought his views more appropriate to the controversies of 1710, but he does not seem to have departed significantly from orthodox Anglican teaching.

Gradually, of course, Jacobite language mellowed into something less fearsome, as the late writings of Charles Hornby illustrate. Once a Tory and clearly later a Jacobite, Hornby still chose to adopt a Whig version of the constitution, though only for purposes of belittling the occupants of the various organs of government: "a Prince led by *Germans,* and by Ministers intirely *Germanized,* a *profligate House of Lords,* and a *House* of Commons, not *duely* elected, have been the *Three*

64. Higgons, *Historical and Critical Remarks on Bishop Burnet's History of his own Time* (London, 1727); and *A Short View of English History* (London, 1723).

65. Echard, *The History of the Revolution and the Establishment of England in the Year 1688* (London, 1725), pp. 21–24.

Estates of the Realm. . . ." If this was loyalty, it assumed uncommonly strong tones, but the charges did suggest that the Whiggish habit of perceiving a limited monarch as an estate was at least acceptable for describing the low company then at Court. Hornby's peroration made another concession to a new era in politics: "It is folly now to talk of *Whig* or *Tory*. The Struggle is between the *Court* and *Country*."[66]

But to portray this as a grudging approach to orthodoxy is to assume that there was indeed a Whig canon that could be followed. In fact, this did not emerge without difficulty, for confusions from the past were not as readily banished as were political opponents. Without doubt, the accession of George I removed inhibitions about mouthing or printing Whig doctrines, and some Whig journalists, veterans of Tory abuse, made much of the fact that many people had experienced a rapid conversion in August of 1714.[67] Now free to express their views, Whigs were still at times confined by strategic considerations, wishing to ingratiate the new order with as many fellow citizens as possible. This surely accounts, for instance, for some odd statements by John Withers, Dissenter and Whig, whose pamphlet of 1710, *The History of Resistance as Practic'd by the Church of England*, ran to some seven editions. An even more successful pamphlet was an effort to exonerate the Whigs from any taint of republicanism. So avidly did he pursue this goal that Withers actually argued that it was in fact the High-Church fanatics such as Sacheverell who were truly anti-monarchical, since they argued that the king was not the supreme power in the state. In attributing a doctrine of co-ordinate power to such an unlikely candidate, Withers was thinking of course of the very special circumstances surrounding the struggle to control the Church. By contrast, the Erastian position of many Whigs emerged here sounding as though it were a general doctrine of royal supremacy: "That the King is not the Supreme Power, or, that there is any Power Superior to, or Co-ordinate with the Regal, is a Principle that has long been exclaimed against as Republican, and imputed to such as utterly disown it."[68] Admittedly, Withers was thinking of supreme executive power and only later mentioned "supreme Legislative Power," resting

66. [Hornby], *The Second and Last English Advice to the Freeholders of England* (London, 1723), pp. 7, 89.

67. *Flying-Post* 3535 (28–31 Aug. 1714); and 3560 (26–28 Oct. 1714).

68. Withers, *The Whigs Vindicated . . . In a Letter to a Friend*, 6th ed. (London, 1715), p. 24.

with King, Lords, and Commons. However, the whole tone of the piece was calculated to understate his special pleading against High-Flyers in the Church while endearing his party to all friends of monarchy. As always, parties wanted to defend positions not easily made compatible with each other. William Oldisworth, for whom the claim of co-ordinate power had been both logically incoherent and the major tenet of Whiggism, was not slow to point out how Withers had destroyed the Whigs' case,[69] and indeed it had been a major prop for at least some Whigs.

Whig arguments were of course much more resilient than that, for they were often shaded and trimmed to command maximum support. The absolute necessity of reconciling as many interests as possible to the Hanoverians and their Whig ministers dictated caution in pronouncements about arguable matters. Thus Francis Squire, Church of England clergyman of Exon and one of the abler Whig pamphleteers, argued that the authority of the government had equally to be maintained by appealing to three schools of thought: those who deemed it to be of purely human origin; proponents of traditional divine right; and also those who believed in the moderate doctrine that government in general was by divine right, though particular forms were dependent upon human choice. Squire actually managed to have it both ways, since he remained dogmatic on the point that the power of government, derived from the people, was sufficient to ensure obedience.[70] His latitudinarian approach thus applied only to the more speculative grounds of authority.

There was not, to be sure, a perfectly free market in ideas, and some—for instance, the argument justifying the Revolution by conquest—soon became unacceptable to all but certain Tories. Nor could any Whig easily afford to tolerate views inconsistent with the supreme legislative power consisting of King, Lords, and Commons. On other matters, there was room to adjust an emphasis to suit the audience, and Whig churchmen sometimes disagreed about the most appro-

---

69. *The Examiner* 2, no. 45 (2–6 Apr. 1715).

70. Squire, *A Treatise Concerning the Supremacy of the Civil Magistrate* (Exon, 1717), pp. 5–7. Squire's views on "passive obedience" had hardened since the previous reign; an earlier pamphlet gave the idea a more positive connotation and contained the admission that sometimes he had supported the Tories. *A Brief Justification of the Principles of a Reputed Whig* (London, 1713), pp. 18, 24.

priate arguments for winning over the non-jurors. Thus when Nathaniel Marshall, a chaplain in ordinary to George I, argued for obedience to the Hanoverians by contrasting, in High-Tory style, the King and the "Estates," he earned rebukes from several sources.[71] The problem of presenting the political system in the most attractive light stemmed from the fact, proclaimed by the Hanoverian Tories and apparently accepted by Whigs of the day, that the nation was predominantly Tory in its prejudices. Nor was a certain nervousness confined to closed counsels of the Whig party; during the debate on the repeal of the Triennial Act, one finds a Whig clergyman, who also hoped to convince non-jurors by argument, naïvely confessing that a Whig Parliament was far from assured unless the king would condescend to use the necessary "Ways and Means" to procure it.[72] Though debate on the high ground of theories of obedience remained central in the years immediately after 1714, apologies for corruption— the concern characteristic of the 1730s—had already begun by 1716. So too had the charge, not without some basis, that Whigs in power would be as arbitrary as Tories.

Though the Whigs managed to consolidate their hold on both Court and Parliament, the strength of Tory sentiment in the country continued to be reflected in doctrines about government. Divine right and the majesty that surrounds a king were more familiar and more comforting sentiments than the colder idiom of a state of nature, of a contract, or of co-ordinate powers. Not only did the older language better lend itself to the medium of sermons, but it might well serve the turn of Whigs as well as High-Churchmen or Jacobites. For the Whigs had now, as the price of their good fortune, inherited the duty of supporting established authority. This proved to be no inhibition to an Old Whig such as Robert Molesworth who continued to perceive authority from a Country, not a Court, perspective. The only change

71. See Arthur Ashley Sykes, *Some Remarks on Mr. Marshall's Defence of our Constitution in Church and State* (London, 1717), p. 45. Earbery's dismissal was more to the point. He wrote that Marshall was naturally unsure of the mechanics of the Gothic constitution, since he had been a fellow Jacobite until after the battle of Preston Pans! Earbery, *Serious Admonitions to Doctor Kennet ...* (London, 1717), p. 126.

72. [Arthur Sykes], *The Suspension of the Triennial Bill, the Properest Means to Unite the Nation* (London, 1716), p. 34.

marked in his opinions was a new readiness to express them.[73] Nor
did the Whig triumph create difficulties for Sir James Montague, Whig
politician and distinguished jurist, whose charge to the grand jury of
Wiltshire, in the summer of 1720, consisted of a lecture on the supremacy of the legislative authority, conceived in strictly Whiggish
terms and with no place for the independence of the Church.[74]

But difficulties and ambiguities there were. The survival of the
tradition of 30-January sermons was one strand that tied the eighteenth century to the seventeenth—and many of these myth-making
acts of remembrance of the death of Charles I ventured upon sensitive
political matters. What should one make, for example, of a sermon
preached before the corporation of London in 1721–22 by John Berriman, chaplain to the Lord Mayor? Berriman depicted Charles I as
"a Sovereign Prince, accountable for his Behaviour before no Tribunal
upon Earth." His judges were not his equals but his "Subjects and
Vassals," and the two Houses of Parliament themselves had been
unauthorized to condemn him.[75] All of this applied to the constitution
of the past, but the implication that the reigning monarch either had
the same prerogatives or was less than a sovereign prince leaves an
uncomfortable impression of things left unsaid. Nevertheless, the
preacher was duly thanked and his sermon published. It cannot be
denied that the vast majority of the sermons were innocuous in their
political content, limited to conventional rebukes to party feeling or
equally unexceptionable cautions that subjects should learn the difference between liberty and licence and act accordingly. The scriptural
text about liberty as the cloak of maliciousness (1 Peter) was often
invoked and was especially useful in the latter part of the century.
Nor were the more sentimental attempts to provoke sympathy for the
sufferings of the royal martyr especially noteworthy, though these
tended to come from clerics whose leanings were other than Whig.
In point of fact, however, there were a considerable number of ser-

---

73. *Franco-Gallia*, trans. Robert Molesworth. The first edition to contain the famous
preface, with its statement of the principles of a "real Whig," was that of 1721. Though
the preface alludes to events of 1716, the bookseller claimed that a version was written
when the translation had first appeared in 1711 but that the political climate had
prevented its publication.

74. *Political State of Great Britain* 20 (Aug. 1720):73–94.

75. Berriman, *A Sermon preach'd before the Right Honourable the Lord-Mayor, the Aldermen
and Citizens of London* (London, 1722), p. 16.

mons employing language suggestive of that view of political authority that had supposedly been supplanted by the accession of George I, if not by the Revolution itself.

The best modern study of the tradition[76] mentions two such sermons delivered on 30 January 1728–29, those of Joseph Trapp (before the Lord Mayor of London) and of Edward Young (before the House of Commons). Equally representative of the genre were sermons belonging to the next anniversary: Samuel Croxall's sermon to the House of Commons and others by Carew Reynell, chaplain to the bishop of Bristol. All of these expressed reverence for the person of the Lord's "Annointed," and all drew the conclusion that the sacred character of kings required obedience from subjects. Trapp, one-time Tory polemecist in Anne's reign, was the most moderate of the four and was concerned chiefly about the attacks of those who wished to abolish occasions for opening old wounds. Croxall, though insisting that kings were God's "Vicegerents," was careful to allow resistance to the measures of a bad king. He also noted that the higher powers to which obedience "both active and passive" was due were King, Lords, and Commons. Reynell went further, emphasizing that God set up and removed kings; and for good measure he repudiated the Whig notion of a state of nature. Most outspoken was Young, now remembered as the author of *Night Thoughts*. Dwelling upon God's choice of Saul, he said: "since the same reason subsists in all ages and nations, (unless forfeited particularly,) why should we think this a personal indulgence to Saul, and not a general endowment of all who receive a crown ...?"[77] None of this, admittedly, was seditious, and there was

76. Helen W. Randall, "The Rise and Fall of a Martyrology: Sermons on Charles I," *Huntingdon Library Quarterly* 10, no. 2 (Feb. 1947):135–67. An excellent guide to the literature, the article says rather little about the content of the sermons. A more recent survey errs in assuming that the sermons lost their High-Church character after 1714. See Byron S. Stewart, "The Cult of the Royal Martyr," *Church History* 38 (1969):175–87. The partisan significance of the commemoration remained alive even in the reign of George III. See *A Collection of Letters on the Thirtieth of January and Twenty-Ninth of May* (London, 1784); this was of Jacobite inspiration.

77. Trapp, *A Sermon Preach'd before the Lord Mayor ... Jan. 30, 1729* (London, 1729), pp. 9, 21; Croxall, *A Sermon Preach'd before the Honourable House of Commons ... Jan. XXX 1729* (London, 1730), pp. 10, 17; Reynell, *Two Sermons on the Fifth of November and the Thirtieth of January ...* (London, 1730), pp. 31, 34; and Young, "An Apology for Princes: or, the Reverence due to Government," in *Complete Works*, ed. James Nichols (1854; reprinted, Hildesheim: Georg Olms Verlag, 1968), 2:396.

ample support in the statute-book for punishment of anyone who compassed the death or discomforture of the sovereign. But such open affirmation of divine right could not have much appealed to, say, William Whiston, who felt that Hoadly (of all people!) was dabbling in dangerous thoughts when he argued the hereditary right of the Hanoverians.[78] For Whiston, nothing but the free choice or recognition of a people could confer a right to govern. But in some sermons of 30 January one finds not only that hereditary right Whiston found distasteful but other elements of the old theory of right divine, expressed in the old language.

These occasions undoubtedly provided opportunities for the expression of loyalties to persons, or at least to doctrines, officially out of favour. But Whigs in power were also subject to the temptation to say similar things, not to keep alive proscribed ideas but simply to enjoin that measure of respect for authority naturally in the interest of the governors. Professor Straka has recorded the presence of a theory of divine providential right that allowed Anglicans who accepted the new order to continue to speak of divine right even after the Revolution.[79] However, there is a good deal of evidence to suggest that this version of divine right did not pass through its "final phase" by 1702, that indeed the seventeenth-century rendering of divine right still had life in it. Certainly the providential theory remained useful for many years thereafter and appealed to others than Anglicans; Samuel Rosewell, a Dissenter, employed it in a coronation sermon of 1714.[80] Another coronation sermon, this time preached by John Potter, bishop of Oxford, to mark the accession of George II, again linked the divine appointment of princes to evidence of the work of Providence in the Revolution of 1688. Potter was roundly criticized for reviving the plea of *jure divino*; yet it was not his references to Providence which attracted fire but his allegedly arguing for

---

78. Whiston, *Scripture Politicks* (London, 1727), p. iii.

79. Gerald Straka, "The Final Phase of Divine Right Theory in England, 1688–1702," *English Historical Review* 18 (Oct. 1962):638–58.

80. Rosewell, *The King's True Divine Right* (London, 1714), pp. 8. 21. See too Gilbert Nelson, *King George's Right Asserted* (London, 1717), pp. 18, 49; Thomas Bradbury, *The Divine Right of Kings enquir'd into and Stated* (London, 1718), pp. 9, 12 (a sermon on 5 November); and Anon., *The Ideas of the Original Rights of Kings and Governors, cooly Consider'd* (London, 1717), pp. 17, 20. This publication had appeared serially, with the title *The Occasional Courant*.

"unlimited Obedience."[81] In the reign of William III, men had said that arguments from Providence would serve only in unsettled times. As it happened though, the credentials of the Hanoverians were subjected to scrutiny for longer than had been anticipated; so there continued to be uses for providential theory. In fact, it was still being heard towards the middle of the eighteenth century in the form of what a Country clergyman called "the True Divine, indefeasible Right of Kings"; this by way of contrast to divine hereditary right, which the preacher rejected as an exploded doctrine.[82] Providence in fact continued to be cited as the basis of all political life, long after it had ceased to be necessary to account for the revolution of 1688.[83] At the time of the '45 Rebellion there was no doubt a good deal of preaching about divine right, and complaints were heard about sermons in favour of "Absolute, Indefeasible, Hereditary Right." The opposite complaint—that sermons were too secular and disrespectful to the memory of Charles I—was also heard.[84]

Sometimes, at least, fears of a resurgence of absolutist teaching were unwarranted. An example is the 30-January sermon delivered in 1731–32 by Francis Hare, bishop of Chichester. Hare was a seasoned Whig who had argued the merits of the Barrier treaty with Swift some twenty years before. His text did cite the New Testament in favour

81. Potter, *A Sermon Preach'd at the Coronation of King George II Oct. 11, 1727* (London, 1727), pp. 3–4. See too "Philalethes," *Hoadly and Potter Compared. Being Remarks upon some Passages in the Sermon Preached at their Majesties' Coronation* (London, 1728), pp. 8, 21. Potter was a High-Church Whig. On the nature of this rare breed see George Every, *The High Church Party, 1688–1718* (London: S.P.C.K., 1956) pp. 125, 156.

82. *The Extent and Limits of the Subjection due to Princes. A Sermon preached on the 30th of January, 1746–47* (London, n.d.), pp. 10, 15. Sometimes attributed to John Butler, bishop of Hereford, the sermon seems to have been the work of James Butler of Royston, Hertfordshire.

83. See, for instance, William Warburton, Lord Bishop of Gloucester, *A Sermon preached before the Right Honourable the Lords Spiritual and Temporal ... Jan. 30, 1760* (London, 1760, pp. 3, 23, and *passim.*

84. See [George Coade], *A Letter to a Clergyman, Relating to his Sermon on the 30th of January* (London, 1746), p. 76. Neither Coade's pamphlet nor the two-volume riposte it prompted from one John Boswell mentioned the name of the original preacher. A variant on the usual theme was the complaint that one 30-January sermon was too secular and Whiggish. See "Philocarolus," *A Letter from an Old Cavalier to the Reverend Thomas Wingfield on Occasion of his Sermon at St. Paul's, on the 30th of January last* (London, [1748–49]), pp. 8–9, 34. Non-resistance and a hint of Filmerite doctrine were the ingredients added.

of obedience to the higher powers but was devoid of most of the emotive phrases that graced many other productions. The doctrine of non-resistance to duly constituted authority was commonly employed in defence of the Whig establishment. In the main, Hare seems to have been advocating that men fear God and honour the king—hardly a startling proposal.[85] Yet this sermon provoked a storm and drew retorts from a number of outraged foes of absolutism, among them, it seems, the Old Whig Thomas Gordon, whose anticlericalism had lain dormant for the previous decade. Hare's most militant critics could not identify any overt sentiment in favour of old-fashioned divine right, but they did accuse him of dredging up a traditional form of passive obedience.[86]

A year later, a much clearer examplar of the passive-obedience genre passed with comparatively little negative comment, presumably because its author was an obscure Wiltshire vicar.[87] Alarms similar to those precipitated by Hare's sermon continued to be expressed from time to time during the next twenty years. Zachary Pearce, the bishop of Bangor, was accused of reviving claims for passive obedience in his 30-January sermon of 1748–49,[88] and in 1753 Thomas Fothergill, of Queen's College, Oxford, provoked the same response. Pearce's contribution was quite innocuous, but Fothergill, with his praise for the constitution as it was at the time of Charles I, no less than for his

---

85. Hare, *Works* (London, 1746) 1:325–54. One of the defences of the sermon is also credited to Hare. Injunctions to obey sometimes used traditional formulas with a High-Church flavour. For one such sermon by Edmond Gibson, bishop of London, see Colley, *In Defiance of Oligarchy*, p. 104. Or the tone could be secular, as in a sermon of 1752 by James Beauclerk, bishop of Hereford, cited in Dickinson, *Liberty and Property*, p. 131.

86. See Anon., *The Principles and Facts of the Lord Bishop of Chichester's Sermon, and the Defence of it, further Examin'd and Remark'd*, 2nd ed. (London, 1732), pp. 8, 45. For the claim that one of Hare's anonymous tormentors was Thomas Gordon see Anon., *The Examiner Examined: Part II* (London, 1732), pp. 4–5. Support for Hare's language in the form of High-Tory constitutional theory cannot have comforted the bishop. See *Fog's Journal* 187 (3 June 1732).

87. See Anon., *An Excellent Sermon in Defence of Passive-Obedience and Non-Resistance: Preach'd on Sunday the 7th of October, 1733* (London, 1733). The publication was intended to embarrass the preacher. For his unembarrassed reply see David Scurlock, *A Caution Against Speaking Evil of Governors and of one Another* (London, [1733]), sig. A2v.

88. See "Phileleutheros Eboracensis," *A Letter to the Right Reverend the Lord Bishop of Bangor Occasioned by his Lordship's Sermon ... January 30, 1749* (London, 1750), p. 14.

description of kings as God's "Vice-gerents,"[89] seems to have earned some rather hard sayings by those whose suspicions of High-Church Toryism had been raised. One wonders only at the comment by a horrified reader that it was difficult to imagine such ideas as belonging to "any man alive." Demonstrably, there were a good many of them alive. The critic also noted, perceptively, how the very expression "God's Vice-gerent" carried with it intimations of passive obedience.[90]

Amid all the numerous false alarms there survived substantial elements of those political doctrines that had sustained Stuart pretensions, and from the provinces came complaints about the ordination of Jacobite clergy and the substance of the rituals of 30 January.[91] Admittedly it was difficult to square an unalloyed claim of indefeasible hereditary right with the situation of the Hanoverians; consequently none but Jacobites were likely to insist upon that strand in the theory of divine right. One preacher who came as close as he dared to the pure doctrine was Richard Venn, a London rector. Venn obviously took claims to hereditary right very seriously and only cleared the Hanoverian title to his own satisfaction by arguing, rather half-heartedly it seems, that possibilities of a sound title, combined with actual possession, made the possessor a lawful king. Furthermore, Venn insisted upon "Passive Obedience" and non-resistance to the supreme power, which he took to mean the king. On the origin of authority, he expressed contempt for proponents of an original contract, with some reservations in favour of the different notion of compact visualized by Pufendorf. Venn appears to have made no concessions to co-ordinate powers, though he allowed that the "States," of which the king was not one, would necessarily decide a disputed title.[92] George I was thereby granted a close decision, based on arguments more suited to supporting the pretender. Arguments similar in tone and

---

89. Thomas Fothergill, *A Sermon* ... (Oxford, 1753), pp. 18, 25.

90. C. P. [Ralph Heathcote], *A Letter to the Rev'd Thomas Fothergill ... Relating to his Sermon* (London, 1753), pp. 5, 22–23, 32. Though emphasizing how Anglicans adapted divine right to support the government of William III, G. M. Straka admits that such expressions smacked of the pre-revolutionary theory of the divine right of hereditary succession. See Straka, *Anglican Reaction*, p. 82.

91. See the letter of a Lancashire tradesman in *Gentleman's Magazine* 19 (Mar. 1749):107; and Anon., *Manchester Politics* (London, 1748), p. 15.

92. Venn, "King George's Title Asserted ..." (1715; reprinted 1734), in *Tracts and Sermons on Several Occasions*, ed. Mary Venn (London, 1740), pp. 30, 47, 51. As late as 1737 Venn continued to preach effusively of Charles I and to rail against republicans.

substance were aired by John Burton in Oxford. In particular, Burton enjoined obedience to the higher powers and left no doubt that he was aware that his views were at odds with opinions supposedly orthodox since the Revolution. "What the higher Powers are, is a point not here determined. ... *Caesar's image* ... on the coin of the country is a sufficient presumptive proof of his Sovereignty."[93]

One need not be surprised that notions of divine right, however hedged about by ambiguity, should still have been abroad in the middle of the eighteenth century. Part of the coronation service instituted for William and Mary referred to the role of divine Providence in placing the king over his people, and this formula continued to be used. Moreover, royal claims of a sacerdotal nature were not merely maintained but in some measure were revived at the coronation of William III, which followed the Revolution. In addition, both the ceremony of anointing and the prayer of 1689 were actually more strongly expressive of divine grace than were the practices in the time of Charles I. True, the words "thine annointed" were deleted from the ceremony, to be replaced by "thy chosen servant," but the prayer itself continued to lend support to High-Church interpretations of the significance of anointing. Finally, the language of that portion of the ceremony known as the "recognition" has been interpreted as a concession to Jacobite sentiment.[94] The symbolism of the régime, then, gave credence to those political conceits that were widely seen at a later date as peculiar to the High-Tory or Jacobite causes.

Another way in which the society formally presented its political arrangements was in those accounts of the constitution that appeared in law books. From the Revolution, this had been an area both sensitive and subject to learned unclarity. Successive editions of some of the more important guides did little to mend the situation. For instance, the 1719 edition of Henry Care's militantly Whiggish *English Liberties* supplied a corrective to his insistence that the king was himself an

---

93. Burton, sermon of 31 January, 1742–43, in *Occasional Sermons Preached before the University of Oxford* (Oxford, 1764), 1:74.

94. Anon., *A Complete Account of the Ceremonies Observed in the Coronations of the Kings and Queens of England*, 2nd ed. (London, 1727), p. 30; Leopold Wickham Legg, *English Coronation Records* (Westminster: Constable, 1901), pp. xvii, xix, 246, 299, 317, 321, 327; Francis C. Eccles, *The Coronation Service* (London: A.R. Mowbray, 1952), pp. 33–34.

estate by citing as well the evidence against the proposition.[95] Leaning in the opposite direction was a new edition, *circa* 1740, of George Petyt's *Lex Parliamentaria*. Here the eighteenth-century editor, Robert Price, reduced some of the earlier confusion created by Petyt, for Price drew attention to the disagreements, extending even to the texts of acts of Parliament, about whether the king was an estate. Despite his own Tory leanings, Price came down on the Whiggish side of the argument.[96] But party politics again appear to have entered in, and the publisher inserted a preface that cast doubt upon the viability of contractual notions in the context of English fundamental laws. Giles Jacob, a prolific popularizer of English law and other subjects, avoided any commitment on the more controversial points. However, his later editors inclined to the High-Church practice of identifying the three estates as lords spiritual, lords temporal, and commons.[97] The Tory or Jacobite view also seems to have had the best of it in a number of similar publications throughout the eighteenth century.[98] The great Blackstone rather fudged the issue of the estates, since he wished not only to honour the Whig concern for a limited monarch but also to give due weight to the antiquarian exactitude that would endorse the bishops, and not the king, as an estate. His conclusions supported co-ordinate power, but this subtle message did not always survive the labours of commentators and abridgers.[99] Edward Wynne, whose bid for legal fame was eclipsed by Blackstone's *Commentaries*, placed greater emphasis upon the political importance of the issue, and after citing

95. Care, *English Liberties, or the Free-born Subject's Inheritance*, 4th ed. (London, 1719), pp. 116–19. This edition contained substantial additions by William Nelson. In other writings, Nelson supported the claim that the bishops were an estate, with the implication that the king was not. See Nelson, *The Rights of the Clergy of Great Britain* (London, 1709), pp. 98–101. A still later compilation, based largely on Care, qualified his views on the estates but ended by accepting his Whiggish position. Anon., *British Liberties* (London, 1766), p. 149.

96. *Lex Parliamentaria* (London, n.d.), pp. 3, 53.

97. Jacob, *A New Law-Dictionary*, 9th ed. ed. Owen Ruffhead & J. Morgan (London, 1772), s.v. "Crown."

98. See Thomas Wood, *An Institute of the Laws of England* (London, 1720), 2:774; T. Cunningham, *A New and Complete Law Dictionary* (Dublin, 1764), s.v. "Parliament"; Anon., *A Law Grammar ...* (London, 1791), p. 157.

99. Blackstone, *Commentaries* 1:56. For a statement, without qualification, that the estates were lords spiritual, lords temporal, and commons see Richard Barton, ed., "Abstract of the First Volume of Blackstone's Commentaries," in *Farrago* (Tewkesbury, 1792), 1:289.

the authorities on either side in his *Eunomus* (1768), he decided firmly in favour of limited monarchy with the king as an estate.

When the laws of the land, not just as embodied in ancient statutes but as understood by lawyers of the day, seemed to pronounce a partisan and supposedly discredited theory of the constitution, the elusive locus of Tory sentiment becomes more sharply defined. When, in addition, the symbolic order surrounding the meaning of the Hanoverian kingship can be demonstrated to harbour the same ethos, and when one contemplates the fact that the prayer-book continued to sustain the shibboleth of High-Tory belief, the pattern becomes clearer still. There was no need to seek out conclaves of enemies of the succession—as displayed in such a fleeting form as political toasts—in order to discover ideas that clashed with the apparent fabric of the state. These ideas were fixed in traditions, laws, and ceremonies that, while owing their existence to party manoeuvres, gained an amplitude that could endure the low fortunes of those with whom they had chiefly been identified. The continuing argument about whether Tories were turned into Jacobites by their proscription need not be settled in order to know that Tory ideas of the seventeenth century lived on, sometimes in unlikely places. For the defenders of the allegedly proscribed doctrines were not just non-jurors or unregenerate Jacobites; conventional supporters of the Whigs in office could be found using terms very similar to one or another tenet of High-Toryism. There was, to be sure, that curious hybrid the Jacobite Whig—Philip, Duke of Wharton, for instance. But much commoner were the Whigs whose views of politics were coloured by ideas not usually deemed Whiggish. This may not be surprising unless one expected co-ordinate power or the original contract. Sometimes it may have been simply the difficulty of shedding a faith that, for all rational purposes, had ceased to be convenient.

A relevant example is Jonathan Smedley, who wrote in favour of passive obedience in the Sacheverell period and continued to defend authority in the reign of George I. However, even as he defended the government of the day, he betrayed the fact that he still deemed the estates of the realm not to include the king.[100] Smedley was con-

---

100. Smedley, *The Doctrine of Passive Obedience and Non-Resistance Stated* (London, 1710); and *A Rational and Historical Account of the Principles which Gave Birth to the Late Rebellion* (London, 1718), p. 66.

sidered, at least in later life, to be a Whig, but one would not know it from his picture of the constitution. Another pamphleteer writing in favour of Walpole's government, and specifically in favour of those bishops who lent it such loyal support, was prepared to reward this loyalty by according the bench of bishops the status of an estate.[101] Of course the urgent issue had ceased to be that of co-ordinate power and had become influence exercised upon the House of Commons. Possibly the significance of the identity of the estates had much declined, and it appeared safe to concede on issues no longer warmly contested in order to prevail on more urgent matters. There was in fact no phalanx of High-Churchmen quoting seventeenth-century statutes, and a Whig who pressed the claims of the bishops could rest assured that they were chiefly Whig bishops.

Bolingbroke himself held no brief for the arguments of Leslie or Oldisworth; and the *Craftsman* was especially insistent on arguments for co-ordinate power, with not a word about the superior status of kings. Bolingbroke challenged the administration's view of government, particularly its readiness to condone the use of influence, but he did so in an idiom far removed from the ideas of Sacheverell: "We shall hear, for aught I know even in this age, that kings are God's vicegerents, that they are ... supreme moderators and governors. We shall hear again, perhaps, of their hereditary, their divine, their indefeasible right, and the rest of that silly cant. ..."[102] This is evidence, not of the death of extreme language of a Tory cast, but of a change of roles that blurred the familiar divisions and, by depriving old formulas of their immediate significance, contributed paradoxically to keeping them in currency. This meant, for one thing, that it would be unwise to infer political loyalties from isolated comments made by people who were unmindful of connotations acquired by phrases some thirty years before. But the same situation created distress for certain loyal Whigs.

---

101. Anon., *The Thoughts of an Impartial Man upon the Present Temper of the Nation* (London, 1733), p. 16. A major defence of influence in the House of Commons also contained a very explicit distinction between the king and the three estates, though again the concerns of the writer were with the new influence and not the old prerogative. See Anon., *A Second Letter to Member of Parliament Concerning the Present State of Affairs* (London, 1741), p. 18.

102. Bolingbroke, "Dissertation upon Parties" (1735), letter 16, in *Works* (1841), 2:144.

Especially distressed was Roger Acherley, remembered for the ve-
hemence with which he defended the contractual basis of government.
Echoing the wishes of Humfrey and others earlier in the century,
Acherley regretted the absence of some epitome of the British constitution, equivalent to the thirty-nine articles. As it was, he complained, one heard continually of "the Constitution," but the term
conveyed no precise meaning.[103] Some clerics approached the matter
through scripture and came to see English kings as though they were
the arbitrary rulers of Judea or ancient Rome. Nor could historians
be trusted not to misrepresent the subject; Acherley had a special
animus against Laurence Echard, generally perceived as rather an
innocuous contributor, because he was unsound on the question of
the Revolution. Writers who insisted that the king was not an estate
were also especially out of favour, provoking Acherley to ask how
anyone could be "so ignorant of the true *British* Constitution." Unlike
Henry Fielding, who in a much-quoted essay advised his countrymen
not to expect any political order to be as abiding as the climate or the
soil,[104] Acherley believed the Whig myth that an unambiguous system
had emerged from the Revolution. Against both High-Toryism, with
its intimation of arbitrary government, and Court Whigs, with their
eloquent defences of influence in the House of Commons, Acherley
stood for King, Lords, and Commons, mutually independent.

Thomas Sherlock, High-Church bishop of Bangor, had argued on
a notorious occasion in 1731 that an independent House of Commons
was unthinkable, and this gave as much offence to Acherley as did
the solecisms of Tory historians.[105] Acherley had captured both of the
major sources of disunion in thought about the constitution in the
reign of George II. The plea for uniformity was naïve, but no more
naïve than the opinions of those who pretended that all Englishmen
were essentially at one regarding the constitution. It was not the diagnosis
that was at fault, only the assumption that the ailment had a cure.

There was, to be sure, some indication by mid-century that all po-

103. Acherley, *Reasons for Uniformity in the State* (London, 1741), also reprinted with
the 2nd ed. of *The Britannic Constitution* (1759).
104. Fielding, "Of the Changes which the Constitution of ENGLAND has Undergone,"
London Chronicle 143 (26–29 Nov. 1757), pp. 514–16. These comments were extracted
from the preface to Fielding's *An Enquiry into the Causes of the Late Increase of Robbers*
(1751).
105. [Acherley], *Free Parliaments* ... (London, 1731), pp. 218, 228–31.

litical malcontents could learn to express their different concerns within a common medium of Country rhetoric about corrupt manners, encroaching ministers, and a prostrate House of Commons. The convergence in the language used by alienated Old Whigs and Jacobites was already apparent in Earbery's assaults on the ministry. In the late 1730s Jacobite money from France supported the paper *Common Sense*, which promoted its aims free of any of the notions about hereditary right normally expected of that party. Thus it was indistinguishable in tone from other organs of opposition. Traces of hostility to the succession are visible, however, in some pamphlets of the late 1740s, notably one attributed to Dr. John Campbell,[106] the busy writer of histories and guides. The most prominent Opposition paper of the 1750s was the *London Evening Post*. Clearly Tory in its sympathies, and expressing openly High-Church opinions on the Jewish Naturalization Bill and in essays in support of Convocation, it generally avoided any offensive statement about the constitution. One issue of 1754 was held, though, to have traduced the Revolution, and the editor, Richard Nutt, was imprisoned.[107] The paper continued to oppose the Whigs but rapidly adapted its idiom to the safe practice of quoting John Locke.[108]

Surprisingly, however, the supposedly vanished doctrines were paraded unveiled in other publications. After the events of 1745, the government was not inhibited about punishing clergymen who sought clemency for rebels, nor was it indulgent to undergraduates who toasted the pretender. But even as these acts were punished, the press came alive with explicitly Jacobite propaganda. First there appeared a magazine, on the model of the *Gentleman's* or *London* magazines. For most of its two and a half years, the *Mitre and Crown* was issued monthly. Like its better-known competitors, it reprinted extracts from the weekly political press; it also had original essays of general interest,

---

106. [Campbell], *Liberty and Right: or, an Essay, Historical and Political, on the Constitution and Administration of Great Britain: Part I* (London, 1747), pp. 53, 65.

107. Francis Ludlow Holt, *The Law of Libel*, (New York, 1818), p. 98n. For comment on the *Post*'s High-Church writers see [John Douglas], *An Apology for the Clergy*, 2nd ed. (London, 1755), p. 14.

108. For its use of Locke as a weapon against the government see *London Evening Post* 4207 (26–29 Oct. 1754). In the provincial press, members of the Farley family were the major presence for much of the eighteenth century, and their politics were strongly Tory, if not Jacobite. See G. A. Cranfield, *The Development of the Provincial Newspaper, 1700–1760* (Oxford: Clarendon Press, 1962), pp. 56–60.

such as a critique of Locke's denial of innate ideas, before such re-thinking had become fashionable. But first and foremost it argued political issues from the vantage-point of a belief in non-resistance, passive obedience, and hostility to the original contract. In 1749, it joined most other journals in reviewing Bolingbroke's *Patriot King*. The reviewer departed from conventional responses in noting that Bolingbroke had neglected to endorse the divine right of kings. On the other hand, the author received full marks for his opinion that there must be an absolute power in every government, though the intent of the original comment was distorted in the telling.[109] Even bolder statements appeared in a pamphlet recommended to readers, and doubtless written by the same hand. Thus George II was granted the assurance that Hanoverians might enjoy the respect of friends to the pretender's cause, if only because the House of Hanover was a branch of the Stuart family![110] Whether this impertinence or some other moved the government is not certain, but the political content largely disappeared after June of 1750. The intrepid author-editor of the magazine seems to have been George Osborn, graduate of Cambridge and one-time member of the Middle Temple.[111]

Before the last issue of the *Mitre and Crown* appeared, in February 1751, a companion publication, known as the *True Briton*, had assumed the burden of upholding the Jacobite presence. The weekly essays in this new venture were less guarded in their language but otherwise comparable in content. Again the public—though a small public, one imagines—learned of kings who ruled by a mandate from God alone, of the necessity of non-resistance and passive obedience, of absolute power residing in the sovereign.

Sometimes the abundance of ammunition became an embarrass-ment, as when a spirited denial of the Whig teaching on the estates and co-ordinate power, based largely on seventeenth-century sources, was followed by borrowings from Montesquieu on the mutual checks

---

109. *Mitre and Crown* (June 1749), p. 509.

110. *The Divine and Hereditary Right of the English Monarchy, Enquire'd into and Explain'd by a Gentleman late of the Temple* (London, 1750), p. 56. The description of the author was the same as appeared on the magazine.

111. So identified in Halkett and Laing. Some details of Osborn's life are recorded in Venn, *Alumni Cantabriginenses: Part I*, 3:28.

and balances among branches of the legislature.[112] The observations were just barely capable of reconciliation, for the king's superiority (as argued by most Jacobites) was not incompatible with the sharing of his legislative power. The two different sources of inspiration were also addressed to different issues, for to deny that the king was an estate spoke to the question of his authority and prerogative and not to the day-to-day relations between executive and legislative powers. In a sense the discordant texts symbolized the Jacobite dilemma: well-disposed to monarchy, they were deprived of an appropriate dynasty to revere; rightly suspicious of the ministers who dominated the House of Commons, they were still unhappy with republican schemes for securing the independence of the popular chamber. In fact, all populist enthusiasms were anathema to the regal theories of Jacobitism, for to speak of fixing power in the people was an expression without meaning. Locke's references to consent in his "so much famed" *Treatises* were thus inoperable: "in this Sense, the People can do nothing either good or bad, not so much as ask what's o'Clock."[113] The one Whiggish dogma that proved convenient to accept, at least for the sake of argument, was that of natural rights. One might then berate Fielding for his harsh thoughts on the manners of the poor, especially their laziness, for such magisterial haughtiness meant that the people of low estate had no such freedoms as the high-born, "and where are those unalterable, unalienable Whig natural Liberties and Privileges of Englishmen, so much boasted of?"[114]

The theoretical bite of the *True Briton* was not primarily the editor's own, but was dependent upon the accumulated sources of Country rhetoric and the Tory reasoning of at least fifty years before. Sometimes, of course, metaphors got mixed, for it cannot have been easy to proclaim a faith fashioned for rulers from the modest station of an insecure subject. But for all the impressive range of talents from which the editor drew—Locke, Montesquieu (badly misspelled), Rousseau, the seventeenth-century republican John Streater, Edward Stillingfleet, the chevalier de Ramsay, and Bolingbroke—there was one

---

112. *True Briton: In which the State, Constitution and Interest of Great Britain will be Considered* 1, no. 24 (12 June 1751); and 2, no. 25 (11 Dec. 1751).

113. *True Briton* 5, no. 19 (29 May 1753). In this, the second last number, the case came to be presented in its essentials, shorn of the trappings of Country-party vocabulary.

114. Ibid. 5, no. 11 (2 Mar. 1753).

source that gave philosophical coherence to the loyalty to which the paper was chiefly devoted. Whenever the question of the basis of Whig government was at issue, Charles Leslie was the well from which the High-Church or Jacobite cause drew.[115] He, above all, had subjected co-ordinate power to the cruelest inquisition, arraigning it before the prayer-book and the statute-book. This, rather than his fruitless loyalty to the Stuarts, has been recognized as the focus of his political thought.[116] Happily for all who stood in need of his help, some of Leslie's political writings, consisting of the essays in the *Rehearsal* and his *Cassandra*, were reprinted in 1750. Thus the most formidable foe of Whig theory came, revived, to do battle in the second half of the century.

3. RENEWAL: 1760–1800

Dr. George Horne (d. 1792), later bishop of Norwich, was introduced to Leslie's political writings, in the form of the six-volume reprint, when he was a young man at Oxford in the 1750s. He was, according to his biographer, much impressed with Leslie's treatment of the arguments of infidels, Dissenters, and Whigs. The same insight given to Horne "must have had its effect on many others; insomuch that it is highly probable, the loyalty found amongst us at this day, and by which the nation has of late been so happily preserved, may have grown up from some of the seeds then sown by Mr. Leslie: and I

---

115. See *True Briton* 1, no. 4 (23 Jan. 1751); 1, no. 25 (19 June 1751); 4, no. 7 (4 Oct. 1752); 4, no. 13 (15 Nov. 1752); and V, no. 17 (16 May 1753). George Hilton Jones recognized Leslie's capacity as a theorist but dismissed in a sentence all literary evidence of Jacobitism after 1714. See *The Main Stream of Jacobitism* (Cambridge, Mass.: Harvard University Press, 1954), pp. 245–46. A similar dismissal of Leslie, which presents him as an irrelevant oddity, is found in Bruce Lenman, *The Jacobite Risings in Britain, 1689–1746* (London: Eyre Methuen Press, 1980), pp. 112–13.

116. See L. M. Hawkins, *Allegiance in Church and State: The Problem of the Nonjurors in the English Revolution* (London, 1928), p. 143. An able study of Filmer's thought has identified Leslie as his most faithful follower but has failed to recognize either that Leslie denied co-ordinate power or the importance of that denial as the vehicle for nourishing High-Toryism throughout the century. See James Daly, *Sir Robert Filmer and English Political Thought* (Toronto: University of Toronto Press, 1979), pp. 136, 167.

have some authority for what I say."[117] The writer, William Jones of Nayland, Suffolk, was among those other people so affected by Leslie's political theory. No doubt George Watson, Horne's tutor at Oxford, was another. Patrick Delany, dean of Down, was associated with the other two and held similar High-Church views.[118] But did Leslie's words from the time of Queen Anne really exercise such an influence? All that one can say is that from 1714 to 1750, when mentioned at all, Leslie usually stood for a set of opinions thought to belong to a political universe forever consigned to oblivion. After the republication of the *Rehearsal*, Leslie's admirers certainly appear to have become more forthright in owning an influence from that source, and Jones, writing at the end of the century, could record a span of fifty years during which the views for which Leslie stood might seem to have been continuously before the public.

This resurgence of High-Church political doctrine was accompanied by another intellectual influence, proceeding from rather different premises. Oxford in the 1750s became the home of a new enthusiasm, if not exactly a brand new cause. This was Hutchinsonianism. John Hutchinson (d. 1738) had denied the validity of Newtonian mechanics, scorned too any assistance from Descartes or Aristotle, and, rather awkwardly for his reputation with learned men, relied upon an uncertain command of the Hebrew scriptures to sustain an alternative cosmology. Physics and politics were joined in this cause, through Hutchinson's hostility to any account of the world that slighted the direct intervention of God as an agent. Newton's account of gravity and of the vacuum fell afoul of this requirement, but so did that understanding of political authority that omitted to award due credit to divine agency. For God did not merely plant the social instincts in

117. "The Life and Writings of Dr. Horne ..." (2nd ed., 1799), in *The Theological, Philosophical and Miscellaneous Works of the Rev. William Jones* (London, 1801), 12:72–75. For Horne's use of Leslie see an undated essay "Some Considerations on Mr. Locke's Scheme of deriving Government from an original Compact," in [William Jones, ed.], *The Scholar Armed Against the Errors of the Time*, 2nd ed. (London, 1800), 2:295. Testimony about Leslie's influence on a High-Churchman who lived until 1855 is found in Edward Churton, ed., *Memoirs of Joshua Watson* (Oxford, 1861), 2:278.

118. Jones, *Works*, 12:18–19. Watson published one sermon with the title *The Scripture Doctrine of Obedience to Sovereigns inforced* (1763), but no copy has been discovered. But see Delany, "The Mutual Duty of Princes and People" (n.d.), a 30-January sermon where he claimed that the office of kingship was "at least" of divine appointment, in *Twenty Sermons* (London, 1750), pp. 319–20.

man; He instructed man in the choice of his governors. It was then absurd "to dream of any sovereign but the first father," and though the line of descent might be unclear, "every man is born under some supreme power, which he ought to submit to without reluctance." Kings were at least "Viceroys of Christ"; indeed, at times Hutchinson made a stronger claim than that: "what he [God] has put into the Hands of these Rulers, his Subjects, by him constituted Governors, he gives by their Hands, (which in Propriety of speaking, notwithstanding the learned Cavils, are his Hands) to the rest of his Subjects. ..."[119]

God had granted all power on earth to kings, and a Christian king might have the same sort of absolute power as Hebrew kings, unless he was restrained by the law of God. Of restraints kings took upon themselves by their own acts Hutchinson had little to say, since they did not affect the principle of absolute earthly power. The political ambitions of Jews, Dissenters, and Roman Catholics were all to be resisted, since the first were not loyal to any king, while the others, especially the Dissenters, challenged kings' right to hold directly under God and tried to relate their authority to human sources. Hutchinson sometimes expressed his alienation from the political current of the time—"I almost despair of making any present advantage by Politicks"[120]—and his followers were not active in partisan manoeuvres, though they did resist the Jew Bill.

Hutchinson's legacy largely assumed the form of a deep distrust of those forces in society that might be seen as undermining authority and hierarchy. This was a theme that grew in strength as the men of the persuasion became more reconciled to the political powers that governed Britain. In Hutchinson's mind, the corrosive effect of free-thinking and notions about popular government had been construed as a conspiracy, which served well to cushion his disappointment at

119. "Moses's Principia, Part II," in *The Philosophical and Theological Works of John Hutchinson*, 3rd ed. (London, 1748), 2:438. For other statements of political principle see "The State of Nature; or, of Instincts" (n.d.), in *An Abstract of the Works of John Hutchinson Esq.* (Edinburgh, 1753), pp. 431–34; "The Religion of Satan, or Antichrist Delineated," in *Works*, 8:96, 116; and "The Use of Reason Recovered by the Data in Christianity, Part II," in *Works*, 9:208, 215–16. Comment on the school is found in Albert J. Kuhn, "Glory or Gravity: Hutchinson vs. Newton," *Journal of the History of Ideas* 22 (July–Sept. 1961):303–22.
120. "The Religion of Satan," p. 109.

the cold reception generally accorded to his silly theories. The New-tonians were presented as "the party" of Newton, a body of ill-disposed men who were thought to have hired John Toland to promote their creed.[121] The Newtonians are now recognized as having had an affinity to a particular political ideology.[122] It is no less true of anti-Newtonians.

Hutchinson had felt betrayed by a one-time collaborator, and the propensity to smell out conspiracies infected his followers' interpretation of any opposition their views encountered. Thus one claimed that the "enemy" had hired scribblers to attack an admirer of Hutchinson who had expressed his views in 1735 at the Bristol Assizes. Unfortunately, there was ample evidence that charges of disloyalty to the Hanoverians were voiced rather freely, and more than one innocent sermon on the duty of obedience had provoked charges of Jacobitism. The Hutchinsonians of Oxford encountered this Whiggish sensitivity when Nathan Wetherell, later master of University College and vice-chancellor of the university, delivered a 30-January sermon in 1755. It provoked a violent response from Benjamin Kennicott, another Oxford man and prominent Hebrew scholar, who accused Wetherell of maintaining

the justly-exploded doctrine of *absolute passive obedience*, and this in terms so extremely gross, as even to have out-*Filmer'd Filmer*: to maintain it to be the indispensable duty of all Christian subjects, under the worst of tyrants, to bow down in the dust or upon the block ... and at last to tell the Congregation, that no man could vindicate Resistance in any case whatsoever, without giving up all regard for the Bible, and all pretension to common Sense.[123]

Since the offending sermon appears never to have been published, one is not to know if it was worthy of such description, though a true follower of Hutchinson would in fact have imbibed the political theory of Sir Robert Filmer. George Horne published a response, called *An Apology for Certain Gentlemen in the University of Oxford*, in which he underlined the basic paradox of a cleric's preaching obedience to King

---

121. *An Abstract of the Works*, pp. 164, 167, 197. These were the comments of the editor.

122. See Margaret C. Jacob, *The Newtonians and the English Revolution, 1689–1720* (Ithaca: Cornell University Press, 1976), pp. 271–72.

123. [Kennicott], *A Word to the Hutchinsonians* (London, 1756), p. 16.

George and then having to face the charge that "you may depend upon it, he is a Pretender's man."[124]

It was indeed an odd conclusion to draw, for increasingly this manner of political controversy reflected nothing so specific as a preference for different ruling houses. Provocations by a few dedicated Jacobites and the memory of a vanished generation of non-jurors had obscured the fact that there were still profound disagreements about the nature of political authority, about ecclesiastical organization, and about the nature of religious guidance for the whole society. These had literally never disappeared, although alarms about the pretender had often veiled the nature of the disputes. In the reign of George III, Horne and his colleagues went over to the Court, and the tension between their situation and their apparent doctrines ceased. Exaggerated claims by displaced Whig politicians that there was a Tory revival at the accession of George III were perhaps not without foundation.[125] But it was less a revival of doctrines than the recognition of traditional High-Church beliefs for what they were: not a covert loyalty to the pretender, but a persistent view of political life that had lacked a proper focus for expression.

There actually seem to have been fewer controversies in the 1760s arising from specific instances of clergymen who preached the "exploded" theories of authority. This probably indicates the effective evaporation of the Jacobite spectre rather than disappearance of the sentiments. George Horne's stronger sermons of the traditional sort all seem to date from the reign of George III. On 30 January 1761, he told an Oxford audience that it was essential to eradicate "the diabolical principles of resistance of government in church and state."

---

124. Quoted in W. R. Ward, *Georgian Oxford* (Oxford: Oxford University Press, 1958), pp. 205–6.

125. For examples of the complaint that *jure divino* and indefeasible hereditary right were again being heard see Anon., *A Derbyshire Gentleman's Answer to the Letter from the Cocoa-Tree* (London, 1762), p. 3; *Craftsman; or Say's Weekly Journal* 417 (13 Aug. 1763); and *Monitor* 423 (10 Sept. 1763). Defenders of the early ministries of George III even felt compelled to disavow adherence to Filmer. See *Auditor* 31 (18 Dec. 1762):198–99. Its editor, Arthur Murphy, came as close as anyone to admitting a Tory complexion to Bute's ministry, but an abler strategy was that of challenging the Opposition to propose abolition of observances of 30 January, thus smoking out the High-Churchmen in their ranks and demonstrating that they were not confined to the government. See Anon., *An Address to Both Parties* (London, 1765), pp. 7–11. This appeared before the Rockingham Whigs came into office.

The next year, preaching before a congregation that included Lord Mansfield, he said that God would "sit as a judge even of them, who by reason of that delegated power, are styled *Gods*," which was not quite the Whiggish conception of kingship. In a sermon of 1769, his theme was the error of supposing a state of nature, and here his Filmer-like position was accompanied by an interesting account of how the misconceptions about the state of nature might have been fostered.[126] Another sermon, delivered on 5 November but undated, called attention to the political assumptions resident in the *Book of Common Prayer*:

Such is the language in the Rubrick in the form of service for this day: whence it must occur to the reader that the doctrine which makes the King one of the three estates of Parliament, is an *innovation*, introduced by Republican Writers; who diminish the Crown to raise *the people*, and in the end to overturn the Government.[127]

Each of these assumptions would have found vehement opponents, but none appears to have provoked the outrage that marked the use of more guarded or innocent expressions in the past.

The American troubles brought with them more urgent need for lectures on the merits of obedience and, accompanying the rise of extra-parliamentary activity, a new readiness in some quarters to challenge any hint of authoritarian language. The Revolution also brought more authoritarian language with which to quarrel.[128] In 1771, the Reverend John Gordon preached at Cambridge against the state of nature and the popular derivation of power. The sermon contained some digs at the discomfort of the one-time Whig oligarchy, but the preacher was careful to dissociate himself from the patriarchial theory. Nevertheless, Dr. Gordon attracted accusations of preaching up divine

126. See Horne, *Sixteen Sermons on Various Subjects and Occasions*, 3rd ed. (London, 1800), p. 37; "The Great Assize," in *Discourses on Several Subjects and Occasions* 5th ed. (Oxford, 1795), 2:300; and "The Origin of Civil Government," in ibid., pp. 306–22.

127. Horne, "The Providential Deliverance from the Gunpowder Treason" (n.d.), in *Discourses*, 2nd ed. (Oxford, 1795), 4:178.

128. An appreciation of the reality of the Tory categories of the 1770s is rare. But see Paul Langford's recognition both of the currency of seventeenth-century language and of a tone of abuse reminiscent of an earlier time in "Old Whigs, Old Tories and the American Revolution," *Journal of Imperial and Commonwealth History* 8 (1979–80):124–25.

right. Similar protests greeted a 30-January sermon before the House of Commons by the King's Professor of Modern History in Oxford. It was, in fact, a sermon very favourable to the Stuarts and quite waspish about Whig historians. Embarrassed, the Commons expunged its vote of thanks, amid suggestions that Sir Fletcher Norton, the Speaker, and others must have slept through the performance.[129] Although this practice of seeking treason under the bed had its comic side, the spectrum of political views had come to be greatly extended by the middle years of the decade. John Wesley poured scorn on radical notions of popular sovereignty and wisely refrained from spelling out his alternative, but he put his case with a new intensity.

However, when Caleb Evans accused Wesley of having dredged up the Jacobite doctrine of "hereditary, indefeasible, divine right,"[130] another Wesleyan—the Swiss-born John Fletcher—came to his defence and rather let the cat out of the bag. For Fletcher's arguments contained elements of the purest patriarchalism, since he linked, in the somewhat mysterious fashion typical of the seventeenth-century writings of Robert Filmer, paternal and magisterial authority. Unashamed, he added; "You may call this Jacobite doctrine, Sir, but such a name does no more make it unreasonable, than your calling Mr. Wesley a slave, deprives him of his liberty."[131] Once committed, he pursued this line of argument in a subsequent pamphlet: "King George the third, is with respect to his children, what Adam was with respect of his posterity. He is a *Father*, and a King. The *first* character he can entail upon all his sons; but the *second* he can entail upon none but the Prince of Wales." Since that observation did not assist his argument in any noticeable way, Fletcher had to press on to counter the normal objection that patriarchal power, if taken seriously, left all men sovereigns. But, Fletcher retorted, this was not so, for "in every country, those that share in the dominion given to Adam and Eve in their

129. Gordon, *The Causes and Consequences of Evil Speaking Against Government Considered in a Sermon, Preached ... Oct.* 25, 1771 (Cambridge, 1771), p. 10; *London Packet or, New Evening Post* 376 (20–23 Mar. 1772); Thomas Nowell, *A Sermon Preached before the Honourable House of Commons ... Jan. XXX,* 1772; and Joseph Towers, *A Letter to the Rev. Dr. Nowell* (London, 1772), p. 6.

130. "Americanus" [Caleb Evans], *A Letter to the Rev. Mr. John Wesley ...* , 2nd ed. (Bristol, 1775), p. 11.

131. Fletcher, *A Vindication of the Rev. Mr. Wesley's "Calm Address to the American Colonies"* (London, [1776]), p. 43.

regal capacity, are as much known as the king and parliament are known in England. ..."[132] Wesley must have felt himself wise in concentrating upon the weaknesses in the case of those who advocated more popular government. Such an exchange indicates how close to the surface patriarchal ideas still lurked, likely to emerge if the disputants on the Tory side were goaded to depart from their strategy of pointing out the problems of government by consent.[133] The barrage of paper between the Wesleyans and the friends of the American Revolution went for several rounds, thus inviting the Wesleyans to reveal their assumptions.

A comparable opportunity and danger lay in store for those High-Tories who wrote substantial volumes on political topics, for here again was the temptation to spell out the underlying rationale of a government that owed nothing to the people for its justification. William Smith, a medical doctor, wrote the most elaborate dissenting opinion on British government to appear in the eighteenth century. Seemingly Jacobite in tendency, his argument was a compendium of all the usual High-Tory positions—divine right, passive obedience and non-resistance, the denial of co-ordinate power, and an unusually extreme affirmation of the absolute character of the English monarchy.[134] Smith also endorsed an unambiguous case for patriarchal power, though he made no reference to Filmer. The most interesting point to emerge from the two volumes was the manner in which Smith argued how the uncontrollable power essential to every government might be located. It was possible, he alleged, for the laws to govern and for magistrates to perform their appointed functions in quiet

132. Fletcher, *American Patriotism Further Confronted with Reason, Scripture and the Constitution* (Shrewsbury, 1776), pp. 36–37.

133. In finding traces of Filmer only in Bentham, Jonathan Boucher, and John Whitaker, Professor Schochet has underestimated its staying power. Nor is it correct to claim that the doctrine was so long dead as to prompt no responses. See Gordon J. Schochet, *Patriarchalism in Political Thought* (Oxford: Blackwell, 1975), pp. 280–81. There were, however, favourable references to the theory that were too fleeting or from sources too obscure to attract much comment. See, for example, John Coleridge, father of Samuel Taylor Coleridge, *Government not Originally Proceeding from Human Agency but Divine Institution* (London, 1777), p. 6; and Richard Munn, *The Loyal Subject, or Republican Principles Brought to the Test* (London, [1793]), p. 12, where kings and fathers are equated.

134. Smith, *The Nature and Institution of Government, Containing an Account of the Feudal and English Policy* (London, 1771), 1:98–99, 123, 126.

times, without their knowing where this power was lodged. However, in times of crisis in the form of wars or revolution, people would seek the supreme power for relief from their afflictions.[135] This is, in effect, the theory of sovereignty associated in the twentieth century with the name of Carl Schmitt! The treatise was of course a curiosity and was neither indicative of the current direction of thought nor influential. It seems to have escaped prosecution, for there were complaints in Parliament that attacks on the constitution from Jacobite perspectives went unnoticed.[136] Nevertheless, it was accorded the courtesy of a review by Dr. Gilbert Stuart, who, notoriously arrogant about his own abilities, was no less respectful about Smith than about the books of most other people.[137] Stuart was understandably most interested in the theory about the location of supreme power and paid tribute to its ingenuity. There is no evidence that Smith was closely associated with other spokesmen for ideas hostile to the establishment, and his work has the air of an enthusiast, not a mercenary. Smith does seem to have profited from reading the writings of High-Churchmen, and in fact he subscribed to Hutchinsonian views of creation.[138]

If one were to choose a time in the eighteenth century when the fragile consensus about British government seemed on the point of disappearing, it would be the years around 1776. Paine and Price had shocked opinion by their different brands of radicalism; James Burgh, in his *Political Disquisitions* (1774) had dismissed talk about the balance among the estates by wondering why more than one estate of the people was needed, a view soon to be put more memorably by Paine and more clearly by the radical Capel Lofft. Bentham, then a Tory, had written his *Fragment on Government* and subjected the ideas of Blackstone to that logical dissection that would continue long after the young Tory had become a radical. Ministerial writers were again, as in the 1730s, contriving sophisticated defences of executive influence over the House of Commons. Their ranks now included John Shebbeare, who had outgrown the covert Jacobitism of his opposition journalism of the 1750s. Amid all the rethinking of government in its origins and its nature, the allegedly proscribed and forgotten formulas of High-Toryism were prominent, leaving the suspicion that

135. Ibid., pp. 188–89.
136. *Parliamentary History* 17 (Feb. 1774):1054–57.
137. *Monthly Review* 45 (Dec. 1771):417–24.
138. Smith, *The Student's Vade Mecum* (London, 1770), chap. 6.

they had never been quite as distant as one might suppose. It seems, in fact, that they had needed only such an opportunity for expression as was afforded by the events in America and the surge of "democratic" aspirations that accompanied those events.

To put the revival of patriarchal ideas in focus, one should recall that there had been very few publications on the origin of government since the disputes of 1710–14, and this is particularly so if one looks only to highly partisan accounts. There had been a sober genre of works on the stages of development of societies—the anthropology of the Scottish enlightenment—but these works had afforded no comfort either to contractarians or to disciples of Filmer. The same factors that account for the incorrect impression that Filmer had long ceased to be relevant also apply to the status of Locke. He had become an authority for the dominant political assumptions without subjection of his views on the origins of political authority to much scrutiny or discussion. The legions of ministerial writers had had no incentive to enquire into the populist implications of Locke, for no administration could hope to gain from speculation about the exact origin of government or, indeed, about the mechanisms for securing consent. Nor had successive Country spokesmen found him as useful as, say, Davenant. When fundamental premises were questioned, as in the 1770s, one should not be surprised that Locke was no more accepted by all points of view than had been the case around 1710. Locke's views were again bandied about, in stark contrast to that honoured neglect to which events had relegated them for many decades. Sometimes, not surprisingly, the attention was unflattering, but usually the friends of authority took issue with the state of nature, the contract, and the popular origins of power without mentioning Locke by name. When Dean Tucker mounted a direct attack on Locke in 1781, he was the exception to the rule. However, there is evidence that some disputants in the 1770s had felt the need of a more direct confrontation with Lockean ideas at their source.[139]

As one might expect, the participants in the debates of the 1770s

---

139. See George Campbell, *The Nature, Extent, and Importance of the Duty of Allegiance*, 2nd ed. (Aberdeen, 1778), a quite moderate sermon that looked forward to the appearance of Tucker's promised work on Locke's theory of government (p. 7n.). An early version of Tucker's *Treatise Concerning Civil Government* was privately circulated as early as 1778. See Robert Livingston Schuyler, ed., *Josiah Tucker: A Selection from his Economic and Political Writings* (New York: Columbia University Press, 1931), p. 41.

were not very conscious of which opinions were startling and which commonplace. Thus when the Reverend Myles Cooper, a returned American Loyalist, preached at Oxford and had his sermon published at the request of George Horne, then vice-chancellor, there was an uproar. The sermon itself was not very strong stuff, consisting of a plea to obey the powers "ordained of God," stated carefully so as not to deny that authority might also have a foundation in the people. Cooper did, however, take a swipe at "Original Compacts which never existed." Predictably, he was held to have resurrected passive obedience and divine right. "Could Leslie or Sacheverel say more?" asked a horrified reader.[140] Clearly they had, but each successive decade of the century saw claims that the currency of these "exploded" ideas was remarkable.

Although it had been necessary to draw upon the early decades of the century in order to assemble traditional Tory ideas, there was no shortage of editors to see such texts through the press. The writings of Dr. William King (d. 1712), supporter of Sacheverell, were reprinted in two different editions in 1776;[141] and a hitherto unpublished essay by Roger North (d. 1734), arguing for the supremacy of the Crown, also appeared in that year. The editor of North's manuscript was William Stevens,[142] a successful hosier, an arch-Tory, and a man quite prepared to express his opinions in his own words. Stung by the Lockean view of the Revolution preached by Richard Watson, later bishop of Llandaff, Stevens set out the traditional High-Church alternative replete with favourable comments on the patriarchal theory. He was naturally hostile to contractarian ideas and to vague talk about the power of the "People"; most of all, however, Stevens con-

140. Cooper, *National Humiliation and Repentance Recommended* (Oxford, 1777), p. 22; [A. M. Shore], *A Letter to the Rev. Dr. Cooper on the Origin of Civil Government* (London, 1777). See too a letter signed "A Disciple of Locke," in *Public Advertiser* 13,189 (21 Jan. 1777), and one signed "Melancthon," in ibid. 13,218 (24 Feb. 1777).

141. See *The Original Works in Verse and Prose of Dr. William King*, 3 vols. (London, 1776); and King, *An Essay on Civil Government ... to which is added a Remonstrance with the Court of Common-Council, on their Presenting the Freedom of the City to Dr. Price* (London, 1776). The addition was said to have been written by Samuel Johnson. Of similar inspiration, but more moderate in tone, was Anon., *A Discourse on Hereditary Right, Written in the Year 1712. By a Celebrated Clergyman* (London, 1775).

142. *A Discourse on the English Constitution* (London, 1776). For Stevens's involvement in the reprinting, see the obituary in *Gentleman's Magazine* 78 (1807):173–75. The author was James Alan Park, Stevens's biographer.

centrated upon that issue that had already figured in the treatise by North—the supremacy of the Crown. Like Charles Leslie and William Oldisworth, Stevens seems to have appreciated that the structure of Whiggish ideas rested upon the simplest and perhaps the most familiar of assumptions—that the government rested with King, Lords, and Commons. Watson had paid conventional homage to this formula, without spelling out the legal niceties that might have been woven around it. It was a signal quality of Whiggism to take the scheme for granted, for few apart from John Humfrey or Roger Acherley had lavished much effort on its exposition, and even Blackstone and de Lolme had skirted most of the difficult constitutional points. But, Stevens argued, the familiar picture of the organs of government was inaccurate. From the time of what Stevens was pleased to call the "Rebellion," it had been claimed "that the King was a part of the Parliament, and one of the three estates, co-ordinate with the two houses of Lords and Commons; but this doctrine, though vulgarly and almost generally believed, is unknown to our law; ... the King not being one of the three estates; but distinct from and superior to them."[143]

For this assertion, Stevens offered two arguments. The first, typically High-Tory, appealed to the office of the Church for 5 November, where prayers were offered for the preservation of "the King and the three estates." The same was implied by prayers to be read in Parliament and by the oath of allegiance. Stevens made the most of these seventeenth-century legal phrases and, in particular, the fact that Watson, as a clergyman, must have subscribed to non-resistance in the form in which it was set out in the prayer-book. The other consideration was an objection, both logical and practical, and one of much longer standing. A mixture of powers, all three of which were supreme, was incoherent as a proposition and incompatible with any lasting constitution. In support, Stevens cited Tacitus. This weapon had not up to that time been much used; in resorting to it great care was needed, for it was both difficult and dangerous to suggest that the British monarchy was other than mixed. Leslie and Samuel Parker had done so, stressing the supposed logical difficulty in visualizing

---

143. [Stevens], *The Revolution Vindicated and Constitutional Liberty Asserted* (Cambridge, 1777), p. 9. As the title suggests, he argued that the Revolution was acceptable, for the simple reason that it had changed nothing but had merely preserved the constitution.

co-ordinate powers; and Leslie had cleverly noted even earlier application of the objection in Harrington's dismissal of the mixed form.[144]
Later, the argument was to prove attractive to various enemies of the
constitution as Watson understood it, appealing both to radical opponents of the unreformed system and to writers who were more
natural allies for Stevens.[145]

It is difficult to estimate the influence of this outspoken champion
of all that was un-Whiggish. To list his friends, who actually came to
form a club, sounds like a roll-call of the figures who were most
conspicuous in combating free thinking and democracy throughout
the nineties and into the nineteenth century.[146] Dr. Horne was his
cousin; Stevens edited the writings of William Jones, who had been
Horne's editor; and numbered among Stevens's friends were the Reverend Jonathan Boucher, a Loyalist returned from America, and John
Reeves, one-time chief justice of Newfoundland and moving spirit in
the Society for Preserving Liberty and Property Against Republicans
and Levellers—that association most in need of an acronym. Other
friends included the Right Honourable Charles Watkin Williams Wynn
(a member of one of the most respected families of Jacobite sympa-
thizers);[147] John Bowdler (brother of the expurgator of Shakespeare);
James Richards Green, who edited the *Anti-Jacobin Review and Magazine* under the pseudonym of "John Gifford"; and John Bowles, an
able political writer in an idiom more Burkean than High-Church,
author of an early reply to Paine's *Rights of Man* and later of many
pamphlets on behalf of Pitt's administration.[148] The views held in

144. *Rehearsal* 49 (30 June–7 July 1705); and 72 (3–10 Nov. 1705).

145. See Gilbert Wakefield, *The Spirit of Christianity, Compared with the Spirit of the
Times in Great Britain* (London, 1794), p. 33.; [Thomas Moore], *Corruption and Intolerance:
Two Poems* (London, 1808), p. 11.; George Ensor, *On National Government* (London,
1810), 1:190; and, representing a view closer to Stevens, Anon., *Pou-Rou: An Historical
and Critical Enquiry into the Physiology and Pathology of Parliaments* (Dublin, 1787), p. 57.
Defenders of the unreformed system also felt the need to come to terms with the
adverse judgement of Tacitus. See the speech by William Young in *Parliamentary History*
25 (1785–86):471–72.

146. See Sir James Alan Park, *Memoirs of William Stevens, Esq., Treasurer of Queen
Anne's Bounty*, 2nd ed. (London, 1814), pp. 161–84; and *The Club of Nobody's Friends*
(privately printed, London, 1938), 2 vols.

147. On the political sympathies of the family see David Greenwood, *William King:
Tory and Jacobite* (Oxford: Clarendon Press, 1969), p. 143.

148. Apparently Bowles wrote thirty-two pamphlets in this cause. See *Parliamentary
Debates* 14 (1809):308–09, 319–21.

common by this group led Stevens and Jones to form the Society for the Reformation of Principles, the reformation of manners having already been pre-empted by Dissenters. High-Church political, social, and religious ideas found a consistent, if moderate, outlet in the *British Critic*, which ran from 1793–1843, outlasting all but the venerable *Monthly Review*.

The *Critic* was edited initially by William Beloe and John Nares with the express purpose of countering the strong dissenting influence in periodical publications.[149] After 1798 High-Tory opinions were also proclaimed by the virulent *Anti-Jacobin* under Gifford and Robert Bisset, the author of one of the earliest book-length assaults on "democracy." Both periodicals gave space to patriarchal theory adapted from Filmer's supposedly dead writings by Bowles and John Whitaker, the historian of Manchester.[150] Both also lionized Reeves after his acquittal in 1796 from charges of writing a seditious libel aimed at reducing the constitutional status of the Lords and Commons and inflating the royal prerogative. Reeves's subsequent publications were reviewed uncritically and at great length, though the *British Critic* was careful not to comment on his pamphlet of 1795 until his acquittal. In its second year, the *Anti-Jacobin* claimed a circulation of 2,500. Since the preferences of the editors of these magazines were more precisely defined than were those in publications of a less conservative political leaning, the High-Tory[151] position was probably better served by the monthly press than was any variant of Whiggism or radicalism.

149. Jones, "A Proposal for a Reformation of Principles" (1792), in *Works*, 12:378–79. The *Critical Review* had ceased in the early 1790s to be sympathetic to Tory views, and both the *Analytical Review* and the *Monthly* were rightly seen as antagonistic. On the political opinions of the reviews see Derek Roper, *Reviewing before the Edinburgh, 1788–1802* (Newark, Dela.: University of Delaware Press, 1978), pp. 175–80.

150. Whitaker, *The Real Origin of Government* (London, 1795), *passim*; and Bowles, "Thoughts on the Origin and Formation of Political Constitutions" (1796), in *The Retrospect; or, a Collection of Tracts Published at Various Periods of the War* (London, 1798), pp. 305–11. For an endorsement of Whitaker's apparent use of Filmer that disavowed any intention on his part to argue for divine hereditary right or absolute monarchy see *British Critic* 5 (Apr. 1795):413–15. The *Anti-Jacobin* warmly received both writers but mentioned Filmer only in a neutral way. See *Anti-Jacobin* 1 (1798):preface, vi; 4 (Dec. 1799):526; 7 (Oct. 1800):176; and 2 (Jan. 1799):10–17.

151. Here I am using the self-characterization of the *Anti-Jacobin*: "We profess ourselves to be Tories and High-Churchmen. Let our adversaries make the most of this declaration ... ," 5 (Feb. 1800):290. Given its obvious admiration for Leslie, the assurance was hardly necessary. See ibid. 1 (Sept. 1798):357–59, and 2 (April 1799):399.

The political teaching of these monthlies was distinctly different from the conventional scorn for popular sovereignty and defence of unreformed institutions that sustained other ministerial prints—such as the *True Briton* of the 1790s, the first so-named paper that was not Jacobite—in the years of Pitt the Younger and after. The avowed aim of most of Stevens's coterie was to reform the public mind; this entailed demonstrating how notions made popular in recent decades, and especially since the French Revolution, were false. There followed an emphasis upon the divine origin of authority, but not, as they were careful to point out, the divine right of kings. However, since they held monarchy to be the only legitimate form of government, the distinction was a fine one. The supremacy of the king was a prominent theme in both High-Church publications, and both found the *locus classicus* for it in Reeves's publication of 1799, *Thoughts on the English Government in a Series of Letters*. The first such letter in 1795 had led to his trial the following year, and the grounds for offence had been the scandalous claim that even were the other branches or Houses of Parliament to be "lopped off," the king, as the supreme power, could carry on the government. Reeves and others favoured the arboreal image of the royal oak and insisted that the monarch was improperly described as a branch of the constitution, since a branch had to exist in relation to some central trunk. This symbol of the royal oak, firmly associated with Charles II, had been primarily favoured by Jacobites. Roger North's earlier work had also supported these arguments, for its central claim had been that the supremacy of the king was the only power in being when Parliament was recessed. North's treatise, as edited by Stevens, was twice reprinted in a collection edited by William Jones.[152]

Having established to their satisfaction the supreme position of the Crown, Stevens and his friends were poised to reach further significant conclusions. Reeves argued that the monarchy could not consistently be called "mixed," though he did not cavil at the word "limited."[153] Furthermore, all presumptions about co-ordinate power were nonsense, for the king was not one of the estates. This point was repeated endlessly by the foes of the French Revolution and of

---

152. See *The Scholar Armed* ... , 2nd ed. (London, 1800), 1:251–65.

153. Again, the Tory monthlies applauded. See *Anti-Jacobin* 4 (Oct. 1799):277; and *British Critic* 14 (Dec. 1799):617.

English radicalism. On one occasion, it was suggested that co-ordinate power was something new: "The application of the expression, *the three estates* to the King, Lords and Commons in Parliament assembled now returning again into common use after having been exploded a century ago is here condemned. ..."[154] More than twenty years before, Stevens himself had suggested that his view of the estates had been overwhelmed by the general acceptance of Whig usage. Though Stevens was closer to the truth, neither statement was correct, since there was scarcely a time during the century when the Whig doctrine was not subject to challenge, and while more writers accepted the claim that the estates were King, Lords, and Commons, their opponents normally argued with a more acute awareness of the significance of such constitutional formulas.

A telling example was provided by the debate of 1788–89 on the Regency Bill. For this issue displayed the opportunism of Charles James Fox when he came perilously close to arguing for indefeasible hereditary right as the foundation of his case for the Prince of Wales. Fox and his supporters opposed the bill by harking back to legislation of the Restoration, which denied any legislative authority to Parliament without the king.[155] Meanwhile, other contributors to the debate referred to the need to supply the "defect of the Third Estate,"[156] meaning the king, an identification that left Reeves and his school quite incredulous. But, in fact, the identity of the three estates had always been an unresolved point, and any issue that entailed analysis, beyond the mere recitation of government by King, Lords, and Commons, raised the difficulty. Normally the Commons were seen as the third estate, but with the growth of concern about the place of the people in politics, either the sovereign or the peers were sometimes relegated to that position. The regency crisis led to frequent quotation of the Bill of Rights, with its references to the estates, and a century after its passage, readers still complained that on crucial issues it was

154. *British Critic* 14 (Dec. 1799):619.
155. For the crucial exchange between Pitt and Fox see *Parliamentary History* 27 (10 Dec. 1788):708–13; and John W. Derry, *The Regency Crisis and the Whigs, 1788–89* (Cambridge: Cambridge University Press, 1963), pp. 68–72.
156. See Anon., *An Impartial Review of the Present Great Question* (London, 1789), p. 27; and for an earlier reference to the House of Lords as the third estate see *Public Advertiser* 13,596 (6 May 1778).

most contradictory and ambiguous.[157] But the High-Church party, with concerns that transcended temporary issues of party advantage, used every constitutional dispute for purposes of affirming values and a symbolic order of no great importance to the bulk of other disputants. In his second *Letter*, Reeves allowed that the arguments by Pitt and Burke on the regency best accorded with his idea of monarchy, but neither side can have been entirely comforting to him, and whenever the regency was discussed the High-Tories insisted on their understanding that the king was none of the estates.[158]

Another inference made from the primacy High-Tories accorded to the king was the discovery that the constitution had not changed with the Revolution but had merely been preserved in that ideal balance between prerogative and liberty known in the reign of Charles II! Reeves insisted that what was then fashionably known as "the Constitution" was nothing more than a collection of statutes. For support, he drew upon North's manuscript.[159] Though the term was not such a neologism as some claimed, the argument was brilliantly conceived for its capacity to puncture elaborate myths about the Revolution. Reeves delighted in pointing out that the managers at Sacheverell's trial in 1710 had said that it was a libel on the Revolution to say that any constitutional innovation had taken place at that time.[160] The writers of the *Anti-Jacobin* improved upon the occasion, observing how this meant that the fundamental laws as described by John Nalson, a seventeenth-century Tory, were still the constitution.[161] When Reeves was brought to trial for his alleged libel, the merit of his argument was well illustrated, for the prosecution was unable to cite any statute, apart from the Bill of Rights, as a basis for condemning the libel; and reference in the bill to prerogative subject to parliaments frequently convened was not sufficiently precise to place Reeve's ar-

---

157. [de Lolme], *The Present National Embarrassment Considered* (London, 1789), p. 42.

158. [Bowles], *A Regent not King* ... . 3rd ed. (London, 1811), p. 6.

159. *Thoughts on the English Government ... Letter the First* (London, 1795), pp. 46–58.

160. Evidence here is mixed. Certainly the speeches by Jekyll and Lechmere at the Sacheverell trial of 1710 had stressed a measure of continuity in English government. See T. B. Howell, ed., *A Complete Collection of State Trials* (London, 1819), 15:98, 193. But see G. M. Straka, "Sixteen Eighty-Eight as Year One," in Louis T. Milic, ed., *The Modernity of the Eighteenth Century* (Cleveland: Press of Case Western Reserve University, 1971), p. 152.

161. *Anti-Jacobin* 4 (Oct. 1799), p. 273.

guments outside the law. Acquittal of the charge was coupled, however, with the reprimand that his pamphlet had been an "improper publication."[162]

It was not, of course, reasonable to insist that only statute law described the system of government, but the merit of a narrow construction of the term "constitution" for supporting reactionary views was undeniable. Reeves's adherence to legal arguments also served to protect him against the wrath provoked by more speculative opinions in the High-Tory repertoire. Thus he denied ever having read Filmer, though he managed simultaneously to commend the general bent of Filmerite thought.[163] In fact, Reeves's legal notions were, in themselves, shocking enough, very similar to those of Timothy Brecknock, whose notorious *Droit Le Roy* had been seized and burned by order of Parliament in 1764. But the times were different, and the fear of republican ideas in the 1790s was an invitation to extremism from the opposite pole. In addition, Reeves was a respectable figure, whereas Brecknock, surviving his dangerous book, had been hanged for a murder in Ireland.[164] Emboldened by his own success, Reeves then claimed that the position taken by the attorney-general, Sir John Scott, in a recent trial for treason endorsed his own claims about the royal prerogative.[165] Clearly, Pitt's government had been no more successful in smoking out political deviance of a Tory character than had the Whigs of 1710, and the government of the 1790s had less incentive to do so. The prevailing immunity enjoyed by notions of absolutism even stilled the clamour of reviewers, and the *Monthly Review*, which in 1796 had begun to mute its advanced political opin-

162. *State Trials* 26:539, 594–95. The claim by one of Reeves's admirers that the jury members could not take the charge seriously is difficult to believe. See [William Beloe], *The Sexagenarian; or, The Recollections of a Literary Life*, 2nd ed. (London, 1818), 2:122. John Whitaker boasted, in a letter of 25 May 1796, that he had publicly maintained Reeves's constitutional views as early as 1761. See R. Polwhele, *Biographical Sketches in Cornwall* (Truro, 1831), 3:107.

163. *Thoughts on the English Government ... Letter the Second* (London, 1799), pp. 161–62n.

164. *Droit Le Roy* (London, 1764), pp. 13–14; *Parliamentary History* 15 (Feb. 1764):1418–19; Anon., *Authentic Memoirs of George Robert Fitzgerald ... together with a Sketch of the Life of Timothy Brecknock* (London, 1786). As Horace Walpole pointed out, the order to take Brecknock into custody was not executed. *Memoirs of the Reign of King George the Third* (London, 1845), 1:384.

165. The claim has some substance. See *State Trials* 24:244.

ions, accommodated Reeves by avoiding reference to "co-ordinate" powers, lest the expression give offence. The reviewer settled on the term "concurrent" for purposes of describing the relations among branches of the legislature.[166]

To fill out the catalogue of High-Tory doctrine by noting that they believed in non-resistance and passive obedience can only seem anti-climactic. They did, of course, hold these beliefs, and given the claim that the king was pre-eminent within British government, it seems probable that he was the supreme power who was to be obeyed; but that point was best left as an inference.[167] In a period of revolutions, injunctions to obey were to be expected. Burke was widely, but wrongly, accused of having become a convert to the ancient principles of divine right and non-resistance,[168] so the presence of some variant of these ideas in the writings of life-long Tories, many of whom were clergymen or devout laymen, cannot have seemed remarkable. Since they had done their utmost to elevate the king above the other organs of government, the High-Tories were not likely to allow reforms of a democratic character. Indeed, they were committed to the proposition that the constitution had not changed since the seventeenth century.

Still, their viewpoint was not immune to insights derived from the political scene before their eyes. Reeves, for example, was most anxious to change that perception of the political system emphasizing a tension between the executive and legislative powers, for this smacked of the detested Whig idea of co-ordinate powers. Thus his fourth *Letter* stressed that the real tension was that between ministerial and opposition parties, with the ministerial group predominating in both Houses and thus ensuring good relations between executive and legislature. The old prerogative and the newer influence were thus served by the same argument. This was elementary enough, no doubt, but

166. *Monthly Review* 32 (May 1800):86. The review was by Samuel Rose, brother of Pitt's patronage secretary.

167. See *British Critic* 9 (Feb. 1797):189, for a very moderate statement of the doctrine of non-resistance. For the claim, more or less correct, that passive obedience was still the teaching of the Church of England see *Anti-Jacobin* 26 (Apr. 1807):337.

168. Examples of this radical paranoia are the following: Francis Plowden, *A Short History of the British Empire During the Last Twenty Months* (London, 1794), p. 37; Benjamin Bousfield, *Observations on the Right Hon. Edmund Bruke's Pamphlet on the French Revolution* (Dublin, 1791), pp. 10, 29; Benjamin Flower, *The French Constitution; with Remarks on some of its Principal Articles* (London, 1792), p. 119; and William Miles, *A Letter to Henry Duncombe Esq.*, 3rd ed. (London, 1796), pp. 7, 55.

it indicates that the sort of reasoning that justified ministerial influence and parties in Parliament was available to this brooder over ancient statutes. Only in this respect did the idiom of the High-Tories approach that of the friends of the ministry, such as George Chalmers or William Playfair, writers whose contributions usually took the form of discussing current advantages and not legal precedents. But by and large the High-Tories were most unlike their less high-flying colleagues. At the same time Chalmers and Playfair, among the more pedestrian and less ideological ministerial writers, gave at least perfunctory support even to the more outrageous assertions by Reeves, though they tended too to minimize the importance of such issues.[169]

The flights of High-Toryism prevalent around the time of the French Revolution have been noted by historians, especially as one moment in the fluctuating reputation of some major figure—Locke or Voltaire.[170] William Jones, ever the zealot, managed to damn both thinkers at once, as he portrayed Voltaire attempting to destroy Christianity with a copy of Locke's *Treatise* in his hand.[171] Locke's use of concepts such as "consent" and "contract" had indeed proved obnoxious to the High-Tories, though it would be easy to exaggerate the extent of their public repudiation of Lockean teaching. The *Anti-Jacobin* was actually quite well-disposed to Locke in several of its references; at times his opinions served to document conservative conclusions. Elsewhere, Gifford was much less kind to the "Great Father of Democracy" and blamed him for the French Revolution.[172] Nor was it difficult to employ Locke's texts—as opposed to what his admirers supposed him to have said—to erect barriers against popular enthusiasms. The Reverend William Hawtayne thus argued for divine right, correctly understood, of course, assisted by quotations from Locke on the limits of the people's power and making use too of Locke's criticisms of

169. Chalmers, *Vindication of the Privilege of the People* ... (London, 1796), pp. 18, 74–75; *Tomahawk* [edited by Playfair] 26 (26 Nov. 1795), and 28 (28 Nov. 1795).

170. For recognition of Stevens, Horne, and others as anti-Lockeans see John Dunn, "The Politics of Locke in England and America," in Yolton, *John Locke*, p. 61. See too Bernard N. Schilling, *Conservative England and the Case Against Voltaire* (New York: Columbia University Press, 1950).

171. Jones, "A Letter to the Church of England ..." (1792) in *Works* (1826), 6:247.

172. Gifford, *A Letter to the Hon. Thomas Erskine*, 6th ed. (London, 1792), p. 55; and *A Second Letter* ... , 4th ed. (London, 1797), p. 80. These popular pamphlets more than compensated for any attenuation of malice in the periodical.

Filmer.[173] But sometimes there could be no compromise, as when Reeves argued, in 1801, that the only possible exemplar of an original contract was the coronation oath. It was undoubtedly true that Locke's authority was much challenged from the mid-1770s. Some chose his theory of mind, as did the Scottish common-sense school; others, among them Jackson Barwis, questioned Locke's position both in philosophy and in politics.

But there was much more to the theorists of church and king than an aversion to Locke, though a willingness to reopen the case on behalf of Filmer was one indication of intense commitment to the cause. Their sympathies seem to have been ungenerous and their vision backward-looking, but one cannot readily dismiss the High-Tory phenomenon as an isolated eddy in a Whig torrent. The doctrines so fervently preached up at the end of the eighteenth century accurately preserved the political aspirations of Leslie and the many others of that persuasion at the beginning of the century. Even allowing for the radical implications of Locke's notion that government might revert to the people, it seems safe to say that Jones and his associates had more successfully guarded the meaning of their inherited beliefs than had admirers of Locke. Nor was the advocacy of Leslie's politics confined to the lucubrations of obscure and powerless men. The High-Tories were well situated in both church and state; the loyal associations of the early 1790s were largely, though not exclusively, theirs; and it is evident that as Britain entered into an era of reactionary government, the unrevolutionary public—never readily and articulately attached to any creed—was more theirs than the creature of the defeated reformers. The triumph involved in Britain's not having a revolution may more readily be appreciated when one recalls that the arguments for divine right could not have seriously been intended to support the indefeasible hereditary right of the Stuarts; the aim was rather to discourage appeals to the populace of a sort that might disturb religion and property. Both, for the time being, remained safe. No more were the disturbing arguments for prerogative intended to be preliminary to dismissing Parliament; instead, when the king wished to dismiss a ministry, as he did in 1807, there were learned men ready to confirm and applaud his actions.

173. [Hawtayne], *A Disquisition on the Divine Right of Kings* (London, 1793), pp. 49, 55–56.

High-Tories were more than the guardians of a flickering, century-old flame, for in the nineteenth century their cause continued to attract adherents who may never have known Horne, Jones, or Stevens or read Leslie. The ambitions of some Anglicans for a revival of Convocation, supported by the ancient argument that the clergy were an estate of Parliament, remained alive,[174] and the Puseyites took up the cry. So too did that version of the creed that expressed less interest in ecclesiastical organization and more for the dignity of the Crown. Contemplating the situation of a Tory minority in the House of Commons, combined with the possibilities inherent in a sovereign who disliked his Whig ministers, the young Benjamin Disraeli lectured the veteran Whigs, such as Grey, about their ignorance in holding that the king was but one of the estates.[175] In the judgements of nineteenth-century historians, Leslie was finally to win that argument, though without any dramatic consequences for the working of government. More importantly, Disraeli preserved an element of continuity with the very first Tories of a century and a half before.

The Tories and the Constitution

The conservative dissent, here called High-Tory, was significant in its own right, but its presence also serves to highlight the fragility of the dominant eighteenth-century view of politics and the constitution. The Whigs of 1689–1714 had shown themselves to be anything but unanimous in their formulations of the constitution, a result that was the joint effect of timidity and confusion. Anyone who assumes that this unanimity came easily after 1714 need only consult the debates on the Peerage Bill of 1719 in which some participants had denied that there was any meaningful "balance" at all in English government.[176] By the 1730s the Whigs had gained a measure of agreement about the political order as it touched, say, the status of the king *vis-à-vis* the houses of Parliament. However, the ministry and the Op-

---

174. [Rev. Thomas Silver], *The Origin of the Constitution; or, the Identity of the Church and State in Great Britain* (London, 1814), pp. 10–19.

175. See the series of articles first published in the *Morning Post* (4–7 Sept. 1835) and reprinted in *Whigs and Whiggism, Political Writings by Benjamin Disraeli*, ed. William Hutcheon (New York: Macmillan, 1914), pp. 102, 105, 109.

176. See, for example, [Charles, Earl of Peterborough], *Remarks on a Pamphlet Entituled, The Thoughts of a Member of the Lower House* (London, 1719), pp. 32, 35.

position gave quite different accounts of that balance that supposedly existed among the branches of the legislature. Government writers sometimes disavowed entirely the notion that there could be equality of power, and on those occasions they eschewed the image of a pair of scales as an apt description of the system.[177] When they did endorse a rough equality of power among King, Lords, and Commons, this sometimes took the form of saying that equal sharing of the executive power was desirable, a claim intended merely to justify ministerial influence though placemen in the House of Commons.[178] The language of co-ordinate power still figured in the *Craftsman* and other organs of opposition, but the issue for debate had shifted to propositions about the degree of dependence or independence belonging to branches of the constitution.

For most of the century political debate was beclouded by images of balance, generally unaccompanied by any precise analysis of what forces were ostensibly in equilibrium and how that state of affairs was maintained. Of course, the very concept of balance was ambiguous, for it might refer to the formal prerogatives of organs of government or else to the resources in force, money, or personal influence at the disposal of their members. These approaches yielded different conclusions, as conclusively demonstrated at the time of the Peerage Bill. Hume clearly stated the difference in his essay of 1741 on the independency of Parliament, and Paley wrote in 1785, contrasting a balance of power based on formal attributes and one of interest that flowed from the designs of political actors. The substance of the eighteenth-century consensus seems to dissolve under close scrutiny. Was the appropriate image that of a pair of scales, or perhaps a "political Trilanx," a "political Steelyard," which crops up on various occasions, or even a scalene triangle? Should the Harringtonian balance of property figure in one's calculations, or had it been superseded by what one administration journalist called the Weight of Employments, or those places to be held by patronage?[179] If this sort of balance was contemplated, then equality of power among the branches of the legislature was unimportant, and control over public affairs had only to be proportionate to the possession of certain resources. Should one

177. For especially virulent attacks on the metaphor of balance see "Francis Osborne" (James Pitt) in *London Journal* 570 (4 July 1730); and 613 (24 Apr. 1731).

178. *Daily Gazetteer* 32 (5 Aug. 1735).

179. Ibid. 46 (21 Aug. 1735).

still favour the common metaphor of a pair of scales, how could one account for three legislative branches? Did the sovereign hold the balance, as was commonly supposed, or was it the House of Lords or the House of Commons? Both had their advocates.[180] Or the significant balance might be seen as that between the people and their government, as was argued by persistent advocates of an effective militia. English Dissenters sometimes flattered themselves that their electoral weight was the true domestic equivalent of Britain's role as balancer of Europe.[181] Little wonder, then, that the young Thomas Pownall, future governor of Massachusetts Bay, published two versions of an essay in which, with Harrington, he despaired of mixed government. Pownall also condemned talk of balance in other than Harrington's terms and was particularly critical of Swift's emphasis on a balance among organs of government, as put forward in his work of 1701.[182] More characteristic of mid-century scepticism about the constitutional balance were the sly thrusts of Dr. John Shebbeare, who was widely held to be a Jacobite. Much of his writing on behalf of the Opposition was standard Country-party cant, but occasionally he had expressed the fear that the Whig principle of a balanced constitution was good only in theory and was unsuited to the coarse materials of daily politics.[183] Less powerful than the logical dissection of Leslie, Shebbeare's critique was better adapted to a time of Whig dominance.

When the coming of the American Revolution proclaimed the bankruptcy of one sector of British policy, the theory of the constitution again came under sustained attack, and the alleged balance was criticized from the left and from the right. There would be no peace on that issue until a new theory gained widespread acceptance around the time of the Reform Bill of 1832. Nor was it only the extremists

180. For the Commons as balance see Charles Lucas, *The Political Constitutions of Great Britain and Ireland, Asserted and Vindicated* (London, 1751), p. 88. Such a role was often suggested for the Lords at the time of the Peerage Bill. See too *Freeholder's Journal* 41 (3 Oct. 1722).

181. See [M. Morgan?], *An Enquiry Concerning the Nature and End of a National Militia* (London, 1757); and William Harris, *The Case of the Corporation and Test Acts Considered ... Part the Second* (London, 1736), p. 21.

182. [Pownall], *A Treatise on Government ...* (London, 1750), p. 29; and *Principles of Polity* (London, 1752), pp. 9, 12.

183. [Shebbeare], *Letters on the English Nation by Battista Angeloni, a Jesuit* (London, 1755), 1:11–12, 23; and *The History of the Excellence and Decline of the Constitution ... of the Sumatrans* (London, [1760]), 1:144–45.

who voiced their scepticism about the vaunted balance. Burke, in a speech of 1784 that deserves to be better known, was credited with saying that theirs was not a government of balances.[184] An important feature of the reconsideration of balance in British government is that it reignited the quarrel between Locke and the High-Tories. The horns of the dilemma on which Leslie and others had attempted to thrust the Whigs were again displayed by the most effective critics of the orthodox constitutional theory. William White, a moderate reformer of the 1790s, dealt succinctly with the sanctified incoherence when he noted that "the story of the balance may be reduced to this alternative, either it does not operate at all in the only case when government is, viz, when it acts, or by preventing action it vitally destroys that government which it is supposed to constitute." Turning to the specifics of some formulations, he noted that it was claimed that one branch might have to resist the force of the two others, "so that the balance is made up of a sort of changeable weight, which charitably deposits itself in the weaker scale, and like the angels of Paradise Lost, who are now giants and now pigmies ... exactly proportions itself to the service performed."[185]

White was not fair in suggesting that this was the only way of conceiving constitutional relations, but it is a perfectly accurate description of some variants of the protean theory of balance. As one Augustan journalist had put it: "In a mixed Government ... every constituent Branch of it must, to all Appearances, physically be a Check upon the other Two. ..."[186] References to a legislative veto belonging to the various branches did not, of course, involve the same difficulties; nor did the notion of a balance arising out of the septennial convention governing the life of Parliament, but this last has been more fully recognized by modern historians[187] than by eighteenth-century actors. More surprising than White's hostility to the balance was the fact that

184. Speech of 14 June 1784, in *Parliamentary History* 24:948.

185. White, *A Dissertation on Government, with the Balance Considered* ... (London, 1792), pp. 36, 45. William Cobbett, while still a Tory, was saying comparable things about inherited Whiggish notions of government by opposed powers. Cobbett, *Porcupine's Works* (London, 1801), 7:29n.

186. *Corn-Cutter's Journal* 18 (29 Jan. 1733–34); *Daily Courant* 5145 (5 Oct. 1732). Nor did the scorn of White and others end the practice. See John Gardiner, *Essays, Literary, Political and Occasional* (Edinburgh, 1803), 2:230.

187. As by Betty Kemp, *King and Commons, 1660–1832* (London, 1968), p. 34.

the experience of a century of balanced government left him with essentially the same bill of particulars as had been presented by Leslie some ninety years before; the system was prone either to immobilism or to instability. Nor were the High-Tory writers of the revolutionary era displeased with criticisms of balanced government, so long as these could be used to promote regal and not popular sovereignty.[188] White himself was, of course, no Tory.

The surprisingly unsettled state of opinion about the constitution lends to High-Toryism an importance that it would not otherwise claim, and this in two senses. The confusion, uncertainty, and disagreement meant that the ideas of zealots such as Stevens, Jones, and Reeves were more serious competitors than would have been the case had constitutional issues been settled once and for all. It is also true that their stubborn adherence to seventeenth-century notions entailed an intellectual integrity of sorts, free of the imprecision of more commonplace opinions. One account of eighteenth-century Tory thought has contrasted the Whigs, in possession of an official doctrine largely bestowed by Locke, and the Tories, pragmatically adrift without the burden or the comforts of metaphysical baggage.[189]

An intriguing and challenging contrast, this is nevertheless unsound history. For one thing, the Whigs were far from clear or unanimous on the theory of the constitution. Some Tories, whatever they might call themselves, did indeed congratulate themselves on their freedom from theories; but usually that was a way of denying any sympathy to abstract ideas they did not like—whether those of Richard Price, or Thomas Paine, or the Jacobins. William Windham sometimes railed at metaphysics, which he seems to have equated with radical theories;[190] but he was one of the parliamentary defenders of Reeves's condemned writings, at a time when the prime minister, Pitt the Younger, joined in the censure by members of the Opposition. Further to complicate matters, Windham saw himself as a Whig! Adherence to Reeves, it should be added, entailed something more than an

188. See *British Critic* 1 (May 1793):66; and *Anti-Jacobin* 7 (Oct. 1800):176. The latter contains a demolition of ideas regarding "political checks, balances and controuls."

189. Donald J. Greene, *The Politics of Samuel Johnson* (New Haven: Yale University Press, 1960), p. 249.

190. For typical statements by Windham see *Parliamentary History* 32 (1795–97):637–44; and *Speeches ... of the Right Honourable William Windham*, ed. Thomas Amyot (London, 1812), 1:193.

endorsement of certain legal precedents, however much both Wind-ham and Reeves may have suggested otherwise. There was, to be sure, a long-standing suspicion of theorizing about political matters, but this was typically an attitude displayed by men in office or at least in tune with the *status quo*, irrespective of their political stripe. At the time of the French Revolution many Englishmen said that what might be speculatively and abstractly true was practically false, an opinion owing much to Soame Jenyns, who had poked fun at notions of con-tract and consent as well as those about divine right.[191] But Jenyns—placeman, poet, and one-time friend of Robert Walpole—was no more a High-Tory than was Windham's friend Burke, the other well-known source of such opinions.

By contrast, High-Tories possessed a theory of government that owed little to the general conservative mood of the country in the 1790s, even though it fitted the times very well. An harmonious blend-ing of arguments for royal prerogative and for influence over the Commons did appear in this period, for the same propositions—the denial of co-ordinate power, for instance—would serve both purposes. Nor was the government loath to embrace firm friends to church and state, even when those friends cherished notions of law and order that challenged the long-standing, if imprecise, tradition of limited government. The higher reaches of Toryism had lacked a role in the many decades separating 1714 and 1789, but the very same charges against popular government that had been the Tory ammunition of 1710 were again in fashion at the end of the century. The major difference was that the Whigs of the reign of Anne had been cari-catured as democrats; but such ambitions were really entertained by the radicals of the nineties.

As the reaction to the French Revolution swept a whole generation to the right, High-Toryism all but disappeared as a separate cause. The marriage between the old Toryism and the new conservatism was all the more readily arranged because writers such as Jones and Reeves lacked that ambivalence towards authority seen in "church-and-king" mobs or in the fascist movements of this century. Certain High-Tories had indeed expressed alienation from the political ethos

191. Jenyns, *A Free Enquiry into the Nature and Origin of Evil* (London, 1757), p. 142. An example of the contempt for theory displayed by anti-reformers of the nineties is Thomas Townshend, *Considerations of the Theoretical Spirit of the Times; on the Inefficacy of Theory to the Formation of Civil Government* (Cork, 1793), pp. 24–25, 53–54.

of Britain, but such feelings were salved as their countrymen retreated from all causes threatening to property and degree. Reeves's vigilante groups were short-lived,[192] and his own brush with authority demonstrated only the weakness of those checks the laws could then pose to an authoritarian political philosophy. Reeves himself rebounded from the prisoner's dock to become King's Printer in 1800, thus symbolizing the acceptability of his doctrines. So it was that in an era of Tory governments the High-Tories found common cause with the articulate nation. For Leslie, Hutchinson, the Jacobite journalists of mid-century, and the friends of William Stevens, their political enemies had been described as "the party"—an amalgam, it seems, of infidels, Dissenters, republicans, and Whigs. The reaction to the French Revolution effectively labelled these unsettling influences as foreign to the British tradition and so, in large measure, endorsed the arrogant Tory ambition to be more than just a party.

An authoritative survey of the period of reaction concludes with the thought that liberty survived and that even self-proclaimed Tories (and that was not all of them) saw themselves as upholding the old Whig constitution.[193] Liberty did, of course, survive, somewhat the worse for wear; but this is not the whole story. Crucial to understanding the High-Tory phenomenon is the fact that there was no agreement on what the old constitution entailed. William White, arch-enemy of balanced government, noted the virtues of belief in what he called the "happy formal constitution," though he saw it as but an elaborate fiction. Modern scholars have similarly remarked on the social benefit of distortions and false images of reality that permit life to go on undisturbed.[194] The persistence of trust in the constitution illustrates the process, for the traditional theme of balance, never very clear, was repudiated by radicals, by ministerial advocates of corrupt influ-

192. On the history of these extra-parliamentary bodies see Austin Mitchell, "The Association Movement of 1792–3," *Historical Journal* 4 (1961):56–77; Donald E. Ginter, "The Loyalist Association Movement of 1792–93 and British Public Opinion," *Historical Journal* 9 (1966):179–90; and Albert Goodwin, *The Friends of Liberty: The English Democratic Movement in the Age of the French Revolution* (Cambridge, Mass.: Harvard University Press, 1979), pp. 264–65.

193. H. T. Dickinson, *Liberty and Property*, p. 317.

194. White, *Dissertation*, pp. 55–56. See too Robert Murphy, *The Dialectics of Social Life* (New York: Basic Books, 1971), pp. 115, 150.

ence, and by the High-Tories.[195] Yet it persisted in the rhetoric of politicians, journalists, and ordinary citizens. This made it easy to endorse an image of the constitutional *status quo*, without thereby committing oneself to saying what exactly it entailed, let alone pronouncing on which theory best explained it. Some people remained attached to the term "balance" but redefined its meaning; others— and this included the Tory ultras—proclaimed the balance a chimera while expressing contentment with the existing institutions. However heated their disagreements with commonplace accounts of the theory of government, Reeves and his associates had no desire to overturn the Glorious Revolution, for they lacked loyalties to any other dynasty. Nor could they readily object to Parliament, though Reeves had argued, amid applause, that the authority of the king was greater. Some old-fashioned enthusiasms could well be forgiven to such a loyal defender of the *status quo*. High-Tories stood for tradition and precedent, and if their obsessions left others cold, at least they posed no clear threat to the ordinary business of government. Most people, save the democratic radicals, endorsed the old Whig constitution either in theory or in practice, but some versions looked back to the Restoration and others forward towards the Reform Bill. Unless one appreciates that point, the nature of the commitment is misunderstood.

One normally conducts scholarship on a small scale, fearful lest broader strokes miss the essential detail. But some matters must be placed in an ample setting, regarding both theme and span of time, if they are to be grasped at all. This approach seems a useful one for charting the intellectual odyssey of the High-Tories. Each generation was the more important by virtue of its self-conscious continuity with revered predecessors. Each generation came too as a surprise to its contemporaries, accustomed to political debate within Whig premises. Each was retrospectively denied existence by later historians, who certified the death of such ideas in some earlier age. Two factors assist in explaining the survival: the confusion of their enemies and the nourishment afforded by those institutions, the law and the Church, that had never fully assumed the garb of Whiggism. Eighteenth-century

---

195. Elsewhere, I have noted the first two schools of thought, but not the Tory contribution. See my "Influence, Parties and the Constitution: Changing Attitudes, 1783–1832," *Historical Journal* 17 (1974):301–28.

Britain could not readily have lived by the letter of the Tory creed, but neither could people make very good sense of the balanced constitution. By viewing the High-Tories within the setting of the diversity of views about the eighteenth-century constitution, we may better understand both of these neglected subjects.

V

David Williams: Organicism and Reform

THE IMAGES in which men have tried to capture the nature of political organization have alternated between the poles of mechanism and organicism. The scientific revolution of the seventeenth century did much to popularize a view of political order founded upon discoveries in mechanics, so that eighteenth-century England was pre-eminently an age of mechanical analogy, with government, even society, being conceived as somehow machine-like. One thinks of John Trenchard's likening a good government to a clock and Mandeville's finding it akin to a spinning wheel. Some version of the balance of the English constitution was familiar to every schoolboy. Although each successive opposition lamented the defects of the machine and imposed its own understanding of the balance, this only confirmed the belief that an equilibrium of prerogatives and interests was indeed an intelligible prescription for political health. Not until the last quarter of the century was the theory of the constitution seriously challenged, and this challenge was quite compatible with the orthodox mechanical vocabulary, as the writings of Paine indicate.

The medieval and Renaissance metaphor of the body politic had already lost much of its point by the time of the English Civil Wars, and it suffered a further decline in the face of Locke's politics and Newton's physics.[1] Whigs of the eighteenth century were not wholly immune to the charms of social organicism, but often they used it, rather inappropriately, to describe the balanced constitution, a notion

---

1. See David George Hale, *The Body Politic; A Political Metaphor in Renaissance English Literature* (The Hague: Mouton, 1971), pp. 121–24, 131.

more readily presented in mechanical terms.[2] Philip Horneck sustained his paper the *High-German Doctor* of 1714–15 on such an analogy, and another paper of the 1730s—inelegantly called the *Corn-Cutter's Journal*—also purported to offer physic to body politic. The inadequacy of the ancient image for Whig purposes was demonstrated when a pamphleteer of the Glorious Revolution pointed out that unlike the head of the body natural, that of the political body could be replaced without doing comparable damage. A further dimension of Whiggish ideology was revealed in Benjamin Hoadly's hostility to the claim that the king was the head of the body politic. In Hoadly's eyes, this too smacked of Tory doctrine, and he much preferred to designate the erstwhile "body politic" as the "Public." If head there had to be, this arch-Whig insisted that it was King, Lords, and Commons combined.[3]

When organic vocabulary appeared later in the century, it was rarely put to new or interesting purposes. The few exceptions were those writers who sought to convey an understanding of processes in public life, for they pointed to the Achilles' heel of a mechanistic idiom. Thus Henry McCulloh, the man who drafted the notorious Stamp Act of 1765, appealed to biological terms for purposes of recommending changes designed to secure the "Circulation of Business through the Channels of the Public Offices." More portentously, he sometimes expressed his concern for clearing the "Channels of Information" in British government.[4] A similar cause that might invite discussion of processes was that of annual parliaments, for it too was describable as a circulation of influences.[5] In the main, however, mechanical images carried the burden of political messages of all sorts.

The waning of typical eighteenth-century habits of mind and the

2. See, for example, Anon., *A Vindication of the Honour and Privileges of the Commons of Great Britain* (London, 1740), p. 16.

3. [Thomas Harrison?], *Political Aphorisms: or, The True Maxims of Government Displayed*, 3rd ed. (London, 1691), p. 7; and Hoadly, *The Measures of Submission to the Supreme Magistrate Consider'd*, 4th ed. (London, 1710), pp. vi–viii.

4. [McCulloh], *General Thoughts on the Construction, Use and Abuse of the Great Offices; with a view to some Further Discourses on the Same Subject* (London, 1754), pp. 19–20; and *The Wisdom and Policy of the French in the Construction of their Offices* (London, 1755), p. 14. Manuscript versions of McCulloh's proposals are to be found in the William R. Perkins Library of Duke University.

5. See [Obadiah Hulme], *An Historical Essay on the English Constitution* (London, 1771), p. 111.

revival of organicism are normally perceived as events of the nineteenth century.[6] The obsessive organicism of several of the German romantics—Schelling, Schleiermacher, and Adam Müller—emerged in the first decade of that century as an ideological response to the French Revolution. Non-German adumbrations of this style of thought came from Burke and de Maistre and were similarly inspired.[7] Of the eighteenth-century writers who questioned the value of mechanistic categories, only Herder has escaped an identification with reactionary sentiments, and it must be admitted that his political message found its most attentive audience among romantic nationalists. However, this initial flourishing of organicism was a state of mind with causes that went beyond the simple desire to cherish past or present arrangements. Dissatisfaction with the conventional political categories of the eighteenth century had a source quite independent of reactions to the French Revolution, for mechanism had uses other than that of threatening the traditions of the privileged orders. After all, throughout most of the eighteenth century a mechanistic vocabulary had served to support institutions. Those desirous of changing these institutions might then begin with an attack on the dominant strain of political metaphor. This in fact happened, and so we must add one radical uncle to the conservative progenitors of nineteenth-century organicism.

A Radical Science of Politics

David Williams (1738–1816) is best known as an innovating school teacher, the translator of Voltaire and founder of the Royal Literary Fund. He was, in addition, a sometime Unitarian preacher and a

---

6. See Francis W. Coker, *Organismic Theories of the State* (New York: Columbia University Press, 1910), chap. 1. Organicism in English social thought has in fact been described as a phenomenon of the 1830s and after. See Walter D. Love, "Edmund Burke's Idea of the Body Corporate: A Study in Imagery," *Review of Politics* 27 (1965):196.

7. On the German organic school see Reinhold Aris, *History of Political Thought in Germany from 1789 to 1815* (London: G. Allen and Unwin, 1936), chap. 10. For the influence of predecessors less attached to the organic idiom see Frieda Braune, *Edmund Burke in Deutschland: Ein Beitrag zur Geschichte des historisch-politischen Denkens* (Heidelberg: C. Winter, 1917), chap. 6; and Elio Gianturco, *Joseph de Maistre and Giambattista Vico: (Italian Roots of de Maistre's Political Culture)* (Washington: Murray and Heister, 1937), pp. 213–17.

tireless writer in the cause of constitutional reform.[8] As a political writer, Williams has been dismissed as a tiresome scold or as a purveyor of metaphysics.[9] Certainly he was a savage satirist, while his prolific writings equally reflect an ambition to transcend immediate issues in the pursuit of the permanent principles of political order. Indeed, it was the fusion of his intense commitment to reform with this interest in discovering the laws of politics that makes his thought important. The result, however, was an unclubbable philosopher, at home neither among the enthusiasms of radical politics nor in the company of complacent beneficiaries of the status quo.

In 1771, Williams published his first political work and there set out a number of the opinions that would inform his writings for the next forty years. Foremost among his priorities was the realization of the interest of the "People," not in itself an unusual concern on the part of English radicals. However, Williams had already reached a number of conclusions that served to place proposals for parliamentary reform in a broader social context than was normal among reformers. For one thing, he qualified the traditional Opposition claim that England could only be enslaved by a Parliament, arguing that

8. Details of William's life are to be found in Thomas Morris, *A General View of the Life and Writings of Rev. David Williams* (London, 1792); E. V. Lucas, *David Williams: Founder of the Royal Literary Fund* (London: J. Murray, 1920); *D.N.B.*; Clarence J. Phillips, "The Life and Work of David Williams" (Ph.D. thesis, University of London, 1951), chap. 1; and Williams's Ms. autobiography, "Incidents in my own Life," Cardiff Public Library, Ms. 2.191. An edition of the autobiography, edited by Dr. Peter France, has been published (1980) by the University of Sussex Library.

Research in the Jefferson papers has shown that he and Williams were friends and that Jefferson consulted Williams as late as 1808. See Nicholas Hans, "Franklin, Jefferson and the English Radicals at the end of the Eighteenth century," *Proceedings of the American Philosophical Society* 98(1954): 406–26. Some useful information on the editions of the major writings appears in Charles F. Mullett, "David Williams, Reformer," *Church History* 13 (1944):111–31. Information about his influence on British contemporaries is contained in my entry for Williams in Joseph O. Baylen and Norbert J. Gossman, eds., *Biographical Dictionary of Modern British Radicals* (Hassocks, Sussex: Harvester Press, 1979) 1:534–39.

9. See James T. Boulton, *The Language of Politics in the Age of Wilkes and Burke* (London: Routledge and Kegan Paul, 1963), p. 197; for the strained relations with both Fox and Burke, as recorded in Williams's amusing autobiography, see Lucas, *David Williams*, p. 17. Contemporaries of Williams tended to identify him with the Literary Fund rather than with his political opinions. See a comment in a letter by Godwin, cited in Charles Kegan Paul, *William Godwin: His Friends and Contemporaries* (London, 1876), 1:71.

Parliament threatened only a nation that was already corrupted. Most people with this opinion tended to avoid the cause of political reform in favour of improving manners. Casting aside the familiar demand that the constitution be brought back to its original principles, Williams denied that he could find in English history any model of an "ancient constitution" to which the nation might return. The false history of those seventeenth-century Whigs and the eighteenth-century Country party, both of whom had stressed the early representation of the people, was therefore irrelevant.[10] To seek freedom in the principles governing "the rude state of society," where people had yet to understand their rights, was chimerical. Rather, one should recognize that civil liberty advanced with the improving state of society and that the "rights of man" grew in proportion to man's capacity to enjoy them. Despite an admiration for King Alfred, Williams generally scorned antiquarian searches for an ancient constitution, for forms of government necessarily responded to environment; "when the circumstances, manners, and principles of a people are totally changed: it would be, like applying the policy of a village to the regulation of a large and populous city."[11]

The positive elements in Williams's early work consisted in a description of those institutions that would best allow the English people to govern themselves. Since his recognition of the fluidity of political life precluded any fixed constitution—already he insisted that government was "ever liable to variation"—Williams was rather casual in describing the institutions that he favoured. Admitting the attractions of "democracy,"[12] he noted that it was not feasible to imitate the system

10. [Williams], *The Philosopher in Three Conversations* (London, 1771), p. 34. The claims of Opposition antiquarianism are discussed in Isaac Kramnick, *Bolingbroke and his Circle*, pp. 128–36.

11. *The Philosopher*, p. 19. As pointed out by Colin Bonwick, Williams claimed no continuity with Saxon forms, for he insisted that that constitution had been entirely effaced by the Normans. See *English Radicals and the American Revolution* (Chapel Hill: University of North Carolina Press, 1977), p. 25.

12. Williams initially used the term to designate an ideal political order, but one that was impracticable. See *The Philosopher*, p. 20. This position was closer to that of Rousseau than to that of the French revolutionaries, who came to see "democracy" as a set of viable institutions. A later reference to "democracy" was more positive. See [Williams], *Letters Concerning Education* ... (London, 1785), p. 204. The term does not occur in Williams's major political writings. On the question of interpreting early favourable references to "democracy" see Jens A. Christophersen, *The Meaning of "Democracy" as Used in European Ideologies* (Oslo: Universitets-forlaget, 1966) chap. 1.

of ancient city-states. The closest modern approximation was not, as some apparently thought, a collection of "little republics," but a scheme of decentralization that employed the tithings, hundreds, and counties as the units in which the popular will was consulted. Beginning with this ascending order of small units, the House of Commons could then be chosen indirectly by the people, through their election of civil officers in the districts. The locally-elected officers would then choose, by ballot, the House of Commons. The primary assemblies provided for in the French constitution of 1793 were not dissimilar in principle and may indeed have been a product of Williams's influence.[13] Williams consistently maintained that such an arrangement had much in common with the divisions of England under King Alfred. Nevertheless, this surprising concession to the admirers of a Saxon constitution left him seeking, not a simple reconstruction of Saxon forms, but a fusion of the decentralization of that system with principles characteristic of modern government.[14]

Writing in 1778 on the American troubles, Williams used, apparently for the first time, the simile that was to guide his future political speculations: "The constitution of a state is in many things analogous to that of the human body. ..."[15] He never explained the source of this assumption; various remarks indicate that he took it to be the view of the best political thinkers throughout the ages. Enlarging upon it in subsequent writings, he made organicism a vehicle of both a partisan dislike of the established order and a more philosophical critique of prevailing modes of understanding. The two concerns were joined in his insistence that current evils—corruption, lack of representation, and the futile squabbles between aristocratic factions—pro-

13. Williams was undoubtedly influenced by French thought, especially that of Rousseau. See Henri Roddier, *J.-J. Rousseau en Angleterre au XVIIIe siècle* (Paris: Boivin, 1950), pp. 151, 208–10, 369–70. For Williams's role as influencer of Girondin opinions on liberty see chap. 6, below.

14. See Williams, *Letters on Political Liberty* ... , 3rd ed. (London, 1789), p. 14. The first edition, differing chiefly in the pagination and in the absence of later appendices, appeared in 1782, and the second in 1783. Extracts from it were subsequently published in *Political Magazine and Parliamentary, Naval, Military and Literary Journal* 6 (Mar. 1784). The *Letters* have won recognition as one of the "eighteenth-century classics of liberal political theory." Albert Goodwin, *The Friends of Liberty*, p. 224.

15. [Williams], *Unanimity in all Parts of the British Commonwealth, Necessary to its Preservation, Interest and Happiness* (London, 1778), p. 1. Another pamphlet, which in its organic metaphors sounds like Williams, is Anon., *The Case Stated on Philosophical Ground between Great Britain and her Colonies* (London, 1777).

ceeded from a failure to discover the principles that underlay properly functioning government. This failure extended to the very intentions and methods employed by students of government, for Williams complained that he could recollect no writer "who has treated Politics, as a science, and deduced his demonstrations from clear or indisputable data."[16]

Current ideas regarding government were diverse and incoherent. Some had treated it as the outcome of climate; others had emphasized force, contract, or a range of "accidental circumstances." But if government were truly a human contrivance, its parts must be constructed according to principles, and these could not be "heterogeneous and discordant," as were the dominant ideas about British government. Here Williams displayed an ambiguity central to his philosophy. He appears never to have distinguished clearly between the claim that all government must be founded upon principles of some sort and the very different proposition that good government required some coherent basis. It is thus unclear in what way imperfect systems could contribute information useful for the science of politics, nor even how good government and political knowledge were to be wedded.

The ambition to be the Newton of the moral world was not, of course, new. Both Hobbes and Harrington had felt the impulse, and the intellectual history of the early nineteenth century was to be strewn with projects outlining the science of human affairs. Such ambitions had been somewhat muted in eighteenth-century England, if only because of the prevailing assumption, fortified by Montesquieu and Blackstone, that the appropriate political forms had already been established by the Glorious Revolution. Hume's rather desultory thoughts on a science of politics had been inconclusive, while the frustration felt by thoughtful men at the anti-intellectual tone of party politics had rarely issued forth in any coherent alternative. The answer of most radicals had been to reassert the balance of the constitution while pouring invective on the personal failings of the politicians. Williams was offering something more, and so his claims for a science of politics were markedly different from the compilations of tradi-

16. *Letters on Political Liberty*, p. 2.

tional opinion that passed for "political science" at the outset of the nineteenth century.[17]

The foundation of the new science of politics had to be a set of principles, self-evident in nature and serving as a standard by which practice could be measured. Williams thus saw it as unphilosophical to assert, with the defenders of corruption, that what was true in theory was false in practice. The insouciance with which politicians treated the obvious disparity between constitutional theory and actual experience led Williams to revert to the seventeenth-century notion that politics might be understood in a manner similar to the truths of geometry, and with equal certainty. Examples of such political truths were the value of political liberty and the means conducive to attaining it, including the governing of all by all. The general rationale for this science was one of the less happy aspects of his political thought. It entailed a naïve belief that ultimate values and instrumental institutions could be justified by an identical process, and it even reproduced Montesquieu's puzzling identification of physical regularities in the universe with moral laws governing human affairs.[18]

Montesquieu, Mechanism, and the Alternative

The balanced constitution and its defects provided the focus for all Williams's early political writings. Comparing his writings to those of most other theorists, one realizes that Williams had striven to escape from that moralistic cul-de-sac in which the eighteenth-century Country party had fulminated against corruption. Whereas even the influential James Burgh had filled the three volumes of his *Political Disquisitions* (1774) with dire reports of venal parliaments and the debasement of civic manners, Williams chose to emphasize the more positive theme of the possibility of a dramatic reshaping of public life. Burgh, to be sure, had sought the usual expedients in arguing for limits on places and pensions, for frequent parliaments, and for freedom to instruct Members of Parliament. Williams's prescription was

17. For examples of the genre see Angus Macaulay, *Rudiments of Political Science . . .* (London, 1796); [R. J. Thornton], *The Politician's Creed; or Political Extracts,* 2 vols. (London, 1799); and John Craig, *Elements of Political Science,* 3 vols. (Edinburgh, 1814).

18. See [Williams], *Lectures on Political Principles; The Subjects of Eighteen Books in Montesquieu's Spirit of the Laws . . .* (London, 1789), p. 6.

more realistic in addressing the question of means and more devastating in its rejection of most received opinions. But first he had to dispose of Montesquieu's praise for an aristocratic constitutionalism that only divided the people's masters. The rebuttal was both democratic in emphasis and couched in a new idiom:

> As in the human body, the functions of each member, are perfectly unembarrassed, though it be united to the body and subject to its general strength: so in a political state, the deliberative and executive parts are free and independent, in their particular exertions, though annexed to the general body; and bound to it, by such ligaments as render them subservient to its collective force.[19]

Montesquieu had, without doubt, intended that the separation of powers be to the advantage of the people; Williams simply argued that this result would be obtained only if the various powers of the state were encompassed in the larger body that they served. It was precisely the necessary connection between government and people that led Williams to restate the basic mechanical premise of the time in a new vocabulary. Previously the alternative conceptions of the constitution had involved either the Opposition's emphasis upon dividing power, in the name of an independent House of Commons, or the ministerial case for accepting a measure of "influence" as the necessary price of making government work. Williams spurned both positions, since neither gave any significant place to popular government. Thus he condemned all current explanations of British freedom as being derived from "romances," with errors progressively enshrined as Blackstone copied from Montesquieu and de Lolme from both.[20]

Writing in 1782, Williams still contemplated a "balance" of sorts as central to the constitution. Some of his phrases indicated the similarities of such a balance to the construction of machines: he wrote of "counteraction and resistance." However he also described the process of limited power in terms of muscles that balanced one another. Only in treating his favourite plan of participation in small units did he

---

19. *Letters on Political Liberty*, p. 64. For Williams's contribution to theories about a separation of powers see M. J. C. Vile, *Constitutionalism and the Separation of Powers* (Oxford: Clarendon Press, 1967), pp. 116–17.

20. *Letters on Political Liberty*, p. 11n.

confine himself exclusively to organic metaphor, explaining how in a state, as in an animal, the arrangements of parts, and not the size of the whole, determined whether the unit was capable of life. The fusion of two different models was not at all unusual; a division of labour between organic and mechanistic imagery has also been found in Burke's political vocabulary.[21] Williams was similarly confined by his desire to defend a variety of different propositions. Both the insistence that governments should be constructed on the basis of known principles and the further emphasis upon the axioms of geometry dictated a mechanistic rationalism, almost Hobbesian in tone. By contrast, Williams's displeasure with received interpretations of constitutional balance and his concern for relating organs of government to the body of the people lent themselves to a more biological form of discourse. It was this latter approach that increasingly gained prominence in his thought.

On the eve of the French Revolution, he published a series of lectures containing the most sustained analysis of Montesquieu's theories that had appeared in English up to that time. Previously Williams had endorsed a mechanical balance of political forces, always with the proviso that all powers were accountable to the people. Now he rejected the whole concept of balance as normally applied to government and referred condescendingly to the "mechanic ingenuity" displayed by Montesquieu. In fact, said Williams, no traces of the "balances, or measured powers of opposition," written of by Montesquieu, had ever been designed in English government. It might happen, Williams conceded, that inhabitants of a nation would benefit from the divisions among their rulers and so enjoy a temporary "suspension of cruelties." Such accidents, he noted acidly, might equally be called the "fundamental constitution of Peru." But Montesquieu not only erred in the "puerile and fantastical" account of the supposed constitutional balance; he was mistaken even in his account of how a machine operated. "The resisting or balanced parts of machines are to create, to accelerate, or perpetuate motion; not to produce inaction or repose."[22]

It was a comparable insight that led champions of influence to conclude that government was a fluid process of mutual accommodation, not a static balance of stalemated forces. In choosing to explore

21. See Love, "Edmund Burke's Idea,"
22. *Lectures on Political Principles*, p. 198.

a more radical alternative to the balanced constitution, Williams combined the Country complaint that constitutional theory was ignored in practice with the awareness, apparent in contemporary discussions of the influence of the Crown, that the organs of government could not function in complete isolation. Williams felt that these organs were rightly independent of each other but should meet in their dependence upon the will of the people. Since he deemed the legislative veto of the king and the House of Lords as outmoded, Williams was in effect asserting the supremacy of the House of Commons, indirectly elected on an adult-male franchise. His analysis paralleled the less radical claim of those politicians of the 1780s who stressed that it was the very pre-eminence of the House of Commons that accounted for the desire of all interests to gain influence there. The importance that Williams attached to relating all legitimate power to the people reduced the importance of his thoughts on a separation of powers. He continued to proclaim the value of an independent judiciary, with popular connection in the form of juries, but failed to indicate precisely how the executive was to be made accountable.

It seems that all traditional wisdom collapsed in the face of a politically active community: "while men are ignorant of any mode of forming the body of the community; to give it perpetual intelligence, will and force; the distribution or balance of legislative, executive and judiciary powers, may well constitute political science."[23] Montesquieu was not preceived as wrong in his comments about a separation of powers, but his formulation had, in Williams's words, "many of the inconveniences of falsehood." Montesquieu, for all his sensitivity to environmental factors, stood accused of abstracting government from its social context, when in fact, all powers had to be the result of "organization in the people" and attached to them as members to a body. Under such an arrangement, the organization of the people assumed enhanced importance, while Williams subordinated his thoughts on the nature of central organs to the overriding truth that they must respond to the community. "In the constitution of the human body, nature is as attentive to a capillary nerve, as to sinews and bones. By subdivisions sufficiently minute, the vote, the will, or the judgment of millions may be obtained; without interrupting the

23. Ibid., p. 206.

occupations of the people; inciting commotions; or hazarding the operations of government."[24]

Williams felt that in the absence of such a guiding image, political speculation would founder on the same errors that had afflicted the statesmen of the ancient world and Montesquieu. Both were guilty of failing to attain more than a mechanical understanding of government. Montesquieu could only describe the machinery of the state; he failed to account for its operation. The ancients, in their failure to develop representative institutions, were also blind to the need to form citizens into "animate bodies." Instead, they tried to arrange men in the same manner as one might order building materials, ignoring the difference between the principles applicable to animate and inanimate realms. A further item in this survey of political unwisdom was an incapacity to deal with change, as evidenced by Montesquieu's concern for avoiding the violation of constitutional forms. But, protested Williams, constitutions were never "stationary." The most direct statement of the general indictment was the judgment that "the idea of government, and that of society, should not be detached, even in speculation."[25]

Taken literally, the dictum proved too much. Admirable for purposes of emphasizing the need for links between government and people, the relationship between government and society was not intended as a blueprint for reforming all social relations. So Williams specifically noted that political equality, in the form of legal protection and of equal voting rights, did not imply "civil" equality. The most that could be expected was that inequalities in talents and property be not unjustly translated into legal privileges. An obvious target here was the accepted notion, sometimes associated with a speech by Lord Camden, that landed property—"blades of grass" and not persons—were represented in Parliament. Williams's attack on this remnant of feudalism showed him at his best, ending with the suggestion that all men should be represented by virtue of their having eaten cattle that had consumed the sacred grass![26] Then likening political arrangements to a horse race, Williams contented himself with urging an equal start in which "in all intercourses of the community with gov-

---

24. Ibid., p. 158.
25. Ibid., p. 146.
26. Ibid., p. 117. See too Williams, *Lectures on Education* (London, 1789), 2:263.

ernment, every citizen is equally a unit. . . ."[27] Coexisting with this
formal equality were the usual social inequalities, which would naturally have their effects on political life. The point was to avoid lending
such natural advantages any artificial support. Williams was then in
the uneasy situation of a political radical who had understood the
connection between government and broader social relations but remained unwilling to propose major changes in the social context. He
combined the optimism of a Godwin with an acceptance of some of
the gloomier concerns of political economy.

Williams's radical principles had their most influential statement in
1790. His *Lessons to a Young Prince* found acclaim in radical circles for
its renewed assault on the fictions of the balanced constitution. It
rapidly reached a sixth edition and was reprinted in New York in
1791. Amid the flood of invective that greeted Paine's *Rights of Man*,
Williams's work was cited as one of the more important statements of
the radical case.[28] In fact, he was even credited with being Paine's
source of inspiration for the notorious opinion that England had no
political constitution.[29] This Williams had been saying, with varying
degrees of candour, for nearly twenty years, but the tensions exac-
erbated by the French Revolution gave new significance to familiar
opinions. The specific comments on the theory of the constitution
were, if anything, more moderate than in earlier works. Williams
simply explained how unlikely an event it would be should the three
powers actually balance one another by "counter-action." The main
novelty in the *Lessons* was Williams's use of diagrams to illustrate the
differences between constitutional forms. He was rather proud of this
graphic mode of presentation, derived no doubt from his experience
as a teacher.

As always, the defects of English government prompted the use of
mechanical analogy. The factors normally credited with preserving
liberty were no more than "stays" and "steel collars." In the same vein,

27. *Lectures on Political Principles*, p. 65.
28. See Jerome Alley, *A Review of the Political Principles of the Modern Whigs. In a
Second Letter Addressed to the Right Honorable Lord Sheffield* (London, 1792), pp. 28n., 40.;
and [T. Gould], *A Vindication of the Right Honourable Edmund Burke's Reflections on the
Revolution in France* (London, 1791), pp. 7–10.
29. See Anon., *The Civil and Ecclesiastical Systems of England Defended and Fortified*
(London, 1791), pp. 6–7n.; and Anon., *A Defence of the Constitution of England against
the Libels that have been lately Published on it* (Dublin, 1791), pp. 5, 9.

the government was portrayed as a "machine acting on the people," when instead the whole society should be animated by attaching the extremities to the seat of government. Each part could then act like the "capillary vessels" in the body natural, both receiving and transmitting impressions.[30] Commenting on the situation of revolutionary France, Williams betrayed his fear that, lacking sufficient decentralization, this new order might come to exclude the people as completely as did English government. The suspicion would grow.

Organicism and a Fading Hope

The French Revolution brought to the fore aspects of Williams's thought previously left inconspicuous by his passion for reform. In 1792–93 he was an honoured visitor in Paris, but the execution of Louis XVI sent him back to England, permanently sobered, by the destructive side of radicalism.[31] Of course, Williams had always been unhappy about the imperfections of worldly activity and had already displayed an intellectual's aversion to the compromises that were so much a part of political life. He had favoured the side of Wilkes on the issue of the Middlesex election, but professed disregard for the man. Supporting the Americans against Lord North, he still reflected that opposition to the war came from factious politicians. A consistent friend of toleration, Williams quarrelled with the tactics of his fellow Dissenters.[32] Even his initial sympathy for the objects of Wyvill's county associations was severely tempered by the thought that the associators comprised no more than a thousandth part of the nation. Captain Morris, Williams's biographer, also credits him with convincing the associators of the futility of addressing petitions for parliamentary

30. [Williams], *Lessons to a Young Prince, by an Old Statesman*, 3rd ed. (London, 1790), p. 82.

31. Ms. autobiography, fol. 30.

32. Williams has normally been identified with English Dissent, even to the extent of interpreting his political writings as primarily intended to defend that group. See Boulton, *Language*, p. 196; and Anthony Lincoln, *Some Political and Social Ideas of English Dissent, 1763–1800* (Cambridge: Cambridge University Press, 1938), p. 66. In point of fact, the scope of the political writings not only went far beyond the interests of Dissenters, but in addition, Williams frequently dissociated himself from their political tactics. See [Williams], *Essays on Public Worship, Patriotism, and Projects of Reformation* (London, 1778), pp. 52–53; *Sermons, Chiefly upon Religious Hypocrisy* (London, 1774) 2:28; *A Letter to the Body of Protestant Dissenters ...* (London, 1777), pp. 3, 17.

reform to a corrupt House of Commons. Ever fearful of mobs,[33] Williams had always argued that popular participation must be orderly. Frequently he noted the presence of a general agreement that power somehow rested with the people. This had usually either issued in raising the masses "undisciplined and unarranged", as he put it, or it had been an empty claim used to mask despotism.[34] Small wonder then that the events in France left him disenchanted.

Before the Revolution, he had written that there was little point in introducing civil liberty into those states that lacked the constitutional arrangements to ensure political liberty. In the reaction that produced the sedition trials of the early 1790s, he apparently concluded that a precipitate move towards political liberty would be equally futile. Williams disliked both Burke's person and his principles, an antipathy that he continued to express as late as 1803. Nevertheless, his portrait of the dangers of rapid political change assumed a distinctly Burkean tone. How, he asked, could order be preserved if a great nation accustomed only to servility were suddenly set free? The resulting joy would require constitutional boundaries, if only to protect erstwhile oppressors. Indeed the whole enterprise demanded a blend of wisdom and integrity that left Williams awestruck with the responsibility. His example of such a premature and abrupt change was the situation of England after the Restoration—a curiously inapposite choice. Obviously his mind was on revolutionary France and its lessons for Britons of 1796. Burke himself might well have written the following.

To stigmatize or to demolish, is within the province of ordinary minds, or of brutal force; but to rescue nations from the ruins and miseries of ancient institutions; and to instruct them to adopt others, formed on different pricnples; requires talents and qualities, which vanity and presumption may readily assume, and which ambition or venality may exclusively affect; but which do not generally obtrude themselves among the contending factions of violent revolutions.[35]

---

33. The Gordon Riots, and later the threat of Napoleon, led Williams to recommend reviving the militia as the instrument of civil order. See *A Plan of Association on Constitutional Principles, for the Parishes, Tythings and Counties of Great Britain* ... (London, 1780); and *Regulations of the Parochial Police*, 4th ed. (London, 1803).

34. *Lectures on Political Principles*, pp. 95–96. See too [Williams], *Constitutional Doubts ... on the Pretensions of the Two Houses of Parliament, to Appoint a Third Estate* (London, 1789), p. 23.

35. Williams, *The History of Monmouthshire* (London, 1796), p. 317.

Was the cause of reform, then, lost? Williams thought not and stressed that men could ultimately be governed by their own reason. However, for the immediate future he advocated caution, recalling that a people wrenched abruptly from old ways might simply return to them disillusioned. This notion was at least as old as the Country propaganda in the reign of Anne, when pamphleteers had described the subtle oppression of "legal tyranny," a government made all the more onerous because its cruelties were masked by an adherence to forms. The only programme now offered was the advice directed to country gentlemen to quit the intrigues of "provincial politics" and to educate their tenants and neighbours in the ways of national improvement. It was thus not political organization but "economical and agricultural societies" that were to lay the foundations of freedom.[36] In this period it was not uncommon for writers to insist that energy was better spent in understanding the truths of political economy than in engaging in partisan political activity.[37] Always an admirer of Sir James Steuart, Adam Smith, and the physiocrats, Williams found in this cause an opportunity to press for social knowledge, no doubt with the added attraction that such activity was politically inoffensive.

In his most radical days Williams had always displayed a respect for custom and tradition. He had berated Montesquieu for his cavalier suggestion that the customs of some corrupt nations should be outlawed. Instead, Williams had argued, superstitions should be dispelled by growing enlightenment. To destroy them by fiat was to forbid an effect without touching the original cause. By 1803 Williams had become increasingly reconciled to the existence of bizarre customs, with no mention of when and how they might be replaced. Reformers were warned not to expect states to have identical properties, for even the "usages" of despotism were "natural and necessary," in the sense that they "hold the society together."[38] Beginning as an image for bridging space in the political order, Williams's organicism had now met with time—and history.

36. Ibid., pp. 359–60.
37. See Sir James Steuart, *An Inquiry into the Principles of Political Economy* (London, 1767), 1:xii; George Edwards, *The Political Interests of Great Britain* ... (London, 1801), pp. 16–17; and Hector Campbell, *The Impending Ruin of the British Empire* ... (London, 1813), pp. 33–34.
38. [Williams], *Egeria, or Elementary Studies on the Progress of Nations in Political Economy, Legislation and Government* (London, 1803), p. 7.

The sensitivity to historical and cultural factors normally associated with organicism pervaded the political writings of Williams's old age—his *Egeria* (1803) and the *Preparatory Studies* (1810). When once he had dismissed all existing governments as sadly flawed, he became more reconciled to British institutions, without benefit of any major improvements in the institutions. Previously he had urgently demanded the creation of a genuine body politic; now the ambition mellowed into the form of a law of social development. This law stated that polities began as irrational bodies in which government ruled by force over "mere multitudes." Ultimately, there would emerge a degree of public awareness sufficient to mould the previously "inorganic" masses into a coherent body politic.[39] Only in these late writings does it become clear that Williams was saying not only that societies should be looked upon as bodies but also that increasing sophistication actually made them more and more analgous to living, rather than to inert, materials. The key to the process of development was an understanding of the growth of a "public mind." To express this truth Williams pursued his organicism far beyond the allusions of his first efforts.

To say that the people had to be integrated into the body politic was an opinion requiring no more sophistication about organicism than had been present in the work of John of Salisbury in the twelfth century. The appropriate image for Williams's message was supplied by the work of Albrecht von Haller (1708–77), the first experimental physiologist. This name figures, however, only in the later writings, and Williams may well have first been influenced by the biological ideas of Charles Bonnet.[40] Haller had argued that some tissues and organs in the human body responded to stimuli only in the form of irritability, whereas others were capable of sensibility. This finding was expressed by Haller in the statement that the parts that were most irritable were least sensible.[41] Applying this to politics, Williams reached

---

39. Ibid., p. 57. In the hands of a later organicist, such as Albert Schäffle (d. 1903), this notion was linked to a focus on social functions and processes, but with a clear repudiation of the individual as a social unit.

40. For use of Bonnet on the "re-production of parts of animals" see [Williams], *An Apology for Professing the Religion of Nature in the Eighteenth Century of the Christian Era*, 4th ed. (London, 1789), pp. 123–24.

41. For Williams's use of Haller see *Egeria*, p. 58; and *Preparatory Studies for Political Reformers* (London, 1810), p. 172. Haller also influenced Herder's organicism, though in a different way. See "Ideas for a Philosophy of the History of Mankind," in F. M. Barnard, ed., *J. G. Herder on Social and Political Culture* (Cambridge: Cambridge Uni-

the conclusion that the primitive irritability of the mass had to be changed into a general sensibility. In 1803 Williams judged Britain to be the only nation in Europe in which the "public mind" really influenced the government.[42] America, spared the presence of the restless classes of the great towns of Europe, shared this privileged status. Still, there was need for improvement, so much so that in 1810 Williams estimated that Britain would not attain the desirable "state of communication" between brain and extremities for another forty years.[43]

The task before the reformer was to stimulate the emergence of a public mind, such that an animated public conveyed all relevant information to the central organs, or "sensorium."[44] Here Williams displayed a degree of uncertainty wholly absent in his earlier statements that he was already in a position to solve all political problems to his entire satisfaction. The early confidence had been based upon the notion that the power of the people need only be invoked in order to balance the arrogance of office. But the simple truths of geometry deserted him when he was faced with the problem of actually creating the necessary state of awareness. Under despotism the people had been treated as an "inert mass." Well aware that the English people were no longer inert, Williams was also conscious that there remained more irritability than sensibility in their responses. This complicated the work of peacefully reforming society. He had placed his faith once in the self-evidence of the claim that the whole people was greater than any part and that the whole should rule itself. Returning to this theme, Williams showed a new appreciation of the difference between politics and mathematics. "In mathematics, all the superfluous portions are thrown into an imagined infinite space; but in politics there is no vacuum; every atom, every person is a part of a mass or body of interested sensibility, and in modern times, every person is a pol-

---

versity Press, 1969), p. 259. It is worth noting that by the time Williams used Haller in his political theory, Haller's conclusions had been superseded in physiology. See Albrecht von Haller, *A Dissertation on the Sensible and Irritable Parts of Animals* (1755), introduction by Owsei Temkin (Baltimore: Johns Hopkins, 1936), p. 4.

42. *Egeria*, p. 313.

43. *Preparatory Studies*, p. 108.

44. This term had previously been current in England only in relation to the individual nervous system. See, for example, [H. Halkerston], *Considerations on Man, in his Natural as well as Moral State* (Edinburgh, 1764), p. 32.

itician."[45] Presumably this was meant to imply not that the sensibility of each citizen was perfect, but that all were more animated than in the past. Paradoxically, it was this very animation that convinced Williams of the need to accept reform as a slow and lengthy process of "instruction." Were modern society simply the unorganized matter that had been perceived by traditional despots, it might be levelled and reconstructed without damage. But it was complex: "it consists of bodies which are not only animated as individuals, but form aggregations which are also animated. ..."[46]

Just as he eschewed the weapon of revolution, Williams seems also to have questioned his previous attacks on the various enemies of social improvement. In the 1780s he had been perfectly aware that a reform of Parliament would not suffice to rid the nation of its political ills. However, he had been quite willing to pour invective on specific villains. As his analytical scheme became more complex, the difficulties of assigning personal responsibility increased. Adhering still to the opinion that government originally had corrupted the people and not the reverse, he became less and less capable of turning this observation to any good purpose. All the possible candidates for attack receded into a maze of social relations, so that he became loath to identify even broad groups within the population as chargeable with general calamities. Kings, priests, nobles and philosophers, parties, the bar and the universities—all had their faults, but they had to be viewed as "parts of a general system."[47]

This insight, of course, cut two ways. From one perspective, Williams was arguing that corruption was general, not localized. At the same time, just because it was so pervasive, the corruption was immune to those measures of constitutional change sought by reformers. For them to rail against corruption in the boroughs or in Parliament was to ignore the "connections and relations" existing among the various parts of the constitution. In fact, Williams went so far as to accept the claim, fashionable among creatures of the ministry, that buying places in the Commons had its advantages, since several of the most independent members had gained their seats by that route. The county associations had once called for a convention to reform institutions,

45. *Preparatory Studies*, p. 150. Cf. the facile optimism of *Letters on Political Liberty*, pp. 54–59.
46. *Preparatory Studies*, p. 203.
47. Ibid., p. 171.

for the plausible reason that a corrupt legislature would never reform itself. Williams improved on this notion, arguing that Parliament was only "a circle within a circle,"⁴⁸ a mere part of a "system, of vast extent and power." This was but a more sombre version of his early claim that governments were usually considered as causes when in fact they were but "effects."⁴⁹ Not only was it then futile to call upon Parliament to correct abuses; the same considerations applied to the society at large. The many beneficiaries of the system would not listen, and the common people lacked (as yet) the understanding to be other than violent. Trapped between the undeserved privileges of the higher orders and the dangerous frustration of the lower, Williams had largely deprived himself of any ground from which to bring leverage.

His disinclination to blame specific persons or groups was rooted in another strand of the organic theory. As the emphasis upon the designs of individuals was replaced by the notion of a system, the scope for conceiving of activity as conscious and intentional was greatly reduced:

In society, no man can be considered singly, but compounded, according to the laws of the political body to which he belongs. As every thing in animals is animalized; so in political bodies, men become component parts, are modified or assimilated to the society by its organic laws, and generally remain under their specific influence. The same man, solitary, and in society, may act by different specific laws.⁵⁰

Williams had long been impressed with the economic theories of Adam Smith and had absorbed the counter-intuitive doctrine of the invisible hand along with the rest of Smith's teaching. With Williams, the idea gained new amplitude. The action of political bodies, like the processes traced by Haller in the human body, was partially involuntary. In his elaboration of this thought, Williams emphasized that there were pro-

48. Ibid., p. 127.

49. *Lectures on the Universal Principles and Duties of Religion and Morality* (London, Paris, Berlin, and Hamburg, 1779), 1:170.

50. *Preparatory Studies*, p. 30. See, by contrast, the very funny broad satire, directed at George III. [Williams], *Royal Recollections on a Tour to Cheltenham, in the Year 1788* (London, 1788). Only two years later, Williams had become more a critic of the system and less concerned with individual failings, arguing that the interests of the corrupt financial system were so entwined with national prosperity that the business of attacking corruption had become a most delicate one. See *Lessons to a Young Prince*, p. 31.

cesses in society not yet clearly "understood or recognized" by the actors.[51] This was different from the observation that large parts of the English people were irritable rather than sensible organs, though the points were related. In denying that the springs of action in the body politic had been fully understood, Williams was recording a failure of understanding on the part of all men, not just of the unruly masses. The moral to be drawn from this confession of imperfect understanding was that the process of change could not readily be charted in advance.

Society had a structure, or as Williams put it, "a continuation of fundamental organisation," and through all changes, this organization persisted. Reformers intruded on the mysterious processes of change at their peril: "Every thing in nature, which undergoes transformation or reproduction, retains a primitive organisation, and all variations, whether for good or for evil, are in consequence of derivative circumstances or arrangements that may be called accidental."[52] It seemed that one could scarcely even plan for freedom—the initial object of Williams's political inquiries. For the events that had weakened the practice of entail in Europe, thus encouraging commerce and releasing classes from slavery, were the result of kings' wishing to break the power of the nobility. Only time and circumstances would bring all estates into the market and thus contribute to a diminution of those privileges that inhibited civil liberty. The example so impressed Williams that he ventured to suggest that "civil liberty is seldom or never the object of the circumstances that produce it."[53] This did not directly contradict his pre-revolutionary belief in constructing a constitution to protect liberty, because he had then been concerned with *political* liberty. Still, it marked a decline in optimism, since he had once poked fun at Montesquieu's complacent tendency to find unintended benefits arising from political evils.[54]

Public Opinion

Surviving throughout the rags and tatters of a reformer's spent enthusiasm was a form of organicism that looked beyond the *status quo*.

51. *Preparatory Studies*, p. 84.
52. Ibid., p. 132.
53. Ibid., p. 97.
54. See *Lectures on Political Principles*, pp. 51–52.

No British writer of the time seems to have thought as much as Williams did about the nature of public opinion and the organization appropriate to expressing it. He began to write of it, after the fashion of the time, as "the public opinion."[55]

Early thoughts on opinion emphasize how it would come to form human character once it was embodied in habits and customs. New opinions, when "formed and fixed" would cease to be effects of the political order but would themselves become causes "and use the constitution which occasioned them as their instrument."[56] In another work of the same year Williams took pains to argue that the social organization of opinion was still a neglected subject. Opinion was the bond holding together "all associations, all clubs, and all parties," for thoughts were "joyless things" unless they could be shared and avowed. But, said Williams, the political potential of this insight remained uncultivated. The first politician to grasp the power of opinion, and especially the unrealized influence of "those who never assemble and never avow any opinions," would change the tenor of public life.[57] Complementing this recognition of the potency of organization was his distress at the manner in which the claims of existing institutions were impressed upon the minds of citizens. Ignorance and hypocrisy joined in the work, for "men have not only false ideas and false consciences given them, but they are also taught to wear masques. ..."[58] This blend of political radicalism and the Nonconformist's suspicion of authority would find no more powerful statement until the publication of Godwin's *Political Justice*.

By 1789 Williams and others had come to refer to the phenomenon without the definite article, and "public opinion" was firmly established in the language. In 1789 Williams explained what he meant by the expression:

A political state is an artificial body; constructed on principles similar to those of the natural. The conduct, or morality of individuals, rests immediately on sensibility to pleasure and pain; and on reflection or judgment, concerning the circumstances which occasion them. The conduct or morality of societies,

55. See *The Philosopher*, p. 43. For the early history of the expression see below, chap. 7.
56. Williams, *The Nature and Extent of Intellectual Liberty* (London, 1779), p. 17.
57. *Lectures ... Religion and Morality*, 1:iv–v.
58. Ibid., 1:207.

rests on sensibility of a similar nature; but hitherto imperfectly formed: and on reflection and judgment in the whole society called public opinion, concerning the causes of its happiness or misery.[59]

There is some truth in the suggestion that developments in the meaning of public opinion were reflected in a great increase in the use of the expression.[60] Public opinion and the weight to be attached to it had been important in the election of 1784, and the voice of the people gained significant recognition in Fox's Libel Act of 1792.

The most sophisticated applications of organicism were directed at explaining how public opinion arose, and these came late in the day when hopes of reform were much abated. "Social communication" existed to some degree in all societies but varied enormously in sophistication. In the early stages of political development the system culminated, at best, in some form of balance among several competing interests. On various occasions Williams suggested that some element of balance would always be necessary in a just social order. However, he also insisted that the ideal state of affairs saw the emergence of a common feeling of "sympathy" within a society, a condition in which there was a genuine community sentiment that served as a "connecting principle." Williams was explicit that this feeling was not the same as Adam Smith's principle of sympathy as expounded in *The Theory of Moral Sentiments*.[61] The latter explained relations between individuals; though to the extent that Smith was writing of the growth of a socialized conscience, one is inclined to object that there was some connection. The difference was primarily one of levels of analysis. Smith had explained how individuals participated in the feelings of their fellows and came to regard social norms as a mirror in which they

---

59. *Lectures on Political Principles*, p. 25. In another book of 1789 Williams professed contempt for the prevailing judgements "of what is denominated public opinion." *Lectures on Education* 3:261. Taken together, the two statements clearly depict his aspirations for the public and his frustration at its unenlightened performance.

60. See P. A. Palmer, "The Concept of Public Opinion in Political Theory," in Carl Wittke, ed., *Essays in History and Political Theory in Honor of Charles Howard McIlwain* (Cambridge, Mass.: Harvard University Press, 1936), p. 236n. Palmer's article, which is still often cited, has contributed to perpetuating several misconceptions about the early history of the concept—specifically, Bentham's alleged novelty in writing of it in 1789 and the supposed primacy of French writings on the subject. See below, chap. 7, n. 24.

61. *Preparatory Studies*, p. 119.

might scrutinize their own conduct and by which their faculties were developed. Williams said little about the individual actor, stressing instead the formation of channels of communication between the people and their government.

In a specific application, Williams contemplated the day when Members of Parliament could be trusted to act in such a manner as they supposed their constituents would act, given the same opportunities for gaining an informed opinion. This he contrasted with the more primitive ambition of instructing members so that they acted as "machines." In another simile, Williams likened the elections in representative government to the operation of "lymphatic vessels," aiding the circulation of the blood by separating matter that could be assimilated from that which was injurious. Just as knowledge of these vessels assisted the circulatory system, so an understanding of how to attain the constant circulation of knowledge and feeling would perfect the representative system.

A major problem with such an inelegant parallel was, of course, that the physical mechanisms for sustaining the purity of the blood did not have to be created, only understood. The development of the public mind entailed activity, perhaps even conscious planning, as well as enhanced understanding. Williams undoubtedly perceived the difference, but such imperfect analogies clouded the message. Again, the claims of science and of reform were joined in his thought, but uneasily: "The channels of social feeling are not yet completely discovered. Human anatomy exhibits the human nerves. Political anatomy has not developed the nerves, by which human feelings and imaginations produce a sentiment and opinion in a whole nation."[62] By 1810, the time of writing, the process of scientific discovery seems to have held more fascination for Williams than did the prospect of substantial improvement. Not that he had disavowed his commitment to reform, but in keeping with the political detachment that increasingly characterized his work, the later writings show him grappling with the abstract dimensions of the problem, scarcely deigning to mention the practical business of changing the electoral system. Thus his discussion of a circulation of knowledge and feeling, a special instance of "vortices" in the moral world, dwells more on the general

62. Ibid., p. 116.

properties of what would now be called "feedback mechanisms" than on the narrowly practical problem of revamping institutions.

Williams was fascinated by the possibility that there were various time-constants appropriate for various social and political activities; for the presence of annual, monthly, weekly, and daily cycles would give substance to the notion that society was indeed, in some sense, corporeal: "Political, like physical bodies, appear to be susceptible of periods or circles in idea and action. ..."[63] The same general interest has been attributed to Williams's contemporaries, the authors of *The Federalist Papers*, with the significant difference that they may be viewed as trying to build certain timed responses into political machinery.[64] Williams, by contrast, was concerned in part with demonstrating the presence of a pattern already developing in society.

One measure for developing a political nervous system was the press—an institution described implausibly as "the stomach of the constitution." In fact, Williams saw it, with all its faults, as quite the best instrument of public information. He took particular comfort from its presence in the gallery of Parliament, for it was "one of the strongest lodgments of liberty in the fortress of power." His consistently low regard for the parliamentary Opposition can only have raised the press in his esteem. Perhaps the most direct impact conceived for an enlightened press lay in its influence on the Cabinet. The press also had a long-term function in instructing the public, but here Williams cherished only a modest ambition:

Society is gradually fashioned by institutions, laws, and manners, to an artificial character, good or evil, which cannot be easily or speedily changed; and that change to be effectual and salutory, must be produced by those general agents which not only stimulate to activity and exertion, but, as aliments, furnish new matter, communicate information, and furnish the principles of moral existence.[65]

Since this vehicle of enlightenment would work only slowly, the first priority was to encourage "men of genius" to strive towards raising its tone. One possible way was to remove all remaining restraints on the freedom of the press, for Williams argued ingeniously that pros-

63. *Egeria*, p. 28.
64. See J. R. Platt, *The Step to Man* (New York: Wiley, 1966), p. 114.
65. *Preparatory Studies*, p. 168.

ecution of journalists only served to drive timid scholars out of the medium, leaving it to professional libellers. However, writing early in the nineteenth century, Williams was led by his disrespect for an irresponsible press even to suggest that the ministry should silence its carping critics.[66]

Since Williams was both student and practitioner of education, one might have expected him to place more emphasis upon the means of instructing the public about its political duties. Curiously enough, his educational theories gave comparatively little support to schemes for immediate reform, and this for several reasons. From his investigations of the learning process, Williams became convinced that the fixed predispositions of adults prevented their readily being given new opinions. Thus he frequently assured his audiences in public lectures that any effect he might have upon their opinions would probably only be apparent in their children. Modes of education still assumed great importance, for the correct procedures might ensure that the next generation would be appropriately responsive to the dictates of reason. It is also worth observing that when Williams discussed plans for improving the instruction of the young, he saw fit to dwell on such topics as the relative merits of teaching by parents or by private tutors, and the dangers of leaving children to the company of servants. Implicit throughout was the assumption that the chief beneficiaries of new pedagogical technique would be the children of the privileged orders. There were no specific references to the classes to be educated, but significantly absent was any endorsement of universal education. The political writings sufficiently establish that Williams was hostile to a uniform system of state education, owing to its tendency to impose opinions favourable to the régime.[67]

The measure in which Williams's educational theories actually inhibited the quest for reform may be seen from a lecture of the late 1780s, "Private Attempts to Reform Public Customs." Here he argued

66. "On the Press" (c. 1803), BL, Add. Ms. 33,124, fols. 78–81. References to the *Egeria* as a current undertaking serve both to date the Ms. and to establish Williams as the author.

67. Thus he was extremely critical of Montesquieu's dictum that systems of education be appropriate to prevailing principles of government. See *Lectures on Political Principles*, pp. 38–46. Williams's theories of education are briefly summarized in Nicholas Hans, *New Trends in Education in the Eighteenth Century* (London: Routledge and Kegan Paul, 1951), pp. 163–64.

that premature attempts to change opinions and habits might actually worsen the condition of society. Those reformers who sought immediate acclaim for systems of abstract principles were thus doomed to abject failure.[68] Before the political universe was shaken by the French Revolution, Williams had thus already come to terms with the inertia of societies. The pessimism displayed in his educational theories was readily transferable to all projects of reform, for the principles on which it was based had already been stated. Indeed, it was in these very educational writings that Williams said that "tyrants and imposters" would vanish if the people but realized their own power. The sober realization that the people would learn slowly provided the foundation for all the subsequent comments about the difficulties of procuring a sound public mind from the passions, ignorance, and bad habits of the multitiude. Reform could proceed only from the growth of "acquired habits." In the absence of these habits, he could only counsel "homages to the prejudices and inconsistencies almost unavoidable in the present condition of society." Long exclusion had "alienated" the people from public business; their ignorance of issues and contempt for politicians dictated great caution in appealing for popular support.[69]

Williams's treatment of public opinion showed it to be the force for lasting reform, tardy and perverse as that force might be. His thoughts on the subject were a decided advance on the unhelpful suggestion of numerous writers from Sir William Temple to Hume that all governments were founded on opinion. In accord with his insight that all régimes claimed a popular mandate, Williams showed conclusively that some governments depended more upon active communication of opinion than did others. It might well be true, as Hume said, that opinion was a necessary support to any system. But, in fact, there was a vast difference between the régime that had a free press and an increasingly literate public and one lacking either. Unsuccessful in discovering existing social equivalents of the human nervous system, Williams nevertheless made clear that there were already traces of such nerves of government. His speculations dated both the autocratic assumption that public sentiment was irrelevant and the populistic misconception that there was a ready-made public will awaiting rec-

68. *Lectures on Education*, vol. 1, lecture 6.
69. *Preparatory Studies*, pp. 145, 140.

ognition. Probably his writings did little to popularize notions about public opinion, but it is just as clear that he was one of the very first to contemplate the subject. By the early nineteenth century, consideration of public opinion and the role of the press had become familiar topics in works on British government, but these had little to add to what Williams had already said, albeit in his own somewhat obscure way.[70]

Organicism Reassessed

Every scheme of political philosophy must, sooner or later, explain what considerations make its conclusions plausible and attractive. David Williams chose to defend his preferences by an appeal to nature, and specifically the structure and growth of living things. The organic analogy first supplied the standard for diagnosing political evils and prescribing a cure. The desirable condition of the body politic changed little over forty years; in 1810 Williams still looked to the day when the tithings and hundreds would realize their potential and come to act like "animal glands," transmitting impressions to the brain. The same organicism that condemned the old order served to express the optimistic judgement that society was indeed capable of improvement and would in fact improve. None of the inhibitions of climate, territorial area, topography, religion, or manners necessarily consigned any people to permanent subjection, and so the early writings stressed the untruth of Montesquieu's correlations between environment and political forms. Having made a case for the possibility of political improvement, Williams spent the rest of his active life discouraging those who pursued it too hastily.

Organicism and an awareness of social complexity had already been united in Williams's most radical writings. Following the Revolution, he emphasized both, for such concerns were better suited to the mood of a subdued reformer than to the cause of immediate and radical change. Paradoxically, as the organic analogy gained in prominence, its heuristic clarity receded. In the 1780s Williams had been confidently in possession of a truth; by 1803 he was quite prepared to

70. For an example of this theme in the period see the treatment of James Mill in Robert D. Cumming, *Human Nature and History* (Chicago and London: University of Chicago Press, 1969), 2:255–57.

admit that analogies might be misused and that language often failed to convey the complex ideas of "political science." To these arguments he added the somewhat plaintive plea that discoveries in politics would certainly be made by seizing analogies, for even a refuted hypothesis would contribute to the store of knowledge.[71] Seven years later, Williams remained insistent that societies bore "strict analogies" to natural bodies. However, the ideal of a "political theory on scientific principles" was still frustrated by the complexity and diversity of the world. Of particular interest is his description of the emergence of the ultimate political good of "national happiness." It ensued from the "conformity of governments to the natural principles of the aggregation of societies."[72] Williams identified the relevant social aggregates as "domestic, social and political"; and elsewhere he had considered the possible causal relations between levels of social organization—specifically family structure and political system.[73] However, he reached no clear conclusions about the pattern of reciprocal influences.

A more famous contemporary shared Williams's uncertainty about the laws governing human groups. When Burke denied the relevance of analogies, drawn by unidentified opponents, between nature and society, he made several points that were also allowed by Williams.[74] The latter would have agreed that polities were "moral," not physical, entities and that the state was, in some sense, the "artificial" creation of human beings. Paradoxical as it may seem, biological categories have generally been used to emphasize mental and moral causes, rather than physical ones. Williams could also have endorsed Burke's comments on the difficulty of understanding social and political change. Burke's repudiation of inquiry based on organic analogy was coupled with selective use of such images, chiefly in dealing with the past. By

71. *Egeria*, pp. 76–77.

72. *Preparatory Studies*, pp. 255–56. An identical notion was expressed by the young Comte in an essay published in 1822. Indeed, the resemblances between Williams's writings and those of Comte are remarkable, extending from an insistence that government always be examined in the context of society to an interest in the physiology of irritability. Both writers also combined an emphasis upon "organic" growth with the ambition of constructing a science of politics; both severely criticized Montesquieu, and for similar reasons. See Auguste Comte, *Early Essays on Social Philosophy*, trans. Henry Dix Hutton (London: G. Routledge and Sons, 1911), esp. pp. 150, 299, 347, 174–76.

73. See *Lectures on Political Principles*, p. 271; and *Lectures on Education*, 2:85–86.

74. "Letters on a Regicide Peace I," in *The Works of the Right Honourable Edmund Burke*, ed. F. Lawrence and W. King (London, 1803–27), 8:78–79.

contrast, Williams pressed the analogy in treating future states of society and, in general, used it more consistently. Was he also correct, or just true to his misconceptions? Certainly Bentham—a thinker of undoubted stature—endorsed a passion for analogy and pursued it in the same direction. Bentham's use of biological language differed chiefly in that it was confined to describing pathological conditions.[75] This Williams also did, as when he likened corruption to an infection or appealed to epidemiology to halt the spread of Jacobinism; but usually organicism described desirable states of affairs.

An adequate assessment of Williams's organicism must record the defects normally attributed to the approach. It is no doubt true that organic analogies have tended to block avenues of inquiry,[76] but this is especially true of organicism intended to overawe those who investigate society in order to change it. Williams identified such obfuscation with tyranny. Admittedly, organicism has often been pretentious and misleading, even when directed by a genuine desire to understand social relations. However, judged by the political theory and the dominant concerns of his time, Williams appears to have been both an innovator and a perceptive student of society. He took up the biological idiom long before it became fashionable; so much so, that reviewers of his last work found the vocabulary of thirty years' standing bizarre and incomprehensible.[77] More important, he used his lonely inspiration to good purpose. For despite the growing opacity of his writing—a failing shared with Bentham—Williams identified major errors in traditional assumptions and offered significant improve-

75. Examples, mostly dating from a period too late to have influenced Williams, are cited in Mary Peter Mack, ed., *A Bentham Reader* (New York: Pegasus, 1969), pp. xxv–xxvi. For another example of commitment to organic analogy for describing society as "an organized system" see Robert Young, *Gnomia; or the Science of Society* (London, 1801), 4:131–35. If Young had learned from Williams, he did not acknowledge the fact.

76. See Kenneth E. Bock, *The Acceptance of Histories: Towards a Perspective for Social Science* (Berkeley and Los Angeles: University of California Press, 1956), pp. 113–15.

77. See the review of twenty-three pages in *Critical Review*, 3rd series, 20 (May 1810):1–23, and especially the puzzlement expressed at what the reviewer called "medical" analogies. A similar impatience with organicism is apparent in the reception accorded to an English translation of Herder. See *Anti-Jacobin Review*, 18 (1804):411, and 19 (1804):83. The *Anti-Jacobin* was notoriously hostile to German literature in general, not just to organic analogies. See V. Stockley, *German Literature as Known in England, 1750–1830* (London: G. Routledge and Sons, 1929), p. 130.

ments. Not only did he lead the way in discrediting a thoroughly inadequate understanding of British government; he also provided a case against revolution that rivalled those of the most committed defenders of the balanced constitution. In broadening the field of political inquiry to social relations, and especially by including the factors that moulded public opinion, he was again relevant in his interests and unfailingly suggestive in his comments.

A major aspect of organic social imagery has been its great attraction for those who wish to explain social development. Alleged parallels between the blood stream and the circulation of wealth, or between the human nervous system and social communication, are certainly seen to best advantage when contrasted with the static machinery of eighteenth-century alternatives. Williams's most trenchant criticism of Montesquieu was that he had distinguished between the structure of government and its principle, thereby making political constitutions subject to an "indefinable spirit." The insertion of "abstract ideas or souls" into governments thus left reformers impotent. Here, anticipating Comte, Williams called the exercise "metaphysical." To counter such conservative mystification, Williams emphasized the potential for growth inherent in all systems: "It is owing to ignorance of the nature of society, men affirm of *any* people, they are incapable of liberty, or incapable of being happy."[78] Subsequent writings did not repudiate this judgement. Williams just came to emphasize factors, chiefly the pressure of excess population and attendant evils, that conspired to perpetuate tyranny. Normally he had qualified or rejected Montesquieu's claims for environmental factors that might appear to condemn a people to permanent subjection. Of course, Williams consistently objected to any explanation that assigned causal primacy to formal government, abstracted from its social setting. In addition, he sometimes emphasized environmental constraints neglected by Montesquieu. This was certainly true with respect to population. In *The Spirit of the Laws* Montesquieu pictured despotic government as depleting population; Williams reversed the direction of influence and noted how the institutions of despotism were secured by over-population

78. *Lectures on Political Principles*, pp. 25–35.

and the resulting poverty.[79] Just as the potential for freedom rested in the body of the people, so the condition of that body determined the rate of improvement for any society. In spite of the harsh logic of political economy, Williams continued to affirm his faith in the dictum that "human society is in a progressive state." He contemplated a long road for society, arguing once that being reconciled to the existing order was comparable to having to breathe air that was three-quarters impure. The two were equally unpalatable and equally necessary.

Modern scholarship has identified two major categories of organic social theory: the positive and the normative.[80] Williams belonged, in a sense, to both. For if his attempt to found a science of society raised important analytical questions, that science was intended only as the handmaiden of a normative quest. He argued that parallels between human bodies and bodies politic were reflections of a uniform scheme of nature. At the same time, he strove towards a level of political development in which society would come increasingly to resemble organic animation, with sensibility replacing the primitive irritability of less perfect societies. Normative organicism has often been seen as sharing all the errors of the positive school and turning its relatively innocuous misconceptions into moral evils. Organicism need not entail the assumption that the state enjoys moral pre-eminence over individuals, but undoubtedly the metaphor has proven attractive to political philosophers given to holism and philosophical realism.[81]

No such charges can be sustained against Williams, who, for all his commitment to organic categories, was a conventional economic individualist and nominalist. In this vein, he complained that it was

79. The most pessimistic comments on the adverse political effects of rapid population growth appear in *Egeria*, pp. 36–42. Sir James Steuart and Benjamin Franklin were the sources of inspiration here, and one reviewer recognized that Williams had been unfamiliar with the contemporary writings of Malthus. See *Critical Review*, 3rd series, 6 (Sept. 1805):65. Williams's familiarity with Steuart's economic theories dated back to the 1780s, and in 1789 Williams announced a series of lectures on the subject.

80. See Werner Stark, *The Fundamental Forms of Social Thought* (London: Routledge and Kegan Paul, 1962), p. 17.

81. For an exoneration of some versions of organicism see F. M. Barnard, "Metaphors, Laments and the Organic Community," *Canadian Journal of Economics and Political Science* 32 (1966):297. The more familiar, and sinister, tendencies of organicism are summarized in Stark, *Fundamental Forms*, chap. 1.

wrong when "the happiness of society is sacrificed to the security of institutions and systems." The welfare of society meant always that of private persons; so, while he condemned states lacking all public spirit, he also insisted that a system with public spirit as the sole determinant of action would be overheated. From Steuart and Smith, Williams had learned that self-interest feeds the world; apparently he never forgot it. His identification of a developed public mind with the common good was quite compatible with this individualism. The public mind was simply a state of general awareness, reflected in the activities of individual citizens. It would knit the interests of government and people through sympathy and not through the mechanical and external instrument of fear, which Williams associated with despotism. Never was will or personality assigned to the system. Even the *Preparatory Studies*—the work most strongly influenced by organicism—reflects Williams's suspicion of demands for self-sacrifice: "The public good, whenever it is really procured, is the result of the combination of all private interests."[82] Such a doctrine provided no basis for elevating the state; the point was rather to bring it down into the local communities, making public business familiar to the people. The German organic school culminated in Adam Müller's admiration for warfare; Williams cultivated instead the gentle virtues of liberal internationalism, praised free trade, and observed that the body politic would thrive on peace. The state gained no stature even as teacher of citizens or the guardian of culture, for Williams chose instead to stress the educational duties of parents. The admirer of dissenting academics would never have joined Schleiermacher in calling for state education.

Armed with the psychology of classical economics, Williams had ventured into a larger world of social relations. A healthy system was sustained by the purposes of individuals, its movement nourished by a universal human desire for happiness. The march of social organization towards perfection required no vitalistic principle; it was rendered unmysterious by universal human needs, informed by emerging science. Thus, while some organicists relied upon instinct to link individuals to society, Williams perceived social integration as a function of the growth of individual reason. In the light of his nominalism and individualism, Williams had a surprising amount to say about society

---

82. *Preparatory Studies*, p. 29.

and little of consequence about individuals. He adhered, for instance, to a wholly conventional version of associationist psychology and described himself, in this respect, as a follower of David Hartley.[83] His original insights were all about social relations and the form of society. However, he avoided the dangers of holism by retaining, unchanged, the individualistic values with which he had begun.

If Williams avoided hypostatizing social relations into a super-person, he also refused to defend those social groups admired by nostalgic romantics. The first nineteenth-century wave of organicism was friendly to hierarchy and feudal privilege. But these concerns were alien to a writer who proclaimed the irrelevance of titled nobility and saw the free circulation of estates as essential for lasting freedom. In fact, the traditional applications of anatomical language were singularly inappropriate for what Williams wished to say about politics. To list the various organs of the state with their functions was helpful chiefly if one wished to discuss the various gradations of worth in a highly stratified society. Normally it had supported an argument for the claims of the regal head. This ancient analogy was revived, especially in the France of the 1790s, and appears to have formed the slender basis of Antoine de Rivarol's *Théorie du corps politique*, sometimes hailed as an imaginative application of biology to politics.[84] Rivarol may well have acquired his ideas during a stay in London in 1793, but Williams can hardly have been his inspiration. Among contemporary French writers on government, only Jean-Louis Seconds seems to have approached Williams's use of organic images to express the processes of political communication, and the echo—if echo it was—sounded only faintly.[85]

Williams seems to have written in the traditional vein only once, when he compared the different "offices" of those parts of body (nails, hair) lacking sensibility with those more vital organs that possessed it. The passage in question is one of the less effective conceits in his work, since he suggested that the failing of an immature polity lay in the absence of functional specialization in its parts.[86] Such a position

---

83. *Nature and Extent of Intellectual Liberty*, p. 18n.

84. Fernard Baldensperger, *Le Movement des idées dans l'emigration française* (Paris: Plon-Nourrit et cie, 1925), 2:134.

85. Seconds, *De l'Art social ou des vrais principes de la société politique*, 2nd bk. (Paris, 1793), pp. 69, 87–88.

86. *Preparatory Studies*, pp. 117–18.

would serve Herbert Spencer well, but it failed to convey Williams's main concern, which was to justify and procure a greater homogeneity in understanding and sentiment within the nation. This required decentralization, but not differential privileges and functions, for even his original emphasis upon a separation of powers had been in the context of subjecting all government activity to the scrutiny of an attentive public. The only important political organs were then the body (people) and the brain (government); the important processes were forms of communication between the two. Biological imagery, applied to social structure, readily lends itself to the conservative injunction to leave things alone. By emphasizing processes, Williams was able to pay some regard to the organization of change.

It is a commonplace of intellectual history that the French Revolution was a watershed: for a host of sensitive minds it signalled a loss of innocence. In the case of David Williams, his loss of innocence took the form of a growing appreciation of the complexity of political change. He never embraced reaction, but undeniably he came more and more to sympathize with the views normally associated with social organicism. Both his values and his social analysis placed him in the vanguard of the political thought of the time. A moderate democrat before Bentham's conversion to that position, Williams was also already sensitized to social complexity before Burke raised the insight into dogma. Williams combined hostility to much that was superficial in the conventional wisdom of the eighteenth century with an ambition that would grow more familiar as the nineteenth century progressed: "It is probable, though that probability appears generally in hope, that science may in time combine the various powers and interests of individuals with the simple and regular laws of arrangement and organization, and submit these laws to calculations. This would produce a political theory on scientific principles. ..."[87]

87. Ibid., p. 257.

VI

A Measure of Liberty

WHEN ENGLISHMEN of the early and middle years of the eighteenth century wrote of their political arrangements, they displayed an apparent unanimity about certain cardinal virtues of the system. Judgements about the administration of the day would naturally differ, and there remained competing accounts of the history both of events and of institutions. But even as the Opposition predicted the imminent demise of liberty, to be greeted by ministerial reports of its robust good health, it was generally accepted that there was liberty to lose. Comforting comparisons with the plight of less fortunate nations— the Turks, the French, or the Danes—expressed a deep-seated satisfaction not readily shaken by partisan wranglings.

Despite this near consensus among the politically articulate, the idea of liberty was not thereby thrust into the background; far from it. Its very centrality as the basic shared assumption meant that a remarkably large proportion of political argument consisted in specifying how liberty might be lost and affirming how it might best be preserved. It was a time when there were few overt disagreements about the desirability of the existing institutions and hardly more regarding most matters of policy, apart from issues of war and peace. This meant that the question of the safety of Britain's peculiar advantages had few competitors. The currency of highly personal jibes at politicians who had offended by the manner in which they took office or resigned attests to the paucity of real issues in the era of the Whig supremacy. Little wonder that orators and journalists found drama and urgency in what was potentially the most compelling issue of all—the future of liberty.

That Englishmen were in some sense free had not been a discovery of the Hanoverian period. One need only consult the writings of

William Prynne, steeped in the precedents of the law, to encounter an elaborate recital of those particular benefits and immunities that formed the tissues of feudal society. Ancient rights, privileges, and franchises had been Prynne's stock-in-trade and that of other polemicists of the seventeenth century. His contemporary John Lilburne was neither as learned nor as tiresome, but he too left an ample record of specific liberties constituting due process of law.[1] Such claims and others found their way into Henry Care's very popular compendium of the 1680s, entitled *English Liberties or the Freeborn Subject's Inheritance*. With the proper relations among the branches of the legislature in dispute until at least 1688, it was a simpler matter to invoke particular liberties than it was to relate them to the overall pattern of government.

It is understandable, then, that the emphasis given to English liberty varied with the occasion. When the status of juries was crucial in the 1670s, as it would be again a century later, the liberty of Englishmen was seen to turn upon this "first-born" of freedoms, as Sir John Hawles once called it. A different account of priorities came to the fore when the charters of municipal corporations were challenged, as by Charles II, though fear muted contemporary comment. Sometimes the symbol of Magna Carta sufficed to plead a case, as when William Penn and William Mead fell afoul of authority in 1670: "First, It asserts *Englishmen* to be free; that's Liberty. Secondly, That they have Free-holds, that's Property."[2] Since Magna Carta was generally taken to be a confirmation of liberties already existing in the thirteenth century, Penn's statement said nothing in particular about the political institutions of his own day. Nor was it a theme that was necessarily denied to the defenders of authority. Even John Nalson, High-Church Tory of the 1680s, gave a positive turn to the claims of "liberty and property" in some of his writings, for who would do otherwise?

---

1. Characteristic examples of their arguments are: Prynne, *A Legall Vindication of the Liberties of England, Against Illegal Taxes* ... (London, 1649); and Lilburne, *The Legal Fundamental Liberties of the People of England Revived, Asserted and Vindicated*, 2nd ed. (London, 1649), p. 5.
2. *The Peoples Ancient and Just Liberties Asserted in the Tryal of William Penn and William Mead* (London, 1670), p. 50.

Liberty's Palladium?

The most general formula for capturing the nature of English liberty seems to have been the creation of Abraham Cowley, now best remembered as a representative of the seventeenth-century Epicurean revival. "The Liberty of a people consists in being govern'd by laws which they have made themselves, under whatsoever form it be of government."[3] Unclear in its expectations about how a people were to contribute to the making of laws under any form of government, Cowley's dictum thus introduced two different dimensions of liberty—the freedom of individuals and the processes of the state—without elaborating upon the crucial connections between the two. Indeed, the disclaimer at the end seemed to vitiate the initial assumption that the people could, in fact, fashion their own laws. Nevertheless, Cowley's opaque aphorism continued to have admirers after the Revolution,[4] especially when Richard Steele, in *The Crisis* (1714), fitted it out for the Hanoverian era with a reference to "consent." Locke was undoubtedly a greater political authority, but his works did not supply, it seems, a comparably serviceable statement.

In order to make sense of their political situation, the Augustans were not really in need of a very precise definition of liberty, which was just as well, since they did not have one. Rather, what was needed was some ranking of the elements of the political scene in order to understand the factors that underlay the nation's happiness. Not surprisingly, it was widely held that the familiar balanced constitution was somehow connected with liberty. Power had to be checked by some other power, or freedom would perish. The general idea allowed for almost endless variations and was not immune to very confused treatment. However, in the eighty years following the Glorious Revolution it was not often denied, especially after the first generation of Jacobites had passed from the scene. Writing in 1705, Defoe couched the notion of balance in Roman dress and visualized it as requiring a rough equality of power and property between the nobles and the

---

3. "Several Discourses by Way of Essays in Verse and Prose" (c. 1668), in A. B. Grosart, ed., *Complete Works in Verse and Prose of Abraham Cowley* (London, 1881), 2:311.

4. L. L. D. J., *Animadversions on a late Factious Book, Entitled Essays upon I The Ballance of Power* ... (London, 1701), p. 3; Anon., *The Present State of Liberty in Great Britain* (London, 1715), p. 9.

commons.[5] After mid-century, those who had read their Montesquieu were more apt to refer to a separation of powers; and soon the claims of party were granted a place in this scheme. In any event, liberty was thereby linked to the relations among the branches of the legislature.

But this was only to say that liberty was a product of the constitution; human ingenuity combined with the vagaries of political struggle could find much more than that to say about the conditions that preserved liberty. For one thing, the alleged balance was a condition too general and, despite the misleadingly simple mechanical metaphor, too abstract to serve as a test for liberty. One had to inquire about the conditions that, in turn, sustained the balance. In addition, the general framework of government was no sooner settled when alarms began to be heard lest a superficial concern for forms might prove illusory. This too contributed to a quest for those conditions that underlay the formal constitution and so laid all manner of political and social processes open for scrutiny. Opposition politicians, ever prone to envisage imminent tyranny, were a powerful spur to increasingly subtle probing of the mechanisms of politics. The liberty of Britons as experienced after 1688 was the subject of both moral exhortation and conceptual refinement, but above all it invited careful analysis of causes. The result, if something less than science, was more than rhetoric.

In order to refer succinctly to the conditions that sustained liberty, the writers on politics often had recourse to the language of classical antiquity. The wooden statue of the goddess Pallas had embodied the security of Troy and had fallen prey to the beseigers, with what result every schoolboy knew. The British palladium had thus to be cherished in the name of national survival. The notion was formulated in diverse ways. In some versions, the palladium seems to have been taken to be liberty itself, and its mode of defence was to be provided somehow by cultivating the intellects of young nobility and gentry.[6] To suggest another extreme, Bolingbroke was once described as Britain's palladium, no doubt with an ironical intent. More familiar though, was the claim that there was a palladium of liberty or of the system of government, a position that broached the essential question.

5. [Defoe], *The Ballance: or, a New Test of the High-Fliers of all Sides* (London, 1705), pp. 19–20; 34–35.

6. See *The Gentleman's and Lady's Palladium* (London, 1750), p. 42. This was an almanac.

Candidates for this responsibility depended upon the concerns of the writer; nevertheless, the list of possibilities was quite restricted. Rarely was the constitution itself or the balance of its constituent parts so described. It was a commonplace that there had to be a balance between sovereignty (or prerogative) and liberty, for the state had to be secured against foreign enemies at the same time as its citizens and their property were secured against government. The more specific understanding of balance—that of social orders or the powers of government organs—was only another way of stating that condition. Since liberty, from one point of view, was then but an element in the balance of the state, it cannot have seemed useful to identify the balance with the palladium of liberty. The closest approach to such a view was the assertion that Parliament, its power and independence, was the palladium. This, for instance, was an opinion held by Samuel Johnson (the Whig, not the dictionary-maker) and by John Toland.[7] As fears grew for the continued integrity and independence of the House of Commons, that body more often figured as the guard of liberty.

Even in this case there were inconveniences in the identification, for talk about preserving liberty came chiefly from the opponents of the administration, and these people were all too aware, in the years of the Whig supremacy, that the Commons belonged to the government of the day. Until the close of Anne's reign, political facts in some measure confirmed the role of one or other house of Parliament as the protector of various freedoms. Thereafter, majorities in both houses were usually in agreement with each other and with the ministers. The locus of the palladium was thus apt, in some minds, to become extra-parliamentary, and so, during the Walpole era, the press came into its own.

Initially presented as necessary for religious and general intellectual freedom, the freedom of the press had already been linked to the whole range of political liberties by the close of the seventeenth century. All writers here took their cue from Milton, but one notes an increased emphasis upon political factors in later arguments. Matthew Tindal, in an essay first published in 1698, said that without the liberty

7. [Johnson], *The Second Part of the Confutation of the Ballancing Letter Containing an Original Discourse in Vindication of Magna Charta* (London, 1700), p. 8; and [Toland], *The State-Anatomy of Great Britain*, 6th ed. (London, 1717), p. 39.

of communicating opinion, no other liberty could be secure. More strongly, he insisted that a free press might well prove to be a sufficient protection for all other liberties.[8] The claim was revived in the vigorous debates that accompanied the scandal of the South-Sea Bubble, and even some ministerial prints allowed that a free press was politically significant. Government-subsidized newspapers were cautious on this point and tended, in the 1720s, to bestow their admiration for this particular liberty rather grudgingly. Thus one dismissed it as no doubt a good thing but still "ranked among the *second-rate Liberties*," while another chose to present it in the innocuous form of an outgrowth of pre-existing freedom, rather than as a foundation or guardian of it.[9]

Promotion to a more exalted status was accomplished rapidly by the Opposition papers. In 1727, the *Craftsman*, destined to be the major engine against Walpole, called freedom of the press "the Chief Bulwark and Support" of liberty. Similar claims were kept current by Eustace Budgell in various publications of the early 1730s, including his paper the *Bee*.[10] Thus when *Common Sense*, in 1738, dubbed liberty of the press as "the Palladium of our Rights," that journal was only echoing a judgement that was becoming part of the ordinary language of politics.[11] Nor did ministerial papers withhold their commendation. In 1735, the *Daily Gazetteer* competed with Opposition papers, such as the *Independent London Journal*, in proclaiming how all other liberties rested upon that of the press.[12] Four decades later, when Junius, in the dedication to the collected edition of his letters, called liberty of the press "the Palladium of all the civil, political and religious rights of an Englishman," he was but following the crowd.

Junius's dictum has been called the best-known and most frequently quoted one on the subject.[13] However, by 1772 the familiarity of such

8. Tindal, "Discourse for the Liberty of the Press; in a Letter to a Member of Parliament" (1698), in *Four Discourses* ... (London, 1709), p. 319, 323.

9. *Commentator* 3 (8 Jan. 1719–20); *St. James's Journal* (25 Oct. 1722).

10. *Bee: or Universal Weekly Pamphlet* (21 May 1733), p. 585; and a broadsheet by Budgell, *A Letter to Every Person in Great Britain* ... (London, 1733).

11. *Common Sense* 49 (7 Jan. 1737–38). Cf. *Flying-Post* 5871 (9 Sept. 1731); and *Old Whig* 107 (24 Mar. 1736–37).

12. *Daily Gazetteer* 104 (28 Oct. 1735). Cf. *Independent London Journal* 15 (25 Oct. 1735), and 16 (1 Nov. 1735).

13. James N. M. Maclean, *Reward is Secondary ... an Inquiry into the Mystery of 'Junius'* (London: Hodder and Stoughton, 1963), p. 348.

an idea was in no way dependent on puffing by any one person, and the words were doubtless repeated by many people who were quite unaware of the particular turn of phrase employed by Junius.[14] Certain writers, who were especially concerned with broadening the mandate of juries in cases of seditious libel, pointed to the jury system as the true palladium. However, given the close connection between effective juries and continued liberty of the press, this late-eighteenth-century idea was very much the original elevation of the press, adapted to changing circumstances.[15]

Searching for the significance of these comments about the political importance of the press, one may offer the thought that this mode of discourse contributed to a clarification of the pattern of politics. For the writers who pointed to the essential role of a free press were not thereby committed to overlooking the contribution of the formal organs of government. It was still obvious that a properly functioning legislature was a crucial support of liberty and that, indeed, the less observable maintenance of some measure of constitutional "balance" was similarly vital. The signal virtue of finding the focal point of liberty outside the formal organs of the state was that a link was then added to those political phenomena that could be perceived as a causal chain; one could then explain more of the workings of the polity than would otherwise be the case. Conversely, when one identified the condition of Parliament or the maintenance of constitutional balance with the preservation of liberty, there was often no related attempt to trace those conditions that ensured the right sort of central institutions. Of course, writers were free to inquire separately into such matters, but this mode of inquiry into the foundation of liberty normally accounted for a comparatively small part of politics.

To appreciate the relative sophistication of inquiries about the palladium of liberty, one need only consult one of those general panegyrics to English liberty that often graced the periodicals of the age. A case in point is William Webster's hymn to liberty in one such

14. So strong was the notion that the press was the palladium of liberty that the phrase even pervaded private correspondence. See the letter of 24 March 1792 from James Anderson, in *The Literary Correspondence of John Pinkerton, Esq.* (London, 1830), 1:403.

15. The connection was spelled out, for instance, in Joseph Towers, "Observations on the Rights and Duty of Juries in Trials for Libels" (1784), in *Tracts on Political and Other Subjects, Published at Various Times* (London, 1796), 2:iv.

publication. The author's great strength as a thinker was his awareness of the abuse of words in polemical works; but he was not equally sensitive to the task of explaining the workings of political forces. Thus Webster chose as his definition of liberty the capacity of acting rationally and properly. He then observed that the subject of a despotic prince was no less free than Englishmen, "so long as he governs them by the same *wise* and *equitable* laws to which *we* are subject. ..."[16] Of course he recognized the fact that such liberty was rarely realized under arbitrary governments, and when it was, the subjects were less safe in their continued enjoyment of it. By way of accounting for this fact, he noted that the power of Parliament to grant or refuse consent to measures was as absolute as the king's power of veto. The "checks" that formed a part of limited monarchy thus preserved English liberty.

Webster did distinguish between the substance of liberty and the means of preserving it, and in this respect he was more coherent than others who alluded vaguely to Magna Carta. But he certainly failed to demonstrate—or even literally to assert—that there were reasons why the quality of the laws might be superior in British government to those of other states. The one mechanism offered by way of explaining the performance of the polity was a formal description of mixed government, deficient both in its failure to indicate that the king was a part of the legislative power and in its unrealistic portrait of immovable forces locked in combat. By contrast, the simple assertion of the contribution made by an unfettered press opened for investigation the actual processes of political strife while suggesting the manner in which the constitution might be related to the freedom of the citizen.

This was especially so in the case of those discussions that presented a free press as a necessary adjunct to continued competition between political parties, and this function of the press was recognized from quite early in the century. In the light of the narrow social sympathies of eighteenth-century parties and the limited good they could be seen to do for ordinary people, the link between the form of the state and the rights of individuals was no doubt still a tenuous one. Therefore, when admirers of a free press pointed out the manner in which it

16. *Weekly Miscellany* 307 (18 Nov. 1738), later reprinted as "An Essay on Liberty," in *Tracts Consisting of Sermons, Discourses and Letters* (London, 1745), pp. 68–74.

could promote the welfare of private interests[17]—and not just those of parties—the structure of liberty became that much better defined. But this was not the only way to political understanding; the second half of the century saw dramatic new claims about liberty and its conditions that went beyond the categories used by admirers of a free press. Meanwhile most of the traditional notions also remained current.

Montesquieu and Liberty

An indication of the direction in which political ideas were developing may be seen in the new connotations acquired by the word "system" around mid-century. Previously a system in political language had most often been a plan or pattern of conduct, either of an individual politician or of the state as international actor. In the latter sense, a book of 1743, entitled *Le Système politique de Grande-Bretagne*, dealt with foreign policy, not with the form of government. In the 1750s, however, one encounters "system" used to refer to the form of government or as a synonym for "constitution," and this was followed by the more explicit "public system," with particular reference to administration.[18] The more recent usage obviously encouraged the search for general patterns and connections among aspects of public life.

With the appearance of Montesquieu's *Esprit des lois*, the analysis of liberty entered a new phase. Montesquieu's contribution can best be seen as leading eventually to a clearer distinction that freedom embodied in the constitution of a state and the freedom enjoyed by private persons. The organization of books 11 and 12 followed this plan, which was explained by the author's observation that the two conditions were separable, it being conceivable that either the citizen or the constitution might be "free" and not the other. This possibility allowed for the distinction, important to Montesquieu's analysis, between liberty that was provided for "by right" and that which was

---

17. See the series of essays on the liberty of the press, later issued as a pamphlet, in *Old England* 187–193 (28 Nov.–9 Jan. 1747–48), and esp. 189 (12 Dec. 1747).

18. A writer who particularly used "system" in a way previously rare was Henry McCulloh. See *The Fatal Consequences of the Want of System in the Conduct of Public Affairs* (London, 1757), pp. 1–2. For the term "public system," see *London Chronicle* 1377 (17–19 Oct. 1765). I am aware that in the previous century both Hobbes and Harrington had given a comparable scope to the term.

enjoyed "in fact." The first, Montesquieu explained, was the result of
that separation of the powers of government that was to become his
best-known idea; the second, he deemed to consist of "security or in
the opinion people have of their security." A further mode of clas-
sifying liberty was to speak of "civil liberty" as opposed to "political
liberty"—Montesquieu's second most influential addition to Anglo-
American political thought—but his distinction played no part in books
11 and 12, both of which treat political liberty.

Had Montesquieu adhered to this complex typology, his thoughts
on liberty would have been difficult to follow; as it was, confusion was
confounded by inconsistencies and definitions inappropriately placed
in the text. Montesquieu was not very precise in identifying civil liberty
and unclear as to whether it admitted of the same divisions as did
political liberty. In addition, the only definition of "political liberty"
to appear in the famous book 11 relates to that liberty as experienced
by the individual citizen—and this, despite the fact that book 11 was
supposedly devoted to liberty of the constitution. The definition stated
that such political liberty was "a tranquility of mind arising from the
opinion that each person has of his safety."

The effect of these notions upon British opinion was neither immediate nor dramatic.[19] Traditionally, Englishmen had thought in
terms of liberty as divisible into civil and religious forms, a point
mentioned, if only in passing, by a host of preachers. The term "political liberty" had not enjoyed much currency, though it was sometimes introduced in order to differentiate talk of liberty in the context
of the necessitarian debate from the use of the term in a quite different
context. It was in this sense that a letter, written to the editor of the
St. James's Journal, complained that the writings of John Trenchard
and Thomas Gordon were a jumble of ideas about "Political Liberty
and Moral Necessity."[20] Montesquieu's initial effect on ordinary vocabulary may perhaps be reflected in certain sermons where conventional references to civil liberty were broadened to read "political or

19. The one study of Montesquieu's reception in England probably exaggerates his
impact in attributing widespread concern about political corruption to his work. See
F. T. H. Fletcher, *Montesquieu and English Politics* (1750–1800) (London: E. Arnold,
1939), p. 159.
20. Henry Grove, *Miscellanies in Prose and Verse* (London, 1739), p. 64.

civil Liberty," an expression found too in Blackstone.[21] The two were not contrasted, and both seemed to be more or less covered by Cowley's well-known definition of liberty in general.

Of Montesquieu's more cogently argued distinction between a free citizen and a free constitution, more can be said. Clearly Englishmen had long been familiar with the notion that individual liberty did not necessarily flourish in a so-called "free state." That had been the refrain of numerous enemies of the Cromwellian experiment. Government writers had also been known to complain that their opponents were prone to stress a particular species of liberty to the neglect of other forms. Thus the Opposition sometimes stood accused of substituting "the Liberty of *particular Persons* for that *of all* taken together."[22] Such an argument would have benefited from a more precise vocabulary. Prior to the *Esprit des lois* there was no reason why one might not entitle an essay primarily concerned with the structure of the central government "A Dissertation on the Liberty of the Subject." It is perhaps attributable to Montesquieu that another essay, of the 1750s, explored the same theme by referring to the "Liberty of Government."[23]

To assess the influence of Montesquieu's distinction it may be useful to compare complaints about the state of liberty before and after the appearance of his book. There had always been some people who expressed disrespect for the blessings of British liberty, and even though this attitude was undoubtedly seriously underrepresented in the surviving record, it is traceable. Matthias Earbery, a Jacobite, was an able spokesman for the interests of the non-jurors and others who failed to flourish under the Whig oligarchy. Earbery said explicitly that the dogmas of the constitution made no significant contribution to the task of making people happy—the true measure of liberty. Put most succinctly, this meant that "Liberty and Ballance of Power are

---

21. Peter Peckard, *A Sermon on the Nature and Extent of Civil and Religious Liberty* (London, 1754), p. 5; and Blackstone, *An Analysis of the Laws of England* (Oxford, 1756), p. 7.

22. *Hyp-Doctor* 133 (5 June 1733).

23. Sir William Keith, "A Dissertation on the Liberty of the Subject" (1737), in *A Collection of Papers and Other Tracts, Written Occasionally on Various Subjects* (London, 1740). Cf. "Dissertation on the Liberty of Government," *Universal Visiteur, and Moralist for the Year 1756* (London, 1757), pp. 15–22. This writer's remarks suggest familiarity with the *Esprit*.

two different Things. ...." Dramatizing the plight of the poor—and the non-jurors, often barred from their professions, were nothing if not poor—he wrote:

The last have no Advantage of the Constitution; there is no *Habeas Corpus* out of *Bridewell*; they have no Power to defend themselves from an arbitrary Justice of the Peace, if one of that Bench should prove tyrannical ... by a modest Computation, one single Attorney may devour four Hundred in a Year, for his proper Share.[24]

That message was heard with increasing frequency after mid-century, for though the whole period was not one of special economic distress, there was a new awareness that some abuses were open to remedy. The 1750s saw a spate of literature that expressed concern about the fate of the poor,[25] who also at times spoke for themselves. Montesquieu's categories did nothing to provoke such sentiments, but they could prove useful for purposes of giving form to them. A tract of 1749, pleading the case of poor soldiers, may well reflect the vocabulary of the *Esprit des lois*, though the Nugent translation was not to appear until the next year. Taking the expressions "free Government" and "free People," the anonymous advocate held that they should imply a nation where the "Right of natural Property" was secured to all. But reality was disappointing:

It by no means necessarily follows, that the Subjects of a free Government are a free People; for, in common Speech, the Term Free Government, is often used, when no more is intended by it, than, that the Government or States governing, are free as to their Acts of Government, free from the Controul of an absolute Sovereign. ... But a Free Government, in a just Sense, as referring to the People governed, must necessarily imply the Freedom of all its Subjects, or the Government over a free People.

Warming further to his subject, he added:

High civil Privileges make a dazling Appearance. ... The Cities, Nobility and Palatinates of Poland are possessed of these to a very high Degree; and there the Justice and Liberty of their Government stops; it proceeds no lower. ...

24. Earbery, *The Occasional Historian* (London, 1731), 2:67–68.
25. See Malvin R. Zirker Jr., *Fielding's Social Pamphlets* (Berkeley and Los Angeles: University of California Press, 1966), p. 35.

That Government then is best, which extends its Freedom, Benignity and Justice the farthest, or to the most, the greatest Number of its Subjects. ... If the Laws will take care of the Poor, the Rich will generally find the Means to take care of themselves.[26]

Of course, Montesquieu's immediate influence is not easily separated from writings that were a product of renewed interest in the social and economic state of the people. For whenever people discussed such matters, nothing was more natural than to contrast the liberty associated with high politics with the indignity and insecurity suffered by ordinary citizens. A prisoner for debt, for example, expressed his disdain for rhetoric about liberty and property in a country where a man's creditor had more power over him than his prince.[27] It was becoming widely understood that liberty might be sustained by extra-constitutional arrangements, but the fact that slavery might be similarly nourished had not received comparable attention. This remained a minor theme in political discourse, though it appeared with greater frequency and urgency later in the century.[28]

For all the stirrings of new ideas at this time, the old ones retained a firm hold on opinion. The most vociferous champion of British liberty at mid-century was Charles Lucas, a sort of eighteenth-century Lilburne, who set his lance against the city council of Dublin. His various publications, including one of 1750 entitled *A Critical Review of the Liberties of British Subjects*, added nothing to the arsenal of Opposition ideas that had not already been present in the reign of William III. In a polity in which the state of liberty was the major topic of debate, any issue might provoke consideration of the health of the liberties of Britons. On one occasion, the closing of roads through Richmond Park gave sufficient warrant for an essay warning of the

26. Anon., *An Inquiry into the Rights of Free Subjects* (London, 1749), pp. 15, 30. Whig journalists sometimes put the issue more brutally, John Henley once saying that popular liberties implied only "those of the Governing Part of the People." *Hyp-Doctor* 133 (5 June 1733).

27. Anon., *The Attempt: or, An Essay towards the Retrieving Lost Liberty* ... (London, 1750), p. 8.

28. See the anonymous tract, probably by James Elphinston, poet and critic, *An Essay on British Liberty* (London, 1777). The savage tone is sufficiently conveyed by his comment that "British liberty precludes nine tenths of the people from the aid of counsellors and physicians ..." (p. 123).

dangers to liberty.[29] A more significant statement was Owen Ruffhead's use of the distinction between the liberty of the constitution
and that of the citizen—an explicit borrowing from Montesquieu—in
order to invoke the familiar charge of ministerial tyranny. According
to Ruffhead, the first sort of liberty, dependent upon fundamental
laws, had already been lost, but the liberty of the citizen lived on,
preserved by manners of the people.[30] For people of Ruffhead's persuasion, the early reign of George III was to be the time when the
liberty of the constitution would be reasserted. But to say, as he did,
that citizens could remain free, owing to the good example of the
sovereign, provided no clear connection between the two species of
liberty. If citizens could enjoy freedom when the constitution was
ostensibly in abeyance, then the virtue of a free constitution was uncertain. An equally complacent version of those ideas was Richard
Hurd's contrast between the "liberty of the subject" and a "free constitution" in order to distinguish England's past from its political state
since the Revolution. Only with the advent of this free constitution,
according to Hurd, was the subject's liberty rendered secure.[31]

The Radical Alternative

It required an ambition other than a simple displacement of the Whig
oligarchy in order to connect the citizen's freedom with that of the
government. To Joseph Priestley fell the task of making an effective
connection. His pamphlets of the late 1760s reflected the new volatility
of extra-parliamentary organization and the beginnings of the demand that a reform of Parliament go beyond the mere removal of
corruption to secure, as well, adequate representation. But this latter
possibility was not Priestley's main ambition, nor perhaps that of any
of his contemporaries, and so his thoughts on political liberty serve
primarily as an introduction to a plan of education.

The major departure was to provide an entirely different rendering
of Montesquieu's notion of political liberty. Ruffhead had equated it
with maintenance of the constitution; Priestley perceived it as a con-

29. *London Evening Post* 3918 (7–9 Dec. 1752).
30. [Ruffhead], *An Appeal to the People in which the Prerogatives of the Crown, with the
Rights of Parliament and of the Privy Council, are Considered*, 2nd ed. (London, 1760),
p. 55.
31. Hurd, *Moral and Political Dialogues* (London, 1765), 2:327n.

dition present "where every member of the society enjoys an equal power of arriving at the supreme offices, and consequently of directing the strength and sentiments of the whole community. ..."[32] Anyone excluded from office or from the capacity to vote for officeholders lacked any share in government, for he had no power over the actions of others, however much "civil liberty or power over his own actions" he might have. Otherwise expressed, civil liberty consisted in peoples' enjoyment of their natural rights, while political liberty was the guardian of civil liberty.

Priestley allowed for some qualifications to his position, since his professed aim was not universal suffrage but greater freedom and political power for the Dissenters, still labouring under the provisions of the Test and Corporation Acts. Thus he accepted the position, commonly identified with Blackstone, that the political activity of dependent creatures would not enhance the cause of freedom in national politics. The requirement of a stake in the country for voters in parliamentary elections—which seems to have been Priestley's position— left the poor with votes for the filling of the lowest offices, and this he deemed as much political liberty as was compatible with the current state of affairs. Priestley had therefore renounced any dramatic eruption of the masses into political life while still posing a substantial challenge to dominant conceptions.

For despite his modesty of language, Priestley understood the novelty of his position when he observed that it was surprising that great political writers had not more often commented on the oddity of expecting citizens to be bound by some renunciation of interests made in the past. This gentle statement was separated only by its tone from Paine's later insistence that each generation be in full command of its destiny. Similarly, Priestley claimed less than was his due when he complained that the similarity between the two forms of liberty had resulted in their often being confounded.[33] One might better have said that rarely had anyone attempted to distinguish between the two, and never had his emphasis been employed. One looks in vain for

32. Priestley, *An Essay on the First Principles of Government; and on the Nature of Political, Civil, and Religious Liberty* (London, 1768), p. 15.

33. Priestley, *Essay*, pp. 17–18, 58. More characteristic of previous opinion was a tract of the same year that invoked Magna Carta, habeas corpus, and various other bases of liberty and that remained very unanalytical. See W. P., *The Foundation of British Liberty* (London, 1768), pp. 8, 15, 29.

any such position in the language of John Wilkes, self-proclaimed personification of liberty, nor had it any place in the well-known thoughts of the Reverend John Brown, champion of a conservative understanding of civil liberty. Priestley challenged established ideas at precisely the point where they appear to have been unquestioned, for he had argued that the vaunted liberty of Britons was far from being secure except in the measure in which these liberties were supported by political power vested in the people. In advocating a new content for political liberty and in emphasizing its role in preserving the familiar natural rights, Priestley had endowed an emerging English radicalism with its vocabulary.

A publication of the following year repeated the general argument by pointing to the manner in which "political rights" served to protect "natural and civil rights."[34] Had Priestley's language remained consistent and strong, the next decade might have been spared a lengthy and confused debate. As it was, his formulation of liberty seems to have made no marked impression on the radical sentiments of the early 1770s. His language appeared in the *Craftsman* in February 1771, but it was absent, for instance, from James Burgh's *Political Disquisitions*. John Wesley's diffuse attack on popular sentiments mentioned Wilkes and Junius but did not come to grips with Priestley's arguments for government by the people.[35] De Lolme's first English edition did meet Priestley's point, without naming him, with the observation that voting was an act of government and the enjoyment of a share of power but did not warrant the term "liberty."[36] Priestley did, however, succeed in influencing Richard Price and with dramatic results.

Price's *Observations of the Nature of Civil Liberty* was a forceful and high-minded defence of the American colonies, which became an instant best-seller. Attempting to ground his case on philosophical premises, Price chose to expound the nature of liberty and especially civil liberty. This he defined as the "power of a *Civil Society* or *State* to govern itself by its own discretion; by laws of its own making, without being subject to any foreign discretion. ..." This sounded like sovereignty or independence within the international community, but the peculiar circumstances of Englishmen in America tempted Price to add a further dimension to his definition. Civil liberty in its per-

---

34. [Priestley], *The Present State of Liberty in Great Britain and her Colonies* (London, 1769), p. 19.

35. [Wesley], *Thoughts upon Liberty by an Englishman* (London, 1772).

36. J. L. de Lolme, *The Constitution of England* (London, 1775), pp. 226ff.

fection then became possible only in those states "where every member is capable of giving his suffrage in person, and of being chosen into public offices." Here he seems to have been following Priestley, for Price insisted that it was especially important for the maintenance of "Political Liberty" (here undefined) that one not be guided by the will of another. The freedom of a state, or its responsiveness only to its own will, was thus equated with government by an assembly of representatives. Though he made passing reference to the freedom of individual citizens, Price failed to connect it either with his comments on political action by citizens or with his more general reference to representation. Rather, a free state was said to secure the freedom of its members by excluding licentiousness and by protecting their property and persons.[37]

Price had tasted enough of the new ideas to give a dangerous turn to his pamphlet, but in the absence of detailed plans for changing the system, he was in no position to add much substance to the Country cry for public spirit as found in *Cato's Letters* half a century before. The fleeting reference to political liberty was enough to raise the hackles of ministerial supporters but otherwise simply confused the issue, all the more so because Price neglected to specify in what measure he sought to approach that perfect civil liberty he identified with the direct democracy of small states. Philosophically audacious when addressing himself to liberty in the abstract, Price was vague about the institutional meaning of his outburst. His faults did not escape notice.

Few pamphlets of the eighteenth century provoked more comment in print, a fact recorded by contemporaries who were at odds about the merits of the argument.[38] One of the more sophisticated replies

37. *Observations* ... , 3rd ed. (London, 1776), pp. 3, 7, 11, 13. Price's pamphlet has received detailed analysis in David O. Thomas, *The Honest Mind: The Thought and Work of Richard Price* (Oxford: Clarendon Press, 1977), chaps. 8, 10. A succinct and helpful comment is to be found in Peter Brown, *The Chathamites: A Study in the Relationship between Personalities and Ideas in the Second Half of the Eighteenth Century* (London: Macmillan; New York: St. Martin's Press, 1967), pp. 148–49.

38. *Edinburgh Magazine and Review* 5 (July 1776):316; and *Weekly Magazine, or Edinburgh Amusement* 32 (20 June 1776):395. Some forty responses, mainly unfavourable, appeared in pamphlet form over the next two years. Carl B. Cone, *Torchbearer of Freedom* (Lexington, Ky.: University of Kentucky Press, 1952), p. 82. According to Priestley, one of them was due to come from Price's fellow Dissenter Israel Maudit, but I have been unable to trace it. John Towill Rutt, *Life and Correspondence of Joseph Priestley* (London, 1831), 1:290, a letter of 9 February 1776.

came from John Lind, with the assistance of Jeremy Bentham.[39] Lind's thoughts endorsed Montesquieu's treatment of "political liberty in a citizen," though the author also confessed to an understandable hesitation about what Montesquieu was actually saying. About Price's notions he had no uncertainty and taxed him with confusing that civil or political liberty that consisted in living under law with "civil or political Security," which ensured that power was employed for the greatest happiness of the greatest number. That condition, he said, could be created by a proper distribution of the powers of government.[40] Another able retort, expressing agreement with Lind's approach, was written by Richard Hey. He too stressed the negative quality of liberty and the inappropriateness of applying the term to powers of self-government. However, Hey saw less to admire in Montesquieu's book.[41]

Some of the most astute criticism focused upon Price's conflation of the liberty of individuals and the independence of a community.[42] For even if one agreed with Price's half-hearted attempt to justify political power in the people, it was difficult to see how his manner of approaching the question could do justice to that theme. The independence of a state was not the same thing as popular government, and nothing better illustrates the trans-Atlantic strain placed upon Price's good will than this attempt simultaneously to serve the needs of American independence and of British radicalism. The critics who argued that liberty was a misleading name for the power of the people were indulging in ideological debate. But the most devasting charge remained the simple and obvious weakness of Price's argument, for it allowed his tormentors to avoid the serious question whether a government responding to popular impulses might not be a better government as measured by its protection of individual interests of all sorts. Not only did Price's analytical solecisms open the door to

39. Timothy L. S. Sprigge, ed., *The Correspondence of Jeremy Bentham* (London: Athlone Press, 1968), 1:309–10n.

40. [Lind], *Three Letters to Dr. Price . . . by a Member of Lincoln's Inn* (London, 1776), pp. 74–75, 88–89.

41. Hey, *Observations on the Nature of Civil Liberty* ... (London, 1776), pp. 9n., 19.

42. See [James Stewart], *A Letter to the Rev. Dr. Price, F.R.S. wherein his Observations on the Nature of Civil Liberty ... are Candidly Examined* (London, 1776), p. 11; John Gray, *Doctor Price's Notion of the Nature of Liberty shewn to be contradictory to Reason and Scripture* (London, 1777), p. 3; and, less clearly, [Thomas Hutchinson], *Experience Preferable to Theory. An Answer to Dr. Price's Observations ...* (London, 1776), p. 15.

attacks upon the vagueness of government by "the people"—an issue already broached by John Wesley in 1772—but they also afforded the opportunity to raise all of the obvious objections stemming from the apparent tension between popular government and a régime that honoured the rights of the individual.

Dr. John Shebbeare, a literary mercenary of considerable ability, exploited the situation to the fullest. Taking as his central theme Price's assumption that liberty lay, not in the nature of laws, but in the organization of the government, Shebbeare had little difficulty in fashioning a contrasting picture. He interpreted Price, not unfairly, as holding that a law approved by the majority of the people could not be taken to annihilate the liberty of a nation, since that very liberty consisted in making laws by such a majority. This raised, perhaps for the first time in eighteenth-century England, the spectre of the tyranny of the majority, and Shebbeare pressed his advantage, asking if this would authorize a popular government to mistreat that minority who professed, for instance, Presbyterian and democratic principles. It then became all too easy for Shebbeare to proclaim civil liberty as the outgrowth of just laws "righteously administered, by whatever kind of government they are instituted."[43] Of course, Price had never wished to argue that a majority of the population had *carte blanche* to persecute their less numerous fellow citizens; his had been a desire simply to assert the good effects of a government more broadly based than the existing one. However, by passing over any coherent discussion of the mechanisms that might ensure wise legislation and sound administration, Price left himself at the mercy of his least charitable critics.

Similar embarrassments flowed from Price's sanguine hope that all good things might prove somehow to be linked in an indissoluble whole. Shebbeare seized upon Price's conventional aspiration for shorter parliaments and readily demonstrated that this criterion of good government was irrelevant to his initial commitment to majority rule, if not inconsistent with it. Here, as before, Price had injudiciously associated a number of conditions with a definition of liberty that could not bear the burden. Montesquieu's book 11 supplied a ready corrective to all such arguments, and the hireling scribbler deftly set out

---

43. Shebbeare, *An Essay on the Origin, Progress and Establishment of National Society*, 3rd ed. (London, 1776), pp. 27–28, 47.

the familiar creed that the power of the people must not be confused with their liberty, that liberty and independence were entirely different conditions, and that true liberty consisted in doing what the laws permitted, not in following one's own will.

Price naturally sought to defend his views, though his *Additional Observations* of the next year represented no dramatic improvement. His shield against charges of seeking a popular tyranny consisted in a disavowal of "pure Democracy" and the allowance that although liberty was the most essential quality in a government, it was not the only good quality. He persevered in the original emphasis on the difference between a free government and a government under which freedom was enjoyed. This was a valid point against the case put forward by Shebbeare, with his emphasis upon results as opposed to structural guarantees.

However, Price again stumbled in his efforts to make clear the various forms of liberty and their relation. He did observe that a free government was one that secured the citizens' liberty by allowing them to be their own legislators. However, he refused to adopt Priestley's distinction between civil and political liberty, while professing admiration for the latter's general argument.[44] Price adhered to his earlier categories to the extent of saying that both civil and political liberty, in Priestley's sense, belonged to the liberty of the citizen. He thus deprived himself of the simplicity of Priestley's view that political liberty was the guard of civil liberty, and by retaining notions such as the liberty of government and of the community, Price again blurred the relations between the situation of individuals and the organization of the polity.

In calling the freedom of a community analogous to that of the individual, Price continued to plead the case of America, without thereby illuminating his central concept. The exposition of the freedom of the citizen and that of the government had undoubtedly gained in clarity, but problems remained. For he chose to view the capacity of legislating for one's self as part of the liberty of a citizen, while a free government was none other than one that provided such an opportunity. No longer was there a gulf between the two loci of freedom; instead they now appeared to amount to much the same

44. Price, *Additional Observations on the Nature and Value of Civil Liberty* (London, 1777), p. 14n.

thing. Still absent was a precise account of the political mechanisms entailed by the definitions. Nor were the definitions themselves satisfactory, for Price had no need of such a concept as the freedom of a government, especially given his separate provision for community freedom. Montesquieu's penchant for multiplying needless entities lived on. Ideas of independence, popular sovereignty and mild government remained in a state of confusion, relieved only by Price's valid distinction between a polity in which individuals might enjoy an accidental and precarious liberty and one in which liberty was rendered secure.

Indeed, this last distinction, as clear as anything Price wrote on the subject, proved acceptable to some readers, without thereby winning their support for the general argument.[45] Price made one further effort to explain himself on the subject of liberty, spurred, it seems by his disappointment at Burke's refusal in the *Letter to the Sheriffs of Bristol* to endorse his views.[46] However, it was left to others to introduce order to a subject Price had brought to the forefront of political discussion. The new prominence of "liberty" was manifested in some writings—notably *Three Dialogues Concerning Liberty* (1776) by Jackson Barwis—that owed nothing to this debate, but for the most part Price provided the context for further thoughts on the subject as they emerged in the 1770s.

Ideas of a conspicuously radical cast had emerged through the American war, and the county associations, beginning in 1779, gave organization and voice to them. The efforts of Priestley and Price had done much to ensure that the shift in emphasis of reformers from constitutional government to popular government would have "liberty," of some sort or other, as its watchword. The forces of reform still had to agree upon a vocabulary, however, for Richard Price's obvious disarray left the defenders of the *status quo* with the prospect of a cheap and easy victory. That victory came anyway in the realm of affairs, for there was no reform of the sort then being sought, but the 1780s saw a significant sharpening of the intellectual issues and

45. See John Stevenson, *Letters in Answer to Dr. Price's two Pamphlets on Civil Liberty* ... , 2nd ed. (London, 1779), p. 79, from letters originally published in the *Public Ledger* and the *Morning Chronicle*.

46. Price, *The General Introduction and Supplement to the Two Tracts on Civil Liberty* ... (London, 1778), p. vi.

something approaching a standard set of concepts for making the case for reform.

The Earl of Abingdon's response to Burke's *Letter to the Sheriffs of Bristol* set the course of the reformers when he observed that Blackstone had erred in failing to distinguish political from civil rights. It was only a passing remark in a crowded pamphlet, but it gave notice that it would be the distinction between two sorts of liberty, and not the relatively clumsy one between free citizens and free governments, that would provide the language of debate. Only the former approach, strangely enough, seemed to offer an intelligible connection between the situations and activities of individuals and the nature of the overall political order.

Efforts to strengthen the position of the Irish parliament provoked David Williams to write his *Letters on Political Liberty*, the major statement that purported to redefine the nature of liberty in political terms. Williams's work was too full of novel ideas to win a large following, but on the meaning of liberty he was relatively clear and apparently influential. Dismissing Montesquieu's contribution as both unhelpful and inconsistently applied, Williams ventured his own definitions. Civil liberty, he said, resulted from laws that defined the "boundaries" of men's actions and otherwise left them unimpeded. His understanding of the companion term was less conventional: "Political liberty has a reference merely to the grand divisions of the state ... and consists in their freedom from the encroachments of each other."[47] A hurried reader might have been forgiven for thinking that this was merely Montesquieu's separation of powers in new dress. In fact, what Williams sought was an arrangement that linked all powers of government to "the constitutional and permanent power of the people." Small units of representation, universal manhood suffrage, frequent elections, and a hierarchy of representatives of tens, hundreds, and thousands of voters, culminating in the national parliament, were the materials from which the desired effect was to emerge.

In a later publication, Williams reflected further upon the difference between the two major forms of liberty and noted how the defenders of American indpendence had taken their stand on the grounds

---

47. Williams, *Letters on Political Liberty*, 1st ed. (1782), p. 8. A study of Williams and his influence is overdue; I have attempted to sketch some aspects of his thought in chap. 5, above.

of "civil liberty," though the concept of "political liberty" would have served them much better. He also made clear that the essence of political liberty was the security that government would not pursue interests separate from the public. At the same time, however, Williams conceded that political liberty would be destroyed, not only by leaving the people at the mercy of government but also in the event that the proper business of the administration were interrupted by popular clamours.[48] Obviously Williams had learned something from the ease with which Price's arguments had been twisted into a case for mob rule. It was an argument ideally suited for countering the facile opinion that civil liberty was secure in the proportion that political activity was restricted. The rise of extra-parliamentary organization and the increase in mob violence lent fuel to this nervous Toryism. But Williams himself had been shocked by the Gordon riots and unhappy with the ineffectiveness of the county associations, and so he had done his best to anticipate the charge.

Liberty and Power: At Home and Abroad

A respectful critic of Williams's views pointed out the basic similarity of the ideas of those writers on government who were also "bred in Presbyterian principles."[49] The particular turn of phrase seems inadequate as a means of identifying Priestley, Price, and Williams, but undoubtedly these were the people so described, and if the divergence of their religious opinions went unnoticed, their political kinship did not. Following the French Revolution, and a great deal more debate about the meaning of liberty, these three figures continued to be associated with the argument for popular government based on the nature and significance of political liberty. Angus Macaulay, a reliable if uninspired student of political ideas, recognized Priestley's originality in pressing Montesquieu's vocabulary to some useful conclusions. Liberty had been understood to have civil and political dimensions before Priestley's statement, but he was perhaps the first "to establish it by definition." Of the other two writers, Price was consigned to the

---

48. Williams, *Lectures on Political Principles*, pp. 134–37, 234–35.
49. Matthew Dawes, *The Nature and Extent of Supreme Power* (London, 1783), p. 17n.

now familiar role of a distressing example of reasoning gone wrong, whereas Williams represented a position quite similar to the author's.[50]

Agreement about who was responsible for a form of discourse did not mean that everyone accepted the implications of the argument itself. The major reaction against populist tendencies was still to come in the 1790s. Nevertheless, the tone of criticism within moderate opinion was much muted from that which greeted Richard Price. William Paley, for instance, confined his negative comments to the verbal level, simultaneously leaving himself free to endorse the main point of would-be reformers. Paley refused to grant the name "liberty" to the process of consenting to laws, for that, he said, was to confound liberty with its safeguard.[51] The objection had much in common with de Lolme's criticism of a decade earlier, but de Lolme had chosen to ridicule the application of the term "liberty" to the act of voting and had dismissed it as a "play on words." Paley's influential book struck a note more in keeping with Pitt's professed commitment to strengthen the voice of the people by adding county members. No call for reform issued from Paley, but neither did he dissent from the proposition that freedom under law required some influence over the government. In fact, he accepted the notion that those conditions known to others as "civil liberty" had to be secured by political means. Others, who largely echoed Paley's argument, made more substantial concessions to the argument that political power was needed to safeguard liberty, and some expanded their understanding of civil liberty to incorporate the processes of consent.[52]

These writers disavowed the arguments of Priestley and Williams while, in varying degrees, conceding the importance of the substantial case. Paralleling this development was a tendency to embrace the language of populist radicalism for purposes of defending other causes.

50. Macaulay, *Rudiments of Political Science, Part the First* (London, 1796), p. 97. Priestley's novelty was also acknowledged by a writer who had no sympathy for his ideas. See Edward Tatham D. D., *Letters to the Right Honourable Edmund Burke on Politics* (Oxford, 1791), pp. 65–66. A radical application of Williams's position, but made without reference to him, is [Daniel Eaton, ed.], *Politics for the People: or, a Salmagundy for Swine* 2, no. 18 (1795):274–75.

51. Paley, *Principles of Moral and Political Philosophy* (London, 1785), bk. 6, chap. 5.

52. See William Belsham, *Essays Philosophical and Moral, Historical and Literary* (London, 1799), 2:185–86; and Thomas Gisborne, *The Principles of Moral Philosophy Investigated, and Applied to the Constitution of Civil Society*, 5th ed. (London, 1798), pp. 351–56.

Charles Francis Sheridan, brother of Richard Brinsley, well exemplifies this variant, for he adhered to the distinction between the two forms of liberty but employed it to defend the *status quo* and specifically to counter the ambitions of Irish Catholics for the elective franchise. Sheridan defined civil liberty in conventional terms of the protection of person and property. Political liberty, applied to individuals, then consisted in their being bound only by laws authorized by a portion of the community that was linked to the interests of the remainder. The formula bore clear traces of the radical side of debate over the previous twenty-five years, but it was also burdened with the legacy of Montesquieu, his complex set of categories, and especially his insistence that liberty and power were not the same. Thus Sheridan introduced the notions of civil power, residing in the officers of government, and the political power of the community, which he equated with the power of legislation. He retained a formal and paper-thin distinction between that power of the community and its political liberty, which, he said, resulted from power and lay in the fact of its possessing a representative body.[53] In effect, Sheridan argued for a disjunction between the liberty of the individual citizen and his political power but fused the two when he contemplated the whole community.

The issue of Roman Catholic rights in Ireland had already given rise to similar thoughts on the part of Henry Flood, who also opposed the removal of political disabilities for Catholics. Though Flood was arguing in this vein before Sheridan, the statement of a nineteenth-century admirer that he had been "one of the first who drew a clear distinction between personal liberty and political power" is nonsense.[54] Montesquieu had adhered to the same view, admittedly without reference to any particular issue, and the hostile response to Price's pamphlets had been a vehement and specific assertion of the traditional and tacit assumption that freedom was unconnected to the political power of citizens. A distinction between liberty and power was nothing more than the substance of traditional teaching; it was the connection between the two that had lacked expositors.

53. Sheridan, *An Essay upon the True Principles of Civil Liberty* (London, 1793), pp. 38, 45–52.

54. *Hibernian Magazine* [unnumbered] (June 1783), p. 328, account of speech in the Irish Parliament, 13 Feb. 1782; and later comment in an unsigned article, "Flood, Part. II," *Dublin University Magazine* 8 (July 1836):93.

The various grudging concessions to arguments about political liberty attest that the language of Priestley and Williams had become the vehicle for future efforts at democratizing British political practices. The need for better mechanisms for securing political liberty came to be accepted in the columns of the *English Review*, most sophisticated of the periodicals in terms of its sensitivity to changing political vocabulary.[55] Talk of political liberty also invaded Westminster in the speeches of Henry Grattan, Flood's Irish rival and sometime ally; Charles James Fox; and the Whig organizer William Adam.[56] Hosts of pamphlets, through the period of the French Revolution, presented the same theme, often in such general or fleeting form that one cannot tell the source of inspiration, whether Priestley, Williams, or a reworking of Montesquieu or Price into more usable form.[57]

A writer who did pause to discuss his sources was Major John Cartwright, one of the most influential of the reformers, if only because of his length of service. Cartwright associated Williams with the careful distinction between forms of liberty, but the Major offered different nomenclature in order to make the same basic point. Liberty, according to Cartwright, existed only when one had an equal vote with others in making laws and otherwise played the role of a citizen. What Williams had denominated "civil liberty" was in fact the condition of "legal protection," a thing valuable enough but not worthy of the name of liberty of any sort. Despite the verbal quibble, Cartwright followed Williams in emphasizing, in particular, "political liberty" and frequently expressed his admiration for Williams's theories.[58] Elsewhere in his voluminous writings, Cartwright gave a somewhat different account of the nature of liberty, but he adhered on the whole to his resolve not to admit the existence of any sort of civil liberty that

---

55. *English Review* 14 (Sept. 1789):238, and 20 (Dec. 1792):477.

56. *The Speeches of the Right Honourable Henry Grattan, in the Irish and in the Imperial Parliament* (London, 1822), speech of 1793 in 3:47; *Parliamentary History* 33 (1797–98):147, and 30 (1792–94):908.

57. Typical of such references is that in a statement attributed to the Medical Society of Edinburgh. See Henry W. Meikle, *Scotland and the French Revolution* (Glasgow: J. Maclehose and Sons, 1912) p. 78n. See too Anon., *Observations sur le gouvernement et la constitution de l'Angleterre* (Paris, 1790), p. 9.

58. Cartwright, *An Appeal, Civil and Military, on the Subject of the English Constitution* (London, 1799), pt. 1, p. 16n. See too *A Letter ... to a Friend at Boston* (London, 1793), pp. 26n., 28.

was separable from political liberty or the capacity of citizens to be self-governing.[59]

A major influence in forming the notion of liberty current among reformers was David Williams. Sometimes obscure in his overall position, he was eminently quotable in short extracts, and British publications took full advantage of his merits.[60] His ideas penetrated France,[61] in part through his association with Brissot de Warville, who seems to have been responsible for the French edition of the *Letters on Political Liberty* and who puffed Williams's opinions in his *Journal du Lycée de Londres*. Williams also exercised an influence on Condorcet—like Brissot, a leading Girondin—in the drafting of the French constitution of 1793.[62] Frenchmen of different political persuasions had long been prone to question the reality of British liberty, and Williams supplied the categories for expressing such thoughts. Judging from those French publications that dealt, prior to 1783, with British liberty, there had been a real need for precise language by which to contrast the condition of personal safety with that of effective control over government.[63] The *Encyclopédie* in 1765 had covered the subject of liberty in two articles by the chevalier de Jaucourt, both of them faithful to Montesquieu. A generation later, Montesquieu seemed not to suffice. For whether one wished to criticize the working and theoretical pretensions of English government, to elevate the majesty of the people, or to condemn the fact of revolution, the twofold nature of liberty was difficult to ignore. Different schools of thought expressed the thought differently, and Jacobins such as Robespierre

59. Cartwright, *The State of the Nation in a Series of Letters to his Grace the Duke of Bedford* (Harlow, 1805), pp. 108–9.

60. See *Political Magazine and Parliamentary, Naval, Military, and Literary Journal* 6 (Mar. 1784):173–74; and *London Chronicle* 4285 (15–17 Apr. 1784):375.

61. For some of Williams's French associates see Claude Perroud, ed., *Lettres de Madame Roland: Tome second, 1788–1793* (Paris: Imprimerie nationale, 1902), pp. 204n., 699, 744.

62. Franck Alengry, *Condorcet: guide de la Révolution française* (1904; reprinted, Geneva: Slatkine Reprints, 1971), pp. 214–15, 386, 822–23.

63. See P. L. Claude Gin, *Les Vrais principes du gouvernement françois* (Geneva, 1777), pp. vi, 92n., where the writer was critical both of Montesquieu and of British government but lacked the concepts to clinch his argument. Some of Linguet's essays in his *Annales* of 1777 have been read as contrasting civil and political liberty, but this seems unwarranted. For a book that seems faithful to Williams's definitions see Pierre Caze, *Comparison des constitutions de la Grande-Bretagne et de la France* (Paris, 1792), pp. 247–53.

and Saint-Just thought primarily in terms of "public liberty," with a distressing lack of emphasis upon conventional notions of individual security. At the other end of the ideological spectrum, intransigent Royalists rejected the association of suffrage and liberty, though its prominence in the arguments of their opponents necessarily brought it to their attention.[64]

The new opinions about the power of the people had first penetrated America before they appeared in France, but they did not take root so readily. Both Martin Howard and James Otis had recognized a difference between personal and political rights as they debated the rights of colonies in 1765.[65] However, neither developed an argument along the lines of that of Priestley or Price. Such radical ideas did find a responsive audience in America, and the votaries included Alexander Hamilton, but their reign was rather brief, and significantly, Thomas Paine did not employ the vocabulary popularized in Britain. Once independence had been gained, interest in stressing the people's participation in government declined, and concern for the suffrage— less of a problem than it was becoming in Britain—waited for another day. A more negative and old-fashioned understanding of liberty again came to prominence, after an absence of scarcely twenty years. Indeed, the tendency in the late 1780s to perceive liberty chiefly as protection against government has been seen by an historian as similar to de Lolme's denial that enjoyment of the suffrage could properly be called "liberty."[66] When the thought of David Williams received notice it was apparently a tribute to his refutation of Montesquieu's opinion that liberty could flourish only in a small state.[67] There is little indication that his views on political liberty were equally welcome.

The post-revolutionary mood did not last, however, for there were

---

64. Examples of *émigré* opinion include Pierre, Baron Malouet, *Interesting Letters on the French Revolution*, trans. William Clarke (London, 1795), p. 24; and J. B. Duvoisin, *An Examination of the Principles of the French Revolution* (London, 1796), pp. 11–15. The English connotations of "political liberty" seem to have made less headway in German writings. Certainly they are absent in the substantial work by Franz Baltisch, *Politische Freiheit* (Leipzig, 1832).

65. Bernard Bailyn, ed., *Pamphlets of the American Revolution, 1750–1776* (Cambridge, Mass.: Belknap Press of Harvard University Press, 1965), 1:535, 538.

66. Gordon S. Wood, *The Creation of the American Republic, 1776–1787* (Chapel Hill: University of North Carolina Press, 1969), pp. 24, 609.

67. Paul Merrill Spurlin, *Montesquieu in America, 1760–1801* (Baton Rouge: Louisiana State University Press, 1940), p. 238.

still battles for political equality to be fought in America. In the nineteenth century, indeed, only the most radical understanding of liberty appears to have satisfied the better-known political thinkers of the new world. A characteristic position may be gathered from the reaction to the ideas of Edward Christian, Cambridge professor of law. He was an opponent of reform in Britain, since he felt that existing institutions sufficiently protected liberty. At the same time, Christian accepted the widespread opinion that political liberty, founded upon the nature of a government, was the necessary safeguard of civil liberty, and he berated Blackstone for his failure to recognize the distinction between the two.[68] This formula had much in common with Paley's but leaned slightly more in the direction of endorsing political participation, though of an undefined sort. The non-committal quality of this familiar statement failed to satisfy the American Nathaniel Chipman, who objected that Christian had defined the purpose of political liberty but had neglected to say what it was. Nothing less than an unequivocal avowal of the popular right of participation through elections would suffice.[69] A similar insistence, provoked by different circumstances, informed the arguments of Richard Hildreth and Francis Lieber, whose important books appeared in the 1850s.

In Britain, where lack of representation was a more serious problem, the cause of political liberty underwent no decline in popularity among those who were reform-minded, though of course the number of such people was severely reduced after the French Revolution. No less a figure than Lord John Russell endorsed the desirability of a form of liberty apart from personal security and the capacity for action not forbidden by the laws. This, Russell called political liberty and defined as "the acknowledged and legal right of the people to control their government or to take a share in it."[70] The Reform Bill and its successors were the outcome of a variety of factors, not all of which fall under the desire to promote political liberty. But undoubtedly they served to entrench the principle that genuine public freedom could not be divorced from some measure of political power. Signif-

68. Christian, *Notes to Blackstone's Commentaries* ... (Boston, 1801), p. 28; and *A Concise Account of the Origin of the Two Houses of Parliament* ... (London, 1810), p. 94.

69. Chipman, *Principles of Government: A Treatise on Free Institutions* (1833; reprinted, New York: Burt Franklin, 1969), pp. 56–66.

70. Russell, *An Essay on the History of the English Government and Constitution*, 2nd ed. (London, 1823), p. 115.

icantly, the argument from natural rights remained in abeyance throughout the period of active reform.[71]

Even the utilitarian tradition eventually came to terms with the new mode of argument, for though the teaching of Bentham remained sufficiently potent to withhold the support of George Cornewall Lewis in his *Remarks on the Use and Abuse of Some Political Terms* (1832), vindication of a sort finally came with the last identifiable member of the school.[72] Of more recent opinion, the field has been shared between those who have remained aware of the historical connection between political liberty and the political efficacy of the common people and those for whom the message was less urgent and precise.[73] Still, the differences between such perspectives have not been as great as one might suppose; certainly much less pronounced than was the case in the 1770s.

The claim for political liberty seemed to many in eighteenth-century Britain a misuse of language and a dangerous ambition in politics. No idea, however, served better to distinguish the concerns of earlier periods from that which saw the stirrings of the people as a regular and constitutional political force. Should one canvass the arguments for a "free state" put forth by John Milton, or by his less memorable colleague Marchamont Nedham, one encounters numerous ingenious considerations in favour of government without kings, but nothing by way of a systematic plea for "political liberty" as understood in the eighth decade of the eighteenth century. Not that it was necessarily a doctrine more distressing than the notions that had horrified Milton's contemporary Salmasius, but it was decidedly a different doctrine. Nor need one deny that the implications of political liberty had long been present in maxims such as the medieval *quod omnes tangit*. ... The radicals of the eighteenth century did not so much discover a wholly new idea as reassert an old one in an institutional setting capable of sustaining it.

The systematic distinction between civil and political liberty did not put an end to the search for Britain's palladium. However, the radical

---

71. As noted by Norman F. Cantor, *The English: A History of Politics and Society to 1760* (London: Simon and Schuster, 1968), p. 448.

72. See Henry Sidgwick, *Elements of Politics* (London, 1891), p. 42.

73. See Ernest Rhys, *The Growth of Political Liberty* (London: J. M. Dent, 1921). Cf. the more learned and more innocent account in A. J. Carlyle, *Political Liberty* (1941; reprinted, New York: Barnes and Noble, 1963).

argument of Priestley, Price, Williams, and Cartwright dated for ever an earlier idiom in which the courts of law, Parliament, ancient statutes, and the modern and free press—among other factors—all figured indiscriminately as possible keys to the condition of liberty. By designating certain freedoms as dependent on a degree of popular involvement in politics, the radicals brought some intellectual order to what had been a cacophony of claims for unrelated aspects of public life. The immunities of the citizen were attached more surely to the processes of government, and their continued enjoyment was proclaimed as contingent on the political offices filled by those same citizens. An ever more minute inquiry into such matters as the attributes of citizens, their organization, and the sources of their opinions would henceforth serve to link polity and society in new and revealing ways.[74]

At the same time the long-standing complacency about the existence of British liberty had been seriously challenged, for finally it could be argued that a crucial dimension of liberty was denied to the politically inert and that in the absence of large-scale participation, no form of liberty was safe. The claims of nineteenth-century conservatives that democracy and liberty were somehow antithetical were still to come, and the salience of economic considerations had scarcely yet been mentioned. Yet one can hardly deny that the division of liberty into civil and political was a milestone both in political analysis and in democratic aspiration.

74. The writings of David Williams epitomize this development.

VII

Public Spirit to Public Opinion

HISTORIANS HAVE LONG BEEN deeply suspicious of the notion of public opinion, seeing it as the last refuge of the politician without vision or the scholar without any better explanation. This may account for the thinness of materials on the subject. The elusive nature of the phenomenon of opinion has had the effect of restricting such literature as there is to the stuff of social rather than intellectual history. Thus the historian has tended to perceive the development of public opinion as a stage in the emergence of modern societies characterized both by growing literacy and political awareness and by institutions—such as elected politicians and an unfettered press—that complement the sophistication of the public. Whether the historians have written of "the supremacy of public opinion" or of a *naissance d'un monstre*, they have agreed that the latter part of the eighteenth century and the early nineteenth century saw changes in western Europe and elsewhere that signalled the arrival of public opinion as a significant force.[1]

Having had the locus of his inquiry provided for him, the student of political ideas is left with the business of trying to discover what the people of that time thought about the alleged change in the political climate. From the perspective of some political histories, one might conclude that there was no conscious recognition of the growth

---

This chapter was first written in 1976–77. In a recent paper, "Public Opinion: Hopes and Fears, 1780–1820," I returned to the theme. My latest effort departs in several respects from the approach taken here, but I have decided to allow the original chapter to stand substantially unchanged.

1. See Elie Halévy, *England in 1815*, revised ed. (London: Benn, 1949), pp. 108–200; Bernard Fay, *Naissance d'un monstre; l'opinion publique* (Paris: Perrin, 1965); and Leon S. Marshall, *The Development of Public Opinion in Manchester, 1780–1820* (Syracuse: Syracuse University Press, 1946).

of public opinion, and of course it is entirely possible that a nation might undergo important social changes without their being marked by contemporaries. Such, however, is not the case here, and so it makes sense to seek out the opinions that political observers had about the subject of public opinion. Nor is this the pursuit of a shadow's shadow. For, admitting the limited explanatory power of the concept of "public opinion," one is left with the widespread expectation that, in a certain sort of society, public opinion will in fact be significant. The task of this chapter is to explore the emergence of that expectation.

Queen of the World

In the writing of intellectual history, the risk of committing prolepsis is constant. Attempts to deal with the idea of public opinion have suffered from anachronisms of two different sorts. In the first place, ignorance of the ordinary language of political discussion has led historians to date the emergence of the term "public opinion" later than was actually the case. This has had the further effect of focusing their attention on France rather than on Britain as the home of the expression. However, it is no less true that certain factors have been responsible for the uncritical assumption that writers were dealing with public opinion, when in fact they had no intention of discussing the modern phenomenon. Sometimes this has been the result of a too-ready substitution of "public opinion" for terms that an author himself used; sometimes it has followed from paying too much atten-tion to the exact words "public opinion," without inquiring about the meaning that was being attached to them.

Beginning with the widespread assumption that dates the use of public opinion from the latter part of the eighteenth century, it is not difficult to establish a contrary position. We shall see that political language at the election of 1734 already included a number of terms for the voice of the people on political matters; moreover as early as 1727 there had been a short-lived government publication called *The Free Briton: or, The Opinion of the People*. More significantly, the account of the parliamentary debate for 16 March 1737–38, as it appeared in Cave's *Gentleman's Magazine*, makes use of such terms as "general Opinion" and "the Opinion of the People."[2] One of the ostensible

2. *Gentleman's Magazine* 7 (Nov. 1738):525, 553. Cf. *Parliamentary History* 10 (1737–38):700. See too a reference to "the Opinion of the Public" in [Corbyn Morris], *A Letter*

speakers was Walter Plumer, but whether the words were really his or William Guthrie's—or even those of the young Samuel Johnson—makes no difference. Some people, either politicians on the floor or journalists in the gallery, saw fit to use the expressions. It is significant too that the sentiments were favourable to this opinion and thus owed nothing to the condescending judgement about vulgar taste and opinion that filled the literary periodicals of the time. The earliest uses of the exact expression "public opinion" do indeed take this form or that of references to the public opinion on the subject of individual reputations. From Mandeville to Adam Smith, various moral philosophers noted the sanction of the world's opinion as it affected personal conduct. But even if we disregard allusions to what one journalist referred to as "the public opinion, as circulated in the modish conventicles of critical inquiry,"[3] there remains clear evidence that the expression "the Opinion of the Public" had political application well before mid-century. Ordinarily the words still carried the definite article.

One looks in vain for any self-conscious inquiry about the meaning of the concept, or even much awareness that the words had become fashionable.[4] Unlike the word "interest," which emerged in the previous century amid considerable discussion of its meaning in political life (and, incidentally, of its French origins), "public opinion" seems

---

from a By-stander to a Member of Parliament ... (London, 1741), p. 9; and another in Nicholas Tindal et al., *A Continuation of Mr. Rapin's History of England* (London, 1759), 8 (of the continuation):101.

Modern scholarship has stressed the phenomenon of public opinion rather than the concept. See W. T. Laprade, *Public Opinion and Politics in Eighteenth Century England* (New York: Macmillan, 1936); and Paul Langford, *The Excise Crisis* (Oxford: Clarendon Press, 1975), chap. 10. Geoffrey Holmes has shown more concern for the vocabulary of the day, though his judgement that the expression was not then current reflects only the usage of the first half of the century. See *The Electorate and the National Will in the First Age of Party* (Kendal: printed for the author, 1976), pp. 7–8.

3. See *Rhapsodist* 2 (31 Jan. 1757). Earlier samples of its use in relation to matters of taste or reputation include "how unwillingly we admit of a Defect that has not been charged upon us by the Publick Opinion," in Aaron Hill's *Prompter* 66 (27 June 1735); and a comment on "the Rectitude of public opinion," in *Old England: or, The National Gazette* 93 (21 Mar. 1752).

4. Christopher Smart's *Midwife* 3 (1753):73–75, contains a whimsical essay on "The Expediency of settling a Standard in order to ascertain the Opinions of People in all Ranks and conditions of Life." The proposal called for setting up an "Opinion-Office" to supply opinions to people who would otherwise lack them.

to have been employed as a natural growth of the English language. To call a political opinion public does seem—on the analogy of public interest and public spirit—to commit oneself to a relatively favourable position.[5] Though the literati might continue to impugn public taste, those who first invoked the expression "public opinion" in political contexts tended to be respectful. The growth in frequency of use most likely reflects the development of extra-parliamentary activity in the second half of the eighteenth century and a corresponding softening of the traditional animus against recognizing the popular voice outside Parliament.

It is unlikely that foreign, specifically French, uses of public opinion had much influence. There is little evidence of the use of the expression *l'opinion publique* prior to its appearance in Rousseau's *Letter à D'Alembert* of 1758, and there it referred only to the general state of manners. More political importance can be attached to the prominent, if highly ambiguous, treatment of *l'opinion publique* by Helvétius, but again it is difficult to discern any impact on British thought. The work most often credited with popularizing public opinion throughout Europe is Necker's *De l'administration des finances de la France*. The year of its appearance, 1784, was certainly a time when Englishmen discussed public opinion as never before. However, as we shall see, there were ample reasons for this in the state of domestic politics, without seeking any narrowly literary influence.

A probable reason why there was little apparent awareness of the novelty of the expression "public opinion" is that the place of opinion in human affairs had long been accorded great importance. When modern authors suggest that Francis Bacon, who wrote in the *Novum Organum* of *opinione*, had things to say about public opinion, they court the danger of mistaking form for substance.[6] But undoubtedly he did have something to say about "opinion." Even Sir William Temple's famous references to "the general opinion" and to "vulgar opinion" may readily be associated with a modernity of sentiment that was

---

5. This point was suggested by Hans Spier's valuable article "Historical Development of Public Opinion," *American Journal of Sociology* 4 (Jan. 1950):378.

6. See Samuel H. Beer, "Two Models of Public Opinion: Bacon's 'New Logic' and Diotima's 'Tale of Love'," *Transactions of the Royal Historical Society*, 5th series, 24 (1974):79–96. For references to Bacon on "public opinion" see Gunter W. Remmling, *Road to Suspicion: A Study of Modern Mentality and the Sociology of Knowledge* (New York: Appleton-Century-Crofts, 1967), p. 123.

simply not there. Temple's comments in his "On Popular Discontents" (1701) were directed towards an explanation of the manner in which all governments were sustained by opinion—even those that habitually imposed upon their subjects. This sentiment was repeated by Hume in the other well-known British contribution to the subject in the *Essays* of 1741–42. Both writers were making an essentially conservative case about the manner in which people might peacefully be ruled. Far from pointing to the emergence of a new popular influence upon government, they were invoking the traditional wisdom about the measure in which a people, judiciously led, could be kept docile.

Hume's debt to earlier thought is revealed by the sentiment that "interest itself, and all human affairs are entirely governed by *opinion.*"[7] It had been fashionable for seventeenth-century individualists to argue that interest ruled the world, and this dictum did good service in various efforts at increased self-expression. An appropriate riposte to those who stressed man's unstinting pursuit of self-interest was that people did not always seek what was objectively good for them; rather, their priorities were governed by their opinions. The same point could of course be made by emphasizing the subjectivity of interests, and sometimes it was. However, the word "interest," in its seventeenth-century applications, increasingly referred to self-seeking by subjects. There was an obvious value in countering this by reminding people that the voice of authority spoke through opinion.

It would be difficult to trace the precise origins of this notion, but clearly it antedates the onset of what anyone would be inclined to call the consciousness of public opinion in the modern sense. Pascal, whose *Pensées* appeared in 1670, had grasped the essentials, without thereby intending to add to our stock of democratic theory: "L'empire fondé sur l'opinion et l'imagination règne quelque temps ... et cet empire

---

7. Hume, "Whether the British Government Inclines more to Absolute Monarchy or to a Republic," in *Essays, Moral, Political, and Literary*, ed. T. H. Green and T. H. Grose (London, 1875), 1:125. On Hume and his successors see Ernst Vollrath, "That All Governments Rest on Opinion," *Social Research* 43 (Spring 1976):46–61. John Pocock and Donald Winch have both suggested to me that I may be too dismissive of this use of "opinion." No doubt some writers such as Smith did emphasize its role in free government. See Winch, *Adam Smith's Politics: An Essay in Historiographic Revision* (Cambridge: Cambridge University Press, 1978), pp. 168–70. By contrast, Davenant's use of this maxim had not furthered his Country-party views, for he had used it purely in regard to relations between states. See "An Essay upon the Balance of Power" (1701) in *Works*, 3:318.

est doux et voluntaire, celui du force règne toujours. Ainsi l'opinion est la reine du monde. ..." But Pascal was not first on the scene. Girolamo Cardano (1501–76), in his *De Consolatione libri tres* (1542), and elsewhere, held "opinio" to rule human affairs. Thus all educated Europeans from at least the sixteenth century would have been familiar with the idea that opinion, in some very general context, was queen of the world. The maxim was applicable to politics, as to other spheres, but had no necessary and specific connection with that activity. The queen of the world was quite as likely to be seen exemplified in the state of learning[8] or in the sanctions imposed by others upon one's moral choices. Even for Helvétius and d'Holbach, both of whom were interested in reforming public life, opinion continued to have associations more congruent with traditional concerns than with factors peculiar to modern politics. Both sometimes rebuked the queen for consorting with error and superstition, but neither—least of all d'Holbach—thought in terms of public opinion as a spontaneous force that influenced government.[9] Instead opinion emanated from government and did its work, for good or ill, on the masses. There was an insight here that British writers were to learn in time, but first they found reason to take seriously the possibility that the direction of the influence was primarily from the people to the government. French writers may well have been correct in finding the sources of public opinion in government itself, but this position encouraged their thinking in terms of how private conduct was moulded and not how public policy came to be subject to popular influences. The halberd of government might indeed be led by opinion, as Quesnay once pointed out,[10] but the older tradition usually involved the insistence that this opinion was largely the creation of the entire culture, if not of its political elite.

It is apparent, then, that British notions of public opinion as a

---

8. See G.-C. LeGendre, marquis de Saint Aubin-sur-Loire, *Traité de l'opinion* ... (Paris, 1735), 1:9.

9. D'Holbach, *Système social* (London [i.e., Amsterdam], 1773), 1:14, 18; and Helvétius, *Treatise on Man* (1773), trans. W. Hooper (1810; reprinted, New York: Burt Franklin, 1969), 2:356. The same can be said for Diderot. See the passages quoted in Anthony Strugnell, *Diderot's Politics* (The Hague: Martinus Nijhoff, 1973), p. 105.

10. Quesnay is sometimes credited with speaking of "public opinion," but he apparently spoke only of "l'opinion." See Léonce de Lavergne, *Les Économistes français du dix-huitième siècle* (1870; reprinted, Geneva: Slatkine Reprints, 1970), p. 108.

restraint upon government did not derive in any straightforward way from traditional dicta regarding opinion as ruler of the world. Temple and Hume were not the harbingers of a new age; they simply participated in a mode of expression that was well established in European culture. Even at the time of the Revolution, French writers adhered to the conventional language for treating public opinion, and so they continued to invoke a general force governing human affairs and avoided more mundane specifics.[11] British usage, it seems, tended to be more specifically political and—from an earlier date—more enmeshed in discussion of the mechanics of popular elections, instructing, addressing, petitioning, and the technicalities of the law of seditious libel. Differences in connotation are revealed in a British response to Mme. de Staël's observation that men did not need to conform to public opinion in the same manner as did women. The response was that "in this country we acknowledge public opinion to be the security and bulwark of our laws, morals and religion; and in proportion as it favours virtue or vice in every society, that society is either virtuous or vicious. ... perhaps *l'opinion publique* may mean something in French different from *the public opinion* in English."[12] This does not succeed perfectly in capturing the distinction, but at least it is evidence of some contemporary awareness of national styles in the treatment of public opinion.

The modern scholarly judgement is that the concept of public opinion was essentially a French creation. This idea has been especially strong in the rich German literature on the subject, and sometimes it takes the form of stating that the world owes the concept of public spirit to English thought and public opinion to that of the French.[13] Though this may accurately record the source of inspiration of such

---

11. Revolutionary tracts that begin by referring to the queen of the world include [J. de Ségur], *Essai sur l'opinion* (Paris, 1790); Anon., *De l'opinion publique* (Paris, 1791); and [A. J. C. Clément], *Devoirs des citoyens fidèles ...* (Paris, 1792).

12. *The Pic Nic* (written by William Combe) 3 (22 Jan. 1803).

13. See Ludwig Uhlig, *Georg Forster: Einheit und Mannigfaltigkeit in seiner geistigen Welt* (Tübingen: M. Niemeyer, 1965), p. 211. Other sources include Hermann Oncken, *Historisch-politische Aufsätze und Reden* (Munich and Berlin: R. Oldenbourg, 1914), 1:225–26; Ferdinand Tönnies, *Kritik der öffentlichen Meinung* (Berlin: J. Springer, 1922), pp. 374–78; Wilhelm Bauer, *Die öffentliche Meinung in der Weltgeschichte* (Potsdam: Akademische verlagsgesellschaft Athenaion, 1930), pp. 233–35; and Ruth Flad, *Der Begriff der öffentlichen Meinung bei Stein, Arndt und Humbolt* (Berlin and Leipzig: W. de Gruyter, 1929), p. 8.

German essayists as Georg Forster and Christian Garve—the people primarily responsible for bringing *öffentliche Meinung* into the German language—it fails to do justice to British experience in the latter half of the eighteenth century. For there is good reason to suppose both that the concept of public opinion first appeared in ordinary political language in Britain and that its use was the outcome of the nation's experiences, not of cultural borrowing.

In Search of Public Spirit

Before so-called democracy, before even popular radicalism, there were already enemies of arbitrary government who appealed beyond the ministerial majorities in Parliament to people in the community. Under normal circumstances there was no disposition to involve masses of private citizens in the business of making decisions; as Locke had said, the actual exercising of supremacy by the community was inconsistent with the retention of government. Thus even the strongest partisans of the cause of civic virtue were less than anxious to solicit the presence or even the opinions of the bulk of the population. Petitioning and addressing might sometimes supplement the franchise, but as citizens sometimes learned to their cost, the bearers of such documents were not privileged, in their persons, as were Members of Parliament. What remained in the arsenal of the concerned patriot was a posture, a habit of mind, known as "public spirit."

It was not a favourite term among the republicans of the seventeenth century; those, like Algernon Sidney, who contemplated a rebellion of the propertied classes, needed stronger fare. Occasionally one finds seventeenth-century references to the need for men with "public spirits," and the term was sufficiently familiar to be condemned as demagogic in a sermon of 1686.[14] Still, this language was far more characteristic of the early decades of the eighteenth century. It found a home in the vocabulary of the Country party under William III, thrived when the Whigs moved into opposition in 1710, and burst forth with great vigour in the rhetoric of an ineffectual opposition at the time of the South-Sea scandal. Thereafter it receded from the

---

14. See the sermon by Robert South, quoted in M. Dorothy George, "Elections and Electioneering, 1679–81," *English Historical Review* 45 (1930):552–78. For another negative comment see S. P. Gent [Samuel Parker], *Six Philosophical Essays upon Several Subjects: Viz. ... III A Public Spirit* (London, 1700), pp. 28–35.

forefront of political language, returning from time to time to challenge luxury, avarice, placemen, and standing armies.

One of the more cogent Country pamphlets on the reign of William made it clear that the requisite spirit might be sought primarily on the part of the governors, not of the people generally. The author was adamant about the right of the freeholders to erect whatever government they chose—a radical-sounding claim—but would apparently have been satisfied by a place-bill that would promote "a public Spirit in the Ministry."[15] Increased responsibilities were thus contemplated for independent members of the House of Commons, without any requirement that the freeholders do anything. Constitutional reforms would cure the ills of society by procuring the necessary attitude on the part of the chief officers of state. Others, more naïvely, sought spiritual improvement in the great men of the community as a prelude to reform.[16] Both positions were in accord with the commonplace of men out of power that a reform of manners had to begin with the great, for it was their example that led others astray. Sometimes, of course, the message was directed to all people and not just those in high office. On such occasions "public Spirit" might mean nothing more than the capacity to escape self-interest in the name of charity and the public good. The version that was especially redolent of traditional moral homilies called for each member of the community to serve the public by performing his appropriate function. The exact sentiment of sixteenth-century sermons on the estates of the world and their several duties lingered in the directive to people to demonstrate their public spirit by being useful in their stations.[17]

Public spirit was thus nothing new in the realm of virtues and very often invited private men simply to maintain themselves honestly and to revere the laws. Richard Steele, who was much given to appealing to public spirit, saw it exemplified in various Roman heroes, as did his friend Addison. Public spirit, for Steele, was "a Character" be-

15. Anon., *The Claims of the People of England Essayed. In a Letter from the Country* (London, 1701), p. 32. A similar argument appears in Andrew Brown, *The Character of the True Publick Spirit ...* ([Edinburgh], 1702), esp. pp. 81–86.

16. [Thomas Baston], *Thoughts on Trade and a Publick Spirit* (London, 1716), pp. 148–204.

17. See Charles Brent, *Persuasions to a Publick Spirit* (London, 1704); Edward Tenison, *The Excellency and Usefulness of a Publick Spirit* (London, 1711), p. 13; and J. Ashe, *Publick-Spiritedness Recommended ...* (London, 1728), p. iv.

longing to persons; he said little about its exact nature, but judging from the number of references in his essays of 1713 to the loss of public spirit, it was obviously a character that abounded in Whigs.[18] Swift disagreed, but his *Publick Spirit of the Whigs* gave no precise meaning to the expression. John Dennis was less partisan than Steele in his Whiggism—he is sometimes wrongly identified as a Tory—but would also have subscribed to the notion that the possession of public spirit was the most desirable of conditions. Dennis identified the character with frugal, traditional manners and patriotism. However, Dennis was more insistent on the role that public spirit played in political life: "What the Spirit of a Man is to the Body Natural, that, Publick Spirit is to the Body Politick. ..."[19] Still, the character portrayed by Dennis was largely an assemblage of negative virtues; one should be uncorrupt and eschew vanities rather than defend liberty in a more active fashion. Hoadly, preaching in 1716 on the nature and duty of a public spirit, made it sound very reasonable, but very unheroic. It was founded upon a virtuous self-love, being just self-interest "rightly understood."

The view of public spirit promoted by Thomas Gordon in *Cato's Letters* suggested a more active and truculent citizenship than had been advocated by many others. Gordon noted, sensibly, that what was demanded by public spirit depended upon the nature of the government under which one lived. But he also contrasted that spirit consisting in "mere Opinion" with a more genuine and active form. In addition, he suggested that it was desirable that arbitrary governments allow the judgements of the people to be expressed. Gordon's Old Whiggism never developed into the advocacy of resistance to a corrupt administration, but his impatience with a phrase, "in every Body's Mouth" but not in his conduct, was evident.[20] The apparent corruption in public life was also a target for other moral censors, and again the panacea was a genuuine "public Spirit."

Too much loose talk about public spirit was, at best, irritating to the government; at worst, menacing. Thus a number of administration newspapers condemned the use of such a "cant Word" by Cato

18. Steele, *Guardian* 33 (18 Apr. 1713); and 58 (18 May 1713); *Englishman* 2 (6–8 Oct. 1713); and 57 (15 Feb. 1713–14).

19. Dennis, *An Essay upon Publick Spirit: being a Satyr in Prose upon the Manners and Luxury of the Times* . . . (London, 1711), p. 1.

20. "Of Publick Spirit," *London Journal* 35 (1 July 1721).

and others. Some writers tried to interpret the term in ways that would ensure passive acquiescence, but more typical was condemnation of the "Jargon of Publick-Spiritedness, which wastes so much of the Time of the busy Part of our Countrymen."[21]

With the subsiding of the wave of literary unrest that accompanied the Bubble, public spirit came to be less recommended. Often in the succeeding decades it was contrasted with the spirit of party and so served the cause of that sort of diffuse concern for moral reform that posed no threat to any administration.[22] In the measure that public spirit entailed a chaste aloofness from place and party, it decried the existing practices without seriously challenging them. In fact, in a curious way exhortations to public spirit often seemed to serve as the same sort of bromide as did 30-January sermons in the mid-eighteenth century. Both warned against party and its works and, in effect, enjoined a passive loyalty. No steely-eyed passion for liberty intruded on the poet who wrote complacently,

> And Publick Spirit here a People show,
> Free num'rous pleas'd and busy all below.[23]

For all Savage's apparent resentment against Walpole (as recorded by Samuel Johnson), his was a lonely passion without a programme or a role for the people. But long before this, Gordon's ardour too had been assuaged, and he had subsided into a pension.

Public spirit was one of the characteristically British political concepts of the eighteenth century. Though the expression came to be known in France—and in fact has been much used by modern historians to describe the currents of ideas in France in the eighteenth century—it seems to have been a late borrowing from English. Mon-

---

21. *St. James's Journal* 1 (3 May 1723). See too *Whitehall Journal* 47 (9 Apr. 1723); and *Pasquin* 56 (13 Aug. 1723). Even *Applebee's Journal*, written largely by Defoe for the Tories, expressed distaste for the more fulsome expressions of public spirit. See the number for 19 Oct. 1723.

22. See Anon., *The Present Necessity of Distinguishing Public Spirit from Party* (London, 1736); Anon., *Public Spirit* (London, 1808), pp. 4–5; W. L. Brown, "A View of the Present Times," appended to John Leland, *A View of the Principal Deistical Writers ... ,* 5th ed. (London, 1798), 2:482; and C. J. Plumer, "Of Public Spirit Amongst the Ancients" (1823), in *Oxford English Prize Essays* 4 (Oxford, 1830):43–44.

23. Richard Savage, *Of Public Spirit in Regard to Public Works. A Poem* (1736), 2nd ed. (London, 1739).

tesquieu certainly had much to say about spirit, including national spirit, but only after currency in English usage had already passed its peak. The British flavour of public spirit, leaving aside the Roman originals on which British writers modelled the public-spirited character, has long been accepted. As a French man of letters wrote in 1820, the English had both created the word and displayed the thing itself.[24] But for all its fame as a shibboleth of political virtue, the notion of public spirit was due to be replaced as the carrier of civic awareness.

Vox Populi to 1780

Though public spirit was a frail reed on which to base national regeneration, there were other resources in eighteenth-century culture for treating the role of the people. Everyone knew that in some imprecise sense *vox populi* was held to be *vox dei*, though familiarity with the maxim was no guarantee of its relevance to British politics.[25] As early as the sixteenth century one finds the poet John Skelton pleading or threatening the claims of *vox populi* in a complaint against taxes. The same cry had surfaced rather often in the tracts of the Puritan Revolution, just as it had in the French *Mazarinades* of the same period, with no great effect. Throughout the seventeenth century, the Court party in England had enough difficulty coming to terms with *salus populi*; *vox populi* in any literal sense was clearly unthinkable as a test of political wisdom. Indeed, Whig adherence to the proverb was systematically exaggerated by their opponents, since there is no reason to believe that most Whigs of 1710 would have dissented from the substance, as opposed to the tone and intent, of Francis Atterbury's insistence that the voice of the people was not the voice of God. Another Jacobite cleverly assailed the Whigs as Jacobites, basing his case on the assumptions that Whigs believed in *vox populi* and that

---

24. Paul-Louis Courier, "Lettres au Rédacteur du *Censeur*" (1819–20), in *Oeuvres Complètes* (Paris: Gallimard, 1951), p. 43. This identification of public spirit with British sources may very well have been a factor in leading European scholars to underestimate the Anglo-Saxon sources of the modern concept of public opinion. An unusually sophisticated work that still displays the tendency is Jürgen Habermas, *Strukturwandel der Öffentlichkeit* (Neuwied am Rhein: Luchterhand Verlag, 1968), pp. 102–16.

25. Indeed, the maxim has been treated by Professor Boas largely in terms more relevant to literature and the arts, than to politics. See George Boas, *Vox Populi: Essays in the History of an Idea* (Baltimore: Johns Hopkins University Press, 1969).

the people, if ever consulted, would support the pretender.[26] Considering the Whigs' frantic efforts to avoid an election in 1710 and their passage, in 1716, of the Septennial Act, there was some truth in the charge that the professed admirers of the people were somewhat chary of an encounter with popular opinion.

Thus we see that no significant party in the state cared to give firm content or consistent application to the principle that the voice of the people was sound in content, much less divine. Even the remaining republicans of the time chose to express their concern for honest government and the political rights of the propertied classes in other terms. If one chooses the broadest possible understanding of the identity of the people, then it is clear that no one literally sought to invoke *vox populi*. Benjamin Hoadly, most Whiggish of Low-Churchmen, sometimes defended the Revolution by reference to *vox populi*, but obviously he had in mind a very different understanding of the people than when he described the public good as that of "every individual Person, of what Rank and Quality soever, besides the supreme Governour."[27] Of course, parties would continue to compare their support as measured by electoral results, petitions, and addresses; such activities, however, entailed no sustained role for extra-parliamentary influences. Parliament could find its inspiration where it wished, and even efforts to promote public discussion of controversial issues might be construed as an unwarranted appeal to ignorance. So argued Sir John Meres in branding agitation over government complicity in the South-Sea debacle of 1720 as based on the unproven principle of *vox populi, vox dei*.[28]

Through the decades of the Whig oligarchy and beyond, the con-

---

26. Anon., *Vox Populi, Vox Dei* (n.p., 1719), p. 3. The alleged printer of this pamphlet was executed. One Brewster, said to have been the author, made his escape. See Joseph Gillow, *A Literary and Bibliographical History, or Bibliographical Dictionary of the English Catholics* (1885–1902; reprinted, New York: Burt Franklin, 1966), 4:219. For another line of enquiry, which makes no reference to Brewster, see R. J. Goulden, "Vox Populi, Vox Dei: Charles Delafoye's paperchase," *Book Collector* 28(1979):368–90. Linda Colley seems to attribute the work to Matthews, the nineteen-year-old printer, but cites no evidence. See *In Defiance of Oligarchy*, p. 28.

27. Hoadly, *Some Considerations Humbly Offered to the Right Rev. the Lord Bishop of Exeter* (London, 1709), p. 43. The fullest treatment of the nature and avenues of public sentiment, as they then existed, came in John Oldmixon's *The History of Addresses*, 2 vols. (1709–11). I have discussed his ideas and those of Defoe in chap. 2, above.

28. Meres, *The Equity of Parliaments* (London, 1720), p. 31.

stitutional position of all administrations remained clear and inflexible: the sense of the nation was to be collected only within the House of Commons, and no other test was admissible. Despite the influence of coffee-houses, daily newspapers, and the volatile population of London, the idea of the public as a constant actor in the political process did not materialize. Instead, when it suited them politicians appealed to opinion in the country, but they accorded it no permanent superintendence over public affairs. Compelling statements of this position appeared in the ministerial press after the election of 1734, as Walpole's writers refused even to allow that the alleged popularity of the Opposition without doors was a sign of merit. The notorious folly of the people indicated, rather, the reverse. Most eighteenth-century elections ended in recriminations about which side had truly won and why. That of 1734, coming on the heels of the furore over the Excise Bill, called forth particularly elaborate positions on the meaning of the result, the Opposition blaming its defeat on corruption and various unfair tactics by the Treasury, the government relying upon its unassailable majority in the Commons.

Although no new constitutional position emerged, the period serves as a landmark in the development of a national political culture, if only because it seems to have been the first at which the terms "the Opposition" and "general Election" were used. The first suggested the maturing of transitory oppositions into a more permanent institution, while the second served to emphasize a national dimension in what might otherwise have appeared to be purely local contests between rival families.[29] The expression *vox populi* became—for a time, at least—less current and was replaced by a host of expressions closer to modern political vocabulary. The pages of the various papers in that summer of 1734 record such expressions as "popular Opinion," "general Opinion," "publick Sense," and, above all, "the Sense of the People." Robert Walpole in particular insisted that it was this sense of the people, rather than its voice, that was significant for his administration. Clearly, the "sense of the people" had a qualitative dimension lacking in *vox populi*.

By the 1750s, events were again pressing the claims of the people to the fore. The so-called Jew Bill of 1753 called forth a host of

29. For references to the forthcoming "General Election" see *Daily Courant* 5212 (22 Dec. 1732); and BL, Add. Ms. 33,344, fol. 85, dating from 1733.

petitions, and even allowing that most of the furore was artificially induced, there was enough of it to worry the government. Furthermore, the useful precedent of having forced the withdrawal of legislation inspired the Opposition to new ventures. The martyrdom of Admiral Byng, as a scapegoat for the loss of Minorca, served to keep alive an awareness of the public voice and its place in the political system. The forces favourable to Byng took comfort in the recent triumph of opinion outside Parliament and cited it as the justification for addressing the Throne. Indeed, the comparatively disorganized Opposition of 1756 seems to have made a good deal more of the importance and propriety of public sentiment than had Bolingbroke's party when it forced the abandonment of the excise scheme in 1733.

Those who were anxious to embarrass the ministry questioned the traditional claim that Parliament was the only reliable guide to the "Sense of the Nation." Parliament might very well be out of step with national feeling, and so it might better be collected from the addresses of grand juries, always provided that the wealth and social standing of the addressers were impressive.[30] For all their proclaimed faith in the reality and virtue of public opinion, writers against the ministry could not fail to be aware that this opinion was manipulated. This awareness is amply reflected in comments that clerks in the victualling office were ordered to burn Byng in effigy and in sardonic queries whether the post office was still the organ of state vested with the responsibility for arranging mobs and bonfires.[31] On the whole the Opposition defended *vox populi*, but its enthusiasm remained qualified by the resentment that had haunted Bolingbroke and his following— a truly enlightened populace would surely support the Opposition! The dilemma of the Opposition, having to appeal to the fount of authority and knowing that it had already been polluted by Treasury money, was vigorously spelled out by a pro-Byng pamphleteer:

---

30. See Anon., *The Voice of the People* (London, 1756), sig. A2, p. 11.

31. [Dr. John Shebbeare], *An Appeal to the People: Containing the Genuine and Entire Letter of Admiral Byng, Part the First* (London, 1756), p. 70; and Anon., *Observations on the Conduct of the Administration; particularly in regard to the Loss of Minorca* (London, 1757), p. 30. For the attribution of the first of these to Shebbeare see *European Magazine* (Sept. 1788):167. Paul Whitehead, poet and satirist, is known also to have written on behalf of Byng, but his contributions have never been identified.

History shews ages are necessary to obliterate national prejudices, when the populace of a nation have once been raised to acts of resentment, by their ministers ... by this means the people are made a party in the cause, and each individual thus imposed on, thinks himself interested, that it should not be proved, he was or could be imposed on. —The multitude therefore never can conceive, that public authority, for the information of the people, has been prostituted and corrupted to inflame their minds. ...[32]

Seeking a term for the *vox populi*, or sense of the people, this writer referred to the "common sense."

It was another writer of the day—in this case a critic of Pitt's courting public favour—who argued against the use of addresses by private citizens. Addresses purported to press the views of greater numbers than actually subscribed to them; they could never indicate the sense of the nation. "The publick Opinion certainly cannot be known, but by public application to the whole Body."[33] This was not an invitation to seek out public opinion, though the writer allowed that it was perfectly proper for people without doors to scrutinize proceedings in Parliament. That, he said, was why the votes were published. It can usefully be noted here that as late as 1738 William Pulteney of the Opposition is recorded as objecting to the general and unrestricted publication of the votes of Parliament or any appeal to the public based on what had been said in Parliament.[34]

Although ministerial writers were understandably reluctant to recognize the right of public opinion to correct government policy, they too appealed to the people. One such spokesman also followed the Opposition in protesting that the public was imposed upon by misinformation and emotional rhetoric, and he complained of those "who watch the Ebb and Flow of Affairs, and every little Change in the

---

32. Anon., *Observations on the Conduct of the Administration*, p. 13.

33. Anon., *A New System of Patriot Policy* ... (London, 1756), p. 63. The tone of this pamphlet, including jibes at Pitt as the British Cicero, is much like that of the paper called the *Test*, begun by Arthur Murphy later in the year.

34. *Parliamentary History* 10 (1738):806–7. Pulteney's objection to the publication of debates was quite conventional, nor would it be surprising had he been concerned about the circulation of division-lists. But the publication of the votes—the decisions that Parliament finally made—had been allowed, with occasional interruptions, since 1680.

Minds of the People, that they may turn even our best Dispositions to the public Prejudice."[35]

If one contrasts this period with that of the excise scheme and the election of 1734, it seems that both the ministers and the Opposition were more favourably disposed to popular involvement in the discussion of issues. It was widely held that the change of ministers in December 1756 had been the direct result of the "Voice of the People," while Pitt's eventual triumph of 1757 was hailed by his admirers as the manifestation of the people's will against the inclinations of the Court.[36] Pitt's enemies, of course, had the ready retort, commonly heard at the accession of George III, that despite the great orator's hold on the people, his alleged source of power had no formal standing, since the people were not engaged in raising supplies. Whatever one's views on Pitt, it was difficult to deny that the events of these years raised the issue of public opinion and its place in British government to a prominence that it never lost thereafter. Smollett's *Adventures of an Atom*, which is filled with a contempt for the vagaries of the populace, was inspired, in large measure, by this period.

Neither side on the Byng question had been anxious to redefine the nature of that body, outside Parliament, whose sentiments were supposed to direct the general policy of government, though the scope of the *pays légal* was increasingly an issue. In 1763, for instance, it came to the fore—once on the character of the addresses on the peace and again on those to mark the birth of a prince. Still, the traditional understanding of the identity of the people survived even the efforts of the freeholders of Middlesex to have John Wilkes as their representative. In asserting the power of the people outside Parliament, the petitions of 1769–70 involved no extension of the politically-active

---

35. Anon., *An Appeal to the Sense of the People on the Present Posture of Affairs* (London, 1756), p. 2.

36. See *London Evening Post* 4531 (20–23 Nov. 1756); and O. M. Haberdasher [*i.e.*, Alexander Carlyle], *Plain Reasons for Removing a certain Great Man from his M——Y's Presence and Councils for ever* (London, 1759), p. 7. The laboured irony of the title is typical of political literature of the time.

A modern and sceptical judgement about the place of public opinion at this time is that of Paul Langford, "William Pitt and Public Opinion, 1757," *English Historical Review* 88 (Jan. 1973):54–80. However, a recent study argues persuasively that, for all the difficulties involved in tracing its effects, the force of public opinion is discernible in Pitt's career. See Marie Peters, *Pitt and Popularity: The Patriot Minister and London Opinion during the Seven Years' War* (Oxford: Clarendon Press, 1980), esp. pp. 272–74.

population beyond the traditional confines of the electorate. Majority and minority parties continued to sound rather alike in their views about who counted outside the walls of Westminster.

Confronted with petitions on behalf of Wilkes and the Middlesex freeholders, Lord North offered only the characteristically mild defence that the majority of the counties had not petitioned and that among the signers were few men of great property, few justices of the peace, and few clergymen. To this Burke replied only that a justice of the peace could hardly be expected to petition the government, being appointed by it, and that North was silly to demand that every member of the community complain before he accepted that there was substantial discontent.[37] More effective than North's solemn pronouncements was Samuel Johnson's famous mockery of petitioners in *The False Alarm*. Neither defence contested the constitutionality of petitioning, nor was the ministerial understanding of the people's identity noticeably less generous than what was claimed by the Opposition. A North supporter defined *vox populi* as that of the "sensible, experienced, and disoppionate part of the community." Even the voice of radicalism as it emerged, independent of and hostile to the Whig magnates, sounds moderate on the subject of *vox populi*. "Under the persons meant by the appellation 'of the people', are presumably included the independent country gentlemen, merchants, capital manufacturers, and opulent tradesmen."[38] The disenchantment with the conventional Opposition already evident in radical circles was quite consistent with loyalty to the substantial elements in the community.

The term "opinion" did not, at this time, figure prominently in the case for popular influences on Parliament. It was in fact supporters of the majority party who wrote to the newspapers warning that disaffection with the decisions of government had the unfortunate effect of weakening both Parliament and ministry in "the opinion of the

---

37. *Parliamentary Spy* 11 (30 Jan. 1770):63–65. The right of petitioning was sometimes linked to the claim to instruct members, based on the assumption that a petition instructed the whole Parliament. See *Freeholder's Magazine: or Monthly Chronicle of Liberty* (July 1770):251. For further relevant distinctions see Betty Kemp, "Patriotism, Pledges and the People," in M. Gilbert, ed., *A Century of Conflict, 1850–1950: Essays for A. J. P. Taylor* (London: H. Hamilton, 1966), p. 42.

38. *London Evening Post* 6594 (8 Feb. 1770). See too "A Marvel" in *The Gazetteer* 12,936 (4 Aug. 1770).

people." This might lead to general ruin, for, as a letter-writer pointed out, "opinion is the sole foundation of power."[39] The exact words had previously been used by Charles Davenant in 1701, the time of the Kentish Petition, though in a different context. As in the past, the dictum about power and opinion was used to urge restraint on the part of the country, not its governors.

But a new awareness of the public without doors did more than to invoke the past; there were also new anxieties. In *The False Alarm* (1770) Johnson had suggested that the science of government might so improve through a knowledge of the nature of man that causeless public discontent would disappear. The same work contained his memorable catalogue of reasons for signing a petition—vexing the parson or proving one's literacy. This scepticism prompted the reply from the Opposition that "discontent is an effect, and no effect can subsist without a cause. The appelation of seditious violence, may be affixed to the most rational, and prudently conducted opposition. ... To study the theory of man, perhaps means to discover what the people will accept, and what they will bear. ..."[40] The entire exchange has an air not quite of the eighteenth century.

As North and Burke in Parliament,—"Junius" and "Modestus" in the press,—strove to identify their respective positions with the people, there remained some who expressed doubts about the whole mode of debate. This was the judgement of one unusually sensible observer:

It is somewhat remarkable that each party insist the people are with them, and one from the complaints of the petitioner, the other from the silence of the greater number of non-petitioning counties. In fact, there can be no such thing as a united voice of a free people, for their very freedom will occasion a discordinancy in sentiments. It is very possible for a bad government to have as many friends, ... and a good one to have as many enemies as the present.[41]

39. *General Evening Post* 5655 (9–11 June 1770). See too *Public Advertiser* 11,042 (17 Apr. 1770).

40. [John Scott], *The Constitution Defended, and Pensioner Exposed in Remarks on the False Alarm* (London, 1770), p. 3. Scott is best known as a minor poet.

41. "Decius" in *Middlesex Journal* 138 (17 Feb. 1770). Surviving runs of London newspapers for this period are incomplete. The best available source, covering the period from November 1769 to October 1770, is *The Repository: or Treasury of Politics and Literature for MDCCLXX*, 2 vols. (London, 1771). It is composed mainly of letters reprinted from the newspapers.

What is surprising, however, is that Lord North and others were prepared to debate the merits of various measures of public opinion without doors. It was left for the young Charles James Fox, who apparently had inherited his father's disrespect for popular opinion, to put the traditional case, and in terms so uncompromising that he must surely have regretted it later. There was no criterion, said Fox, for judging the sentiments of the people but the views of a majority of the House of Commons: "I can never acknowledge for the voice of the nation what is not echoed by the majority of this House."[42] In a curious way Fox would return to this position in the course of his tortuous defence of the coalition of 1783, but not before he had strayed from it on various other occasions.

The Triumph of Public Opinion?

By 1780 the voice of the people had found a new vehicle—the county associations—and debate shifted, in some measure, from the propriety of petitioning and instructing to the status of these extra-parliamentary bodies. The Wilkesite cause had, of course, produced an association in 1769, but not with the same pretensions as that which sprang up in Yorkshire in 1780. By this time Fox had changed his opinions and heatedly denied that he had ever claimed that the public voice might be found only in the House of Commons. Answering the charge by Henry Dundas that he had been inconsistent, Fox insisted that he had always allowed that the voice of the people was also present in petitions. Normally this voice was collected in those of members of Parliament, but only "until they acted in opposition to the voice of the people in the original capacity."[43]

A more inflammatory version of this doctrine was propagated in the country by the one-time Cambridge radical Dr. John Jebb. Taking for granted that the members of the lower house were but proxies for their constituents, Jebb argued that it was not improper for the people to treat directly with the King and the Lords as the other main branches of the constitution. Indeed, the very existence of the House of Commons "ought ... to be regarded as annihilated, when the voice

---

42. *The Speeches of the Right Honourable Charles James Fox ...* (London, 1815), 1:5.
43. Ibid., pp. 256–57.

of the principal shall be thus distinctly heard."[44] The modern parallel presumably would be the redundancy of a provincial or colonial governor in the presence of the head of state. Jebb's extraordinary claim that an association of county assemblies could unilaterally declare the House of Commons dissolved touched the farthest reaches of eighteenth-century radicalism. Only a republicanism that refused to recognize the rights of the other branches of government could have asked for more.

Amid all the talk about gathering the sense of the people from a great national congress or convention, the ordinary political machinery continued to function, and in the autumn of 1780 there was a general election. The outcome served to weaken North's support in the Commons, and modern historians are still in disagreement about the place, if any, of public opinion in that election. It is quite clear, however, that contemporaries were becoming ever more aware of public sentiment and were anxious to devise some way of measuring it. Commenting on the failure of a reforming petition at Nottingham, the *Public Advertiser* suggested that the number of names attached to any such document was a poor indication of the weight of opinion. Instead, Parliament should take pains to determine the weight of real property for and against a petition, and this would ensure that "every *petitioning* County will also be a *protesting* one." Nor was the business of gauging opinion in such popular constituencies as Westminster and Surrey an easy one. Richard Tickell, a ministerial pamphleteer, made fun of the claim that the sense of the nation could be perceived in these conspicuous contests. Referring to the fact that two admirals, Rodney and Keppel, had been returned in these elections—not to mention Keppel's fellow Rockinghamite Charles James Fox—Tickell observed with mock gravity that there was a striking similarity in the successful candidates. On this basis, he pronounced the two constituencies "a common and equal standard of national opinion" and "the great political parallelogram of public spirit."[45]

Tickell's irony underlined the obvious difficulty of determining what

44. "An Address to the Freeholders of Middlesex ... on Monday the XXth of December, MDCCLXXIX" (from the 4th ed. of 1782), in John Jebb, *Works* (London, 1787), 2:475–76.

45. [Tickell], *Common-Place Arguments Against Administration* ... (London, 1780), pp. 91–92, 96–97. The county of Surrey was not always politically volatile, but it showed independence in this election.

the people thought. That difficulty combined with the modern scholar's knowledge of the machinery of influence as detailed in the private correspondence of the time, might lead us to suppose that the small electorate and obvious corruption left no scope for genuine public opinion. It is difficult, though, to get around the fact that increasingly people were conscious of current opinion in the country, to such an extent in fact that the term "public opinion" slipped—more or less unheralded—into the everyday language of politics. Though the earliest uses of the term can be traced far back into the first half of the century, only after 1780 did the press refer with any frequency to "the public opinion." Fox again serves as an indicator of shifts in attitude. In 1770 he had denied the value of consulting the people outside Parliament. By 1783 Fox's words were recorded to the effect that "he had contended, and he ever would contend, that no ministers who acted independent of the public opinion, ought to be employed. The public opinion alone was the basis, in his mind, on which an administration should be formed."[46] One finds that after 1783 the definite article was commonly discarded, and "public opinion"—whether or not it existed—stood forth in its modern form.

Historians have often looked to the election of 1784 as a signal example of public opinion in eighteenth-century political life. In a sense, the two sides in the election divided on the same basis as have twentieth-century accounts of the election and its significance. Pitt had gone to the country to gain a mandate and could not be blamed for feeling that he had gained it most convincingly. Modern sceptics about the reality of public opinion in this election find their eighteenth-century parallel in the routed Opposition. Like Bolingbroke's apologists after Walpole's less overwhelming victory of 1734, Fox's people cried "foul." The election, they said, proved only that the Treasury purse was longer than that of the Opposition. The Treasury built in an unfair advantage, rendering appeals to the people farcical, "for to adjust the public opinion with any degree of exactness, those only who have no sort of connection whatever ... with the Court, ought

---

46. Fox, *Speeches*, 2:148. Cf. Catherine Macaulay, *The History of England from the Revolution to the Present Time* (Bath, 1778), pp. 20, 42, where the equivalent expressions are "the opinion of the public" and "the public opinion." Paul Kelly's claim that the expression was in "general use" in the 1760s does not find support in the newspapers of the time. See Kelly, "Radicalism and Public Opinion in the General Election of 1784," *Bulletin of the Institute of Historical Research* 45 (1972):83.

to be fairly divided."[47] Burke's speech of 14 June made the same point, with some typical embellishments, when he pointed to the ominious aspect of appealing to the sense of the people. There was, he said, now a double House of Commons: that in Parliament assembled and that in "corporation and county meetings dispersed." By playing one off against the other, an artful minister might prevail over both.[48] Interestingly enough, some of the other Foxite complaints suggest that there had indeed been a contest for public favour, although perhaps not an equal one. The Opposition complained that Pitt had cheated by dating his letter of canvass to the electors of the University of Cambridge before the dissolution. But such tactics were a far cry from a simple *Diktat* from the Treasury. More revealingly, the Opposition protested that Pitt had offered himself at more than one place, raising the possibility that as prime minister "he was therefore to be made the representative of all the boroughs in the kingdom. ..."[49] That particular objection brings visions not of dark dealings in close boroughs but of something more akin to the outcry at Gladstone's Midlothian campaign of 1879.

The political historian's case for there being a meaningful public opinion in 1784 rests on several compelling facts. It was demonstrably true, for instance, that a number of groups, such as the English Dissenters, deserted the coalition; whereas the large meetings in Yorkshire and the addresses of thanks to the king for dismissing the coalition were quite real. One might add the arresting discovery by Mrs. George and by Professor N. C. Phillips that expressions of public feeling and conviction were by no means confined to the act of attending the poll, but that the state of the public mind was a most significant factor in determining whether a formally contested election would really be required. An unopposed return might thus signal nothing more than an aspirant had gauged his chances and, finding insufficient support,

---

47. *Gazetteer and New Daily Advertiser* 17,288 (10 May 1784).

48. *The Speeches of the Right Honourable Edmund Burke* ... (London, 1816), 3:12. The lamentation was echoed by others. See [Thomas O'Beirne], *A Gleam of Comfort to this Distracted Empire* ... (London, 1785), p. 27; and Sir Brooke Boothby, *Observations on the Appeal from the New to the Old Whigs* ... (London, 1792), pp. 249–50.

49. *Gazetteer* 17,263 (10 Apr. 1784).

had judged it "inexpedient to trouble his friends any further," as the standard phrase went.[50]

Another consideration, founded on less meticulous research, but reasonable under the circumstances, was simply that the influence of the Crown was in retreat as a result of the reforms that began in 1782. The effect of some of these measures would not yet have been evident in 1784, but we have the testimony of John Robinson, Pitt's election manager, that they had already made a difference. A somewhat more independent House of Commons would still, naturally, have its local magnates, so apparently there was some scope for influences other than those that proceeded from the Treasury. Some of those influences could appropriately be labelled as that complex phenomenon called public opinion. One need not rule out local dignitaries and their extensive influence, for it would be a hopelessly demanding standard of public opinion that refused the name to any but electors under no conceivable influence save their own consciences.

We have evidence from as late as 1831 that suggests the tendency for the great families to get their way on major issues, thus creating in some parts of the country an interesting patchwork of returns—for or against the Reform Bill—depending on the preferences of the politically influential.[51] But it would scarcely be news to modern believers in public opinion that there are such people as opinion-leaders or "influentials," and that finding need not inhibit references to public opinion. No public is a *tabula rasa,* and all publics seem to lose their innocence in one way or another, if one looks sufficiently closely. Hobbes may not have been correct in calling the will the last appetite, but there is nothing extraordinary in saying that opinion, in an individual or in a public, is the last push. There were family favours and Treasury money; there was also the canvass.

There is some irony in the claim that an increasingly independent House of Commons opened the door to the influence of public opin-

---

50. M. Dorothy George, "Fox's Martyrs; The General Election of 1784," *Transactions of the Royal Historical Society,* 4th series, 21 (1939):133–68; and N. C. Phillips, *Yorkshire and English National Politics, 1783–1784* (Christchurch: University of Canterbury, 1961), pp. 16, 26. For similar conclusions about the election of 1780 see Phillips, "The British General Election of 1780: A Vortex of Politics, " *Political Science* 2 (1959):3–22.

51. D. C. Moore, "The Other Face of Reform," *Victorian Studies* 5 (Sept. 1961):16–17.

ion,[52] for those eighteenth-century figures who especially paid their respects to this new phenomenon were, in many cases, precisely the same politicians who tried to justify the remaining elements of royal influence. The normal ministerial argument had always consisted in saying that the public voice must not intrude into the business save for the occasional recourse to it at elections. Defending royal influence against the Whiggism of Richard Watson, recently appointed bishop of Llandaff, Richard Cumberland wrote that "if a Minister shall attempt to govern by the Opinions of the Public, this Country will soon be found in a State of Anarchy and Confusion."[53]

These words were written in 1783. After the election of 1784, however, an attitude more favourable to public sentiment is apparent in literature. Pitt was generally allowed to have captured the support of the nation and the king to have appealed, successfully, to the people against the express wishes of the majority of the House of Commons. The Foxites might grumble about the impropriety of selecting the people in the country as an alternative to the will of their representatives—and the force of the argument assumed that ignoring the country in favour of a compliant House of Commons would remain part of the ministerial repertoire—but they could hardly deny that they had suffered a severe rebuff. When North resisted parliamentary reform because of the existing degree of popular influence on government, and the Pittite Henry Beaufoy retorted that this most popular of Parliaments had a mandate for reform,[54] they agreed on one thing: public opinion had become of supreme importance.

No publication expressed more enthusiasm for the implications of the premature dissolution than did the *English Review*. This sophisticated magazine was, to begin with, written largely by Gilbert Stuart, the historian, and by Dr. William Thomson. After Stuart's death in 1786, the bulk of the political writing seems to have been carried on by the prolific Thomson. From the beginning, the *Review* portrayed the events of 1783–84 as marking a new era. The people, it claimed, now functioned as the final arbiter in all disputes between the various branches of the legislature. Indeed, even before the dissolution of Parliament, the *Review* had traced the probable outcome of events

52. See Sir William Anson, *Law and Custom of the Constitution*, 2nd ed. (Oxford, 1896), 2:37, 137.
53. Quoted in *Public Advertiser* 15,298 (9 June 1783).
54. *Parliamentary History* 24 (1783–84):990, 993.

and had called insistently for an opportunity for "public spirit" to pronounce decisively against the majority of the Commons. Only such an appeal to the people would dispel all doubts about the propriety of the king's dismissal of the coalition:

If the general opinion that the people are on the side of the Crown shall be rendered suspicious by counter addresses, or even by the silence of the counties, there is not a doubt that either the Sovereign must yield up his prerogative and the rights of the people to the ruling faction in the House of Commons, or that an immediate effort must be made for their preservation by a dissolution of parliament.[55]

The healing principle of public spirit would revive the king's otherwise obsolete veto and would ensure the continued rectitude of public measures.

From the events of 1784 the writers of the *Review* drew very far-reaching conclusions about the drift of national affairs. They proclaimed the growth of a "Spirit of Association" that embraced the politics of all parts of the British Empire and, in fact, all nations that knew any liberty. "The progress of knowledge, and commercial intercourse has opened the readiest avenues of intellectual and social communication. ..." In arbitrary governments, such as that of Russia, the gates of cities were closed in times of tumult, and the "communication of the people" was cut off in the interests of good order. By contrast, a free government gave scope to public sentiment—as by the flood of addresses against the India Bill on precisely those occasions when such popular intervention was needed. Especially in constitutional crises the people would be decisive, and no danger need be apprehended about the power of the Crown or the possible weakening of Parliament, since the recent exercise of royal prerogative had been "approved and supported by the general voice of the nation."[56]

Nor was the popular intervention of 1784 meant to be any aberration in the political system; the *Review* expressed concern in 1786 that public life seemed to have sunk into a sort of "stupor." As an antidote to this morbid condition, the magazine recommended a strengthening of the bonds of political parties, a firmer adherence to principle, and a "regular and systematic" spirit in their operations.

55. *English Review* 3 (Feb. 1784):157–58.
56. Ibid. (June 1784):478–80; and 5 (Jan. 1785):80.

Only then, it suggested, would the "uniformity of conduct" in the part of public men serve to "draw the multitude along with them." To this end, it applauded the growing practice by Members of Parliament of writing out parliamentary speeches and delivering copies to the press. The same viewpoint lay behind the comment that the published accounts of parliamentary debates were satisfactory evidence of the opinions of public men. For even though there would be difficulty in verifying "an individual expression" for use in a court of law, "there are sufficient grounds, and stronger than the general strain of testimony, to influence the belief, and determine the opinion, of the public."[57]

Again and again the *Review* hailed the virtues of a free press and the manner in which the liberty to comment upon public affairs was related to all other liberties. In a free government with parties, it made no sense for only one side to claim an exclusive privilege of publishing its views. The press and its freedom were also connected with such unique British institutions as trial by jury and habeas corpus; for all these stood or fell together. Not only did a free press serve as an essential support of the vital institution of an opposition, it also rendered all forms of dissent less formidable to a government. For those humours that, deprived of expression, might lead elsewhere to conspiracy and insurrection would simply "evaporate" when freely voiced. Freedom of discussion, as practised in press or coffee-house, would render tribunals, prisons, and scaffolds ever less relevant to political life. Rather more grandly, the *Review* envisaged a time when the press would advance to new heights of significance, with the establishment of a daily newspaper that would have a greater compass than any hitherto existing. In its columns men of all persuasions would converse and reason, contributing to the enlightenment of the public. More pretentiously, there were reciprocal influences at work among "literature, liberty, government, and manners," since liberty encouraged certain forms of literature that in turn acted upon the political mores to render liberty yet more perfect.[58] The awareness by these writers of the interaction of a great number of social forces was not the least of their merits. For over fifty years the press had been described as the "palladium of liberty," but never before had its manifold

---

57. Ibid. 7 (April 1786):261–62; and 9 (Jan. 1787):40.
58. Ibid., 9 (Apr. 1787):313–18.

connections with every part of the political system—Parliament, Opposition, the courts, and private associations of all sorts—been spelled out. The press had absorbed the political functions of the pulpit and, as the necessary stimulant to public opinion and vehicle of it, increasingly dominated the political system. Earlier praise of the press as the bulwark of freedom was, by contrast, tainted by the fact that the opinion of the people was accorded little respect and no constitutional status.

But all was not right in Eden, for increasingly Pitt came to be perceived as failing to realize his promise. He had risen to power on influence and had then been confirmed by public opinion, but he was decidedly reluctant to push away the ladder of influence or to abide by the public sentiment that had served him in 1784. The *Review* served notice in 1790 that the honeymoon was over and expressed great disappointment that Pitt's accomplishments in domestic policy had not been nearly so impressive as those in foreign affairs. It was a time when those who had been temporarily converted to the merits of influence by the peculiar events of 1784 came to reassess their position. Often they recalled, for the prime minister's benefit, how his power was founded on a remarkable demonstration of public support. Such reminders continued throughout Pitt's career.[59] In one of its milder warnings the *Review* again summarized some of the major tenets in its analysis of the newer features in politics. As with previous efforts, the essay is noteworthy for its grasp of political life as a coherent assemblage of related factors:

In the present situation of affairs, there is no British minister but who MUST pay regard to the public opinion, which, in all public dissensions, casts the balance. ... The people, by taking part with ministry, are able to support them if they are in the right, or overturn them ... , by supporting opposition. The chain of arteries that runs throughout, and connects and bestows vitality on the British constitution is this: as ministers must pay regard to the voice of the members of parliament, and these to that of their electors; so the electors

---

59. See "Simon Search," *The Spirit of the Times* 3 (1790):64; [Sir Brooke Boothby], *A Letter to the Right Hon. Edmund Burke in Reply to his Reflections ... by a Member of the Revolution Society* (London, 1790), p. 49; and [Maurice Montagu], *Friendly Remarks upon some Particulars of his Administration, in a letter to Mr. Pitt*, 2nd ed. (London, 1796), p. 32. All of these reminded Pitt of his debt to what the first of them called "PUBLIC OPINION." The words were commonly capitalized at this time, apparently to mark their relative novelty.

themselves, on all great and momentous occasions ... dare not to resist the unanimous sentiments of their neighbours.[60]

Some of this was an exercise in wishful thinking, but it serves admirably to portray a sophisticated understanding of how the political order, at its best, could function.

This sort of optimism was not easy to sustain in the political climate that followed the French Revolution, as we shall see. Those who managed found evidence for their conclusions in comparisons of the sophistication of British opinion with that of nations less cultivated and less free. This was true, for instance, of Dr. John Moore, physician and novelist. Combining a liberal concern for freedom with a certain complacency about the British constitution, Moore wrote, in the era of the treason trials, as though liberty and popular influence remained unimpaired. But even Moore's apparent insouciance left room for at least a hint of anxiety:

Any material alteration in the opinions and prejudices of a whole nation took much longer in former times to be brought about. Since material alterations in the public opinions may ... be effected with infinitely more rapidity than heretofore, it is of more importance now than ever for all Governments, particularly those of free countries, to be alert in attending to those alterations as they occur, that they may be able in time to preclude the mischiefs which arise from the current of public opinion bearing one way, and the measures of Government another; for, to maintain tranquility, one of two things must be done: a Minister must either adopt his measures to the public opinion; or, which is a much more difficult task, and requires very uncommon talents to accomplish, he turn around the public opinion in favour of his measures. ...[61]

The feat was perhaps a simpler one than Moore was inclined to admit. Certainly if his optimism had been entirely typical of educated men,

60. *English Review* 15 (Apr. 1790):319. The major writer of the *Review* at this time was still probably William Thomson, who ultimately became its owner. For an extended example of his mode of political analysis, which also records his growing discontent with conditions in Britain, see his *Letters from Scandinavia*, 2 vols. (London, 1796).

61. Moore, *A View of the Causes and Progress of the French Revolution* (London, 1795), 1:90–91. See too vol. 1, chap. 12, part of which is entitled "Reflections on the Influence of Public Opinion"; also 2:269–70, 379.

there would have been fewer expressions of concern about the state of public opinion in the nineties. Even so, the years immediately after the election of 1784 saw faith in public opinion at its height.

Public Opinion and the Constitution

The writers of the *English Review* were not the natural friends of the influence of the Crown, and their admiration of Pitt had been founded in large measure on revulsion against the coalition and on the expectation that the young minister would persevere with his planned reform in the representation. A more significant body of sentiment was expressed by those Pittites who feared a further diminution of influence and who had no intention of accepting any change in the franchise. Appeals to the importance of public opinion thus entered into the language of ministerial pamphlets, and this was reflected in political argument of the 1790s.

A dominant theme in the defence of the *status quo* was the ingenious plea that the obvious defects of the English constitution were, in truth, the very source of its strength. An early example of this approach was put by a Scottish hydrographer, Alexander Dalrymple. Dalrymple was not very explicit about the various benign corruptions in the state, but he was most explicit in denying that parliamentary reform was advisable and in asserting the importance of public opinion. Especially, it seemed, this opinion was to be deemed valuable in a government that checked the excesses of popular impulses. In a popular assembly, opinion might be moved by demagogic oratory, but the degree to which the House of Commons was not popular accounted for the happy fact that public opinion was not easily moved or "blown into a Flame." Indeed, any well-meaning effort at changing the representation would doubtless just augment the aristocratic part of the constitution by rendering public sentiment less respectable, "because *at present* the *weight* of the *people* depends on the *Wisdom* of its Members to guide the *Publick Opinion*, and not on their *wealth* or *numbers*." Without specifying quite how the system worked, Dalrymple stole a leaf from the book of some radical reformers by his unstinting praise of the popular elements in the system: "the whole is subjected to the *controul* of *Publick Opinion*: This although no part of the *nominal Constitution*: is paramount to all: and what makes The *Government* of *This Country* The best that *ever existed*." Such a "*Balance* of *Corruptions*" as existed in Britain could never be worked into the constitution of a new state.[62]

Dalrymple did not make it clear whether public opinion was itself one of those corruptions so subtly blended into the constitution, and in this he was followed by others. The reason for this ambiguity is that the enemies of reform were necessarily ambivalent about the role of the people in politics. Those who stood against a reform in the representation were by definition anxious to confine popular influences to their current level. But the old constitutional shibboleths would no longer do, for the events of 1784 had given the people's voice a more pronounced public function than had previously been admitted. It was important, then, to resist reform by insisting that the forces arrayed against the ministry and the influence of the Crown were already as powerful as was consistent with good government. Thus public opinion joined the institution of the Opposition in that curious status assigned by ministerial writers to political factors that should be recognized as apparent counterweights to the advantages that belonged to the Treasury Bench. The rules of this new game required that one pay generous compliments to the popular or antiministerial forces while emphasizing that their current level of effectiveness was the optimum.

Even Professor John Wilde of Edinburgh, a stern opponent of constitutional innovation, had to admit that the constitution recognized the voice of the people in the legitimacy of petitions and addresses. His fears were directed at any attempt to institute the general will as a direct and ordinary part of government, a position that Wilde associated with Rousseau. Wilde regretted that the voice of the people, which, according to him, was deemed rebellion in 1769, had now come to be acclaimed as the promptings of reason. Resolutely against the populism either of radicals or of Pittite opportunists, he could offer only the traditional judgement that the public will could be known only through the House of Commons.[63] Very different was the emphasis of the new breed of anti-reformer, such as the Earl of Selkirk. Selkirk actually professed to be an advocate of parliamentary reform, but like many others of his kind, he never found the time to

---

62. Dalrymple, *Parliamentary Reform, as it is called, Improper in the Present State of the Country*, 2nd ed. (London, 1792), pp. 15, 22, 34.

63. Wilde, *An Address to the Lately Formed Society of the Friends of the People* (London, 1793), pp. 530–39, 563.

be ripe. Pursuing a point already made familiar by others, Selkirk saw a place for the will of the people even inside the House of Commons. According to him, the twin evils of the political system were the excessive influence of wealth and that of popular ferment. Happily though, the two met and were reconciled within the lower House. No longer could men in power "venture to despise public opinion," for it occupied an honoured place as a check to any sinister influence that might proceed from wealth. To this end, parliamentary demagogues might bring vulgar prejudices into public business without harmful effect; indeed, they served the useful function of checking "the opposite vices of a different portion of the House."[64]

Neither the rejection of public opinion nor the practice of greeting it with unlimited encomiums was a useful basis for fitting the phenomenon into any coherent theory of the constitution. Rejection suggested only the traditional balanced constitution—widely condemned by the 1790s as an inadequate description of British politics. On the other hand, anyone who wholeheartedly endorsed the untrammelled reign of public opinion seemed to commit himself to a sort of mob rule, incompatible with the king and the Lords, incompatible even with the House of Commons as then constituted. There remained the intermediate position of integrating the fact of the *vox populi* into a theory of the constitution that could encompass all the newly recognized and extra-constitutional aspects of the balanced constitution. The influence of the Crown and that of the people could thus be depicted as blending with all other influences to form the complicated processes that were evident in the modern House of Commons.

This understanding of the constitution increasingly became the common property of both the government spokesmen and their moderate Whig opponents of the early nineteenth century. Courted by both, belonging exclusively to neither party, the factor of public opinion bulked especially prominently in the constitutional doctrines of all those who sought to assert the essential well-being of existing arrangements. It was a matter, then, not of hailing the future triumphs of the popular will but rather of establishing that it already dominated political life, counteracting and rendering innocuous the alleged abuses

---

64. Selkirk, *A Letter Addressed to John Cartwright, Esq. ... on the Subject of Parliamentary Reform* (London, 1809), pp. 14–15. Selkirk also voiced some of his thoughts on public opinion in a speech of April 1807 defending the king's dismissal of the Talents.

on the part of the Crown or the nobility. The revolution had come, apparently unnoticed. Growing literacy, the swarms of publications, and the ever greater publicity accorded to parliamentary debates were cited along with the specific changes wrought by Fox's Libel Act of 1792. All such developments seemed to lend substance to the conclusion of a pamphleteer that the basic conditions of politics, foreign and domestic, had undergone a dramatic change:

> Governments, I suspect, cannot any longer be maintained, under the new and peculiar exigencies of these times, by the old maxims they have found in their offices, or the political testaments of their predecessors. The public has drawn nearer to them, the middle space has been contracted, and the common interests and union of the people and the state are become more intimate and visible.[65]

Oddly enough, one of the familiar maxims had been that government rested upon opinion—words equally at home in the mouth of an attorney-general and of democratic radicals[66]—but the well-worn phrase gained new content in the light of the emergence of unprecedented facilities for expressing political opinions. The novelty of "that restless, resistless power, which men call Public Opinion" called forth a poetic effusion from the Tory writer and future Member of Parliament Horace Twiss. The institutions from which public opinion sprang, he declared, had gained their importance within living memory, and to spell out the effects of the phenomenon "would be to retrace the whole history of our own times." Typically, Twiss refrained from bestowing any conventional praise upon either the rectitude or the moderation of this opinion; its simple presence provoked expressions of awe. It was a subtle spirit, protean and unpredictable: "It moves in darkness; it speaks in thunder. ..." To write of it in terms of darkness was no mere rhapsody, for Twiss noted how the public had been caught, powerfully but inconveniently, in a temporary "twilight of the mind." The truth of affairs was not yet clearly perceived, but the giant was already awake, and if the people lacked as yet

---

65. [Thomas Richard Bentley], *Considerations upon the State of Public Affairs, in the Year MDCCXCVIII, Part, the Third* (London, 1798), p. 46.

66. See the speech of Sir John Scott in Howell's *State Trials* 24 (1794):273; and a pamphlet attributed to Major Cartwright's friend, T. Holt White, *Letters to William Paley ... on his Objections to Reform* (London, 1796), p. 4.

sufficient light to guide their steps unerringly, they had already experienced too much to remain asleep. Public opinion was not necessarily benign in its movements, but its very existence lent assurance
that no powers belonging to Crown, ministry, or nobility could pose
any danger to the rights of the people. Whatever sinister influences
might make their way into the people's House of Parliament, the
people could take comfort that a ready check lay in the "gigantic
importance of Public Opinion."[67] Reliance on this factor seems, for
at least some politicians of the age, to have been genuine. Expression
of the idea was not confined to public statements but also informed
private correspondence.[68]

This recognition of the place of public opinion took the same course
as the process whereby the role of the Opposition gained legitimacy.
Indeed, though the two developments were not entirely simultaneous,
they were closely related, for in both cases the crucial stage was an
admission by the government that forces actually or potentially hostile
to it were nevertheless integral parts of the political scene. Since public
opinion, as in 1784 and in 1807, seemed to endorse the cause of the
Court party, one might have expected a more genuine and hearty
acceptance of that phenomenon than of a parliamentary Opposition
that would necessarily try to check the king's ministers. In fact, the
claims of the Opposition to a respectable place in politics was more
readily conceded than were the cries of the populace in the country.
Both the Opposition and the sentiments of the public could usefully
be adduced as mitigating the evil effects of placemen and Treasury
funds. However, all politicians, even the secure Tories of the early
nineteenth century, could contemplate the possibility of reverting to
opposition, and so the institution of the Opposition was not difficult
to accept. By contrast, few men in public life could with confidence
assign any permanent and coherent functions to public opinion. It
was too inchoate, too unpredictable, and really far too dangerous to
be embraced uncritically as the saviour of the constitution. Its status
thus remained ambiguous and unresolved for longer than was the
case with respect to the Opposition. *Vox populi* had possessed certain
favourable connotations long before an Opposition party had been

67. Twiss, *Influence or Prerogative?* (London, 1812), pp. 14–21.
68. See the views of one Whig politician whose fear of reform led him very close to
the Tories, *Letters of the Earl of Dudley* [J. W. Ward] *to the Bishop of Llandaff* [Edward
Copleston] (London, 1840), letter of 17 June 1822, pp. 320–21.

at all respectable, but uncertainty continued to surround reactions to public opinion long after most Englishmen had become reconciled to the propriety of a formed opposition.

Twiss had been unusually forthcoming in his tribute to the new-found influence of the people, for some defenders of the *status quo* deemed the Opposition and the diversity of interests within the Commons a sufficient counterweight to the ministry. James Jopp, for instance, published a lengthy treatise on the constitution in which he managed to say very little about public opinion. Though the book appeared in the same year in which Twiss proclaimed the dominion of the public mind, Jopp limited his recognition to the statement that government should submit to the will of a clear majority of the populace. Many in the previous century would have disagreed, but the concession remained an empty one, since Jopp refused to allow that the true voice of the people was expressed in demands for reform.[69] Yet another position on the spectrum of attitudes towards public opinion was occupied by a writer who alleged that the "popular voice" had at least an indirect influence upon both king and Lords, as in the business of creating peers. But the weight of this manifestation of opinion must have seemed slight even to the author, for he went on to condemn annual parliaments because of the excessive importance they lent to a factor as fluctuating and unsatisfactory as "public opinion."[70]

The year 1812 witnessed the most elaborate and enlightening discussion of the unreformed constitution that had yet taken place; only on the eve of the Reform Bill of 1832 was the press again so full of material on the complex of forces that might be seen as maintaining a new form of political balance. Brand's reform motion of May sparked the parliamentary debate, and an even abler dissection of the political system occupied the attention of informed observers outside Parliament. Prominent in the business of reassessing the constitution were Francis Jeffrey and, to a lesser extent, Henry Brougham of the *Edinburgh Review*. These two had been largely responsible for popularizing the theory that the effective balance of the constitution now lay within the House of Commons, and their opinions on the matter, which had

69. James Jopp, *Historical Reflections on the Consitution and Representative System of England, with Reference to the Popular Propositions for a Reform of Parliament* (London, 1812), pp. 383n., 406.

70. [W. J. Ching], *England's Danger: or, Reform Unmasked* (London, 1819), pp. 16, 31.

begun to appear in 1807, were already being quoted, not only by their fellow Whigs but also by the supporters of the ministry.[71] The Whigs of the *Review* were in the odd situation of being responsible for sup-plying the ministry with much of its ammunition against reform, for the party that was eventaully to pass the Reform Bill took a very long time to make up its mind.

Earlier essays by Jeffrey had made reference to the importance of an informed public that could readily have its intelligence mobilized in defence of its "public rights and interests." The essay of 1812, ostensibly a review of a book by Gould Francis Leckie, is important because the compliments paid to the voice of the people were not simply for the purpose of allaying fears about excessive influence on the part of the Crown and its officers. Popular influences were de-scribed as both inevitable and, on the whole, beneficial to the polity. At the same time, Jeffrey was careful to couch his defence of popular influences in terms of a long historical process of increasing maturity of the nation. His ideal—a polity in which all significant public sen-timents were communicated instantly to the whole—was to be the fruit of a society that had attained its "full measure of civility and intelligence." Clearly, he did not perceive the condition as already attained, but he did emphasize how far British society had actually departed from the primitive mode of governing in which intolerable conditions eventually provoked bloody revolt. Much of the essay con-sists in his portrait of the traditional state that Sir Richard Burton would later call "despotism tempered by assassination." This Jeffrey contrasted with the mechanisms, then emerging in Britain, for antic-ipating the demands of the people and for satisfying their wants before the populace became explosive.

Consistent with his studied moderation, Jeffrey made no mention of the conventional stock of radical panaceas; shorter parliaments, a wider franchise, the instructing of members, and the exacting of pledges from them were all absent from his analysis. The promise of a better order lay in conditions that reflected the manners and institutions of a complex, commercial society. It was not apparently to be realized by precipitate changes in the constitution. Since Jeffrey had been quite as critical of radicals such as Cobbett and Sir Francis Burdett as he

71. I have treated some aspects of this view of affairs in "Influence, Parties and the Constitution: Changing Attitudes, 1783–1832," *Historical Journal* 17 (1974):301–28.

was of the ministers, he took pains to specify how the perfection of government could be realized:

> The whole difference, indeed, between a good and a bad government, appears to us to consist in this particular, viz. in the greater or the less facility which it affords for the early, the gradual and steady operation of the substantial power of the community upon its constituted authorities; while the freedom, again, and ultimate happiness of the nation depend on the degree in which this substantial power is possessed by a greater or a smaller proportion of the whole society—a matter almost independent of the government, and determined in a great degree by the progress which the society has made in civilization and refinement.

The relevant indices of the degree of access afforded to the people were therefore the normal accoutrements of a prosperous and sophisticated society: the press, general literature, provincial magistracies, the courts of law, the stage, the pulpit, and what Jeffrey called "all innumerable occasions of considerable assemblage for deliberation on local interests."

Combining the long-standing aphorism that all government relied upon opinion with rather minute observation of British institutions, Jeffrey noted that all governments did indeed rest upon the support of some people apart from the immediate rulers but that the nature of the controlling power differed with the political system. While there was no such thing in the world as an absolute monarch who ruled only for himself, there were crucial differences between those governments that lived in a cycle of oppression and rebellion and a government such as that of Britain. The merit of the British government thus lay in its provision for "authoritative and uninterrupted communication" between the governed and their government. Jeffrey had sufficiently qualified his case against the excesses of reform. His peroration breathed a liberal optimism:

> The dissensions of a free people are the preventions and not the indications of radical disorder—and the noises, which make the weak hearted tremble, are but the natural murmurs of those mighty and mingling currents of public opinion, which are destined to fertilize and unite the country, and can never become dangerous till an attempt is made to dam them up, or to disturb their level.[72]

---

72. *Edinburgh Review* 20, no. 1 (Nov. 1812):345.

It is perhaps not surprising that Jeffrey, the Whig in opposition, should have provided this able analysis of the place of opinion in politics. Public opinion, perceived as the general force that defined constitutional government, served as a substitute for fundamental reform in the system of representation. Jeffrey and others were thus free to dismiss specific manifestations of sentiment in the country, secure in the knowledge that the constitution gained legitimacy through its provision for the expression of opinions. Radicals and Tories had made up their minds about reform, but Jeffrey's celebration of the process of communication between governed and governors shows that the position of the *Edinburgh Review* was precariously balanced among a variety of incompatible viewpoints. Public opinion in the abstract was held to be a major redeeming feature of the unreformed system. At the same time, Whigs of this era were just as likely as Tories to resist extending the suffrage for fear that the weight of popular influences would become excessive. Brougham opposed Sir Francis Burdett's reform motion of 1818 for precisely this reason and, in so arguing, placed himself in the company of numerous other opponents of reform. Charles Jenkinson and George Canning—in defence of so-called Tory ministries—were also prone to press that considera-tion.[73]

An important factor allowing the Whigs room for manoeuvre was the expectation, rather obliquely voiced by Jeffrey, that the public would grow in responsibility and in enlightenment. This alone served to make intelligible the tendency to acclaim public opinion while re-sisting any reform that might strengthen its immediate impact on government. Writers in the Tory *Quarterly Review*, for instance, were more consistent in their rejection of reform and also more candid in citing the current shortcomings of public opinion. Following the lead of Horace Twiss, Robert Southey wrote of the peculiar difficulties of a period in history in which the public had graduated from its tra-ditional ignorance only to wallow in a sea of misinformation. The times, he said, suffered from "a kind of half knowledge" that was inimical to common sense.[74] Southey was still disposed to rely upon

73. *Parliamentary Debates* 38 (1818):1172. Cf. Jenkinson in *Parliamentary History* 30 (1793):812–13; and Canning in *Parliamentary Debates* 17 (1810):158.

74. Southey, "On the State of Public Opinion and the Political Reformers" (1816), in *Essays, Moral and Political* (London, 1832), 1:329, 376, 414. The same language was used by a journalist who, unlike Southey, had not lost his radical views. See Charles Knight, *Memoirs of a Working Life* (London, 1864), 1:260–61, an observation of 1821.

the power of the *vox populi* to balance the influence of the Crown and was especially impressed by the augmentation in the power of the people simply from the publication of parliamentary debates. He was also forthright about the need to direct the new currents of opinion into appropriate channels. Such a sense of mission befitted an ex-radical such as Southey and was quite consistent with his loyalty to the administrations of the early nineteenth century. By contrast, the notorious vacillation of the Whigs made them irresolute as mentors to the people—simultaneously wary of the demagogic appeals of radicals and envious of the public support enjoyed by the ministers.

Insofar as a direction can be discerned in the flow of Whig and Tory opinions—and attributing coherent opinions to these privileged knots of politicians seems almost as difficult as attributing substance to public opinion in general—the Whigs retreated from Jeffrey's theory and the Tories held fast to it. In the debates of 1831 on the first Reform Bill, Twiss continued to argue for the presence of a balance of forces within the House of Commons, with public opinion regulating the relations between ministers and the Opposition.[75] The Tories were also left with the dilemma that had confronted Jeffrey and others. How could one pay one's respects to public opinion as a legitimate force in politics while ignoring both the substance of extra-parliamentary demands and any change in the institutions originally framed for a people that generated little public opinion? Sir Robert Peel's anguish seems to have been genuine when he observed, in a letter of 1820, that it was very difficult to widen the "vents" in the political system in proportion to the size and force of the currents pressing upon them. He remarked upon the oddity that the people should demand increased influence on government at precisely the time when public opinion enjoyed unprecedented sway. He worried too that public opinion was moving ahead of the policy of the government. Above all, then, he was repelled and fascinated by "that great compound of folly, weakness, prejudice, wrong feeling, right feeling, obstinacy, and newspaper paragraphs, which is called public opinion. ..."[76]

Much nineteenth-century political thought turned on this feeling

---

75. *Parliamentary Debates*, 3rd series, 2 (1831):1132.

76. Letter to J. W. Croker, in *The Croker Papers*, ed. Louis J. Jennings, (London, 1884), 1:170.

that a great beast was now—not entirely improperly—out of its cage and had somehow to be tamed. An acceptable answer to Sir Robert's problem was simply to insist that any force correctly identified as public opinion would necessarily be compatible with unreformed institutions. This position informed the most elaborate study of the phenomenon to appear prior to the Reform Bill—William Alexander Mackinnon's book of 1828.[77] Refining some of the notions current in the *English Review* of the 1780s, the author identified certain attributes of the population as "requisites for the formation of public opinion." This allowed him to assert that the growth of a large middle class, accompanied by the necessary facilities for transport and communication, would invariably beget public opinion. Mackinnon ingeniously argued that effective communication among the people would be possible only with a proper sense of religion. Thus his prerequisites included factors ensuring that only sentiments acceptable to the higher classes would count as public opinion. A less subtle indication of bias was Mackinnon's lame argument for close boroughs. For all its faults, however, his book was an able blending of two themes: an eighteenth-century optimism about the growth of civilization and the conservative case against political reform.

The Tyranny of Public Opinion

The change in Whig attitudes in the 1820s was epitomized by Lord John Russell, whose adherence to an extension of the franchise was accompanied by the explicit repudiation of all talk about an existing equilibrium of forces within the unreformed Commons. Russell aptly characterized the prevailing constitutional doctrines by noting that it was "the fashion" to neutralize demands for reform by emphasizing the growing influence of public opinion. Although he allowed that the publication of debates and the diffusion of "political knowledge" had made a significant change in politics, he argued against any heavy reliance on public opinion to check the pretensions of the executive. Only when opinion was conducive to protecting legitimate liberties was it to be accounted valuable. But sometimes it countenanced oppression of religious minorities or encouraged a government to

77. Mackinnon, *On the Rise, Progress and Present State of Public Opinion in Great Britain, and other Parts of the World*, 2nd ed. (London, 1828).

undertake unwise foreign adventures. In various ways the presence of public opinion served to inhibit and divide the opponents of a government, without imposing shackles of equal weight upon the ministers. For instance, the public's familiarity with the views of politicians served often to discredit the arguments of Opposition—just because they seemed inconsistent with a previous stand. Men in power might more readily withstand such a charge, finding "in the rewards of office a solid compensation for any hooting they may undergo."[78]

The discovery that public opinion might be less an instrument of popular control than a device for entrenching the administration was not new; it had been implicit in the century-old complaints that the governors who used parliaments might be more secure, even in their wrongdoing, than those who did not. After the elder Pitt's acclaim by the people, and even more so following the victory of his son, the Opposition had become painfully aware that more extensive communication between government and people might not make it any easier to unseat ministers. The popularity of the wars with France was a signal lesson in this respect and led to charges that the ministry misled public opinion.[79] The bright prospect of 1784 was fading.

It was no secret that Walpole had spent large sums of public money in financing administration newspapers, but the practice had declined under the Pelhams. During the Grafton and North ministries there had been ministerial writers—even Treasury poets—but no massively subsidized press, for the columns of papers such as the *Public Advertiser* had been open to all. In the 1790s there was a return to government newspapers, and these tended to spend a good deal of effort in justifying their own existence. William Playfair's abrasive print, the *Tomahawk*, poured scorn on the claims of the Opposition to speak for the people and the public opinion. Playfair also expressed concern at the neglect, shown by defenders of the *status quo*, for "the conducting

78. Russell, *An Essay on the History of the English Government and Constitution*, 2nd ed. (London, 1823), chap. 35, "Public Opinion—Restrictive Laws," and esp. pp. 429–30, 441, 445. The same reservations about the efficacy of public opinion are expressed in a remarkably well-argued critique of Russell's fellow Whigs. See Anon., *Statement of the Question of Parliamentary Reform; with a Reply to the Objections of the Edinburgh Review, No. LXI* (London, 1821), pp. 39–41, 125–29.

79. See M. M. de Montgaillard, *The Situation of Great Britain in the Year 1811* (London, 1812), p. 51; and the letter, written in 1793, by a disillusioned supporter of Pitt in *The Correspondence of William Augustus Miles on the French Revolution, 1789–1817*, ed. Rev. C. P. Miles, (London, 1890), 2:12.

and guiding of public opinion."[80] Considering the prominence in 1792–93 of quasi-official societies for discouraging reform, Playfair's concern might seem to have been misplaced, but by 1796 the organizations of church-and-king extremists had declined while the equally Tory, but less militant, Society for the Reformation of Principles had yet to make its mark.[81]

Perhaps the most startling proposal for manipulation of opinion came from the pen of Robert Fellowes, philanthropist and one-time editor of the *Critical Review*. Fellowes subscribed to all the soothing commonplaces about the role of public opinion as a political censor, but he added an important dimension to the anti-reform position. As a sometime journalist, Fellowes as conscious that the processes labelled public opinion involved a two-way flow of attitudes and information: the light came from people to the government and also from government to the people. Wise politicians would thus not await the impulse of popular feeling but would "anticipate its movements." Seemingly carried by his enthusiasm, Fellowes pressed ahead to explain how necessary it was to lead the public: "the government which had rendered the public opinion ductile to its will, would possess a sort of unlimited sway both over the minds and the bodies of the people." Leaving no doubt of his intentions, he wrote of the power of the government that "converted the public opinion into an obsequious auxiliary."[82] Then, almost as an afterthought, he conceded that, with an enlightened public only measures of public utility could be expected to gain public support. Obviously, this provided no qualification at all to the basic concern that the lower orders had to be imbued with correct principles.

This was a major aim of all the anti-revolutionary activities after 1790 as large numbers of propertied men became aware that unless the common people could be won over to existing institutions, Britain might well go the way of France. Hannah More's *Village Politics*, huge numbers of which were distributed by the Society for the Preservation

---

80. *Tomahawk* 82 (30 Jan. 1796). See too *Looker-On* [ed. William Roberts] 23 (26 May 1792).

81. On the activities of the extreme anti-reformers see Eugene Charlton Black, *The Association* (Cambridge, Mass.: Harvard University Press, 1963), chap. 7; and Austin Mitchell, "The Association Movement of 1792–93," *Historical Journal* 4 (1961):56–77.

82. Fellowes, *The Rights of Property Vindicated, Against the Claims of Universal Suffrage* (London, 1818), pp. 137, 145–46.

of Liberty and Property against Republicans and Levellers, epitomized the message that the poor and humble should be satisfied with their lot. A more explicit indication of the nature of the task of the anti-reformers may be gained from the full title of Arthur Young's publication of 1798—*An Enquiry into the State of the Public Mind Amongst the Lower Classes: and on the Means of turning it to the Welfare of the State.* No talk here of collecting public sentiment only within Parliament; Young sounds very much like radical democrats in his description of how one was to take the pulse of the common people. His venture, however, was in the interests of suppressing discontent and the threat that it posed to political and social institutions. Nineteenth-century Tories sometimes congratulated themselves on their belief that a Tory Opposition was far more responsible than a Whig one, since Tories were profoundly sensitive to the credulity and folly of the public. This low estimate of the public mind was held to be a guarantee that Tories in opposition would not offer demagogic appeals. The case may be sound in some respects, though it failed to come to terms with Whig ambivalence about the voice of the people. But it was undoubtedly incomplete in failing to comment on the way in which the party in power might strive to turn public opinion to its advantage.

Only by bearing in mind the effectiveness with which a succession of so-called Tory governments rode the waves of public opinion can one understand the reservations with which the presumed friends of the people approached the supposedly sovereign public. The voice of the people acclaimed the royal choice of ministers in 1784 and again in 1807, and the dangers posed by Jacobinism, and later by Bonaparte, served far better to silence domestic disaffection than had the bogey of Jacobitism in earlier decades. Of course, it was no new thing for the defenders of constitutional government to regret the presence of public applause for overgrown ministers, and Blackstone had expressed an eighteenth-century commonplace when he supported an electorate of independent men as the only protection of liberty. But a new amplitude for this fear of the poor, the venal, and the ignorant became apparent with the rise to prominence of public opinion.

Especially, it seems, the advantages of office showed themselves in guiding opinions about foreign affairs. Before it became *de rigueur* for British governments to warn about the ambitions of France, the younger Pitt had sought closer relations with that country. Contemplating the difficulties of opposing this departure, Sir Robert Adair had noted the strong situation of an administration that had gained the public confidence: "with the publick opinion, however adverse to some late measures, either acquiescing in their general principles, or voluntarily blind to their effects, they can attempt any thing with security."[83] The same weary disenchantment with public opinion is a recurring theme in the correspondence of Opposition politicians of the Napoleonic era. The people had acquiesced in the suppressing of liberty, and their sentiments appeared to approach clarity and enthusiasm only in support of bad causes. Francis Horner, a passionately intellectual Whig Member of Parliament, greeted such movements of sentiment with a sad contempt. Commenting on the rhapsodic support in 1814 for the restoration of the Bourbons, he wrote that "the state of public opinion is an amusing subject of observation at the present moment; I never knew it more violent or more nearly unanimous."[84]

Even the dictum that all governments rested upon the favourable opinion of at least a portion of the public became tainted. It had always been double-edged, pointing to the limited place of force in politics and to worrisome similarities between despotisms and governments that were ostensibly liberal and popular. Francis Jeffrey would be able to distinguish between good governments and bad only by the fact that the latter rested upon a narrower base of support and tended to provide less effective channels of communication between government and governed. Others, less complacent about the slow progress of improvement, suggested that all existing governments shared the same defect in that none rested upon spontaneous and genuine public approval. A very moderate reformer, the wealthy William Burdon, thus wrote of a subject destined for a long and controversial future—"the tyranny exercised by means of public opinion." Burdon's animus against the prevailing opinion gained a specific focus in his dismay at the popularity of T. J. Mathias, a vulgar tormentor of reformers in any shape, whose *Pursuits of Literature* was much read. Burdon's despondency about the prospects of reform rested on his awareness that a government could even resist public opinion for a long time by the resort to force. In countries, such as England, where the authorities did not favour the use of force, they "govern by public

83. [Adair], *The Principles of British Policy Contrasted with a French Alliance; in Five Letters from a Whig Member of Parliament to a Country Gentleman* (London, 1787), p. 6.

84. Letter of 25 Feb. 1814 to J. A. Murray, in *Memoirs and Correspondence to Francis Horner, M. P.*, ed. Leonard Horner (London, 1843), 2:169.

opinion," managing it to suit their purposes. Until public opinion was freed from ministerial control, there was no hope of any lasting improvement in society.[85]

An awareness that the public was easily imposed upon hangs like a dark cloud over the British radicals of the revolutionary period. In proportion as reformers harboured ambitions for the people their hopes were repeatedly dashed by events. John Cartwright, the father of radicalism, reflects the progress of disenchantment through forty years of political argument. In 1784, a banner year for expectations about the growth of the public mind, he rebuked Soame Jenyns and his placeman's creed with the lofty claim that he was "vainly hoping to stem the tide of truth and the current of public opinion."[86] By 1789 he had begun to doubt Pitt's commitment to reform. At the turn of the century, Cartwright was no less ardent in his concern for public enlightenment, but the way seemed ever more strewn with difficulties. Public opinion might err, he now conceded. Furthermore, it had become clear that it was not always readily discernible and had to be winnowed out by consulting people in the parishes where they lived. New machinery was required to collect this opinion, and it had then to be united with the parliamentary Opposition. Public opinion remained the "Archimedian lever" by which despotism could alone be overturned, but now Cartwright called, with ever more anxiety, for a press that could mould an enlightened public.[87] The friends of reform, like its enemies, were coming to recognize that public support had to be cultivated.

In 1805 we find the old radical complaining that the government functioned in defiance of public opinion, suggesting that at least the opinion could be identified with the cause of public improvement. However, in 1812 a discouraged Cartwright wrote of the prevailing

85. Burdon, *Various Thoughts on Politics, Morality and Literature* (Newcastle Upon Tyne, 1800), pp. 8–10. Burdon is not much discussed by his contemporaries or by twentieth-century scholars. But see J. E. Cookson, *The Friends of Peace: Anti-War Liberalism in England, 1793–1815* (Cambridge: Cambridge University Press, 1982), pp. 112, 282.

86. Cartwright, *Internal Evidence; or an Inquiry How Far Truth and the Christian Religion have been Consulted by the Author of Thoughts on a Parliamentary Reform* (London, 1784), p. vii.

87. Cartwright, *An Appeal Civil and Military, on the Subject of the English Constitution* (London, 1799), pp. 55, 90, 261; and *To Christopher Wyvill ...* (n.p., 1801), pp. 16, 61–62.

system of "concealed Despotism"—a response, it seems, to talk of a moderate change in the franchise that would further reduce prospects of manhood suffrage.[88] Here was one reformer whose every aspiration for change depended on reform in the political machinery. Cartwright had little to say of public attitudes on any other issue, and so his faith in the effectiveness of public opinion fluctuated with the prospects for reform. His hopes for reform hinged upon the capacity "to instruct the public mind ... to arouse the public spirit . . . and to unite in one focus the public opinion. ..."[89] To find him, in 1812, invoking the traditional rhetoric about legal tyranny suggests a very different view-point from that present at the bright dawn of 1784.

Others were certainly less inclined to despair. The poet John Thelwall was an ardent democrat who expressed great confidence in the spread of his principles. Thelwell, however, seems never to have probed much into the actual content of public opinion, and his fierce commitment to the people was thus little more than superficial rhetoric. He did leave some interesting thoughts about the ways in which one might identify public sentiment, and he spelled out a crude sampling tech-nique for testing public feeling as it was expressed by strangers in inns and stage-coaches.[90] His advice about not accepting as typical the views of one's acquaintances was no doubt sound. However, in seeking reform contrary to prevailing prejudices, it is questionable whether he followed his own counsel.

On the whole, though, there is little evidence that reformers were confident about the development of public opinion. It was one thing to express good will towards the people and quite another to be able to respond in other than slogans to the age-old Tory taunt that the people and its voice either spoke the harsh tones of the rabble or were undiscoverable. Popular sovereignty never has been an easy political faith to expound with any degree of analytical sophistication, and one suspects that the Whigs of the Glorious Revolution had a much easier

---

88. Cartwright, *Six Letters to the Marquis of Tavistock, on Reform* (London, 1812), pp. 19, 22. See too *The State of the Nation in a Series of Letters to his Grace the Duke of Bedford* (Harlow, 1805), p. 5.

89. Letter of 5 Feb. 1801 to Thomas Hardy, in *The Life and Correspondence of Major Cartwright*, ed. Francis D. Cartwright (1826; reprinted, New York: A. M. Kelly, 1969), 1:292.

90. Thelwall, "Report on the State of Popular Opinion ... ," in *The Tribune* (London, 1796), 2:189–90.

time defending their doctrine of the popular origins of authority than had later radicals with their wavering faith in public opinion. The doctrine of social contract had been a moral claim, founded not on fact but on the apparent rightness of harnessing power to the good of the community. The later commitment to public opinion was too vulnerable to the rude shocks administered by day-to-day contact with ignorance, prejudice, and a servile loyalty to powerful ministers and traditional institutions.

It has sometimes been argued that the British reformers' suspicion of state education was directly attributable to the tradition of religious dissent,[91] and the dissenting background of such political reformers as Priestley, Godwin, and David Williams serves to document the claim. However, another factor that may help equally to explain this pattern is the conventional fear of the eighteenth-century British Opposition that tyranny lurked behind a façade of ostensibly free institutions. Such a worry was not very relevant to the situation of the absolute government of France where the absence of liberty was sufficiently evident to invite no further subtleties of analysis. But in Britain, the radicals of the revolutionary era improved upon the alarms voiced by the patriot oppositions of the Augustan age. Thus fears about bribed electors and packed parliaments came to be translated into the new political idiom, and this entailed taking a jaundiced view of the meaning of public opinion. If most reformers were convinced that the people would need education in order to exercise their responsibilities, they were equally persuaded that this instruction could not be entrusted to the government. Such confidence as there was in the *vox populi* was confined, as with Cartwright, to the people's readiness to embrace parliamentary reform. Prior to such fundamental improvement, there could be little reason to suppose that popular intervention in public business would serve the cause of freedom.

The conclusion may sound unlikely, but careful attention to what political reformers of the nineties actually said about public opinion suggests a very uncertain trumpet. Those who wrote, with apparent confidence, of the decisive quality of public opinion were still not in a position to assert that this opinion invariably would endorse their plans for national improvement. Sometimes the language of reform

---

91. See John Passmore, *The Perfectability of Man*, 2nd ed. (London: Duckworth, 1971), chap. 9, where British and French views on state education are contrasted.

was belied by the circumstances of the writer. Thus one reads in a pamphlet of 1808 the optimistic-sounding claim that "public Investigation and public Opinion are superior even to juries." Recalling that the use of juries in libel cases was held to increase the power of the public, one might easily overlook the fact that the statement was normative and not descriptive. The substance of the tract makes clear the depressing state of political reformers, for it records both the imprisonment of two newspaper editors—William Cobbett and Henry White—and the author's lack of respect for reforming editors even when they managed to stay out of jail.[92] Clearly, the friends of social improvement often failed to agree among themselves about how public opinion was to be found and expressed. The more they examined the state of opinion, the more their cause for concern lest there be no coherent public voice or one muted or distorted by the agents of misrule. A relative optimist who wrote of "the Growth of Reason, and Extension of Public Opinion" noted as well the deficiencies of "public spirit" and placed great reliance upon an apparent tendency for politicians to canvass votes with more candour and less condescension than had previously been used.[93]

Complacency about the prevailing state of public opinion was consistent only with a concern for relatively limited reform, and this may account for the fact that Christopher Wyvill, who did not share Cartwright's enthusiasm for manhood suffrage, seems to have been less quickly disillusioned. Even those moderates who relied heavily upon the salutary influence of a large middle class were aware that it might be difficult to collect the opinions of that public and translate them into policy. Public opinion might indeed be irresistible, but its "pure and genuine voice" was liable to be counterfeited.[94]

Nor was the cold rationalism of William Godwin sympathetic to public opinion as then constituted. No one said more often than Godwin that all government was founded upon opinion, but neither did any radical of the period express greater anxiety about the capacity of the rich and powerful to mould the attitudes of humbler citizens.

92. [William P. Russel], *British Liberty and Philanthropy . . . by a Philanthropist* (London, 1808), p. 13.

93. Sampson Perry, *The Argus: or, General Observer: A Political Miscellany* (London, 1796), pp. 632–33; 418–19.

94. [John Fenwick], *Oeconomist, or Englishman's Magazine* (Newcastle upon Tyne) 1–4 (Jan.–Apr. 1798):8, 38, 89.

This fear lay behind Godwin's refusal to contemplate the educating of opinion by government. Normally a government would employ the opportunity only to perpetuate itself, and indeed, Godwin insisted, even a government interested only in educating its citizens could not fail—if only incidentally—to convey its political prejudices. Godwin's animus against forcing the pace of enlightenment extended even to the place of "political associations," and so he rejected the conventional arguments in their favour. Such organizations could not be justified by virtue of their "generating a sound public opinion,"[95] and they were equally unnecessary as mechanisms for ascertaining or executing the public will. Nothing, in fact, save a general movement towards equality would convince Godwin that the opinions of the community sprang from a source not already defiled by the interests of the rich. Improvement, then, had to be a gradual process. Until the slow growth of knowledge had improved the public mind, its products would give no comfort to the reformer. Developing a theme familiar to twentieth-century readers, Godwin observed that "it is one of the evils of a corrupt state of society, that it forces the most virtuous unwillingly to participate in its injustice."[96] From such a premise, there could be no confidence in the role of opinion in day-to-day politics. A provincial writer, seemingly much influenced by Godwin, developed the theme in more specific terms as "the Art of Leading the Public Mind."[97] Given such suspicions, it is not surprising that those who were most committed to the vision of a free and enlightened people were equally certain that such a condition could be only the product of time.

Godwin's concern for developing the life of the parish was paralleled by the nostalgia of radical circles for reviving the ancient divisions of the Saxon kingdom—tithings and hundreds. For Granville Sharp

---

95. Godwin, *Enquiry Concerning Political Justice and its influence on Morals and Happiness*, ed. F. E. L. Priestley, from the 3rd ed. of 1798 (Toronto: University of Toronto Press, 1946), 1:285–86. In the first edition of 1793, Godwin wrote of "the opinion of the people."

96. Ibid., 2:310. See too the slogan of Robert Fleming Gourlay—later to figure in efforts at reform in Canada—that "Government should grow out of education—not education out of government." *A Specific Plan for Organizing the People and for Obtaining Reform Independent of Parliament* (London, 1809), p. 122.

97. See the articles signed "Philalethes" in *The Cabinet* (Norwich, 1795), 2:295–303; and 3:97–105. Most contributors have been identified, but not this one. See Walter Graham, "The Authorship of the Norwich Cabinet, 1794–5," *Notes and Queries* 162 (Jan.–June 1932):294–95.

and Major Cartwright, the supposed government of Alfred's England supplied the appropriate units both for defence and for mass participation. To the more erudite and thoughtful reformers, this offered more than the impractical scheme of a national convention. As an anonymous book, probably influenced by Williams, put it: "How to estimate and regulate,—improve and use the *public mind* or opinion, seems not yet well understood."[98] The answer lay in an appreciation of how political organization could clarify and focus that public mind.

Some reformers of the day were disheartened by the knowledge that a very imperfect government could not be trusted to reform itself; that had been the sole point of the radical enthusiasm for a convention independent of Parliament. But increasingly it became apparent that an unenlightened public would not seek reform; did not want it. Public education seemed to be the only answer, but it too was rendered difficult by the government's enormous influence over the prevailing stock of ideas. Thus concern about the current idiom of politics added to the reformers' fear of *vox populi*. Assuming that the hegemony of the ruling classes was not wholly the product of fear but a testimony to their imposing on the minds and the emotions of the common people, the very language of politics became a potent weapon. Complaints that the privileged orders corrupted the understandings of the people were already old. However, the new prominence of public opinion could only lend urgency to existing concern. When the Independent Whigs of the reign of George I had attacked the use of tendentious language to overawe the people, they were contributing to a tradition of critical inquiry into the *instrumenta regni*. Similar in tone were the complaints of Chatham's opponents that the public applause, which so strengthened his hand, posed dangers to the system. Understandably, such complaints appeared with increased vigour during his son's time in office.

Major John Cartwright put the point succinctly when he wrote that "words govern public opinion."[99] John Horne Tooke, who was well known for his attachment both to reform and to philology, might be expected to have pursued this tack. Actually, though widely credited with combining the two interests, his *Diversions of Purley* effected no

98. A. D. R. S., *An Essay on Civil Government, or Society Restored* (London, 1793), p. 151. The work was ostensibly translated from Italian, but this seems unlikely.

99. Cartwright, *The Commonwealth in Danger* (London, 1795), p. 126.

useful integration. Tooke was quite capable of basing his defence against charges of high treason on the claim that the chief law officers of the Crown were ignorant of the correct usage of the conjunction "that"; he was not, however, particularly sensitive to the nuances of political language. Tooke's religious orthodoxy and his reservations about some of the more far-reaching schemes for constitutional reform meant that he was not as alienated from the dominant institutions as were many others who were less conspicuous in their opposition.

One of these obscure radicals was James Gilchrist, an admirer of Tooke's studies in philology. Gilchrist's main point was that political bondage was closely linked to moral bondage, the latter being imposed by an official political language. Rendered submissive by their education, citizens were incapable of generating a "manly and independent public opinion." Part of the blame rested, according to Gilchrist, with the uncritical admiration of Greece and Rome that was inculcated by British education. This was an odd claim for one who admired Hobbes's contributions to an understanding of language, for Hobbes had expressed just the opposite worry—that excessive attention to antiquity bred unquiet subjects. Descending to specifics, Gilchrist denied that there existed any genuine freedom of the press and railed at the obfuscation and evasion practised by the party system. How, he asked, was public opinion formed and expressed? "There must be parties; for such is the enslaved state of intellect, that the multitude are fit only for being the multitude, going ever as they are led. If the Tories have a bold leader, they will be the popular and prevailing party, ..." Men were constantly bemused by false appearances and cheated "under the disguise of affected significant phrases." Disappointingly though, his examples were trite and were confined largely to the etymology of the names "Whig" and "Tory." Gilchrist was unequivocal in his respect for Bacon, Hobbes, and Tooke, each of whom had managed to penetrate the defences of language to grasp the nature of "intellectual weapons." He was effective too in his general charge that, despite appearances, citizens were confined by "authorized opinion."[100] But all his learned fulmination served only to

---

100. Gilchrist, *Reason the True Arbiter of Language; Custom a Tyrant; or Intellect set free from Arbitrary Authority* (London, 1814), pp. 67–68. See too his *The Labyrinth Demolished; or, the Pioneer of Rational Philology* (London, 1815), pp. 34–38; and *Philosophic Etymology, or Rational Grammar* (London, 1816), p. 201.

state preliminaries to an argument the details of which never appeared.

Complaints that party warfare was largely a matter of the misleading use of words were anything but new. They were part of the traditional objection to political parties. In the reign of Anne, for instance, it had not been unusual for commentators, tired of the bickering of Whig and Tory, to insist that the survival of those factions owed much to the persistence of party names, enduring symbols of loyalty that disguised the inconsistencies and lapses of principle on both sides. In the early nineteenth century, especially after 1820, it again became more common for public persons to call themselves Tories. It was natural, then, for the complaint about party names to revive, couched now in terms of the way in which inflated language served to mislead public opinion. The "tyranny of names" was a familiar theme in radical literature of the 1820s and after, and increasingly it was related to current distortions in the formation of public opinion. Indeed, most political topics were discussed in terms of the issue of public opinion, for, as one journalist noted, "in society—and in books—we find few things of which there is more said, or more written, than what is called '*public opinion*'. ..."[101]

Much of what was then said dealt with impositions on the public mind. Stating the issue in general terms, one dissenting clergyman, Robert Hall, noted how the orthodox theory of the constitution deluded the populace into acquiescence. Faced with constitutional theory that was a "satire" on the practice and with a government that was deemed to promote intellectual thraldom, Hall ventured the doubt whether the liberty of the press was perhaps not more a detriment than an advantage to the cause of improvement.[102] Nothing better illustrates the distance between the familiar optimism about the fruits of a free press and the pessimism that overwhelmed the reformers who actually examined the state of public opinion.

William Hazlitt expressed the same point somewhat less poignantly when he developed Locke's observation that most people took their wrong opinions from others. Locke had seen here the basis of the

---

101. *The Umpire* 2 (11 Jan. 1823), and 5 (1 Feb. 1823), the article "On Public Opinion."

102. "An Apology for the Freedom of the Press, and for General Liberty" (1793), 3rd ed. (1822), in *The Miscellaneous Works and Remains of the Rev. Robert Hall*, ed. John Foster (London, 1846), pp. 217–19.

cheerful conclusion that there were really fewer different wrong opinions in the world than one might think. For Hazlitt, the inference was
less sunny, for his expectations were much more demanding. "Neither
are the opinions of the people their own, when they have been bribed
or bullied into them by a mob of Lords and Gentlemen. ... The *vox
populi* is the *vox Dei* only when it springs from the unbiassed feelings
and unfettered and independent opinions of the people."[103] Hazlitt
also sounded a resonant chord when he observed that it was not
interest only, but "prejudice or fashion" that swayed mankind: "Opinion governs opinion." This would hardly have surprised Cardan, who
appears to have known it three centuries before; and certainly Hume
shared this view. It might have seemed obvious as well to the Opposition of 1734, who were ungracious when Treasury influence won
the election. But for a time, at least, some people had assumed that
the election of 1784 had ushered an era of public opinion as clear-
sighted as it was benign. Hazlitt was providing the corrective to such
optimism, speaking for a generation of radicals who knew that "opinion flies before, and interest comes limping after."[104] Hazlitt wrote
much about public opinion; even his relatively apolitical essay "On
Public Opinion," in the *London Weekly Review* of 1828, emphasized
how opinion was controlled. The world was ready for the concept of
false consciousness long before it became available.

An Ambiguous Legacy

After generations of constant debate about corruption and the influence of the Crown, political thinkers sought new explanations for
national ills. Without displacing talk of corruption, the factor of public
opinion served as a means whereby radicals could explain their hu-
miliating failure to set abuses right. The spring of liberty had indeed
been poisoned at its source, not just in the traditional sense that emphasized the venality of electorates and representatives, but in respect
to the governing assumptions of public life. Many of the strains of

---

103. Hazlitt, "What is the People?" (1818), in *Political Essays, with Sketches of Public
Characters* (London, 1819), p. 323. The same odd demand that the electorate be uninfluenced has led some modern historians to deny that public opinion played any part
in public life. See W. T. Laprade, "Public Opinion and the General Election of 1784,"
English Historical Review 31 (1916):224–37.
104. "On Court-Influence" (1818), in *Essays*, pp. 269–70.

thought of the frustrated reformers centred in this point. Their rationalism and desire for a science of government necessarily required a more precise political vocabulary than that associated with, say, Burke's traditions and prejudices. Constant misrepresentation of their intentions also drove radical reformers to seek more accurate expression, in the hope that they might lose their unfortunate association with metaphysical schemes imported from France. The development of a science of government was often perceived as an essential preliminary to reform, thus discouraging reliance upon uninformed opinion. The very sophisticated arguments against political reform also invited an equally adroit rejoinder. It was often argued, for instance, that the enormous complexity of society rendered any effort at a mere reform of the representation ineffectual. Similarly, the defence of fictions and salutary untruths—based on the assumption that they were necessary for reassuring the masses[105]—goaded some radicals to attempt to pierce the veil of illusion with an analysis equal in subtlety to this defence. In this they largely failed. However, in their disenchantment, some did perceive that a major instrument of change lay in an enhanced understanding of the phenomenon of public opinion. This served both to identify the source of earlier failures and to prescribe the direction of peaceful change.

Of course, there remained the dilemma of a public that required enlightenment before it could seek reform or use it to good purpose, although that very enlightenment seemed dependent upon changing the political order. That particular chicken-and-egg relation, perceived with varying degrees of clarity, was enough to dampen reformers' enthusiasm for public opinion. Too great an alienation from established institutions made the prospect of peaceful reform seem impossible, since there remained nothing uncorrupt on which to build. The alternative attitude, more favoured by literary folk, was the vague hope that advancing civilization would do what agitation had failed to achieve. In the short run, at least, despair was not uncommon, and men marvelled at Major Cartwright's enthusiasm, sustained over half a century. More representative of the response of would-be reformers was the reply of Sir Philip Francis to one of Cartwright's interminable

105. For a sophisticated defence of social fictions see the Rev. John Owen, *The Retrospect; or, Reflections on the State of Religion and Politics in France and Great Britain* (London, 1794), p. 36.

schemes for an association to promote reform: "I doubt the actual existence of an English public for any great national purpose; and, if it exists, I am not its debtor. ... the mass of the English population is inert."[106]

Only after the Reform Act did intellectuals have good reason to contemplate the gradual enlightenment of the populace through the experience of participation in government, and then it was largely a middle-class notion that relied upon a measure of influence, by the elite, over the lower orders. The general idea of an improvement in the quality, and not just in the communication, of opinion had been present in schemes for decentralization of government to parishes or tithings, though it never seems to have been spelled out with any precision. The expectation that people's sophistication would expand with increased public duties was occasionally expressed by Cartwright. It appeared too in a work by Benjamin Heath Malkin of Trinity College, Cambridge,[107] but the notion was rare before 1832. For most, the unreformed, and apparently unreformable, Parliament cast a pall over the imagination. In the years leading to the reform of 1832 it was generally conceded that public opinion was a significant aspect of public life, and few endorsed Benjamin Disraeli's claim of the 1830s that public opinion had been equally prominent in the seventeenth century. The problem was what to expect of the public and its newly powerful voice. For Edward Lytton Bulwer, hoping to improve upon Mackinnon's thoughts on the subject, the phenomenon proved too "vague" to supply material for an article in the *Edinburgh Review*.[108] It thus seems that the more genuine and widespread a nation's opinion was, the more difficult it was to describe and analyse it. Eighteenth-century Frenchmen encountered little real public opinion but wrote confidently about it.

Before the late eighteenth century, public opinion was most often an object of ridicule. It then enjoyed a brief period of universal favour as opponents of change invoked its presence to justify inaction while reformers expressed confidence in its growing enlightenment. The reformers were only the first to be disappointed.

Nor did the Reform Act do anything to reconcile political minorities,

---

106. Letter of 2 Apr. 1811, in *Life and Correspondence of Major Cartwright*, 2:4.

107. See Malkin, *Essays on Subjects Connected with Civilization* (London, 1795), p. 156.

108. Letters of 6 Feb. and 1 Mar. 1831 to Macvey Napier, in *Selection from the Correspondence of the late Macvey Napier*, edited by his son (London, 1879), pp. 103–4.

whether radical reformers or just the Opposition of the day, to public opinion. One would not expect that it would, for those not in control of a government naturally suspect those forces that sustain it. Surprisingly, though, it seems that public opinion as a political force was destined to have no fast friends in public life—certainly not among politicians of the old style. Too mercurial and unstable to give security even to those who benefited from established institutions, public opinion continued to be blamed by all those whose projects had not been blessed by public support. Impossible to ignore in any adequate understanding of nineteenth-century politics, it was unlikely either to attract constant admirers from other than the ranks of journalists. Peel's lament of 1820 had expressed the feeling of many public men that the business of politics had become more difficult and uncertain because of public opinion. But a more subtle and worrisome complaint was voiced by those reformers who saw that the public mind was all too receptive to government influence.

Modern social science encourages the view that scepticism about government by public opinion was a product of the early twentieth century and of the works of men such as Gabriel Tarde, Graham Wallas, and Walter Lippmann.[109] But these students of opinion came late in their hopes and in their fears; the essential problems had long been apparent. The last word belongs to the Right Honourable John Wilson Croker, an influence both in the Tory party and in the republic of letters, and certainly not a person who should have felt that the world was conspiring against his interests.

The Reform Bill established the broad principle of governing by representation, and on that basis had been erected into omnipotence what was formerly a valuable subordinate agent, now called public opinion: she was of old the queen of the world; she has now become its tyrant. ...[110]

109. On these and other contributors see Francis Graham Wilson, *A Theory of Public Opinion* (Chicago: H. Regnery Co., 1962), esp. chap. 6.
110. Letter of 21 July 1854 to Lord Brougham, in *The Croker Papers*, 3:339.

Index

195; on public opinion, 297–98; view of constitution before Reform Bill, 298; name revived, 311. *See too* High-Church; High-Tories
Towgood, Micaiah, 56–57
Townsend, Joseph, 118
Trapp, Joseph, 140, 151
Treasury Bench, 71, 72
Trenchard, John, 13, 25, 28, 238; on corruption, 19–20; on corporations, 52–53; on standing army, 53–54; on good government, 194
trial by jury, 230, 235, 286, 307
Triennial Act (6 & 7 Wm. and Mary, c. 2), repeal of, 63, 78, 112, 149
True Briton (of 1751–53), 162–63
True Briton (of 1790s), 178
Tucker, Josiah, 173
Tufton, Sackville, 45
Turner, Francis, 121
Tutchin, John, 132, 138
Twiss, Horace, 292–94
Tyrrell, James: on local autonomy, 48; on identity of estates, 126; on "co-operative" power, 126

Ulster volunteers, 84–85
unintended consequences, in Mandeville, 104, 119
Union of England and Scotland, 76, 124
Universal Spy, 144
Universities Bill (1716), 51

Venn, Richard, 155
Vertot, René Aubert de, 101, 111
veto: power of, as sign of estate, 55, 81, 82, 124; of King and Lords deemed outmoded, 204; King's absolute, seen as revived, 285
"Vice-gerent" of God: significance of expression, 155
Voltaire, F-M. Arouet de, 183; Williams translates, 196
vox populi: Defoe on, 76; Oldmixon on, 77; Atterbury on, 78; assumed basis for government after 1784, 87; reformers come to fear, 309
Vox Populi, Vox Dei, 141

Wade, John, 40n
wages, views of after 1750, 116
Wake, William, Archbishop, 137
Wallas, Graham, 315

Walpole, Sir Robert, 7, 12, 22, 23, 24, 25, 40, 46, 56, 60, 61, 65, 98, 109, 190; as prime minister, 68; Mandeville's alleged hostility to, 104–5; defends luxury, 113–14; on "sense of the people," 273; victory in 1734 election, 79, 273; financing of newspapers, 300
Waltham-Black Act (9 Geo. I, c. 22), 63
Warburton, William: his *Alliance Between Church and State,* 51
Ward, Edward ("Ned"), 46
Watson, Richard, 174–75, 176
Webster, William, 235–36
Werenfels, Samuel, 20
Wesley, John: on the people, 82–83, 247; on popular sovereignty, 170; his followers, 170–71
West, Richard, 35–36
Wetherell, Nathan, 167
Wharton, Philip, Duke of, 24, 158
Whigs: tendencies in power, 11; propensity to form associations, 46–47; commercial affinities, 47; intolerance of competing bodies, 50; on church and state, 51; split of 1718, 65; views on the people, 74–80; triumph in 1714, 78; version of reason of state, 102; constitutional theory, 106; ahistorical positions, 125, 198; unclarity of constitutional views after Revolution, 125–26; their newspapers, 136; ambiguities of views on royal supremacy, 137–38, 147; tentative in 1713, 138–39; need to support authority, 149; doctrine of natural rights, 163; take constitution for granted, 175; constitutional uncertainties, 185–89; misrepresented as democrats, 190; accused of Jacobitism, 271–72; hesitancy about reform, 295, 297; optimism about public, 297; embrace extension of franchise, 299; and social contract, 305–6. *See too* Old Whigs
Whiston, William, 152
Whitaker, John, 171n, 177, 181n
White, Henry, 307
White, Rev. John, 56–57
White, William, 188–89
Whitehead, Paul, 274n
Wilde, Dr. John, 290
Wilkes, John, 30, 82, 207, 244, 276–77
William III, King, 15, 18, 22, 48, 70, 112, 121, 125, 126, 153, 267